Derivative Actions and Corporate Governance
in China

ASIAN COMMERCIAL, FINANCIAL AND ECONOMIC LAW AND POLICY

Series Editors: Douglas Arner, Xian Chu Zhang, *University of Hong Kong* and Chin Leng Lim, *Chinese University of Hong Kong*

Asia is home to the world's most dynamic and increasingly interlinked economies. At the heart of their future development are issues of commercial, financial and economic law and policy. This series brings together volumes addressing related issues, across the region, in individual economies and between Asia and the rest of the world.

Titles in the series include:

Derivative Actions and Corporate Governance in China

Jingchen Zhao

Professor of Law, Nottingham Law School, Nottingham Trent University, UK

ASIAN COMMERCIAL, FINANCIAL AND ECONOMIC LAW AND POLICY

Edward Elgar
PUBLISHING

Cheltenham, UK • Northampton, MA, USA

Published by
Edward Elgar Publishing Limited
The Lypiatts
15 Lansdown Road
Cheltenham
Glos GL50 2JA
UK

Edward Elgar Publishing, Inc.
William Pratt House
9 Dewey Court
Northampton
Massachusetts 01060
USA

A catalogue record for this book
is available from the British Library

Library of Congress Control Number: 2022946671

This book is available electronically in the **Elgar**online
Law subject collection
http://dx.doi.org/10.4337/9781784719111

ISBN 978 1 78471 910 4 (cased)
ISBN 978 1 78471 911 1 (eBook)
Printed and bound by CPI Group (UK) Ltd, Croydon, CR0 4YY

Contents

Figures

Tables

Acknowledgements

I wish to thank a number of people and organisations. My grateful thanks to Nottingham Law School and School of Law, University of Leeds Law for awarding me research grants and scholarships that enabled me to go to academic meetings while finishing this book. The research is kindly supported by Economic and Social Research Council [grant number ES/P004040/: Boosting Growth through Strengthening Investor and Creditor Protection in China: How China Can Learn from the UK experience].

Special thanks are due to Professor Andrew Keay, Professor David Milman and Professor Gerard McCormack for their continuing support, stimulating suggestions and encouragement in helping me to write this book. Jenny Chapman and Professor Jonathan Doak and from Nottingham Law School and Professor Joan Loughrey and Professor Janine Griffiths-Baker have also provided immense support and inspiration, for which I am hugely indebted.

I would also like to express my sincere gratitude to my friends and colleagues Shuangge Wen, Wangwei Lin, Ziyu Yan, Kerri Gilbert, Yin Liu, Ding Chen, Zhong Zhang, Chuyi Wei, and to my proof-reader Louise Maskill for her excellent and efficient work. Special thanks are also due to my publisher, and to all the reviewers for their helpful comments and suggestions.

Finally, as always, I am extremely thankful to my parents Guoqing Li and Gang Zhao and my brother Rongchen Zhao for their encouragement, understanding and support.

Abbreviations

CSDC	China Securities Depository and Clearing Corporation Limited
CSRC	China Securities and Regulation Commission
JSLCs	Joint stock limited liability companies
LLC	Limited Liability Company
NPC	Standing Committee of National People's Congress
OBOR	One Belt, One Road
OECD	Organisation for Economic Co-operation and Development
Provision IV	Provisions of the Supreme People's Court on Some Issues about the Application of the Company Law of the People's Republic of China (IV)
QFII	Qualified Foreign Institutional Investor
SME	Small- and medium-sized enterprises
SOE	State-owned enterprise
SPC	Supreme People's Court
UK CA	United Kingdom Companies Act
UNCTAD	United Nations Conference on Trade and Development

1. Introduction to derivative actions and corporate governance in China

China has achieved unprecedented economic growth since 1980, becoming the second-largest economy in the world and with per capita GDP increasing from one of the lowest in the world to a level that is firmly in the middle of the international ranks.[1] The country has seen a number of economic miracles since the opening up policies and reforms that were introduced by the national government in the late 1970s; it has become a global economic powerhouse at an incredible speed, and its meteoric rise has fundamentally changed international trade and investment patterns. Incredibly, China's success to date has been achieved without key elements that are regarded by Western scholars as essential for long-term success, such as a well-functioning market, private property rights, an efficient and impartial legal system, and a shareholder-centred economic corporate governance regime.[2]

However, China's miraculous success has attracted many scholarly discussions and a certain amount of criticism. In terms of its corporate governance, many studies have compared practices in China with those in mature markets, offering various suggestions and recommendations in order to improve the effectiveness, accountability, transparency and efficacy of corporate governance in the Chinese environment.[3] My intention in writing this book is to criti-

---

[1]   See the World Bank Ranking of GDP per capita, available at http://data .worldbank.org/indicator/NY.GDP.PCAP.CD?page=6 (accessed 20 July 2022).
[2]   R. Morck and B. Yeung, 'Corporate Governance in China' (2014) 26(3) *Journal of Applied Corporate Finance* 20, 20.
[3]   For example, see C. Mutlu, M. Van Essen M.W. Pengd, S.F. Salehb and P. Durane, 'Corporate Governance in China: A Meta-Analysis' (2018) 55(6) *Journal of Management Studies* 943; L.H. Tan and J.Y. Wang, 'Modeling an Efficient Corporate Governance System for China's Listed State-Owned Enterprises: Issues and Challenges in a Transitional Economy' (2007) 7(1) *Journal of Corporate Law Studies* 143; Y. Gao, 'Corporate Social Performance in China: Evidence from Large Companies' (2009) 89(1) *Journal of Business Ethics* 23; H.W.C. Yeung, *Chinese Capitalism in a Global Era: Towards a Hybrid Model*, (London: Routledge 2004); K.L.A. Lau and A. Young, 'Why China Shall Not Completely Transit from a Relation Based to a Rule Based Governance Regime: A Chinese Perspective' (2013) 21(6) *Corporate Governance: An International Review* 577; R. Mead, *International Management: Cross-cultural Dimensions*, (Oxford: Blackwell 2005); R. Morck and B. Yeung,

cally analyse the current legislations related to derivative action in China, and examine their application. A very direct question that will be applicable to the discussion in the book is whether derivative action can be developed to provide a more effective solution for shareholder protection in China. The book offers a critical reading of the existing scholarship on corporate governance and shareholders' rights in China, and uses doctrinal, theoretical and empirical approaches to discuss this contemporary topic.

The rule in *Foss v Harbottle*[4] provides a negative answer to the question of whether an individual shareholder is able to bring a complaint before the court if an irregularity has been committed in the course of a company's affairs, or if some wrong has been done to the company. Initially derived from English and US law, the derivative action mechanism works as an exception to the rule that defines the company itself as the proper person or legal entity to bring action when seeking redress, offering a solution in situations where the wrongdoers are in control of the company. The mechanism enables individual shareholders to act in support of the rights and interests of the company, and it has been seen as a useful tool to both mitigate the dominant power of controlling shareholders and deter opportunistic behaviour by boards of directors.[5] It provides that if a shareholder can establish a case in which the action harming the company constitutes a fraud on the company and where the wrongdoers control the company, s/he will be permitted to initiate proceedings which derive from the company's right to institute proceedings. Different from direct minority protection mechanisms such as unfair prejudice remedies[6] or winding up[7] in common law countries or their equivalents, the derivative action process was designed to protect the company, allowing shareholders to bring an action on behalf of the company. Shareholders may benefit from successful recoveries since the value of shares will increase *pro rota* as the assets of the company improve in value.[8] This protection mechanism has since been inserted in legislation in a number of countries with developed markets, such as the United

'Corporate Governance in China' (2014) 26(3) *Journal of Corporate Finance* 20; J. Yang, J. Chi and M. Young, 'A Review of Corporate Governance in China' (2011) 25(1) *Asian Pacific Economic Literature* 15.

[4]   *Foss v Harbottle* (1843) 2 Hare 461.

[5]   S. Tenev, C. Zhang and L. Brefort, *Corporate Governance and Enterprise Reform in China: Building the Institutions of Modern Markets*, (Washington, DC: World Bank and the International Finance Corporation 2002) 149.

[6]   Section 994 of the UK CA 2006; *O'Neill v Phillips* [1999] 1 WLR 1092.

[7]   Sections 122(1)(g) and 124(1) of the Insolvency Act 1986; *Re J E Cade & Son Ltd* [1991] BCC 360; *Re Thomas Brinsmead & Sons Ltd* [1897] 1 Ch 406; *Re Yenidje Tobacco Co* [1916] 2 Ch 426.

[8]   Z. Zhang, 'Making the Shareholder Derivative Actions Happen in China: How Should Lawsuits Be Funded?' (2008) 38 *Hong Kong Law Journal* 523, 526.

Kingdom, Hong Kong,[9] Australia,[10] Canada,[11] Japan,[12] New Zealand[13] and Singapore,[14] as well as in countries with emerging markets including India,[15] Brazil[16] and Russia.[17]

Although China does not follow the rule of common law, after much consideration and public consultation the derivative action mechanism was introduced with high expectations during a Chinese Company Law reform in 2005, coming into effect on January 1, 2006. The rule was adopted to address one of 12 defects in the old Chinese Company Law which were proposed to the Standing Committee of the National People's Congress in February 2005. The changes regarding derivative action are part of a series of changes surrounding shareholder protection, especially for minority shareholders. The Chinese legal system is still distinguished from other jurisdictions by the underlying Chinese market and its legal institution in the context of a control-based corporate governance model.[18]

---

[9]   Sections 731–738 of the New Companies Ordinance 2012 (Cap 622) (the section commenced operation on 3 March 2014).

[10]   Part 2F.1A of the Corporations Act 2001; see L. Thai, 'Australian Statutory Derivative Action – Defects, Alternative Approaches and Potential for Law Reform' in C.B. Picker and G. Seidman (eds), *The Dynamism of Civil Procedure – Global Trends and Developments*, (Heidelberg: Springer 2016) 237.

[11]   Sections 232 and 242 of the Canadian Business Corporations Act 1985; see also B. Cheffins, 'Reforming the Derivative Action: The Canadian Experience and British Prospects' (1997) 1 *Company Financial and Insolvency Law Review* 227, 234; D.H. Peterson and M.J. Cumming, *Shareholder Remedies in Canada*, (Ontario: LexisNexis, 2nd ed. 2009).

[12]   Articles 847–848 of the Japanese Company Law 2005; see also H. Oda, 'Shareholder's Derivative Action in Japan' (2011) 8(3) *European Company and Financial Law Review* 334.

[13]   Sections 165 and 166 of the Companies Act 1993 (New Zealand); see also P. Prince, 'Australia's Derivative Action: Using the New Zealand Experience' (2000) 18 *Company and Securities Law Journal* 493; S. Watson, 'A Matter of Balance: The Statutory Derivative Action in New Zealand' (1998) 19(8) *Company Lawyer* 236.

[14]   Section 216 of the Companies Act 1994 (Singapore) (Cap 50); see P. Koh, 'The Statutory Derivative Action in Singapore: A Critical and Comparative Examination' (2001) 13(1) *Bond Law Review* 64; A.K. Koh, 'Excusing Notice under Singapore's Statutory Derivative Action' (2013) 14(2) *Australian Journal of Asian Law* 1.

[15]   Section 245 of the Companies Act 2013 (India); see also V. Khanna and U. Varottil, 'The Rarity of Derivative Action in India: Reasons and Consequences' in D.W. Puchniak, H. Baum and M. Ewing-Chow (eds), *The Derivative Action in Asia: A Comparative and Functional Approach*, (Cambridge: Cambridge University Press 2012) 369.

[16]   Articles 155 and 157 of the Brazilian Civil Code 2002.

[17]   Item 2 of Article 71 of Russian Joint Stock Companies 2007.

[18]   X. Huang, 'Derivative Action in China: Law and Practice' (2010) 6(1) *Cambridge Student Law Review* 246, 246–247; see also J. Zhao and S. Wen, 'Promoting

In detail, derivative action was introduced to China in Article 152 of the Chinese Company Law 2006[19] in the form of a short provision:

> the shareholders in the case of a Limited Liability Company (LLC), or a shareholder that has independently held, or the shareholders that have held in aggregate, 1% or more of the shares of the company for more than 180 consecutive days in the case of a JSLC, may request in writing the board of supervisors, or the supervisors, in the case of a LLC without a board of supervisors, to institute proceedings with the People's Court; where the supervisors fall under the circumstance set forth in Article 149 hereof, the foregoing shareholders may request in writing the board of directors, or the executive directors in the case of a LLC without a board of directors, to institute proceedings with the People's Court.

The provision was renumbered as Article 151 in the Company Law 2013 reform, but the content was wholly preserved and remains in full force today.

The mechanism functions as part of a series of changes surrounding shareholder protection and shareholders' rights.[20] Notwithstanding the significance of derivative action in modern China, the ability and/or eligibility of shareholders to bring derivative actions have been largely overlooked by scholarly works in this fast-growing nation. Indeed, analyses in the following sections reveal that despite the fact that Article 151 is a relatively brief and seemingly straightforward provision, a detailed examination of its nature, designated scope and relevant data from securities markets concerning its practical effects exposes major problems hindering its application in Chinese joint stock limited liability companies (JSLCs).

Stakeholders' Interests in the Unique Chinese Corporate Governance Model: More Socially Responsible Corporations?' (2010) 21(11) *International Company and Commercial Law Review* 373.

[19]   This legislative amendment came into effect on January 1, 2006. It was originally enshrined into Company Law 2006, art. 152, and subsequently renumbered as Company Law 2013, and most recently in 2018 art. 151. X Huang, 'Shareholders Revolt? The Statutory Derivative Action in China', Comparative Research in Law and Political Economy Research Paper 49/2009 (2009) 4–6; H. Huang, 'The Statutory Derivative Action in China: Critical Analysis and Recommendations for Reform, (2007) 4(2) *Berkeley Business Law Journal* 227.

[20]   In detail, two distinct litigation techniques have been introduced for shareholders to protect their interests in the company on occasions where the directors' fiduciary duties are breached by key members of the company such as directors, supervisors, senior management executives or controlling shareholders. The shareholder remedy mechanisms include direct suits and derivative suits, enabling them to bring legal action against the controllers of the company in accordance with arts 152–152 of Company Law 2018.

1.1   AIM OF THIS BOOK

The current provisions in Chinese Company Law show both convergence and divergence characteristics when compared with statutory derivative action provisions in other legislations. The reforms in the new Chinese Company Law reflect a compromise in relation to the efficiency of Chinese Company Law and procedure law in terms of the protection of shareholders, especially minority shareholders. It is vital to combat the abuse of derivative action in China, a country with an emerging corporate governance model, a weak legal system and inefficient enforcement measures.

This book aims to examine several deficiencies in the current Chinese implementation of derivative actions, with the purpose of arguing for a more effective and positive derivative action rule for the benefit of shareholders and their companies, and also for the development of Chinese Company Law and the reconstruction of the Chinese corporate governance system. The book focuses on how to build more an effective, accessible and balanced mechanism for derivation action in order to promote more sound corporate governance in China, examining two significant problems, namely the possibility of transplanting legal regimes and rules from other jurisdictions, and the practical experiences from the last 15 years.

1.2   METHODOLOGY

This is a library-based study utilising a mixed methodology consisting of doctrinal, theoretical, comparative, socio-legal and empirical research. Parts of this research will adopt a doctrinal approach, with findings based on analysing and contextualising relevant legal authorities, primarily statutes and case law. We will also take an integrated theoretical approach, using philosophical, sociological and economic theories to rationalise lawmaking and law reform endeavours in derivative actions. In detail, corporate governance theories such as agency theory, stakeholder theory, legal transplant and path dependence theory will be used as theoretical arguments for a more effective and enforceable derivative action system in China.

We are aware the Chinese case is unique, characterised by a controlling hybrid corporate governance model due to its state shareholding, the position and power of shareholders, and China's history, culture and traditions. In particular, we will pay attention to 'transplant' bias in legal reforms, and path dependency and its application to corporate law. Changes in Chinese corporate law primarily come from transplants or borrowing. At the same time, we are also aware of the possibility of inefficiencies when law is transplanted into an 'alien' implementing or enforcing environment. An ideal good fit of foreign with domestic law can be increased by the meaningful adaptation of imported laws to local conditions, but economic factors, legal doctrine, historical, cultural and political issues can all cause the legal system to develop in a path-dependent fashion. While laws will change and adapt to new circumstances, the changes in Chinese corporate law have been affected by adapting existing legal concepts rather than by introducing new ones.

This also evidences the interdisciplinary nature of the research. While theoretical analysis forms a central thread in the book, the discussions of the application and enforcement of law are also inherently socio-legal; after all, the law is a social phenomenon, as pointed out by Cotterrell.[21] Lady Hale, the former president of the Supreme Court of the United Kingdom, also highlighted the significance of this approach, particularly the fact that a number of socio-legal studies had been cited in court.[22] The approach is functional and appropriate to interpret and clarify an ambiguous field of law like shareholders' rights in China, against the background of its social context of more than 200 million investors in China's securities market of February 2022,[23] and an incredible 80 per cent of urban Chinese households which are or were formerly investors in the equity market and their reluctance and inability to bring legal actions against controllers of the companies.

In terms of comparative analysis, legal transplant will be used as a conceptual tool to investigate the movement of law from different jurisdictions or legal systems to China. Against the backdrop of the Law and Development Movement that has dominated research in recent decades, seeking to promote an international order of economic and social institutions similar to those in more advanced economies,[24] some scholars have suggested that the first and foremost purpose of borrowing activities in China should be to prepare for the international unification of law during the process of globalisation.[25]

---

[21] R. Cotterrell, *Law's Community: Legal Theory in Sociological Perspective* (Oxford: Oxford University Press 1995) 296.

[22] B. Hale, 'Should judges be socio-legal scholars?' Socio-Legal Studies Association 2013 Conference (2013).

[23] China Securities Depository and Clearing Corporation Limited (CSDC), The number of investors in the securities market exceeded 200 million [证券市场投资者数量突破2亿大关], available at http://www.chinaclear.cn/zdjs/gsdtnew/202202/a88e4b4e0b7848f9b5a5ed1d9577a3b3.shtml (accessed 21 July 2022).

[24] T. Ginsburg, 'Does Law Matter for Economic Development? Evidence from East Asia' 34(3) *Law & Society Review* 829, 829 (2000); B.Z. Tamanaha, 'The Lessons of Law and Development Studies' (1995) 89 *American Journal of International Law* 470, 471.

[25] O. Kahn-Freund has identified three prime purposes of legal transplantation: first, with the object of preparing the international unification of the law, secondly, with the object of giving adequate legal effect to a social change shared

Appreciating that the nation's relative lack of experience of marketisation has not been adequate to distil a complete set of normative standards in the field of company and commercial law, it is also logical for Chinese lawmakers to turn to legal systems in mature market-oriented economies for inspiration. Echoing the powerful rhetorical appeal of aligning Chinese corporate law more closely with that of other developed economies, much scholarly ink has been spilled in China commending this legislative change as the '*legal cornerstone underpinning China's future economic development*'[26] and advocating its effectiveness in prompting the growth of the private economy.

1.3 ORIGINALITY AND SIGNIFICANCE OF THE BOOK

Compared with pre-existing legislations, uncertainties about derivative suits in China have been reduced by the amendments brought in by Chinese Company Law 2018. However, in terms of the newly established derivative action mechanism, ineffective aspects within the new statutory system stipulated in Chinese Company Law 2018 still hinder the enforcement of an investor-friendly derivative lawsuit system in China. Doctrinal and political obstacles severely limit the function and efficacy of the derivative suit as a device for policing management malfeasance. These deficiencies rest on the eligibility of claimants, scope, demand requirements, the cost of litigation and, most importantly, the unique role played by public enforcers and public agencies such as the China Securities Investor Services Centre. Reform suggestions have been made regarding each deficiency in the system, with the purpose of building a new and efficient framework that maintains a balance between granting rights to minority shareholders and avoiding frivolous suits. A number of large corporations in China are dominated by insiders who wield excessive political power that exceeds their formal economic or management power.

---

by the foreign country with one's own country, and thirdly, with the object of promoting at home a social change which foreign law is designed either to express or to produce.
O. Kahn-Freund, 'On Uses and Misuses of Comparative Law' (1974) 37(1) *Modern Law Review* 7.

[26] J. Liu, 2013 *Nian Xingongsifa Shi Dazao Zhongguo Jingji Shengjiban de Falv Jishi (2013年新公司法是打造中国经济"升级版"的法律基石) [The 2013 New Company Law is the Legal Cornerstone of China's Economic Development]* (May 12, 2014), available at http://www.ccpit-ah.com/news/detail/id/5629.html (accessed 29 July 2022).

Beyond the focus on legal reforms, the book also offers discussions and arguments related to legal issues that hinder the efficient and sound enforcement of derivative claims. Suggestions are made clearer by discussions of theoretical support from corporate governance theories including agency theory and path dependence theory. It is suggested that derivative action in China must include a few specific local variations to fit with the many unique characteristics of China's history, culture, economy and society. While appreciating the force of globalisation in inducing legislative changes and the inherent formalist view of law suggesting that legal transplants associated with market-based economies can induce analogous market reforms in developing countries,[27] it would be a mistake to reduce analytical rigour by eliding the force of complex contextual specifics in China, evidenced in the political-economic dynamic and the instrumental nature of corporate lawmaking. For example, careful consideration of path dependence factors such as the deeply embedded non-litigious culture, *guanxi* and *renqing*, the judicial system, and government interference will also add originality to the discussion. Derivative action provides an authoritative remedy for shareholders to question the misconduct of insiders, and provides a powerful political tool for weak shareholders who may otherwise be ignored and may not have a significant voice in corporate decisions. The balance of power of the Chinese state, as the most important shareholder in the market, and the power of the Communist Party which controls the government and the state will be also discussed, especially in terms of state-controlled listed companies, half of whose voting shares are held by the Chinese government or the resolutions of whose shareholder meetings can be substantially influenced by the state.

Although there is a substantial body of literature in the field of derivative action in the form of journal articles, current publications tend to go into detail about the problems related to legislation, with less attention paid to the reasons underlying the legal framework and the relationships between efficient derivative action and other factors in a sound corporate governance model. The book aims to discuss derivative action from an interdisciplinary perspective and in the light of case studies from China, which is a novel and rare approach for research like this. In detail, this book is original since it represents the most complete case study to date, covering all available cases from 2006 to 2020.[28] It is challenging to provide a complete picture of all derivative actions, as there is

---

[27] J. Gillespie, 'Transplanted Company Law: An Ideological and Cultural Analysis of Market-Entry in Vietnam' (2002) 51(3) *International & Comparative Law Quarterly* 641, 644.

[28] We are not going to explore cases from before 2006 as they have been discussed elsewhere in detail; see S. Lin, *Derivative Actions in Chinese Company Law*, (Alphen aan den Rijn: Kluwer Law International 2015).

no single, comprehensive source of data on the issue. Hence, this research uses different means to piece together a full picture of China's derivative actions. It looks at cases from two databases, *Beida Fabao* and *China Judgments online*, and it also employs direct online searches using Chinese search engines and the websites of various courts.[29]

The uniqueness of the Chinese context makes the resulting arguments multi-faceted and complicated. For example, rather than simply criticising the problems caused by cultural factors, we see these issues as double-edged swords that may have both positive and negative impacts on the development of derivative action in China: shareholders may decide not to initiate litigation in order to *la* (pull) or *baochi* (maintain) *guanxi*. Meanwhile, they might also make collective action possible in JSLCs to satisfy shareholders due to their close *guanxi* with other shareholders.

Another distinctive feature of this book is that it fills a gap in the existing literature, integrating discussions of corporate governance with relevant legal aspects that are critical for future entrepreneurs or potential corporate practitioners who need an acute legal and commercial awareness. The chapters in the book work together as a coherent project for shareholders' remedies, catering for the needs of researchers in the field of corporate law and governance and for postgraduate students who need a holistic understanding of the subject. The theoretical enquiry advanced in this book is predicated on the observation that in order to be effective, legal reform and regulatory measures must possess a functional capacity to affect minority shareholders' incentives to bring derivative action, in order to attain the social objectives of law enforcement.

Currently, there is a shortage of similar examinations published in the English language. Regarding Chinese Company Law 2018, this book takes a closer look at related provisions aiming to codify the legislative basis for shareholders' remedies, and goes further to suggest sophisticated remedies for shareholders who object to certain decisions made by corporate controllers. Suggestions for how to enforce these laws more effectively and efficiently will be discussed with reference to current legislations in UK law, US law, Japanese law and Korean law.

This research should provide an essential primer for legal practitioners and in-house counsel who deal with shareholder litigation and corporate governance issues on a regular basis, and for legal and business theorists on corporate

---

[29]   Previous empirical research has only examined cases from *Beida Fabao* since *China Judgments online*, the official website for case reports in China, was established fairly recently in 2014; see H. Huang, 'Shareholder Derivative Litigation in China: Empirical Findings and Comparative Analysis' (2012) 27(4) *Banking and Finance Law Review* 619; S. Lin, 'Derivative Actions in China: Case Analysis' (2014) 44 *Hong Kong Law Journal* 621.

law and governance. The discussions in the book will also be helpful for legislators and policy makers who need to understand potential problems related to the application of law and directions for reform. Also, it will enable practitioners to comprehend and prepare for inconsistencies and complications that may arise when different courts interpret and apply the law in different ways.

1.4   KEY TERMS

1.4.1   Shareholder Protection

Shareholder protection has emerged as a significant topic for discussion in China since the launch of the Shanghai and Shenzhen Stock Markets made the trading of shares possible for listed companies. Breaches of duties by directors, supervisors and senior management executives will lead to civil, administrative and criminal liabilities under corporate law, China Securities and Regulation Commission (CSRC) rules, or criminal law in China. In terms of civil liability, the Company Law 2018 provides not only consequential liability for violating fiduciary duties, but also judicial avenues for enforcing those liabilities. As for shareholders' remedies, they have gained routes to protect their rights and enforce the duties of management teams through administrative action,[30] criminal prosecution[31] or civil litigation.[32] While the first two legal regimes in general terms punish wrongdoers with no compensation to shareholders whose rights have been harmed, civil ligation is identified as private litigation that enables shareholders to sue wrongdoers in order to seek damages. It has been argued that when the securities laws in 49 jurisdictions were assessed, private enforcement was found to be more positively correlated with financial development than public enforcement.[33] Compared with fines or criminal liability, private enforcement may be the only way to enable shareholders and companies to recover the losses they have suffered.

As far as public enforcement is concerned, an enforcer for public companies could be a securities commission, a central bank, or a unique supervisory body in a jurisdiction. Jackson and Roe presented a study in 2009 demonstrating that good public enforcement can contribute to the efficacy of private

---

[30]   CSRC Provisions on Banning the Entry into the Securities Market 3 March 2006.

[31]   See art. 169 (1), Criminal of the People's Republic of China.

[32]   See arts 148–149, Chinese Company Law 2018.

[33]   R. La Porta, F. Lopez-de-Silanes and A. Sheifer, 'What Works in Securities Law' (2006) 61 *Journal of Finance* 1, 11.

enforcement.[34] However, the effectiveness and function of public enforcers[35] have been questioned, and their powers have been described as 'insufficient to identify and prosecute most violators'. Furthermore, they 'may be susceptible to political influence, local protectionism and other forms of corruption and similar problems'.[36]

This research aims to offer a critical analysis of the existing legal protection of the interests of minority shareholders in China, and identify possibilities for how China could benefit from the UK's experience in building its legal infrastructure. This will include learning from what the UK has enforced or offered as possible legislative reforms in order to promote the interests of minority shareholders, such as public enforcement. We are aware of the importance of learning appropriately from experience and responding sensitively to local conditions, and we recognise that the development of the financial system in China has proceeded with uniquely Chinese characteristics. With regard to minority shareholder protection, it has been suggested that this pathway to growth will continue due to the Chinese economy's state shareholding, economic development stage, government policy, political system, history, culture and tradition. The rapid growth of the Chinese stock market necessitates an effective and rigorously monitored minority shareholder protection mechanism that is fit for purpose in the growing market and amenable to use by market participants, especially since a large percentage of such shareholders in emerging markets characterised by rapid growth will find themselves in a vulnerable position.

Creating a more competitive financial and legal system with increased opportunities for all is crucial for sustainable economic growth in China. The thrust of this project is therefore to explore a mechanism to improve the effectiveness of the shareholder protection regime in China in order to reduce the vulnerability of minority shareholders, improve the poor enforcement of company law, contribute to the fairness of corporate governance in China, and explore the possibilities of referring to legislative experiences in the UK company law from the doctrinal, comparative, empirical and historical perspectives.

We hope that suggestions from the research will be helpful for commercial practice, stock market structures and government policy, so that minority

---

[34] H. Jackson and M. Roe, 'Public and Private Enforcement of Securitas law: Resources-Based Evidence' (2009) 93(2) *Journal of Financial Economics* 207, 208.

[35] In detail, the CSRC for all listed firms, the State-owned Assets Supervision and Administrative Commission (SASAC) for listed state-owned companies.

[36] B. Anderson and B. Guo, 'Corporate Governance under the New Company Law (Part 2): Shareholder Lawsuits and Enforcement' (May 2006) 20(4) *China Law & Practice* 15.

shareholders can use the protection mechanisms in good faith. Suggestions will be advanced to achieve purposes such as the enhancement of the protection of minority shareholders, the provision of a device for managing officers and directors of companies who may be dominated by the majority shareholder, especially in state-owned enterprises (SOEs), and the resolution of power imbalances between directors and shareholders and between minority and majority shareholders and directors, to name but a few.

1.4.2   Different Types of Corporations in China

With the development of the Chinese domestic and international economy, many types of companies have been introduced in China. During the period between 1949 and 1956, when the new China was being established under the leadership of the Chinese Communist Party, the Provisional Regulations on Private Enterprises 1950 and Implementing Methods for Provisional Regulations on Private Enterprises were passed in order to encourage private enterprises to continue to operate in China. According to the Regulations, at that time there were five types of private companies in China, including: unlimited liability companies (*wuxian zeren gongsi*); LLCs [*youxian zeren gongsi*]); JSLCs [*gufen youxian gongsi*]); companies formed by one or more shareholders with unlimited liability and one or more shareholders with limited liability (*lianghe gongsi*); and companies formed by one or more shareholders having unlimited liability and one or more shareholder having liability limited to their share contributions, with the company capital divided into equal shares (*gufen lianghe gongsi*).[37]

As well as these private enterprises, SOEs have always played a significant role in the Chinese economy. More than two-thirds of the companies in the Fortune 5000 are SOEs, excluding banks and insurance companies. The largest and most important of the companies are controlled by a central holding company known as the SASAC, which is the world's largest controlling shareholder. Traditionally SOEs were more than corporations wholly owned by the state as the only shareholder. They are more 'aptly seen as a division or aggregation of productive assets within the loosely organised firm of China, Inc.'.[38] The post-Mao period saw a stage of reform characterised by efforts to change SOEs, which were plagued by low productivity, unresponsiveness to

---

[37]   Art. 3, Provisional Regulations on Private Enterprises 1950.

[38]   D.C. Clarke and N.C. Howson, 'Pathway to Minority Shareholder Protection: Derivative Action in the People's Republic of China' in D. Puchniak, H. Baum and M. Ewing-Chow (eds), *The Derivative Action in Asia: A Comparative and Functional Approach*, (Cambridge: Cambridge University Press 2012) 243, 244.

economic signals and waste.[39] The changes also involved a re-evaluation of the roles of directors, which are closely related to the bureaucratic hierarchy and powerful political positions. Since 1980 the SOEs have gradually lost some of their primacy and advantage with the introduction of the Chinese government's policy on the separation of government functions and business operations, and some SOEs are converting to other forms of companies according to the Chinese Company Law, including companies limited by shares, limited liability companies or wholly state-owned LLCs.

The application of Company Law could be different for LLCs and JSLCs under the current company law and the regulatory framework may rest on codified law, regulations from other levels and SPC's provisions. For example, derivative action as it was introduced in Chinese Company Law puts a threshold of '1% or more of the shares of the company for more than 180 consecutive days' for a JSLC to bring actions.[40] Unlike in common law countries such as the UK, where inadequacies may be alleviated by demonstrating a *prima facie* case (section 261(2)) or case law[41] and corresponding procedure rules,[42] the legislative legal basis of derivative action and the relevant rules regarding its procedure in China rest on the Civil Procedure Law 1992 and the Measures for the Administration of Attorneys' Fee 2006, supplemented by the Provisions of the Supreme People's Court (SPC) on Some Issues about the Application of the Company Law of the People's Republic of China (IV) 最高人民法院关于适用＜中华人民共和国公司法＞若干问题的规定（四） (Provision IV).

---

[39]   Ibid.

[40]   This legislative amendment was introduced in 2005 and came into effect on January 1, 2006. For the purpose of this discussion, this Company Law version will be referred to as the 2005 Company Law. The numbering in the Company Law changed with the third amendment of the Chinese Company Law on December 28, 2013. Therefore, Section 151 here may be confused with Section 152 of the 2005 Company Law in some of the literature written before the third amendment. X. Huang, 'Shareholders Revolt: The Statutory Derivative Action in China' [2009] 49 *Comparative Research in Law & Political Economy*1, 4–6; H., Hui, 'The Statutory Derivative Action in China: Critical Analysis and Recommendations for Reform' (2007) 4(2) *Berkeley Business Law Journal* 227.

[41]   See *Wallersteiner v Moir (no 2)* [1975] QB 371 at 391; *Carlisle & Cumbria United Independent Supporters' Society Ltd v CUFC Holdings Ltd.* [2010] EWCA Civ 463; [2011] BCC 855; *Stainer v Lee* [2010] EWHC 1539 (Ch). [2010] EWHC 1539 (Ch).

[42]   Rule 19.9E of the Civil Procedure Rules.

1.4.3   Corporate Governance and Agency Problems in China

Corporate governance makes headlines. Exemplifying and influencing different styles of capitalism, the diversity among corporate governance models has been widely recognised not only as a commercial theme, but also as a central political and economic issue around the world.[43] From the beginning of the new century, there has been a series of commercial crises, from the corporate collapse of Barings Bank to the collapse of Enron, and from the financial scandal surrounding Royal Ahold to collapse of HIH in Australia. A consensus view has emerged that problems and shortcomings in the way the companies were run and managed could lead to these huge collapses and serious consequences. The collapses were due to a lack of efficient control, ineffective and incorrect external audit and accounting reports, a lack of transparent directors' duties and remuneration packages, and poor information disclosure. An obvious and immediate observation was that the sacrifice of the long-term health of the company in order to maximise share prices significantly contributed to those corporate failures.[44] It is argued that corporate governance has shifted from its traditional focus on agency conflicts[45] to address issues of ethics, accountability and transparency in the post-Enron years.[46] Research on the framework, style and reconstruction of corporate governance in China is becoming more and more important and has accompanied the steady opening up of the Chinese economy to greater market-based fair competition and enhanced market monitoring. Along with the sound corporate governance, an awareness of the importance of legal protections in China began to establish a modern framework for legal protection from mid-1980s.

According to the conception of 'corporate governance' given by Julien and Rieger,[47] corporate governance is the system within an organisation that 'protects the interest of its diverse stakeholder groups'. One of the most important group of stakeholders are shareholders, particularly the minority shareholders. As part of the national business framework, a corporate governance system has significant national-persistent path-dependent sources, which include not

---

[43]   J. Kay and A. Silberston, 'Corporate Governance' in F.M. Patfield (ed.), *Perspectives on Company Law 2* (London: Kluwer Law International Ltd. 1997) 49.

[44]   L. Cerioni, 'The Success of the Company in s. 172 (1) of the UK Companies Act 2006: Towards an 'Enlightened Directors' Primacy?' (2008) 4(1) *Original Law Review* 8, 11.

[45]   See H. Demesetz and K. Lehm 'The Structure of Corporate Ownership: Cases and Consequences' (1983) 93(6) *Journal of Political Economy* 1155.

[46]   A. Gill, 'Corporate Governance as Social Responsibility: A Research Agenda' (2008) 26(2) *Berkeley Journal of International Law* 452, 453–454.

[47]   R. Julien and L. Rieger, 'The Missing Link in Corporate Governance: Risk Manager's Role in Corporate Governance' (2003) 50 *Risk Management* 32, 33.

only random historical accidents but also other components of the national business system and complementary elements within the matching social and political systems.[48] The persistence of those sources contributes to the stability of domestic corporate governance systems; and the further diversity of corporate ownership and governance among the worlds' advanced economies.[49] It is argued that a domestic corporate governance system is composed of various complementary elements; meanwhile, it is also complementary to other domestic governance systems, such as the financial system, the political system and so on. Such institutional interdependencies obstruct the transformation of one single institution within the regime. Therefore, even if the corporate governance convergence is going to happen, the convergence is far more complicated than moving to a single archetype model.

The economic and social development in China since its opening to the world in 1978 have highlighted the intense policy focus on corporate governance.[50] China launched its stock market in 1990s and began to establish modern companies, in which corporate governance practices in listed companies have emerged and become increasingly signifanant alongside this global trend. The corporate governance and the institutional and regulatory environment have progressed dramatically.[51] There is evidence to suggest that good corporate governance mitigates agency problems, and this is especially and particularly necessary in the case of China because of its unique double agency problems, namely conflicts between boards of directors and shareholders and conflicts between controlling and minority shareholders. The latter problem may well involve state and government agencies,[52] which are often controlling shareholders and decision makers in their role as representatives of the State. They tend to dominate corporate boards in SOEs, and act as the regulators of companies and corporate actions. Therefore, discussions of the history, nature, problems and future of administrative corporate governance in China

---

[48] R.H. Schmidt and G. Sprindler, 'Path Dependence, Corporate Governance and Complementarity' (2002) 5(3) *International Finance* 311.

[49] L. Bebchuk and M.J. Roe, 'A Theory of Path Dependence in Corporate Governance and Ownership' (2000) 52(1) *Stanford Law Review* 121.

[50] J. Allen and R. Li, 'Awakening Governance: ACGA China Corporate Governance Report 2018'. Asian Corporate Governance Association (2018); M. Ararat, S. Claessens and B.B. Yurtoglu, 'Corporate Governance in Emerging Markets: A Selective Review and an Agenda for Future Research, (2021) 48 *Emerging Markets Review* 100767.

[51] F. Jiang and K.A. Kim, 'Corporate Governance in China: A Survey' (2020) 24(4) *Review of Finance* 733, 734.

[52] See Q. Yang, 'On Governance Control of Corporation' (2008) *Wuhan University Journal (Philosophy & Social Sciences)* 38; see also Y. Zhang, *Large Chinese State-Owned Enterprises: Corporatization and Strategic Development*, (New York: Palgrave MacMillan 2008).

are particularly important in order to offer a complete picture that reflects the country's stages of economic development, political policies, social needs, international policies, shareholder structure, market conditions, financial systems and foreign policies, all of which have had an impact on the Chinese economy.[53] Accordingly to the more recent survey on corporate governance in China, the dominant agency problem in China is still the horizontal agency conflict between controlling shareholders and minority shareholders as the result of the concentrated ownership structure.[54]

China's economic success and the unique Chinese characteristics of its economic development make its transition path a fruitful subject with profound impact for researchers. As far as corporate governance development is concerned, this area of research also offers potential benefits for other jurisdictions with emerging markets, or even jurisdictions with mature markets where there is government interference in the content and process of the corporate governance scheme. Chinese corporate governance has also been described in different ways and based on various focuses and classifications.

The discussions on corporate governance are key for the book to constitute a complete picture for analysis of derivative action. Because of the concentrated ownership structure and imperfect law and regulations, the key agency problem in China is the conflict of interest between the controlling shareholder and minority shareholders. The controlling shareholder holds power through control of the board and managers. The book will then explore the effectiveness of monitoring mechanisms through private enforcement, trying to deter or correct the misconduct of the controller.

1.5   THE LAYOUT OF THE BOOK

This book offers a comprehensive and critical analysis of the derivative action mechanism in China, with a focus on codified law, possible reforms, and the role of the mechanism in promoting more sound corporate governance. The book is organised in seven chapters. Chapter 1 provides an introduction with discussions of some of the basic terms and concepts that will be used throughout the book, such as shareholder protection and agency problems in China, as well as the classification and definition of companies in China as recognised

---

[53]   This unique nature does not only compromise the independence of corporate boards and the efficiency of corporate governance. In fact it may also have positive effects in a jurisdiction like China because of its unique economic and historical development and the profound impact of culture on governance, such as a mitigation of the serious information problems faced by investors and regulators.

[54]   F. Jiang and K.A. Kim, 'Corporate Governance in China: A Survey' (2020) 24(4) *Review of Finance* 733, 733.

by Chinese Company Law. Chapter 2 presents a detailed analysis of the regulatory framework in China, including an analysis of the corresponding legislative attempts to establish derivative action at different levels.

Transformative corporate governance in China will be discussed in Chapter 3. This issue is attracting increasing attention from lawyers, economists, corporate directors and government policy makers as a result of external push factors such as corporate governance convergence and Organisation for Economic Co-operation and Development (OECD) principles, and internal drivers such as the significance of shareholder protection.

Chapter 4 offers doctrinal, comparative and empirical analyses of the eligibility of claimants to bring derivative action in JSLCs, together with proposals for how the effectiveness of the regime in China might be improved in the hope of increasing the effectiveness of the mechanism and the enforcement of company law and contributing to the fairness and accountability of corporate governance.

Chapter 5 focuses on a key element of the derivative action mechanism, namely litigation fee-related issues, and aims to establish a balanced and effective approach in order to eliminate the obstacles that hinder the smooth operation of derivative action, thereby protecting the interests of companies and their shareholders. A fixed fee and a contingency fee supported by a common fund, with substantial tests pioneered by a localised approach, are proposed as methods for the effective enforcement of the mechanism.

Chapter 6 offers an empirical analysis of the enforcement of derivative action in China by looking through all 466 reported cases of derivative action from 2006 to 2020, and addressing the question of whether the mechanism has been consistently and authoritatively used by shareholders, particularly in terms of promoting accessibility, effectiveness and the mechanism's balancing function.

Chapter 7 examines the force of socio-cultural specialties in shaping the distinct nature of laws in relation to derivative action, in particular, the historical and cultural emending and implications. Reform proposals will be offered to promote the accessibility and effectiveness of a balanced derivative action mechanism. We will also consider the significance of private enforcement backed by a public regulator to improve derivative actions along each of the three criteria.

2. The regulatory framework and development trajectory of derivative actions in China

Over the last decade much attention has been given to Chinese corporate governance as a worldwide research topic, both in practice and in theory. It has become a concept that has increasingly engaged the minds of corporate regulators and the stock exchange in China. Attention is mostly focused on the debate concerning how China can develop an effective corporate governance system to improve the performance of its listed companies and protect their minority shareholders and stakeholders. The improvement of corporate governance for Chinese corporations is an ongoing battle that requires the participation of parties such as regulators, market participants and academics.[1]

In light of the granting of permanent normal trade relations to China from other WTO members and also of China's participation in the WTO from December 2001, many more investment opportunities in China are becoming available and the potential market is massive. China has entered a new stage of economic transformation and integration within the world economy.[2] At the same time, the legislation on corporate law has been subject to increasing pressure for reform. The study of Chinese company law is particularly important, and has been at the forefront of international scrutiny due to the dominant positions of Chinese listed companies and the vast numbers of companies and investors in China.[3]

---

[1]   J. Zhao, *Corporate Social Responsibility in Contemporary China* (Cheltenham: Edward Elgar 2014) 90.

[2]   S. Voss and Y.W. Xia, 'Corporate Governance of Listed Companies in China', paper presented at Track 8 of IFSAM VIIIth World Congress 2006, hosted by VHB, Berlin Germany, September 2006, available at https://www.researchgate.net/profile/Stefan–Voss–3/publication/256000571_Corporate_Governance_for_Listed _Companies_in_China/links/565c9c9608aeafc2aac716d2/Corporate–Governance –for–Listed–Companies–in–China.pdf (acessed 21 July 2022), p.11.

[3]   There were 4,698 listed companies with the total market value of 79.88 trillion yuan in China up to April 8, 2022 available at http://www.csrc.gov.cn/csrc/c105936/c2334165/content.shtml (accessed 21 July 2022).

2.1   CODIFIED LAW

It is stipulated in the Legislation Law of China that 'the National People's Congress and its Standing Committee will exercise the legislative power of the state as the national legislature'.[4] Legislation related to this project, including Company Law, Securities Law, Insolvency Law and Civil Law, are all such laws made by the National People's Congress and its Standing Committee. They are the legislations that can be designated as 'laws (*Fa Lv* 法律)'.

Company Law 2005 is the legislation, at the level of *Fa Lv* 法律, that this stream of the project will focus on. At the Fourteenth Meeting of the Tenth National People's Congress, from 25–28 February 2005, six defects were proposed to the Standing Committee of the National People's Congress, including: the registration of companies; corporate governance-related issues including the rights and liabilities of shareholders' meetings, boards of directors and supervisory boards; the protection of minority shareholders and creditors including a more effective derivative action system; issuing, transferring and listing of shares; the supervision of listed companies; and the fiduciary duties and the related liabilities of board directors and supervisors.

The introduction and enactment of new laws in the form of a Company Law in 2006, a Securities Law in 2006, and a new Insolvency Law in 2005, provides evidence of progressive legislative reform. The new Chinese Company Law 2006 is an almost completely rewritten version of the Company Law 1993, and represents completely new legislation. This new law brought many improvements and relaxed a number of restrictions on business incorporations and operation in China, including a reduction and later abolition (after a revision of Chinese Company Law in 2013 and 2018 and Chinese Securities Law in 2019) of capital requirements,[5] enhanced shareholder and creditor protection, and improved rights for shareholders to file lawsuits against directors, including derivative actions.

2.2   LAWS PRODUCED BY LOCAL GOVERNMENT, MINISTRIES AND COMMISSIONS

In addition to laws made by the National People's Congress and its Standing Committee, the following laws or normal documents have been drafted by

---

4   Art. 7 of Legislation Law of People's Republic of China.

5   For details of the revision see 'Decision of the Standing Committee of the National People's Congress on Amending Seven Laws Including the Marine Environment Protection Law of the People's Republic of China' 全国人大常委会关于修改《中华人民共和国海洋环境保护法》等七部法律的决定' (2013).

different government organs at different levels, including administrative regulations (*Xingzheng Fagui* 行政法规) made by the State Council in the form of, measures (*banfa*办法) and provisions (*guiding* 规定), departmental rules (*Bumen Guizhang* 部门规章) made by Ministries under the State Council, Local Enactment (*Difang Fagui* 地方法规) at provincial and city levels, Judicial Interpretations (*Sifa Jieshi*司法解释), and rules made by self-regulatory organisations such as the Shanghai and Shenzhen Stock Exchanges.

One group of key legislators that is closely linked with the stream of the project includes the 29 ministries and commissions in China. Departmental rules and judicial interpretations need additional clarification to provide a solid background for further discussion in this project. In terms of departmental rules, a few State Council ministries and commissions are involved in legislation in areas that are related to the project. First, the China Securities Regulatory Commission is the most active when it comes to shareholder protection. It provides listed companies with corporate and securities rules, corporate governance, corporate finance, information disclosure and the listing and delisting of companies.

Apart from government legislation related to corporation law, the CSRC has played an active role in improving corporate governance. In September 2018, the CSRC issued its Code of Corporate Governance for Listed Companies in China. This Code, like many other similar instruments elsewhere in the world, contains broad and vague language describing guiding principles, rather than explicit regulation. It contains considerable evidence of convergence with international corporate governance guidelines, since the draft largely relied on the G20/OECD Corporate Governance Principles,[6] and almost all the provisions contained in it have parallel provisions in the law of the UK and the US or in the Code of Corporate Governance of the former. Despite the fact that there are many doubts about whether the OECD Principles are appropriate in an emerging economy like China,[7] the Code of Corporate Governance does propose good practices for corporate governance, including the requirement for active boards of directors, independent outside directors forming the majority of boards, and protecting the interests of minority shareholders and stakeholders, which all require strong free markets and economic governance with minimum government interference. The State Administration of Industry and Commerce also makes rules in this area, such as the Regulations of the

---

[6]   G20/OECD, OECD Principles of Corporate Governance 2015.

[7]   See V.Z. Chen, J. Li and D.M. Shaprio, 'Are OECD-Prescribed "Good Corporate Governance" Practices Really Good in an Emerging Economy' (2011) 28(1) *Asia Pacific Journal of Management* 115.

People's Republic of China on the Administration of Company Registration. The Ministry of Commerce makes rules concerning foreign participation in Chinese-incorporated companies. The Ministry of Finance makes rules in relation to companies' accounting standards. Focusing on SOEs, the State-owned Assets Supervision and Administration Commissions enact rules in this area, viewing them as state assets and directors as civil servants.

2.3   ROLE OF THE COURT AND ROLE OF THE SUPREME PEOPLE'S COURT

As a country with a civil law system, the decisions of courts do not have the power to become laws. Despite this, the Judicial Interpretation acts as 'a rudimentary system that may be able to interpret as the functional equivalent of case law' in common law jurisdictions.[8]

In practice, the Supreme People's Court (SPC) has been stretching its interpretative power and one can argue that there is an emergence of 'judicial activism' in China.[9] The SPC makes laws in a more direct and visible manner[10] by issuing interpretation (*jieshi*), provisions (*guiding*), decisions (*jueding*) or responses to enquiries from lower courts (*pifu*).[11] Upon the requests of the lower courts, the SPC will give 'replies' regarding the adjudication of individual cases. The replies are 'final' in the sense that both the lower courts and the appellate courts have to comply with them. The replies have, in fact, nullified the right to appeal by the private party. They have also undermined the judicial independence and discretion of the lower courts, however, many courts are willingly giving up their adjudicative power as in doing so they can shift their responsibility to the SPC. As argued by some, the guiding cases can be more effective than replies in guiding lower courts in the adjudication of specific cases.[12]

Besides substituting lower courts' decisions with its own 'replies' to individual cases, the SPC has also been issuing ponderous judicial interpretations on the general application of the law. Admittedly, the judicial interpretations

---

[8]   A.H.Y. Chen, *An Introduction to the Legal System of People's Republic of China* (Hong Kong: Lexis Nexis 2004) 118.

[9]   C. Wang, 'Law-Making Functions of the Chinese Courts: Judicial Activism in a Country of Rapid Social Changes' (2006) 1(4) *Frontiers of Law in China* 524.

[10]   R. Peerenboom, 'Courts as Legislators: SPC Interpretations and the Need for Procedural Reforms to Increase Transparency and Public Participation', [2006] *Oxford Foundation for Law, Justice and Society Policy Brief* 1.

[11]   Provisions of the Supreme People's Court on the Judicial Interpretation Work, art. 6.

[12]   F. Liu, 'The Definition and Exercise of Judicial Interpretation Authority [司法解释权限的界定与行使]' (2016) 3 *China Legal Science [中国法学]* 207.

issued by the SPC have filled in the gaps left by the slow-paced lawmaking of the National People's Congress (NPC) and its Standing Committee, which is often criticised for being unable to meet the needs of the fast-changing society. However, in doing so, the SPC has transformed its major role as an adjudicator to a quasi-legislative institution.

It has been observed that the SPC has been increasingly proactive in issuing judicial interpretations, the evidence being the decreasing intervals between the major commercial legislation and the relevant judicial interpretations.[13] The judicial interpretation is usually not based on the accumulation of knowledge through the adjudication of individual cases, but formulated in accordance with the reading of the legislation by the SPC. Moreover, the judicial interpretations sometimes deviate from the legislative purpose and assert the SPC's policies which find no basis in the 'legislative spirit'.[14]

Interpretation is the most commonly seen form of a legislative document issued by the SPC in China. They deal with the application of specific laws or types of cases in practice. So far, the SPC has enacted four issues of 'Provisions on Some Issues about the Application of the Company Law of the People's Republic of China', SOE restructuring, and dispute settlement measures where there is involvement from foreign invested companies.[15]

The SPC's power to issue judicial interpretations comes from the delegation of the Standing Committee of the NPC.[16] The Standing Committee has limited the SPC's judicial interpretation power to the 'specific application of laws and decrees in court trials',[17] while the Standing Committee of the NPC will provide interpretations for clarification of legislation.[18] The Standing Committee will supervise the judicial interpretations issued by the SPC.[19] The judicial interpretation regarding the specific application of law should address specific provisions of the legislation in accordance with the objectives, principles, and original meaning of the legislation. As to the clarification of the specific meaning of provisions or the application of the law in new

---

[13]   S. Chen, 'Analysis of Constructing Concept of Judicial Interpretation' [司法解释的建构理念分析]' (2012) 2 *Chinese Journal of Law [法学研究]* 3.

[14]   Ibid.

[15]   See J. Wang, *Company Law in China: Regulation of Business Organizations in a Socialist Market Economy* (Cheltenham: Edward Elgar 2014) 15–16.

[16]   Resolution of the Standing Committee of the National People's Congress Providing an Improved Interpretation of the Law [全国人民代表大会常务委员会关于加强法律解释工作的决议](Adopted at the 19th Meeting of the Standing Committee of the Fifth National People's Congress on June 10, 1981).

[17]   Ibid., art. 2.

[18]   Ibid., art. 1.

[19]   Art. 31, Law on the Supervision of Standing Committees of People's Congresses at Various Levels [各级人民代表大会常务委员会监督法] 2007.

circumstances, the SPC could only request the Standing Committee to issue a legislative interpretation.[20]

As the Standing Committee shares the legislative power with the NPC,[21] the legislative interpretations issued by the Standing Committee have the same binding effect as the legislation.[22] However, the legal effects of the judicial interpretation remain unclear in relation to its legal hierarchy compared with codified laws (*Fa Lv* 法律). The SPC has declared that its judicial interpretation is a formal source of law.[23] However, the SPC is only authorised to issue judicial interpretations in respect of the specific problems in the application of the legislation in trials whereas a judicial interpretation can only be valid within this scope and has the same authority as the legislation it interprets.[24]

The SPC has also emulated the 'democratic' feature of the legislature by soliciting public opinions from 'any citizen and organisation' to improve the legitimacy of its judicial interpretations.[25] The SPC's efforts in 'democratic' lawmaking give rise to doubt whether the judiciary should sacrifice its role as an impartial adjudicator for a 'democratic' function. According to Chinese Constitution, the NPC and its Standing Committee has the lawmaking power and is at the apex of the representative democracy.[26] By becoming a 'democratic' lawmaking institution, the SPC illegitimately challenges the legislative power of the NPC. The judiciary should perform a different role from the legislature and only the latter offers the forum for the rivalry of the interest groups subject to strict procedural controls. Without the rigorous procedural checks imposed on the lawmaking power of the NPC, the SPC is susceptible to the capture by interest groups. Thus, the Constitution should be strictly applied and the interpretative power of the judiciary should be limited to finding the legislative purpose, rather than changing the substance of law and altering the rights of private parties.[27]

---

[20]   Arts 45 and 104, Legislation Law 2000.

[21]   China has a unified legislative system in which the NPC and its Standing Committee is supreme and have the ultimate lawmaking power. See arts 7, 56, 63, 71, 73. Legislation Law 2000.

[22]   Art. 50, Legislation Law 2000.

[23]   Provisions of the Supreme People's Court on the Judicial Interpretation Work, art. 5: 'The judicial interpretations issued by the Supreme People's Court shall have full legal force.'

[24]   C. Wang, 'Research on the Effects of the SPC Judicial Interpretation [最高法院司法解释效力研究]' (2016) 28 *Peking University Law Journal [中外法学]* 263.

[25]   K. Shen, 'Democratization' of Judicial Interpretation and the Supreme Court's Political Function' (2008) 29(4) *Social Sciences in China* 33.

[26]   Art. 3, Constitution of People's Republic of China (effective in 1982, amended in 2004).

[27]   Ibid.

The establishment of the guiding case system[28] by the SPC can be viewed as a good example of executing SPC's legitimate role in providing guidance to specific issues in the adjudication. Since 2010, the SPC has started to issue guiding cases in order to improve the uniformity and consistency of adjudication among the different levels of courts.[29] For this purpose, the SPC has set up an Office for Case Guidance Work[30] to select typical cases[31] that can offer guidance for the future adjudication. Courts are required to cite the guiding case in their adjudication although guiding cases are not explicitly binding on the local courts.[32]

The establishment of the guiding case system has injected an element of *stare decisis* into China's codified civil law system, however, it is doubtful to what extent it will fulfil the objective of unifying the application of the law. First, the guiding cases distinguish from the binding precedents in common law as they are not an independent source of law and could only be cited as a reason for adjudication instead of the basis.[33] Second, the guiding cases cover limited issues and in total there are only 92 cases at the present.[34] On the other hand, the quotation of the guiding case in adjudication remains infrequent.[35] Third, guiding cases are still a product of top-down lawmaking, as they are selected and edited by the SPC, in contrast with the accumulative judge-made law in common law jurisdictions.[36] However, despite these reservations, it is

---

[28]   See Provisions on Case Guidance [关于案例指导工作的规定] (No. 51 [2010] of the Supreme People's Court); Detailed Rules for the Implementation of the Provisions on Case Guidance [关于案例指导工作的规定实施细则] (No. 130 [2015] of the Supreme People's Court).

[29]   Art. 1, Detailed Rules for the Implementation of the Provisions on Case Guidance.

[30]   Art. 3, Provisions on Case Guidance.

[31]   Art. 2, Provisions on Case Guidance.

[32]   Art. 9, 10 Provisions on Case Guidance.

[33]   Ibid.

[34]   See guiding cases on the official website of the SPC, available at http://www.court.gov.cn/fabu–gengduo–77.htm (accessed 21 July 2022) 1.

[35]   M. Jia, 'Chinese Common Law? Guiding Cases and Judicial Reform' (2016) 129(8) *Harvard Law Review* 2213; M. Gechlik, Stanford Law School China Guiding Cases Project, 'China's Guiding Cases System: Review and Recommendations' (August 2016), available at https://cgc.law.stanford.edu/guiding–cases–analytics/issue–5/ (accessed 21 July 2022).

[36]   Common law has been described as growing spontaneously through case-by-case analysis. The common law has been regarded by some as superior to the codified civil law, as it builds piecemeal in response to immediate situations, in contrast to the civil law in which the legislature is making a doomed attempt to amass a totality of knowledge necessary for designing law top-down. See F.A. Hayek, *Law, Legislation and Liberty: A New Statement of the Liberal Principles of Justice and Political Economy* (London: Routledge 2012) 112.

safe to say that the guiding case system is more legitimate and sustainable than general judicial interpretations that have the danger of encroaching the legislative power of the NPC.

2.4   SOFT LAW

The regulatory framework is enriched by soft law approaches. Research on the framework, style and reconstruction of corporate governance in China, including minority shareholder protection, has become increasingly important and has accompanied the steady opening up of the Chinese economy to fairer market-based competition and enhanced market monitoring. For example, the Chinese Corporate Governance Code has played a significant role in promoting the standards of corporate governance in China, and signalled a new direction for corporate governance development. It was designed to serve as a benchmark for evaluating whether a listed company has a good corporate governance structure. In Section 33 the directors are required to act 'faithfully, honestly and diligently in performing their duties for the best interests of the company and all the shareholders'. However, there is also a whole chapter in the Code of Corporate Governance for Listed Companies in China on protecting the interests of various stakeholders.

The opening up of the Chinese market clearly calls for further improvements in corporate governance practice within Chinese corporations. Moreover, the listing of Chinese corporations on both domestic and foreign stock exchanges has accelerated the commitment to transparency and corporate disclosure practice in China. At the same time, the promotion of corporate governance practices in both non-listed companies and non-government controlled Chinese companies will also be increasingly significant, since private companies in China represent more than half of the country's annual economic growth. China is going through a transition from a planned economy to a market-oriented economy. What China needs is an institutional corporate governance framework, including a well-defined corporate legal system, well-structured boards, rigorous law enforcement and well-functioning financial markets.[37] In detail, it will be essential that the framework entails a corporate legal system and board structure which will require directors to consider the interests of stakeholders while maximising the interests of shareholders, not only in SOEs but also in private companies. Further law reform must act to protect stakeholders' interests and make corporations more socially responsible. Therefore, there is a particular need for research focused on a special corporate governance

---

[37]   Q. Liu, 'Corporate Governance in China: Current Practices, Economic Effects and Institutional Determinants' (2006) 52(2) *CESifo Economic Studies* 415, 419.

system, necessary because of China's unique institutional setting and the need to regulate its transitional economy. If a hybrid corporate governance model is adopted in China,[38] this research may offer suggestions on how to protect the interests of stakeholders and promote CSR in order to maintain the healthy development of Chinese corporations.

2.5   LEGAL TRANSPLANT

Choruses of praise notwithstanding, the fit of these Western inspired corporate law principles within the Chinese context thus far has not been given adequate thought. The passage of these amended rules, including the provisions on derivative actions, intrinsically rests upon the powerful metaphor of the '*legal transplant*',[39] holding that laws associated with advanced market economies are an autonomous set of formal, apolitical rules unconstrained by political and cultural borders, which can function and bring about analogous market development in developing countries, just as the case of China.[40] In the meantime, one has to appreciate that even today under the ever-increasing force of globalisation, in many aspects China remains a metaphor for notable differences, distinct from its Western counterparts: the fact that SOEs continue to dominate primary and pillar industries of the economy and enjoy privileges in various aspects challenges key assumptions of the free market economy and the hegemony of economic liberalism.[41] Rooted in Confucianism and reflecting Marxist theory, the dominant instrumental view of law as a means of securing the reign of public ownership of the means of production, represented and exerted by the Party-State, also sets its face against the '*multibillion-dollar rule of law*'[42] concept that Western legal scholars have come to hold dear. Scholars

---

[38]   J. Zhao and A. Keay, 'Transforming Corporate Governance in Chinese Corporations: A Journey Not A Destination' (2017–2018) 38(2) *Northwestern Journal of International Law and Business*.

[39]   G. Teubner, 'Legal Irritants: Good Faith in British Law or How Unifying Law Ends Up in New Divergences' (1998) 61(1) *Modern Law Review* 11, 12.

[40]   J. Gillespie, 'Transplanted Company Law: An Ideological and Cultural Analysis of Market-Entry in Vietnam' (2002) 51(3) *International & Comparative Law Quarterly* 641, 644; G. Lan, 'American Legal Realism Goes to China: The China Puzzle and Law Reform' (2014) 51(2) *American Business Law Journal* 365, 367.

[41]   J. Williamson, 'The Washington Consensus as Policy Prescription for Development', a lecture in the series "Practitioners of Development" delivered at the World Bank, Jan. 13, 2004.

[42]   R. Peerenboom, 'Introduction'*, in* R. Peerenboom (ed.) *Judicial Independence in China—Lessons for Global Rule of Law Promotion* (Cambridge: Cambridge University Press 2009) 1; R. Tomasic, 'Company Law Implementation in the PRC: The Rule of Law in the Shadow of the State' (2015) 15 (2) *Journal of Corporate Law Studies* 285, 285; A. Grosman, I. Okhmatovskiy and M. Wright, 'State Control and Corporate

have developed widely touted labels such as the '*Beijing Consensus*', a '*China Model*', or '*Chinese exceptionalism*'[43] to encapsulate China's unique mode of development. Although the provenance of such uniqueness remains debatable, it has been contended that the ideologically inspired Party-State control over economy and law is one major factor in the list of distinctive '*Chinese characteristics*'.[44] The fact that transplanted corporate law principle including the derivative actions are embedded in a complex economic, political, and ideological system that is unique and distinct from its Western counterparts provides compelling reasons for thinking again about their practical effectiveness.

On a broad spectrum, decades of research have yet to arrive at a coherent view of the general theme of legal transplantation, with two main schools of thought forming the polar extremes of the discourse. On the one hand, advocates hold to the rhetoric of the mobility of law, suggesting that 'the amount of innovation in law is small and borrowing and imitation is of central importance in … the course of legal change'.[45] Endorsed by multilateral organisations such as the IMF and the World Bank, core commercial law principles and governance structures associated with a mature market-oriented economy are regarded by convergence theorists as universally applicable.[46] While not explicitly stated, the mobility of law hints a formalist understanding, viewing laws as autonomous, apolitical rules that can be applied by neutral judges, unconstrained by either national political or cultural borders.[47] This nomadic vision of law also works to combat the criticism of developed countries interfering with the internal affairs of developing nation – after all, legal transplantation is more a matter of borrowing for developing countries and

---

Governance in Transition Economies: 25 Years on from 1989' (2016) 24(3) *Corporate Governance: An International Review* 200, 201.

[43]   E.g., S. Kennedy, 'The Myth of the Beijing Consensus' (2010) 19(65) *Journal of Contemporary China* 461; S. Breslin, 'The China Model and the Global Crisis: From Friedrich List to a Chinese Mode of Governance?' (2011)87(6) *International Affairs* 1323, 1323–4; L. Tang, 'The China Model and Its Efficacy in a Comparative Context' (2016)1(1) *Journal of Chinese Governance* 174; B. Naughton, 'China's Distinctive System: Can It be a Model for Others?' (2010) 19(65) *Journal of Contemporary China* 437.

[44]   R. Peerenboom, 'What Have We Learned about Law and Development? Describing, Predicting, and Assessing Legal Reforms in China' (2006) 27(3) *Michigan Journal of International Law* 823, 825–6.

[45]   E. Örücü, 'Law as Transposition' (2002)51(2) *International & Comparative Law Quarterly* 205, 206.

[46]   E.g., H. Hansmann and R. Kraakman, 'The End of History for Corporate Law' (2001) 89(2) *Georgetown Law Journal* 439; B. Black and R. Kraakman, 'A Self-Enforcing Model of Corporate Law' (1996) 109 *Harvard Law Review* 1911.

[47]   P. Legrand, The Impossibility of Legal Transplants (1997)4(2) *Maastricht Journal of European & Company Law* 111, 112.

an exportation process for advanced economies. As such, contemporary legal transplantation discussions tend to focus on subjects in the private law realm, so as to marginalise the social and political embedding of legal transplants. Rules on the shareholders' rights including right to bring derivative actions, emulating the market-based ideology that commercial law is not a political form of law, are thus well received as part of the transplantation package.[48]

A contrasting theme, originating from Montesquieu's thesis,[49] perceives law as a *'fait social total'*[50] that cannot supersede cultural boundaries. This school of thought was reinforced by the development of path dependence theory, which advocates long-lasting national systematic differences in the ideological, institutional, and economic compositions of home and host countries.[51] As such, mobility opponents do not hesitate to use strong vocabulary to denote transported rules in the host context, describing them as *'contaminants'*[52] or *'irritants'*[53] to the host country's system. Meanwhile, it must be appreciated that even in the eyes of many comparative lawyers who hold to Montesquieu's thesis, sociological factors would not impact on all transplanted subjects. There would likely be socio-cultural barriers when transplanted laws relate to contextually-sensitive subjects, such as family law in the private sphere and constitutional arrangements in the public realm.[54] However, when it comes to corporate and commercial law, a matter 'so very remote from the sociolog-

---

[48] I. Ramsay, 'Commentary: The Politics of Commercial Law' [2001] *Wisconsin Law Review* 565, 572; M.J. Horowitz, *The Transformation of American Law, 1780–1860* (Harvard: Harvard University Press 1977) Chapter VII, 211.

[49] As Montesquieu commented, 'The political and civil laws of each nation must be proper for the people for whom they are made, so much so that it is a very great accident if those of one nation can fit another.' C. de Secondat, B. de Montesquieu, *The Spirit of Laws* (first published in 1748, translated by T. Nugent in 1752 and republished by Batoche Books in 2001); E.W. Orts, 'The Rule of Law in China' (2001) 34 *Vanderbilt Journal of Transnational Law* 43.

[50] M. Mauss, *"Essai sur le don", Sociologie et anthropologie,* (Paris: Presses Universitaires de France, 6th ed. 1995) 274–275.

[51] E.g., L. Bebchuk and M. Roe, 'A Theory of Path Dependence in Corporate Governance and Ownership' (1999) 52(1) *Stanford Law Review* 127.

[52] E. Örücü, 'Law as Transposition' (2002)51(2) *International & Comparative Law Quarterly* 205, 206.

[53] G. Teubner, 'Legal Irritants: Good Faith in British Law or How Unifying Law Ends Up in New Divergences' (1998) 61(1) *Modern Law Review* 11, 12.

[54] For instance, O. Kahn-Freund used Japan as an example in distinguishing commercial law and family law subjects when it comes to the feasibility of legal transplantation:

 Before the First World War Japan adopted the German law of contract, of civil delict and of property, but the principles of family law only with modifications, and even as modified, we are told, they largely failed to mould the 'law in actual operation' as distinct from the 'law in books.

ical and cultural essentials of life',[55] Montesquieu's contention of the match between local conditions and the law will most likely lose its force.

While the fit of a transplanted foreign norm in general, and the applicability of the Anglo-American motivated corporate law rules in China in particular, are matters of controversy, which can lead to distinct conclusions of a half-full or a half-empty glass depending on one's subjective stance,[56] at least three considerations help one gain an insight into the fit and feasibility of legal transplantation. First, there is the issue of the purpose of legal borrowing, i.e., the role that a transplanted norm is expected to serve in the host country. Although some might imagine the needs of the borrowing country to be the same as those of the source society, practice has shown that this is rarely the case.[57] Second, the borrowing society's distinguishing economic, political, and social institutions, which the transplant will be rooted in, are a significant factor. A complex interplay between the transplant and socio-cultural forces may well cause the transplant process to be far from straightforward. Third, there will likely be additional consequences of the transplanted rule when it seeps into the idiosyncrasies of the new legal environment, i.e., possible spill-over to connecting areas. When the background social institutions are different, using regularities and tendencies in the original context to predict future effects in a new environment has often proved premature.[58]

2.6   SHAREHOLDERS' RIGHT AND SHAREHOLDER PROTECTION

Studies by La Porta, Lopez-de Silanes, Shleifer, and Vishny (LLSV) on corporate ownership worldwide demonstrate that diffuse ownership is relatively uncommon and most companies are controlled by large shareholders.[59]

O. Kahn-Freund, 'On Uses and Misuses of Comparative Law' (1974) 37(1) *Modern Law Review* 1, 7.

[55]   Ibid., 4.

[56]   E. Örücü, 'Law as Transposition' (2002)51(2) *International & Comparative Law Quarterly* 205, 209; D. Clarke, 'Lost in Translation? Corporate Legal Transplants in China', (2006) GWU Law School Public Law Research Paper No. 213, available at   http://scholarship.law.gwu.edu/cgi/viewcontent.cgi?article=2259&context=faculty _publications (accessed 21 July 2022), 1, 'At what point do we say that a norm is so new, and its source so different, that it counts as a transplant into a particular body of law, and not simply an internal development of that body of law?'

[57]   Clarke, ibid., 2.

[58]   B. Bix, *Jurisprudence: Theory and Context 16*, (London: Sweet & Maxwell, 6th ed. 2012).

[59]   R. La Porta, F. Lopez-de-Silanes, A. Sheifer and R. V. Vishny, 'The Quality of Government' (1999) 15(1) *The Journal of Law, Economics & Organization* 222; R. La

A primary corporate governance problem has developed and expanded from mitigating agency conflicts between directors and diffuse shareholders to protect minority shareholders from expropriation by a controlling shareholder or a director (or the board of directors).[60] LLSV also identified the linkage between law and corporate performance, arguing that companies in countries with better investor protection are more valuable than companies in countries with poorer investor protection.[61]

For the Chinese case, Zhang also argued, from the law and finance point of view, that the law is critical to sustaining growth in China for the development of the stock market. He asserted that the trajectory of development is growth first followed by law, and the improvement of law is both caused and supported by market growth.[62] Because of the high proportion of minority shareholders in Chinese listed companies and the implication of this for information asymmetry, the protection offered to them (and shareholder protection in general) is regarded as a highly significant mechanism. This is currently embedded within a regulatory framework across National Company Law, Securities Law, the Corporate Governance Code, and documents from local government, stock exchanges, and the highest court in China.

Shareholder protection, especially minority shareholder protection, is key for maintaining the sustainable development of the Chinese stock market. It is a relatively new notion in China which has been introduced to the Chinese stock market for the following reasons. First, shareholder protection is important under China's hybrid corporate governance model because of the involvement of administrative power. A unique model has been implemented in building socialism with Chinese characteristics. There are still characteristics of a centrally-planned economy, such as the continuing prevalent position of SOEs. The dominance of SOEs and state shareholders makes the protection of minority or non-state shareholders critically important. Second, the problems of information asymmetry make it almost impossible for minority shareholders, especially those in JSLCs, to have a voice in company management, due to the fact that they do not understand daily company decision strategies, and may not be willing or have the resources to do so.

Porta, F. Lopez-de-Silanes, A. Shleifer and R. W. Vishny, 'Law and Finance' (1998) 106(6) *Journal of Political Economy* 1113; C.G. Holderness, 'The Myth of Diffuse Ownership in the United States' (2009) 22(4) *Review of Financial Studies* 1377.

[60] A. Shleifer and R. W. Vishny, 'A Survey of Corporate Governance' (1997) 52(2) *Journal of Finance* 737.

[61] R. La Porta, F. Lopez-de-Silanes, A. Shleifer and R. W. Vishny, 'Investor Protection and Corporate Governance' (2000) 58(1) *Journal of Financial Economics* 3.

[62] Z. Zhang, 'Law and Finance: The Case of Stock Market Development in China' (2016) 39(2) *Boston College International & Comparative Law Review* 283.

In terms of shareholding structure, traditionally speaking, many listed companies within the scope of JSLCs in China are still SOEs and the largest shareholder normally refers to the state, which dominates the shareholding in listed companies. It is reported that an average of 31.27 per cent of the shares in these companies are held by the government.[63] This ownership by the state may suggest concentrated shareholding as a characteristic of Chinese corporate governance in terms of shareholding structure, due to the dominance of state shares in China. However, a detailed investigation into the share ownership composition of listed companies would suggest diversity rather than concentration: numbers of individual and non-state institutional shareholders have increased dramatically in the last ten years. This increasingly dispersed share ownership makes it important to introduce eligibility provisions for JSLCs with the purpose of preventing boards of directors or the courts from being overloaded with lawsuits. In comparison, LLCs must be invested in and established by no more than 50 shareholders.[64] Shareholders in LLCs are thus more likely to have a substantial share ownership percentage.

Furthermore, especially after 2001 when the regulatory framework in China started to move beyond a unified state regulatory system, the Chinese government began to put emphasis on shareholder protection and law enforcement, driven by stock market crises such as the bear market crisis that started in 2001 and corporate scandals such as the Vanke incident.[65] In terms of the bear market crisis that started on June 14, 2001, the Shanghai Composite Index breached the symbolic low point of 1,000, the lowest since February 24, 1997.[66] Investor confidence decreased dramatically, which was reflected in the fact that more than two-thirds of the trading accounts in Shenzhen in 2005 did not hold any stock.[67] The market capitalisation decreased from more than 4.8 trillion Renminbi to less than 3.25 trillion, and the ratio of market capitalisation to GDP decreased by 266.67 per cent.[68] The ineffective stock market gave the government a wake-up call, and provided an opportunity to identify and address potential problems. Some extremists actually pushed the idea of closing down the market completely in order to restart it, due to various

---

[63]   Y. Thanatawee, 'Ownership Structure and Dividend Policy: Evidence from China' (2014) 6(8) *International Journal of Economics and Finance* 197, 199 quoted by OECD, OECD Survey of Corporate Governance Frameworks in Asia 2017.

[64]   Art. 25 Chinese Company Law 2005.

[65]   Z. Zhang, 'Law and Finance: The Case of Stock Market Development in China' (2016) 39(2) *Boston College International & Comparative Law Review* 283, 311.

[66]   *China Daily*, China's Stock Markets Slumping to 8-Year Lows, (June 6, 2005); available at http://www.chinadaily.com.cn/english/doc/2005-06/06/content_448880 .htm (accessed 29 July 2022).

[67]   CSRC, China Capital Market Development (2008), 153 and 269.

[68]   CSRC, China Securities and Future Statistical Yearbook (2012) 6–9.

factors including ineffective supervision from the CSRC and problems with low public confidence.[69] However, even with legislative attempts, the level of minority shareholder protection is at a moderate level based on the calculations of MacNeil,[70] in which an index score of 2 was awarded to China, with a global average score of 3 and a maximum of 6.[71]

Crises and corporate scandals re-highlighted the importance of investments from institutional shareholders, public investor protection and the ultimate monitoring role of shareholders, who have been encouraged to become more actively involved in the corporate operation and take supervisory responsibility for the management of companies.[72] In detail, provisions in Chinese Company Law and Chinese Securities Law have given shareholders more say in relation to key decisions in their companies. Offering minority shareholders more protection through direct suits, derivative suits and shareholders' rights to file a request to dissolve a company with the People's Court have been non-exceptionally adopted as goals of these legislations.[73]

Even with the enactment of Chinese Company Law, Chinese Securities Law and the SPC issued Provisions on Several Issues Concerning the Application of the Company Law, it has been suggested that the pathway minatory shareholder protection in China to growth will continue due to the Chinese economy's state shareholding, economic development stage, government policy, political system, history, culture and traditions.[74] Moreover, administrative and criminal penalties have been regarded as inadequate in China in deterring inefficient corporate governance practices in Chinese companies, while the government is reluctant to impose a heavy administrative burden to avoid a negative impact on company performance and the imposition of criminal liability, except in particularly serious circumstances.[75]

---

[69]   Y. Pan, 'Debate on Should the Government close Down the Current Stock Market for A Revolutionary Change? [大辩论：股市是否要推到重来，闹场革命风暴?]' *China Youth Daily* (November 26, 2001).

[70]   I. MacNeil, 'Adaptation and Convergence in Corporate Governance: The Case of Chinese Listed Companies' (2002) 2(2) *Journal of Corporate Law Studies* 289.

[71]   R. La Porta, F. Lopez-de-Silanes and A. Shleifer, 'Corporate Ownership around the World' (1999) 54(2) *Journal of Finance* 471.

[72]   B. Gong, *Understanding Institutional Shareholder Activism*, (Abingdon: Routledge 2015) 172–198.

[73]   See arts 150, 151 and 181, Chinese Company Law 2018.

[74]   B. Anderson and B. Guo, 'Corporate Governance under the New Company Law (Part 2): Shareholder Lawsuits and Enforcement' (May 2006) 20(4) *China Law & Practice* 15.

[75]   Ibid.

2.6.1   Principle of Chinese Company Law and Shareholder Protection

The rapid growth of the Chinese stock market necessitates a more effective and rigorously monitored shareholder protection mechanism that is fit for purpose in the growing market and for use by market participants, especially since a large percentage of these are in a vulnerable position in countries with emerging markets and rapid growth. Creating a more competitive financial and legal system with increased opportunities for all is crucial for sustainable economic growth in China. The thrust of the sub-project is to explore a mechanism to improve the effectiveness of the regime in China, in order to benefit the vulnerable position of minority shareholders, improve the poor enforcement of company law, contribute to the fairness of corporate governance in China. Implications may be proposed to achieve purposes including the enhancement of the protection of minority shareholders, the provision of a device for managing officers and directors of companies, who may be dominated by the majority shareholder, especially in SOEs, and the resolution of power imbalances between directors and shareholders and between minority and majority shareholders and directors, to name but a few.

In terms of the general principles of Chinese Company Law, it is enacted 'in order to protect the lawful rights and interests of companies, shareholders and creditors'.[76] The interests of shareholders as well as creditors, as primary stakeholders, were explicitly mentioned in this book along with the interests of shareholders and the company itself. Furthermore, more applicable to minority shareholders protection, all shareholders are required to 'abide by laws, administrative regulations and the articles of association of the company and exercise shareholder's rights according to the law, and may not abuse shareholder's rights to harm the interests of the company or other shareholders'.[77] This is a provision of principle, but it is often triggered by minority shareholders in corporate lawsuits against majority shareholders. It is further affirmed that the controlling shareholders should not use their affiliation to harm the interests of the company, the interests of controlling shareholders or the interests of minority shareholders collectively, with the possibility of imposing liabilities.[78]

---

[76]   See art. 1, Chinese Company Law 2018.
[77]   See art. 20, Chinese Company Law 2018.
[78]   See art. 21, Chinese Company Law 2018.

2.6.2   Right to Access Financial Information

According to Article 33 of Chinese Company Law 2006, shareholders shall have the right:

> to examine and reproduce the articles of association of the company, the minutes of the board of shareholders, the resolutions of the meetings of the board of directors, the resolutions of the meetings of the board of supervisors and the financial and accounting reports.

They may also 'request to examine the account books of the company'. These provisions are further clarified and ascertained in the Provision IV, to make them more enforceable. It is clarified that the People's Court should decide the specific time and location, or facilitate an agreed location, for the company to provide the opportunity for shareholders to examine documents, with clarified rights for shareholders to examine the original versions of all documents. This right to access information is vital for shareholders to know the 'health condition' or the financial condition of the company they invest in, which is fundamental for their potential controlling rights over the companies through voting or the private enforcement of directors' duties. It will help shareholders to make informed decisions when they make decisions based on their right to vote or exit.

More detailed provisions regarding the provision of financial information for all shareholders may address information asymmetry problems between minority shareholders and corporate controllers, either as the result of shareholders' limited access to information or their ignorance and/or lack of understanding of the available information. This may place minority shareholders in a disadvantaged position in terms of triggering private enforcement measures such as derivative actions.[79] Through these measures, shareholders are required to gather facts in order to evaluate the rationale for, or to assess the strength of, any potential action.[80] Therefore, information is an important precondition and incentive for successful litigation via private enforcement. Minority shareholders may not have effective access to enough information; their access is likely to be limited to information already available to the public. This may be another reason why a more functional and effective shareholder remedy system should be promoted in China for JSLCs, including listed companies.

---

[79]   J. Oliver, W. Qu and V. Wise, 'Corporate Governance: A Discussion on Minority Shareholder Protection in China' (2014) 6(3) *International Journal of Economics and Finance* 11, 11.

[80]   See L. Field, M. Lowry and S. Shu, 'Does Disclosure Deter or Trigger Litigation?' (2005) 39(3) *Journal of Accounting & Economics* 487.

2.6.3   Rights to Vote

If the right to access to information is fundamental for shareholders to know about the company in which they invest, the voting system gives shareholders a voice and makes sure it has an impact on corporate decisions, especially the election of directors and supervisors. Voting rights are regarded as the basic right of shareholders in controlling companies. Their rights to appoint or remove their agents in the board of directors and the supervisory board, to decide their remuneration in Chinese companies[81] and to examine any proposed resolution and thereby have a dramatic impact on the company's performance, will be all carried out through a voting system at the shareholders' meeting. In contrast, resolutions of a general meeting must be adopted by more than half of the shareholders present at the meeting.[82] The voting rights are exercised in LLCs through the default rule that voting power is exercised by shareholders at the meeting pro rata of their capital contribution, unless otherwise stipulated in the articles of association of the company.[83] The principle of 'one share one vote'[84] is adopted in JSLCs[85] due to their more dispersed ownership and the lack of an upper limit on shareholder numbers. It is stated that 'shareholders shall exercise voting rights at general meetings in proportion to their capital contribution, unless otherwise stipulated in the articles of association of the company'.[86] However, in order to protect the interests of minority shareholders, cumulative voting systems have been introduced in China in order to change the situation whereby majority shareholders could control the company by electing their preferred directors.[87] The system will give all shareholders the opportunity to have a voice in corporate control, in order to have

---

[81]   See art. 37(2), Chinese Company Law 2018.

[82]   Ibid.

[83]   See art. 43, Chinese Company Law 2018.

[84]   See H. Hansmann and M. Pargendler, 'The Evolution of Shareholder Voting Rights: Separation of Ownership and Consumption' (2014) 123(4) *The Yale Law Journal* 862; R. Adams and D. Ferreria, 'One Share – One Vote: The Empirical Evidence' (2008) 12(1) *Review of Finance* 51; M. Burkart and S. Lee, 'One Share – One Vote: the Theory' (2008) 12(1) *Review of Finance* 1; A. Khachaturyan, 'Trapped in Delusions: Democracy, Fairness and the One-Share-One-Vote Rule in the European Union' (2007) 8(3) *European Business Organization Law Review* 335.

[85]   See art. 103, Chinese Company Law 2018.

[86]   See art. 42, Chinese Company Law 2018.

[87]   See art. 105, Chinese Company Law 2018; see also Y. Chen and J. Du, 'Regulatory Reform of Cumulative Voting in Corporate China: Who were Elected and its Impact' available at http://papers.ssrn.com/sol3/papers.cfm?abstract_id=2556157 (accessed 21 July 2022); see also C. Xi and Y. Chen, 'Does Cumulative Voting Matter? The Case of China: An Empirical Assessment' (2014) 15(4) *European Business Organization Law Review* 585.

a more diverse influence on the voting process and protect their own interests. It is argued that cumulative voting will encourage minority shareholders to participate in corporate governance and contribute their opinions in relation to the company's interests, maintaining balance among all shareholders in corporate governance.[88]

The questions then arise as to whether shareholders with no voting rights, such as the preference shareholders that the Chinese government has been trying to reintroduce since late 2012[89] or holders of the non-voting shares offered to employees as part of employee shareholding ownership schemes,[90] have the right to bring a derivative action. For these shareholders, giving up voting rights is generally compensated or balanced by the value of the priority that they enjoy in the payment of dividends and in the payment queue in the event of a liquidation.

Voting rights are closely connected to the controlling rights of shareholders through shareholders' meetings, where decisions are made collectively. However, derivative action is designed as a shareholder remedy that an individual shareholder could bring, in the interests of the company, against an individual wrongdoer who has injured the interests of the company. It operates to deter mismanagement by imposing the threat of liability, and therefore provides a strong incentive for directors and other key players to act in the interests of the company and its shareholders to enhance corporate governance.[91] The former is the direct collective controlling right via the shareholders' meeting, and the latter is an indirect controlling right, facing the threat of personal liability with the aim of soundness and competitiveness of corporate

---

[88]   J. Liu, *Modern Corporation Law* [现代公司法], (Beijing: Law Press, 3rd ed. 2015) 416–417.

[89]   See State Council, Guiding Opinions on the Pilot Launch of Preference Shares 2013, CSRC, Administrative Measures for the Pilot Scheme on Preference Shares 2014; see also W. Cai, 'Use of Preference Shares in Chinese Companies as a Viable Investment/Financing Tool' (2016)11(2) *Capital Market Law Journal* 317; see also common law cases such as *Webb v Earle* (1875) LR 20 Eq 556; *Scottish Insurance Corpn Ltd. v Wilson and Clyde Coal Co. Ltd.* (1949) AC 462.

[90]   For general discussions on employee share ownership scheme see A.M. Robinson and H. Zhang, 'Employee Share Ownership: Safeguarding Investments in Human Capital' (2005) 43(3) *British Journal of Industrial Relations* 469; S. Sengupta, K. Whitfield and B. McNabb, 'Employee Share Ownership and Performance: Golden Path or Golden Handcuffs?' (2007) 18(8) *The International Journal of Human Resource Management* 1507.

[91]   A. Reisberg, *Derivative Actions and Corporate Governance: Theory and Operation*, (Oxford: Oxford University Press 2007) 23; see also E. Ferran, 'Company Law Reform in the UK' (2001) 5 *Singapore Journal of International & Comparative Law* 516; J.C. Coffee, 'Privatization and Corporate Governance: The Lessons from Securities Market Failure' (1999) 25 *The Journal of Corporation Law* 1.

control. They are independent rights and there is no logical link between the two, and it is not rational to argue that shareholders who do not have controlling rights will automatically lose the right to derivative action. Derivative claims are proceedings in respect of a course of action, brought by members of a company who are vested in the company and seeking relief. Despite the fact that derivative actions are brought on behalf of the company against wrongful acts and fraud that have been perpetrated against the company, rather than the shareholders, there will be an injury to the shareholders, including those without voting rights. The result of a derivative action needs to be shared by all shareholders. It is thus only fair that this remedy should be kept for minority shareholders who do and do not have voting powers, which in itself does not change the position of minority shareholders.

In addition to a cumulative voting system, the interests of minority shareholders are further considered by two instruments in company law, namely: a restriction on shareholders' voting rights on matters that they are involved in and subject to a resolution adopted by the shareholders' meeting;[92] and a proxy system.[93] These have been adopted to improve corporate governance, focusing on the goal of fairness. In detail, the restriction on voting has been designed to avoid conflicting interests between the company and its controlling, or *de facto* controlling, shareholders. This may be achieved through restricting or invalidating the voting rights of controlling shareholders which could potentially generate a conflict of interests. The proxy system has been designed to meet the transformation of the Chinese stock market and the economy's dispersed ownership pattern. The proxy system helps shareholders with limited information, time and energy to exercise their voting rights.

---

[92] Art. 16 (3), Chinese Company Law 2018. This states that:
any shareholder set forth in the preceding paragraph or controlled by a de facto controller set forth in the preceding paragraph may not participate in voting on any resolution specified in the preceding paragraph. Such resolution shall be adopted by the other shareholders that are present at the meeting and represent more than half of the voting rights.

[93] Art. 106, Chinese Company Law 2018. This states that 'a shareholder may appoint a proxy to attend a general meeting on his behalf. The proxy shall submit the shareholder's power of attorney to the company and exercise voting rights within the scope of authorisation'.

2.7   DIRECTORS' DUTIES IN CHINA AND THE ENFORCEMENT OF DIRECTORS' DUTIES

2.7.1   Directors' Duties in China

The directors' duty of loyalty is no longer statutorily absent since China's 2005 Company Law reform introduced the common law categorisation, in the hope of conforming to prevalent international business standards and developing a market-based economy in this fast-growing nation.[94] Taking English law as an example, the directors' duties that will mainly be relevant to this book include the duties central to the role of directors. These are traditionally drawn from two broad non-statutory sources, and are manifest as fiduciary duties and expectations drawn from common law. The fiduciary duties emphasise the need for trustworthiness and the essence of acting in the best interests of the company, while the common law expectation is concerned with ensuring that directors exercise reasonable care and show requisite skill and diligence.[95]

An occupant with fiduciary duties was defined by Millett LJ in *Bristol & West Building Society v Mothew*[96] as someone who has undertaken to act for or on behalf of another in a particular matter in a circumstance which gives rise to a relationship of trust and confidence. In the case of a company, since directors have complete power and management responsibility over the company and the company's assets, they should indisputably be fiduciaries.[97] Furthermore, as there is no single set of fiduciary duties that applies to all fiduciaries,[98] the fiduciary duties applicable to company directors are well developed and revolve essentially around the core fiduciary obligation of loyalty.[99] Fiduciary duties to which directors are subject to include: the duty to act *bona fide* (in good faith)[100] for the interest of the company and not for other collateral

---

[94]   S. Wen and J. Zhao, 'Trends and Development of the Directors' Duty of Loyalty in China: A Case Analysis' (2021) 13(15) *Sustainability* 8589 available at http://dx.doi .org/10.3390/su13158589 (accessed 21 July 2022).

[95]   Section 174 (1) UK CA 2006.

[96]   *Bristol & West BS v Mothew* [1996] 4 All ER 698 at 711.

[97]   P.D. Finn, 'The Fiduciary Principle' in T.G. Youdan (ed.), Chapter 1, *Equity, Fiduciaries and Trust* (Toronto: Carswel 1989) 46; *Regal (Hastings) Ltd. v Gulliver* [1942] 1 All ER 378 at 395.

[98]   See *Henderson v Merrett Syndicates Ltd.* [1995] 2 AC 145 at 206; per Lord Browne-Wilkinson; see also L.S. Sealy, 'Fiduciary Relationships' (1962) *Cambridge Law Review* 69.

[99]   B. Hannigan, *Company Law,* (Oxford: Oxford University Press, 2nd ed. 2009) 170–172.

[100]   *Re Smith & Fawcett Ltd.* [1942] Ch 304 CA; *Re W & M Roith Ltd.* [1967] 1 All ER 427; *J J Harrison (Properties Ltd.) v Harrison* [2001] BCLC 158.

purposes;[101] the requirement that a director must not put himself in a position where there is an actual or potential conflict between his personal interests and his duty to the company;[102] and the duty of not acting to make secret personal profit from any opportunity resulting from their positions, even if they are acting honestly and for the good of the company.[103]

While their fiduciary duties impose a largely negative obligation on directors to do nothing that conflicts with the company's interests, common law expectation requires them to exercise whatever skills they possess with reasonable care. Three basic principles were established for the duty of skill and care in *Re City Equitable Fire Insurance Co. Ltd.*:[104] first, it is recognised that directors are not experts in everything, and they need only display the skills they actually possess; second, a director need not devote his continuous attention to the business; and third, directors are entitled to rely on the experience and expertise of their co-directors or other employees of the company. It is explicitly stated in Section 174(2) of the UK Companies Act (UK CA) 2006 that a director must display the care, skill and diligence that would be exercised by a reasonably diligent person in a situation where (a) they have the general knowledge, skill and experience that may reasonably be expected of a person carrying out the same function as the director in relation to that company, and where (b) the general knowledge, skill and experience that the director actually has reflected the development in case law[105] and similar tests laid down for assessing whether a director is liable for wrongful trading by Section 214 of the Insolvency Act 1986.[106]

The statutory inauguration of the directors' duty, as well as the soundness of the investor protection regime, including for foreign investors, has become even more significant because of its potential impact beyond China's domestic

---

[101] For directors using their power to raising capital for other purposes, see *Punt v Symouns & Co. Ltd.* [1903] 2 Ch 506; *Hogg v Cramphorn Ltd.* [1967] Ch 254.

[102] See Section 175 UK CA 2006 on avoiding conflict of interests; see also *Aberdeen Rly Co. v Blacikie Bros* (1854) 2 Eq Rep 1281; *Knight v Frost* [1999] 1 BCLC 364; *Jonathan Bell v Eden Project Ltd.* (11 April 2001, unreported); *Bhullar v Bhullar, Re Bhullar Bros Ltd.* [2003] EWCA Civ 424, [2003] 2 BCLC 241.

[103] See *Regal (Hastings) Ltd. v Gulliver* [1942] 1 All ER 378, HL; *Gencor ACP Ltd. and Others* [2000] 2 BCLC 834.

[104] [1925] Ch 407.

[105] See in particular *Norman v Theodore Goddard* [1991] 1BCLC 1028 at 1030–31; *Re D'Jan of London Ltd.* [1993] BCLC 648 at 648; *Re Westmid Packing Services Ltd.* [1998] 2 BCLC 646 at 653; *Re Baring plc (No 3)* [1999] 1 BCLC 433 at 489; *Equitable Life Assurance Society v Bowley* [2004] 1 BCLC 180 at para 4; *Re London Citylink Ltd.* [2005] EWHC 2875 (Ch).

[106] A. Alcock, J. Birds and S. Gale, *Alcock, Birds and Gale on the Companies Act 2006*, (Bristol: Jordan Publishing Ltd. 2009).

market.[107] In 2005 Chapter 6 of the Chinese Company Law set out the general duties that directors owe to the company, and these have remained the same despite major amendments to the Chinese Company Law in 2013 and 2018. Compared with the Chinese Company Law 1993, major improvements were made in the revised version of the law with regard to the duty of loyalty, seeking to improve the clarity of laws by way of initiating a duty framework entailing a 'common law style classification' consisting of both the duty of loyalty and duty of care.[108] Directors owe duties of loyalty and diligence; according to the Company Law, to:

> the directors, supervisors and senior managers shall comply with the laws, administrative regulations, and by law. They shall bear the obligations of fidelity and diligence to the company. No director, supervisor or senior manager may accept any bribe or other illegal gains by taking advantage of his powers, or encroach on the property of the company.

In order to improve the coherence of provisions and provide more explication of the implications of the duty of loyalty, Article 148 §2 aggregates and presents a list of individual duties that were originally scattered in Articles 60–62 of 1993 Company Law. This detailed list specifies the acts that directors, supervisors and senior managers are not allowed to commit; these include:

(1)   Misappropriating the company's funds;
(2)   Depositing the company's funds into an account under his own name or any other individual's name;
(3)   Without consent of the shareholders' meeting, shareholders' assembly, or the board of directors, loaning the company's funds to others or providing any guarantee to any other person by using the company's property as in violation of the bylaw;
(4)   Entering a contract or trading with the company by violating the bylaw or without consent of the shareholders' meeting or shareholders' assembly;
(5)   Without consent of the shareholders' meeting or shareholders' assembly, seeking business opportunities that belong to the company for himself or any

---

[107]   As of 2014, foreign corporations have invested $128.5bn in China, making this fast-growing nation the top destination for foreign direct investment. BBC, *China Overtakes US for Foreign Direct Investment*, Jan. 30, 2015, available at http://www.bbc.co.uk/news/business–31052566 (accessed 21 July 2022).

[108]   G. Yang, *Gongsi Dongshi Yiwu Falv Tixi Goujian: Yuwai Jingyan yu Zhongguo Shijian (*公司董事义务法律体系构建：域外经验与中国实践*) [The Construction of a Legal Framework concerning Company Directors' Duty: Foreign Experience and Chinese Practices]* [2014] 5 *Commercial Law Research [*商业研究*]* 185, 189. See, art. 147 Company Law 2018.

other persons by taking advantage of his powers, or operating a similar business to the company for which he works for himself or for any other persons;

(6) Taking commissions on the transactions between others and the company into his own pocket;

(7) Illegally disclosing the company's confidential information.[109]

In addition, a new catch-all provision is also added in paragraph (8) of this sub-article, in the hope of grasping the fluid nature of the duty of loyalty and affording judges more discretionary power by way of prohibiting all 'other acts inconsistent with the obligation of fidelity to the company'.[110] Moreover, in order to conform to international business standards and incentivise investors, the company law transplants an equity remedy through the disgorgement of unauthorised profits.[111] Article 148§2 enlarges the remedial realm by clarifying that 'the income of any director or senior manager from any act in violation of the preceding paragraph shall belong to the company'.[112]

As far as academic researches on directors' duties are concerned, scholars have investigated the topic through different lenses, After examining the development of the legal framework regarding fiduciary duties of directors in China, Xu et al. argued that the implementation of fiduciary duties in China has encountered considerable obstacles because of the inherent weakness of the legal system, such as the vague and rigid legal texts.[113] They held the view that in the enforcement process, formalised judgments have placed limitations on precedent creation, thus reducing the deterrent effect, and the judicial system has shown reluctance to intervene in matters related to directors' duties in listed companies.[114] From an empirical standpoint through an analysis of 526 cases on the basis of eight attributes, Wen and Zhao discovered some commendable features, including increasing accessibility of the law and a differentiation of various types of directors' duties of loyalty.[115] They tried to reshape the conventional transplantation ideal that commercial laws are easily transferable, suggesting the construction of a broad collateral regime for greater congruence between laws and existing institutions.[116] Moreover,

---

[109] See art. 148§1 (1)–(7), Company Law 2018.

[110] See art. 148§1 (8), Company Law 2018.

[111] S. Wen S and J. Zhao, 'Trends and Development of the Directors' Duty of Loyalty in China: A Case Analysis' (2021) 13(15) *Sustainability* 8589.

[112] See art. 148§2, Company Law 2018.

[113] G. Xu, T. Zhou, B. Zeng, et al. 'Directors' Duties in China' (2013) 14(1) *European Business Organization Law Review* 57, 57–95.

[114] Ibid.

[115] S. Wen S and J. Zhao, 'Trends and Development of the Directors' Duty of Loyalty in China: A Case Analysis' (2021) 13(15) *Sustainability* 8589.

[116] Ibid.

through comparative analysis of regulations on directors' duties in different jurisdictions, Wei argued that the current Chinese law on directors' duties is a combination of both Anglo-American and Continental European influences; most importantly, however, the law has been generally shaped by the corporate development and enterprise reforms in the China itself.[117] Cao researched the problems of director's duty of loyalty in practice in China and giving the suggestions through an intensive analysis of the empirical study.[118] Lee argued that without the concomitant incorporation of the English equity jurisprudence, the revised Chinese Company Law has not fully embraced the fiduciary doctrine, so he evaluates the feasibility of transplanting an equitable concept to a civil law jurisdiction, and the pitfalls that may be encountered.[119] Lin and Lin adopted an empirical and comparative approach in reviewing Chinese duty of care cases in comparison with the UK and the US, arguing that there is lack of a specific standard for the duty of care in the legislation.[120] Xu mainly analysed the problems existing in the practice of the legal provisions on directors' duty of care from the judicial cases. And then proposed feasible methods to complete the judgement standards of directors' duty of care from the legislative perspective and the judicial perspective.[121] This book will primarily focus on the private enforcement of directors' duties through shareholder litigation.

2.7.2   Enforcement of Directors' Duties

Shareholder protection can be implemented through the public and private enforcement of company law. In terms of private enforcement, it is done by the enforcement of directors' duties. This enables shareholders to sue wrongdoers in court in order to seek damages, while any fines as the result of criminal or administrative liability go to the state rather than the shareholder in the domain of public enforcement. Since public enforcement by the CSRC or the government is susceptible to political influence, local protection and different forms

---

[117] Y. Wei, 'Directors' Duties Under Chinese Law: A Comparative Review' (2006) 3(1) *University of New England Law Journal* 36.

[118] J. Cao, 'Director's Duty of Loyalty In China: An Empirical Study Based On Cases' (9 April 2020), available at https://scholarbank.nus.edu.sg/handle/10635/174055 (accessed 22 July 2022).

[119] R.W.C. Lee, 'Fiduciary Duty without Equity: Fiduciary Duties of Directors under the Revised Company Law of the PRC' (2007) 47(4) *Virginia Journal of International Law* 897.

[120] S. Lin and L. Lin, 'Directors' Duty of Care in China: Empirical and Comparative Perspective' (2021) 13(2) *Tsinghua China Law Review*, 295.

[121] H. Xu, 'Judgment Standards for Directors' Duty of Care In China' (9 April 2020) available at https://scholarbank.nus.edu.sg/handle/10635/174063 (accessed 22 July 2022).

of corruption, private enforcement is becoming increasingly important during China's transition on its route from an administrative governance model to a hybrid framework with elements of both administrative and economic governance.

Breaches of duties by directors, supervisors and senior management executives will lead to civil, administrative and criminal liabilities under corporate law. The Chinese Company Law provides not only consequential liability for violating fiduciary duties, but also judicial avenues for enforcing those liabilities. As for shareholders' remedies, they have gained routes to protect their rights and enforce the duties of management teams through administrative action,[122] criminal prosecution[123] or civil litigation.[124] While the first two legal regimes in general terms punish wrongdoers with no compensation for the shareholders whose rights have been harmed, civil litigation is identified as private litigation that enables shareholders to sue wrongdoers in order to seek damages. When the securities laws in 49 jurisdictions are assessed, private enforcement is more positively correlated with financial development than public enforcement.[125] Compared with fines or criminal liability, private enforcement may be the only way to enable shareholders and companies to recover the losses they have suffered.

There are two litigation mechanisms available to shareholders to preserve their interests in the company under Company Law, especially when fiduciary duties are breached by the directors, supervisors or senior management executives, and sometimes controlling shareholders. They are the direct suit and the derivative suit. These mechanisms, both available through private enforcement, have two functions, namely deterring potential wrongdoers from making harmful decisions and offering remedies for injured shareholders. They are designed so that shareholders may bring litigation against those key players under Company Law.[126] While the subject matter of derivative actions is always the wrongs done to the company, direct suits are always due to personal interests or reflective losses.

Article 152 of the Chinese Company Law prescribes the rule for shareholders to bring direct suits. The direct suit is a mechanism for shareholders

---

[122] CSRC, Provisions on Banning the Entry into the Securities Market, 3 March 2006.

[123] See art. 169 (1), Criminal Law of the People's Republic of China 2020.

[124] See art. 151, 152, Chinese Company Law 2018.

[125] R. La Porta, F. Lopez-de-Silanes and A. Sheifer, 'What Works in Securities Law' (2006) 61(1) *Journal of Finance* 1, 11.

[126] See arts 151, 152, Chinese Company Law 2018.

to mitigate their limited participation and controlling rights in corporations.[127] Shareholders may institute proceedings in a People's Court if a director or senior officer violates the provisions of laws, administrative regulations or the articles of association of the company, and the violation harms the interests of the shareholders.[128] This section enables shareholders to bring law suits in their personal capacities, in order to protect their rights as shareholders. Differing from derivative actions, the causes of these actions belong to the shareholders in their own capacity, rather than being on behalf of and in the interests of the company, or of all shareholders collectively.

It is not always a straightforward exercise to determine whether the harm is suffered by the company or by the shareholders.[129] A few grounds for raising direct actions include those such as enforcing shareholders' entitlement to informational rights,[130] redressing the oppression of or fraud enacted on minority shareholders,[131] actions to withdraw from the company, actions to dissolve a company, false statements in listed companies,[132] and defects in resolutions.

A few of these grounds will be clarified in slightly more detail. In terms of actions to withdraw from the company, a shareholder may only bring a direct suit in a LLC, since shareholders in listed and public companies should be able to deal their shares freely. However, a shareholder in a LLC, when transitioning their shares to a person other than another shareholder, must obtain the consent of more than half of all shareholders.[133] Furthermore, if there is a breach of duty or misconduct by board members, the shares may not be as valuable and attractive to other shareholders if they are also aware of these decisions. In such scenarios, shareholders are given rights that enable them to sell their shares to the company under the following circumstances:

> the company has not distributed its dividends to shareholders for five consecutive years, while the company has been profitable for five consecutive years and meets the conditions for the distribution of profit stipulated herein; the company is merged or divided, or transfers its major property; or the term of operation specified in the articles of association of the company expires or any other reason for dissolution specified in the articles of association arises, and the general meeting has adopted

---

[127] J. Wang, *Company Law in China: Regulation of Business Organizations in a Socialist Market Economy*, (Cheltenham: Edward Elgar 2014) 222.

[128] See art. 152, Chinese Company Law 2018.

[129] B. Anderson and B. Guo, 'Corporate Governance under the New Company Law (Part 2): Shareholder Lawsuits and Enforcement' (May 2006) 20(4) *China Law & Practice* 15.

[130] See also art. 33, Chinese Company Law 2018.

[131] See also arts 20 and 21, Chinese Company Law 2018.

[132] S. Lin, *Derivative Action in Chines Company Law*, (Alphen aan den Rijn: Kluwer Law International 2015) 76–88.

[133] See art. 71, Chinese Company Law 2018.

a resolution to amend the articles of association to allow the continued existence of the company.[134]

If the shareholders cannot reach an agreement with the company in terms of a share purchase agreement, the shareholders may bring a direct suit.

In relation to defects in resolutions, a direct suit may occur when resolutions are passed which prejudice the interests of minority shareholders. Two types of defects were clarified in the company law, including defects as the result of illegal content or illegal procedures:

> a shareholder may, within 60 days of the adoption of the resolution, petition a People's Court for the cancellation of the resolution if the procedure for convening the board of shareholders or general meeting or the meeting of the board of directors, or the method of voting, violates laws, administrative regulations or the articles of association of the company, or if the contents of a resolution violate the articles of association of the company.[135]

As the result of this litigation, a claimant shareholder can receive compensation directly in an individual claim.

Lastly, it may be worth mentioning the possibility of direct lawsuits based on information fraud in securities law, which applies to listed companies in China. It is stated that shareholders may bring a direct lawsuit against any damages they suffer due to false financial statements, listing reports, annual reports or other reports in the process of securities trading. The issuer of the listed companies or the directors, supervisor and senior managers shall be subject to the joint and several liability of compensation.[136]

In addition to direct suit, the Chinese Company Law also gives shareholders representing more than 10 per cent of the voting rights in the company to request the courts to dissolve the company where severe difficulties have occurred in the operational management of a company, where continuing to exist or trade will cause heavy losses to shareholders, and where there is no other way to solve the problem.[137] It seems that four requirements have to be simultaneously satisfied before the litigation can be initiated: first, the company must face serious difficulties; second, the difficulties cannot be solved in any other way and dissolution is the only way forward; third, the difficulties will lead to considerable damages; and finally, the percentage threshold for shareholders who qualify for the litigation must be satisfied in order to avoid malicious litigation. This is a particularly important issue considering

---

[134] See art. 74, Chinese Company Law 2018.
[135] See art. 22, Chinese Company Law 2018.
[136] See art. 69, Chinese Company Law 2018.
[137] See art. 182, Chinese Company Law 2018.

the number of shareholders in China, especially in JSLCs. A typical example in which eligible shareholder(s) may bring a direct suit to dissolve a company would be where the company is in a deadlock situation.[138] In this scenario, a division of opinion among shareholders may lead to a dysfunctional board, and the company may be dissolved as a preferred option.[139]

Shareholder protection has also emerged as a significant topic for discussion since the result of the launch of the Shanghai and Shenzhen Stock Markets made the trading of shares possible for listed companies. The launch also represented a significant step towards market-oriented corporate governance reform and corporatisation in China, as it was one of the main events that marked the transformation from a purely administrative model to a hybrid one. In this hybrid model, the government aimed to boost SOEs' output, profits and the efficiency of their employment patterns with the involvement of market power and the participation of private and foreign investors. The stock markets served as a conduit to channel the investment of domestic citizens and passive foreign investors into ailing SOEs.[140] The reform adopted market mechanisms that played an innovative role in aligning the interests of the government and public investors.

In addition, the CSRC has wide-ranging powers in respect of authorisation, rulemaking, investigation, and the enforcement of all aspects of the securities markets.[141] It is expected that a specialised and efficient regulator should provide an effective substitute for judicial enforcement in China in terms of shareholder protection.[142]

Shareholder protection through public enforcement is carried out through the effective regulatory function of the CSRC. As far as public enforcement is concerned, an enforcer for public companies could be a securities commission, a central bank, or a unique supervisory body in a particular jurisdiction. Jackson and Roe presented a study in 2009 demonstrating that good public enforcement

---

[138] S. Lin, *Derivative Action in Chines Company Law*, (Alphen aan den Rijn: Kluwer Law International 2015) 80.

[139] Ibid.

[140] D.A. Caragliano, Administrative Governance as Corporate Governance: A Partial Explanation for the Growth of China's Stock Markets' (2009) 30(4) *Michigan Journal of International Law* 1278, 1293.

[141] S. Zhu, *Securities Regulation in China*, (London, UK: Simmonds & Hill Publishing Ltd. 2000).

[142] S.H. Berkman, R.A. Cole and L.J. Fu, 'Political Connections and Minority Shareholder Protection: Evidence from Securities-Market Regulation in China' (2010) 6(45) *Journal of Financial and Quantitative Analysis* 1391, 1392; see also E. Glaeser, S. Johnson and A. Shleifer, 'Coase versus the Coasians' (2001) 116(3) *Quarterly Journal of Economics* 853.

can contribute to the efficacy of private enforcement.[143] However, the effectiveness and function of enforcers[144] have been questioned and described as 'insufficient to identify and prosecute most violators'. Furthermore, they 'may be susceptible to political influence, local protectionism and other forms of corruption and similar problems'.[145]

2.7.3   Private Enforcement of Directors' Duties: Derivative Action as an Emerging Mechanism in Chinese Company Law

The rule in *Foss v Harbottle* is that, in general, 'where a wrong is done to a company, only the company may sue for the damages caused to it; a shareholder has no right to bring an action on behalf of the company in order to protect the value of his shares'.[146] Two principles stem from this general rule, namely the elementary principle[147] and the principle of majority rule.[148] A derivative claim emanates from the 'fraud on the minority' exception to the rules enshrined in *Foss v Harbottle*, which was designed by the court to be a device to allow minority shareholders to bring a claim against those who control the company. In such a legal claim, the minority shareholders, instead of enforcing a right that belongs to them, are vested in and therefore derived from the company[149] and are therefore in the representative capacity of the company.[150] In the UK, the new statutory derivative action, as provided in Sections 260–264 of the CA 2006, is built on principles developed by the courts over the last 150 years. With regard to civil law countries, in Germany for instance, AktG, the legislative framework governing derivative claims for public limited companies, was set out in Section 148 of the German Aktiengesetz introduced by Article 1 Nr15 of the Act on Corporate Integrity and Modernisation of the Right of Avoidance (*Gesetz zui Unternehmensintegritat und Moderniserung des Anfechtungsrechts, UMAG*).[151]

---

[143]   H. Jackson and M. Roe, 'Public and Private Enforcement of Securities Law: Resources-Based Evidence' (2009) 93(2) *Journal of Financial Economics* 207, 208.

[144]   In detail, the China Securities Regulatory Commission (CSRC) for all listed firms, the State-owned Assets Supervision and Administrative Commission (SASAC) for listed state-owned companies.

[145]   B. Anderson and B. Guo, 'Corporate Governance under the New Company Law (Part 2): Shareholder Lawsuits and Enforcement' China Law & Practice' (May 2006) 20(4) *China Law & Practice* 15.

[146]   *Newbriggin-by-the-Sea Gas Co. Ltd. v Armstrong* (1879) 13 Ch D 310.

[147]   *Konamaneni v Rolls-Royce Industrial* [2002] 1 BCLC 336.

[148]   *Carlen v Drury* (1812) 1 Ves and Bea 149.

[149]   See *Percival v Wright* [1902] 2 Ch 421 Ch D.

[150]   *Cooke v Cooke* [1997] 2 BCLC 28 Ch D.

[151]   Bgbl I P 2802.

The emergence of derivative action in China is the result of the rapid development of the stock market. Chinese stock exchanges, including the ones in Shanghai and Shenzhen, developed very quickly after 1990 and by 2008 China's stock market had grown to become the second and fourth largest stock exchanges in Asia in December 2020. By 17 December 2020, there were 4,128 listed companies with a total capital of 77.47 trillion yuan RMB.[152] One of the interesting characteristics of the Chinese capital market is the large percentage of small investors (owning less than one million RMB in cash worth of shares), accounting for 99 per cent of the total number of capital accounts.[153] In order to counter the booming capital market packed with unsophisticated individual investors, the problems of inadequate shareholder protection are becoming increasingly important for securities regulators.[154]

Logically, since the coming into force of Company Law 1993, the Central Committee of the Communist Party of China shifted the corporate objectives of reform in SOEs from power-delegating and profit-sharing to the establishment of a modern enterprise system, in the context of which company law was a significant factor.[155] However, in Chinese Company Law 1993 there was no explicit section allowing for derivative action on the part of shareholders. Article 111, the only provision referring to shareholders' action in Chinese Company Law 1993, gave shareholders legitimate rights of action but failed to indicate whether derivative action would be permitted. Claimants in a derivative claim can sue based on the corporate right of action, and the right provided in Article 111 of Chinese Company Law 1993 was a typical direct action, rather than being derived from the rights of the company. No substantial or procedural rules have been provided in Article 111 for derivative claims to make the claim fundamentally different from shareholders' personal actions, and therefore the article cannot be regarded as a legal basis for derivative action in China.[156]

Legislative interpretation completed the positive position of derivative action when Mr. Guogang Li, the ex-deputy president of the SPC, concluded

---

[152] See China Securities Regulatory Commission, Statistics Data of December 2020; available at http://www.csrc.gov.cn/ (accessed 22 July 2022).

[153] See China Securities Regulatory Commission, *China Capital Markets Development Report* (18 December 2020) p. 269; available at http://www.csrc.gov.cn/pub/newsite/scb/gzdt/sckb/202012/t20201222_389114.html (accessed 22 July 2022).

[154] X. Huang, 'Shareholders Revolt: The Statutory Derivative Action in China' (2009) 49 *Comparative Research in Law & Political Economy* 1, 5.

[155] F.X. Hong and S.H. Goo, 'Derivative Action in China: Problems and Prospectus' [2009] 4 *Journal of Business Law* 376, 377.

[156] However, there is controversy about this, since it has been argued that the right to derivative action can in fact be implied elsewhere in art. 14(2) and art. 63 of Chinese Company Law 1993.

that courts would accept derivative action in his speech to the Meeting of China's Court Adjudication Work for Civil and Commercial Affairs on 11 December 2002. The legitimate position of shareholders in bringing a derivative claim was further confirmed in 'Opinions on Some Issues in Trials for Legal Actions Related to Company Disputes (No. 1)' promulgated by the Shanghai People's Court in 2003 when the system was first introduced in China. Further, 'Opinions on Some Issues in Trials for Legal Actions Applied with Company Law', promulgated by the High People's Court of Jiangsu Province in 2003, and 'Opinions on Some Issues in Trials for Legal Actions Related to the Company Disputes' promulgated by the Beijing High Court one year later also stipulated the rules for shareholder derivative action. However, these judicial opinions were only for judges to use for reference, and as such they did not have legally binding effect. Due to the disparities in procedural requirements and the lack of experience and common law support, it was still very difficult for shareholders to successfully bring derivative claims.[157]

A few cases need to be discussed here to illuminate the Chinese derivative action system pre-Chinese Company Law 2006. Despite the fact that derivative action is accepted by both the local courts and wider legislation, not many suits had been brought against companies, especially publicly listed companies, either before or after the formal introduction of the system in Chinese Company Law 2006. Derivative suits filed by minority shareholders declined due to the fact that there was no legal basis for derivative action. The Shanghai Intermediate People's Court refused to entertain it in *Zhongtian v Bichun* in 1996. The courts first acknowledged a derivative action lawsuit in the case of *Zhangjiagang Fibre Company* in 1994, where the SPC was asked for guidance on the question of whether a factory, a Chinese investor in a Chinese-foreign equity joint venture, was able to represent the joint venture in bringing a lawsuit against a vendor to the joint venture. The SPC held that the Chinese factory could exercise the litigation right of the cooperative joint venture. Despite the fact that the case was hedged with many conditions and

---

[157] See *Zuigao Renmin Fayuan Guanyu Zhongwaihezi Jingying Qiye Duiwai Fasheng Jingji Hetong Jiufen, Kongzhi He Ying Qiye De Waifang Yu Maifang You Lihai Yuanxi, Heying Qiye De Zhongfang Yingyi Sheide Mingyi Xiang Renmin Fayuan Qisu Wenti De Fuan* 1994 (Reply from the Supreme People's Court on the issues in whose name shall the Chinese side of the joint venture file a lawsuit to the People's Court when a Chinese foreign equity joint venture has an external controversy over an economic contract, and the foreign side which controls the joint venture has a direct interest relationship with the seller 1994); see also D.C. Clarke and N.C. Howson, 'Pathway to Minority Shareholder Protection: Derivative Action in People's Republic of China' in D.W. Puchniak, H. Baum and M. Ewing-Chow, *The Derivative Action in Asia: A Comparative and Functional Approach* (Cambridge: Cambridge University Press 2012), 243, 265.

had limited broader applicability, this was the first specific acceptance of a derivative action where shareholders were given legitimacy to take an action to redress a wrong where a company was unable to do so. The response from the SPC was used and cited in cases such as *Zhejiang Wu Fang Zhai* in 2001, and in decisions by the Guangdong Higher People's Court in *Gungzhoui Tianhe Scitech* in 2003. However, because the judgement in the *Guangdong Tianhe Scitech* case was issued after 1 January 2006, Chinese Company Law 2006 could have been applied although the court chose not to.

Regarding listed companies, three cases have been filed by minority share-holders, without exception due to the misappropriation of companies' capital by controlling shareholders. In the case of *Mr. Shao v Zhao Xinxian* (000999), Mr. Shao, as a minority shareholder of Sanjiu Medical and Pharmaceutical Co. Ltd., filed a lawsuit against Zhao Xinxian, the chairman of Sanjiu, due to misappropriations in Sanjiu on 8 April 2003. The law suit was rejected on the grounds that 'derivative action shall be brought based on the interests of all shareholders and Mr. Shao needs the permission of all shareholders for filing the lawsuit', which was impossible in the case of Sanjiu considering the shareholding ownership structure at the time, according to which the two largest shareholders owned more than 70 per cent of the shares and were both involved in the misappropriations. The court denied the enforcing effect of the Corporate Governance Code 2002[158] and took a cautious attitude in the absence of litigations on derivative action. In addition to the case of *Sanjiu*, derivative action was accepted in another two cases with unknown subsequent developments, including *Henan Lianhua Weijing* (600186)[159] and *Shenzhen Xingdu Hotel* (000033).

In order to promote the position of shareholders and improve the incomplete and unsatisfactory legislative approach in Chinese Company Law, the Chinese Company Law received in 2005, 2013 and 2018 provides the shareholder with cumulative voting rights,[160] the right to request the companies to repurchase their shares at a reasonable price[161] and the right of viewing important company documents.[162] Most innovatively, the provision for statutory derivative action was introduced in Article 151 of Chinese Company Law 2018. The provision

---

[158] See art. 4 Code of Corporate Governance for Listed Companies 2002.
[159] For the case report see: http://www.sse.com.cn/cs/zhs/scfw/gg/ssgs/2004–07–23/600186_20040723_1.pdf (accessed 23 July 2022).
[160] See art. 105, Chinese Company Law 2018.
[161] See art. 75, Chinese Company Law 2018.
[162] See art. 34, Chinese Company Law 2018.

of a mechanism for shareholder derivative action can also be found in Chinese Securities Law 2020:

> Where an issuer's director, supervisor, or officer violates the provisions of any law or administrative regulation or the company's bylaws in performing corporate duties, causing any loss to the company, or where the issuer's controlling shareholder or actual controller, among others, infringes upon the company's lawful rights and interests, causing any loss to the company, an investor protection institution may, if holding shares of the company, institute an action in a people's court in its own name in the interest of the company, not subject to the provisions of the Company Law of the People's Republic of China regarding the shareholding ratio and holding period.[163]

Moreover, the new securities law provides that:

> an investor protection institution may, as authorised by 50 or more investors, participate in actions as a representative, and according to the provision of the preceding paragraph, register right holders confirmed by the securities depository and clearing institution with the people's court, except for investors who have expressly indicated their reluctance to participate in the actions.[164]

There was an increase in the number of lawsuits brought by minority shareholders based on Section 152 after the enforcement of the derivative claim action in Chinese Company Law 2006.[165] However, most of these lawsuits have been focused on LLCs, with a striking absence of actions targeted at companies limited by shares.[166] As for listed companies, there has only been one lawsuit brought by shareholders and subsequently accepted by the Shandong Higher People's Court on 11 December 2009. The *Sanlian Shangshe* case (2009), as the first shareholder derivative lawsuit against a listed company

---

[163] See art. 94, Chinese Securities Law 2020.

[164] See art. 95, Chinese Securities Law 2020.

[165] Y. Ji and L. Zhu, 'Dissuasions of Jurisdictional Issues of Shareholder Derivative Lawsuit in China [*Qiantan Gudong Paisheng Susong Anjian de Guanxiaquan Wenti*] [浅谈股东派生诉讼案件的管辖权问题]' (2008) available at http://old.chinacourt.org/html/article/200812/09/334742.shtml (accessed 23 July 2022); see cases such as *Li Xiaozhang and twenty other shareholders v Xiao Wuyong & Zhang Dingzhong re: Nnanchuan Municipal Hardware Infrastructure Electric Chemical Industry Company Limited* (2006); *Dong Fengchang v Fang Yishu re: Shanghai Zhongjian Enterprise Company Limited* (2008); *Zhu Yongjun and twenty other shareholder plaintiffs v. Liu Huanren, Zhu Yongjun and Ma Zhonghua re: Shizuishan Municipal Autonomous Region Shizuidshan Municipal Intermediate People's Court* (2009).

[166] See D.C. Clarke and N.C. Howson, 'Pathway to Minority Shareholder Protection: Derivative Action in People's Republic of China' in D.W. Puchniak, H. Baum and M. Ewing-Chow, *The Derivative Action in Asia: A Comparative and Functional Approach*, (Cambridge: Cambridge University Press 2012) 243, 275–276.

after the enforcement of Chinese Company Law 2006, has important practical significance. However, the case is still *sub judice* and the filing of the case is relatively slow. Unlike classic derivative action cases, this case involves an attempt by the plaintiffs, 78 shareholders of *Shanlian Shangshe*, to bring a derivative claim against the former controlling shareholder. From discussions on the reality of applications of derivative action pre- and post-Chinese Company Law 2006, it is obvious that derivative action in China has been used in a very limited fashion by minority shareholders, despite extensive reports of the power abuse by controlling shareholders and directors. In the next chapters, a few factors that hinder the application of the system and related proposed reform suggestions will be discussed with reference to two corporate governance theories.

3. Corporate governance in China

Corporate governance issues in China have received much attention both in theory and in practice, in the last decade. The attention is mostly on how to develop an effective corporate governance system in China to improve its listed companies' performance and protect their shareholders and stakeholders. The improvement of corporate governance is an ongoing battle that calls for the participation of parties such as regulators, market participants and academics.[1] The Chinese corporate governance model is essentially fashioned on a combination of the external market-based German two-tiered model, with firms having both a main and supervisory board, and the Anglo-US model in that companies are listed on the stock market. The Chinese corporate governance model should more accurately be defined as a controlling hybrid model which is unique to China, due to its state shareholding, history, culture and tradition. The system is a combination of the shareholder value model and a co-determination model[2] based primarily on the insider model of institutional control, supplemented by good practice from the two basic models.

After more than 40 years of economic reform since the reform and open-door policy of China, China continues to transform its economy from a planned and administrative economy into a fully market-oriented economy. SOEs are still playing a key role in the Chinese economy, and 'there is still significant ownership owned by various government levels'.[3] The derivative action is the route by which shareholders are powered to enforce the companies' rights where the duties of directors or other controllers have breached their duties. The mechanism is a significant aspect of the continuing debate about corporate governance in China. The theoretical inquiry of the derivative action system advanced in this book needs to be built on the rich context of development and characteristics of corporate governance in China.

---

[1]   Q. Liu, 'Corporate Governance in China: Current Practices, Economic Effects and Institutional Determinants' (2006) 52 *CESifo Economic Studies* 415, 416.

[2]   S. Vob and Y. W. Xia, 'Corporate Governance of Listed Companies in China', paper presented at Track 8 of IFSAM VIIIth World Congress 2006, hosted by VHB, Berlin Germany, September 2006.

[3]   D. Cumming, V. Verdoliva and F. Zhan, 'New and Future Research in Corporate Finance and Governance in China And Emerging Markets' (2021) 46 *Emerging Markets Review* 100792.

3.1   SETTING THE SCENE

China has achieved unprecedented economic growth since 1980, with per capita GDP increasing from one of the lowest in the world to a level that is firmly in the middle of the international ranks.[4] China has seen the advent of economic miracles since the opening up policies and reforms that were introduced by it in the late 1970s; it has become a global economic powerhouse at an incredible speed and has changed international trade and investment patterns. The success of China to date has come about without key elements that are regarded by Western scholars as essential for long-term success, such as a well-functioning market, private property rights, an efficient and impartial legal system and a shareholder-centred economic corporate governance.[5] In 1992 the Chinese central government altered its policy from seeking to have a 'combined planned and market economy' to having a 'market economy with Chinese characteristics'.[6] If the adjective 'socialist' characterises the political system, the term 'market economy' clearly guides the direction of the reform goals in China.[7] These reforms have significantly increased and enhanced the scope of the market, while a shift can be seen from central planning to market regulation. It has been argued that enterprise and economic reform in China since the 1980s has been a process that is aimed at establishing a suitable corporate governance mechanism.[8] A suitable and ideal corporate governance model has not yet been developed despite innovative reforms and the undertaking of a variety of comparative studies and some empirical research.[9]

---

[4]   See the World Bank Ranking of GDP per capita. From 1980–1984 to 2010–2014.

[5]   R. Morck and B. Yeung, 'Corporate Governance in China' (2014) 26(3) *Journal of Applied Corporate Finance* 20, 20.

[6]   This is a model with a competitive market system in which public ownership predominates.

[7]   In addition to this fundamental change, the rapid growth of the private economy, joint ventures, wholly foreign-owned enterprises, collectively-owned enterprises, farmers' special cooperatives and the corporatisation and reconstruction of state-owned enterprises have meant that Chinese business organisations are very diverse, forming a truly 'mixed ownership economy'. See G. Liu, 'The Dialectic Relationship between Peaceful Development and China's Deep Reform', in S. Guo, *China's "Peaceful Rise" in the 21st Century: Domestic and International Conditions*, (Aldershot: Ashgate 2006) 1, 23.

[8]   P.F. Yang, 'The Two Models of Corporate Governance and the Institutional Reform of Chinese Enterprise', in M. Nakamura (ed.), *Changing Corporate Governance in China and Japan: Adaptions of Anglo–American Practices*, (Basingstoke: Palgrave Macmillan 2008) 15.

[9]   For example F. Jiang and K.A. Kim, 'Corporate Governance in China: A Modern Perspective' (2015) 32(6) *Journal of Corporate Finance* 190; W. Shen, Q. Zhou and C. Lau, 'Empirical Research on Corporate Governance in China: A Review and

Chinese corporate governance is clearly distinct from the German-Japanese insider model, the Anglo-American outsider model or the south-east/west Asian family-oriented corporate model,[10] having moved on from learning lessons from the German experience of corporate governance with strong employee participation and two-tier boards in the 1980s, to learn from the American experience in developing a strong stock market and introducing a system of independent directors in the 1990s.[11] The transition process of the Chinese corporate governance model is one that is ongoing, and is constituted by a hybrid model which has both administrative and economic dimensions.[12] Both elements of governance are expected to co-exist and develop to provide an equilibrium in China over a long period, during which there will inevitably be various institutional and ideological obstacles to be overcome.[13] This hybrid model continually changes as in line with economic growth and the initiation and development of a series of reform attempts, primarily dominated by corporatisation and transformation of the role played by the government and the Communist Party. It is unlikely that the transition of the corporate governance model will ultimately lead to a full economic model due to the political system

---

New Directions for Future' (2016) 12(1) *Management and Organization Review* 41; S. Claessens and J.P.H Fan, 'Corporate Governance in Asia: A Survey' (2002) 3(2) *International Review of Finance* 71; G.S. Liu, 'Comparative Corporate Governance: the Experience between China and the UK' (2005) 13(1) *Corporate Governance: An International Review* 1; S. Estrin and M. Prevezer, 'The Role of Informal Institutions in Corporate Governance: Brazil, Russia, India, and China Compared' (2011) 28(3) *Asia Pacific Journal of Management* 41; R.V. Aguilera and G. Jackson, 'Comparative and International Corporate Governance' (2010) 4(1) *The Academy of Management Annals* 485.

[10] W. Li, A. Qiu and Z. Gu, 'Dual Corporate Governance Environment, Political Connections Preference and Firm Performance – Study on Governance Transition of China's Listed Firms (*Shuangchong Gongsi Zhili Guanjing, Zhengzhi Lianxi Pianhao Yu Gongsi Jixiao*) [双重公司治理环境_政治联系偏好与公司绩效: 基于中国民营上市公司治理转型的研究]' (2010) 6 *China Industrial Economics* 85, 85–86.

[11] P.F. Yang, 'The Two Models of Corporate Governance and the Institutional Reform of Chinese Enterprise', in M. Nakamura (ed.), *Changing Corporate Governance in China and Japan: Adaptions of Anglo–American Practices*, (Basingstoke: Palgrave Macmillan 2008) 16.

[12] For discussions on the hybrid corporate governance model see J. Zhao, 'The Emerging Third Way in the Corporate Objective Debate in Company Law' (2011) 62(3) *Northern Ireland Legal Quarterly* 361; J.Y. Lee, 'Hybrid Corporate Governance: The Case of Asia' (2014) 3(4) *Review of Contemporary Business Research* 21; A. Rasheed and T. Yoshikawa (Eds.), *The Convergence of Corporate Governance: Promise and Prospects*, (Basingstoke: Palgrave Macmillan 2012).

[13] See W. Li, X. Chen and Q. Yuan, *Chinese Corporate Governance: Road to Transition and Perfection* (*Zhongguo Gongsi Zhili: Zhuanxing yu Wanshan Zhilu*) [中国公司治理：转型与完善之路], (Beijing: China Machine Press 2012) 140.

which is dominated by a very powerful Communist Party ('the Party') and deeply-rooted traditional factors including the devotion to a business regulatory culture, the influence of dominant ideology, China's long-term preoccupation with state ownership of property with its cautious embrace of capitalism accompanied by ownership that involves Chinese characteristics, including a Chinese top-down regulatory system.[14]

This chapter examines the transition of corporate governance in China, with a special focus on the nature, problems and necessity of administrative governance in order to lay a foundation for our proposal of a unique derivative action in China as a private enforcement measure supported by public enforcer and its agents. The chapter assesses whether administrative power will hinder corporate governance transformation in China on its journey toward a sound and sustainable model. If there are unavoidable barriers that reflect deeply rooted views within China's political system, as well as China's culture, history and shareholding structure, should administrative governance be seen as a positive advantage that is useful, necessary and functional under the current economic development stage in China? In order to be able to do this, we offer an in-depth analysis of the corporate governance transition in China on its route from an administrative governance model to a hybrid one with elements of both administrative and economic governance, and a critical examination of the role played by administrative power that has been wielded by the government in shaping corporate governance.

3.2 A HYBRID MODEL WITH ECONOMIC AND ADMINISTRATIVE CORPORATE GOVERNANCE

Economic corporate governance involves governance that is rooted in economic considerations. The central idea remains constant – the primacy of private and contractual solutions for reducing agency costs. For instance, in Anglo-American systems there tends to be a focus on the economic power of companies, and as far as many companies are concerned this involves the directors running the company so that it makes as much profit as possible, and in such a way as to lead to the maximisation of the wealth of shareholders. The company is viewed as a contractually-based, profit-maximising entity founded on this norm. Therefore, in these jurisdictions traditionally directors' duties are exclusively owed to the company, and the maximisation of the wealth

---

[14]   C. Shi, *Political Determinants of Corporates Governances in China*, (Abingdon: Routledge) 18–19.

of the shareholders is the fundamental purpose of their fiduciary duties.[15] According to efficiency theory, it is more efficient if directors run companies with the aim of maximising shareholder wealth since the least cost is expended in doing this. The directors can work more efficiently if they are focused on one objective only,[16] without any unpoliced managerial discretion.[17] Besides, in contractarian theory, which arguably underpins the nature of the company in Anglo-American jurisdictions, the contracts between the firm and its shareholders are implicit as all these contracts simply amount to a claim on the company's residual cash flow.[18] In Anglo-American companies there is now arguably a greater concern over CSR issues, and consideration is given to the social and environmental as well as the economic (known often as 'the triple bottom line'), but clearly economic concerns still predominate. Under the economic model there is no room for government intervention in private transactions between companies and their stakeholders, and companies rely more on stock and bond markets for external financing. It is believed that a contractual rather than a mandatory model of corporate governance is optimal for achieving economic efficiency, and the market should prevail in shaping the structure

---

[15] See J. Fisch, 'Measuring Efficiency in Corporate Law: The Role of Shareholder Primacy' (2005) 31 *Journal of Corporation Law* 637; S.M. Bainbridge, 'Director Primacy: The Means and Ends of Corporate Governance' (2003) 97(2) *Northwestern University Law Review* 547; S.M. Bainbridge, 'In Defence of the Shareholder Wealth Maximization Norm: A Reply to Professor Green' (1993) 50(4) *Washington. & Lee Law Review* 1423; W. Lazonick and M. O'Sullivan, 'Maximizing Shareholder Value: a New Ideology for Corporate Governance' (2000) 29(1) *Economy and Social* 13; H. Hansmann and R. Kraakman, 'The End of History for Corporate Law' (2001) 89(2) *Georgetown Law Journal* 439; S. Wen, *Shareholder Primacy and Corporate Governance: Legal Aspects, Practices and Future Directions*, (Abington: Routledge 2013).

[16] M. van der Weide, 'Against Fiduciary Duties to Corporate Stakeholders' (1996) 21(1) *Delaware Journal of Corporate Law* 27, 56–57; see also J. Fisch, 'Measuring Efficiency in Corporate Law: The Role of Shareholder Primacy' (2005) 31 *Journal of Corporation Law* 637; L.A. Stout, 'Bad and Not-So-Bad Arguments for Shareholder Primacy' (2002) 75(5) *South California Law Review* 1189; M.C. Jensen, 'Value Maximization, Stakeholder Theory, and the Corporate Objective Function' (2001) 14(3) *Journal of Applied Corporate Finance* 8; R. Daines, 'Does Delaware Law Improve Firm Value?' (2001) 62(3) *Journal of Financial Economics* 525; G. Subramanian, 'The Disappearing Delaware Effect' (2004) 20(1) *Journal of Law, Economics and Organisation* 525; L.A. Bebchuk, A. Cohen and A. Ferrell, 'Does the Evidence Favor State Competition in Corporate Law' (2002) 90(6) *California Law Review* 1775; L. Lin, 'Effectiveness of Outside Directors as a Corporate Governance Mechanism: Theories and Evidence' (1996) 90 *Northwest University Law Review* 892.

[17] A.K. Sundaram and A.C. Inkpen, "The Corporate Objective Revisited", (2004) 15(3) *Organization Science* 350, 354.

[18] Ibid., 355.

of corporate governance.[19] The model prevails in many common law countries with an effective legal enforcement of shareholder rights, but aspects of the model have been applied around the world. Corporate law under this model provides relatively extensive protections for shareholders, and courts are also relatively active in enforcing those protections. Corporate law is designed out of economic consideration for corporate development and survival, rather than with the objective of fairness or paternalism in mind.[20]

Administrative corporate governance has its own different characteristics which involves various forms of government and administrative interference and participation. As the chapter demonstrates China began its journey with a totally administrative corporate governance framework. The characteristics of administrative corporate governance can be observed in relation to share ownership, corporate control, and corporate objective and the result being profit distribution, which is typical in those jurisdictions with elements of a planned economy. First, administrative corporate governance is always connected with the ownership of shares by the government and the historical dominance of SOEs in which the state owns the shares and controls the companies with what is often seen as a detrimental presence. SOEs have been rising in influence in the global economy over the past decade and based on a study by PwC SOEs increased from 3 per cent of all companies in 2005 to 15 per cent in 2014.[21] Despite the fact that the percentage of listed SOEs has dropped 74.86 per cent to 37.88 per cent from 2003 to 2014, they still function as a crucial part of China's economy, carrying great economic weight by making up of 64.36 per cent of the total market capitalisation.[22] To date over 150,000 SOEs are active at the national and local level, with half of listed companies under their control. These SOEs also seem to do relatively well in global competition: they control an astronomical $690bn in assets abroad, with 47 centrally-owned firms ranked in last year's Fortune Global 500.[23]

Secondly, the dominance of state ownership always led to control-based corporate governance. Therefore, the corporate objective is subject to the

---

[19]   F.H. Easterbrook, 'International Corporate Differences: Markets or Law' (1997) 9(4) *Journal of Applied Corporate Finance* 23.

[20]   F.H. Easterbrook and D.R. Fishchel, *The Economic Structure of Corporate Law* (Cambridge, MA: Harvard University Press, 3rd ed. 1991) vii.

[21]   PwC, State-Owned Enterprises: Catalysts for Public Value Creation? (2015), available at http://www.pwc.com/gx/en/psrc/publications/assets/pwc–state–owned–enterprise–psrc.pdf (accessed 22 July 2022).

[22]   T.J. Wong, 'Corporate Governance Research on Listed Firms in China: Institutions, Governance and Accountability' (2016) 9(4) *Foundations and Trends in Accounting* 259, 271–272.

[23]   W. Leutert, 'China's State Enterprise Reform: Bigger, Yes, but Better?' Brookings Institute, April 23, 2015.

interference of government and political policies. Many listed companies, especially SOEs, do accommodate objectives other than profit maximisation and these might include administrative goals. Apart from making profits, these companies have other more immediate administrative missions such as the maintenance of urban employment, other social and environmental purposes or various administrative tasks required by the CSRC in order to regulate China's stock market. Administrative interference aims to serve the state's interests and strategic plans by controlling or influencing multifarious issues of business operation.[24] The administrative approach stems from the government policy in maintaining a full or controlling ownership in companies so as to achieve direct control of key industries such as energy, banking and telecommunications.[25] Furthermore, it can entail direct involvement in upstream industries due to their strategic importance in sustaining the growth of downstream industries.

Companies subject to administrative power pursue the often-conflicting goals of maximising profits on the one hand and contributing to national welfare on the other.[26] Connecting with its unique corporate objective, the decisions relating to CSR, rather than being voluntary in nature, may be a part of orders given to companies by the government or be part of their corporate mission as constituting an element of political strategy. Many listed companies in China are carve-outs or spin-offs from large SOEs which were set up after the establishment of the Chinese stock exchanges in the early 1990s. Therefore, they share personnel functions, capital and assets with their parent companies.[27] Their corporate strategy and profit distributions are closely related to the needs of administrative planning and policy, and their board members always have a close relationship with the government and civil servants. It is argued by Mead that the mode of corporate governance in China, in relation to

---

[24] H.X. Wu, 'Accounting for the Sources of Growth in Chinese Industry 1980–2010' in L. Song, R. Garnaut and C. Fang (eds), *Depending Reform for China's Long-term Growth and Development*, (Canberra: The Australia National University Press 2014) 431,432–433.

[25] Q. Liu and Z. Lu, 'Corporate Governance and Earnings Management in the Chinese Listed Companies: A Tunnelling Perspective' (2007) 13(5) *Journal of Corporate Finance* 881, 884; see also L.S.O. Wanderley, R. Lucian, F. Farache and J.M. de Sousa Filho, 'CSR Information Disclosure on the Web: A Context-Based Approach Analysing the Influence of Country of Origin and Industry Sector' (2008) 82(2) *Journal of Business Ethics* 369.

[26] Z. Wang, 'Corporate Governance under State Control: The Chinese Experience' (2012) 13(2) *Theoretical Inquiries in Law* 487, 488.

[27] Q. Liu and Z. Lu, 'Corporate Governance and Earnings Management in the Chinese Listed Companies: A Tunnelling Perspective' (2007) 13(5) *Journal of Corporate Finance* 881, 885.

the administrative approach, can be accurately described as 'patrimonialism', a combination of paternalism, hierarchical order, mutual obligation, familialism and personalism.[28] Under the administrative governance, governments at all levels act as a guardian of the public and an arbitrator in organising enterprise interests and social interests to effectively supervise SOEs in fulfilling their CSR by way of administrative intervention and economic control.

A good example of the administrative corporate governance approach in China was the quota system that was introduced officially from 1993 to 2000, and which continued to exist on a *de facto* basis until 2002. This system relied on decentralised administrative governance as a key feature of market management during the transition period. The quota system served two functions while it operated including mitigating the serious information problems faced by regulators and investors and incentivising local bureaucrats to select viable companies.[29] From 1993 to 2000 the CSRC had a quota on the number of corporate listings in any given period. It assigned control of this to the planning commission at the provincial level, and the commission distributed listings to IPO candidates, and corporate restructuring was also organised in a way that was based on the actual quota an IPO firm obtained.[30] This was a system that involved allocating critical resources among the regions of China, and the annual quota for each region was established during intense bargaining between regional governments and relevant central agencies. The system played an important role in the era of economic development that was dominated by the planned economy. It was regarded as a basic feature of regional economic management prior to and during the Chinese economic reform process.[31] It facilitated ordered market entry so that the government could, on one hand, maintain certain levels of controlling power over the size and stability of the stock market, and on the other assure an appropriate level of equity

---

[28]   S.G. Redding, *The Spirit of Chinese Capitalism*, (New York: deGruyter 1990).

[29]   D.A. Caragliano, Administrative Governance as Corporate Governance: A Partial Explanation for the Growth of China's Stock Markets' (2009) 30(4) *Michigan Journal of International Law* 1278, 1311.

[30]   Q. Liu and Z. Lu, 'Corporate Governance and Earnings Management in the Chinese Listed Companies: A Tunnelling Perspective' (2007) 13(5) *Journal of Corporate Finance* 881, 884; see also Q. Liu, 'Corporate Governance in China: Current Practices, Economic Effects and Institutional Determinants' (2006) 52(2) *CESifo Economic Studies* 415; J.P.H. Fan, T.J. Wong and T. Zhang, 'Politically Connected CEOs, Corporate Governance, and Post-IPO Performance of China's Newly Partially Privatized Firms' (2007) 84(2) *Journal of Financial Economics* 330.

[31]   Z. Chen, 'Capital Markets and Legal Development: The China Case' (2003) 14(4) *China Economic Review* 451, 454.

financing for the state sector.[32] However, the system also generated problems. The system provided opportunities for corruption and enabled local bureaucrats to have 'rent-seeking' opportunities as the local bureaucrats selected the companies to be IPO candidates and this created the chance for the to extract benefits from expectant companies. Additionally, through the aforementioned control the government manipulated the market. From 2000, the system was abandoned in order to foster the market economy. Therefore, it is clear that the trajectory of administrative governance in China varies and depends on many factors, such as government policies and the state of economic development.

3.3 HISTORICAL PROGRESS OF CORPORATE GOVERNANCE TRANSITION IN CHINA

In this part, some of the major milestones and key transformative issues will be discussed in terms of the development of corporate governance in China in order to identify reasons for, and evidence of, transition and to demonstrate the kind of transition that has occurred.

3.3.1 Pre-1978

Before 1978 only the system of administrative governance existed. SOEs largely operated under the centrally-planned economy and these companies were managed by the committee of factory management, consisting of the head of the factory, management staff and employee representatives.[33] However, the arrangement was abolished after the state launched the first Five-year Plan to carry out socialist transformation where private capital was integrated into public ownership pursuant to the basic Soviet development model of command planning.[34] Under this model, resource allocation decisions were made in response to the command from government planners in the administrative hierarchy instead of responding to the market. The distinct characteristics of this model were discussed by Prybyla as having vertical information flows, centralised coordination and property, and limited and

---

[32]   D.A. Caragliano, Administrative Governance as Corporate Governance: A Partial Explanation for the Growth of China's Stock Markets' (2009) 30(4) *Michigan Journal of International Law* 1278, 1313.

[33]   Art. 2 7, Decree on Establishment of Factory Management Committee in State-operated and Public-operated Factories [关于国营、公营工厂建立工厂管理委员会的指示], 1950.

[34]   K.T. Liou, *Managing Economic Reforms in Post-Mao China*, (London and Westport: Praeger) 28.

concentrated participation in economic decisions.[35] SOEs were, under the model, not independent commercial entities and were owned by the people and functioned as tools by the government in order to deliver economic strategies and business management.[36] They were employed as branches or affiliates of government departments under highly centralised and planned management.[37] Prior to 1978, administrative governance was characterised by features such as public ownership,[38] state plan-directed production activities, price controls with a system of commodity allocation, and state investment and financial control systems.[39] The lack of an efficient market economy mechanism and the contribution by the private sector of only 22 per cent to China's total industrial output at the time characterised the Chinese economy through this period.[40]

3.3.2   1978 to 1986

Following the cultural revolution that attacked all forms of traditional Chinese culture, including the Chinese economy, 1978 was regarded as a key turning point in the development of the economy when the government adopted policies that encouraged greater autonomy for SOEs and granted more decision-making power to the management team, in line with the commence- ment of economic reform and the implementation of the opening-up process.[41] As for corporate governance in China, a top-down approach was implemented by the Party in order to initiate the reform in late 1978[42] and this approach has been dominant, being a logical result of the absolute leadership by the Party in

---

[35]   See J.S. Prybyla, *Reform in China and Other Socialist Economies*, (Washington, DC: AEI Pres 1990); J.S. Prybyla, *Issues in Socialist Economic Modernization*, (London and Westport: Praeger 1990).

[36]   C. Shi, *Political Determinants of Corporates Governances in China* (Abingdon: Routledge) 116–117.

[37]   S. Hong and Z. Nong, *China's State-Owned Enterprise: Nature Performance and Reform* (Danvers: World Science Publishing 2013) 1.

[38]   This includes predominant state ownership and collective ownership.

[39]   A. Huang and C. Xun, 'China' in R. Ma, *Financing Reporting in the Pacific Asia Region* (Singapore: World Scientific Publishing 1997) 159.

[40]   F. Allen, J. Qian and M.J. Qian, 'Law, Finance, and Economic Growth in China' (2005) 77(1) *Journal of Financial Economics* 57.

[41]   See Third Plenary Session of the 11th Community Party Central Committee, People's Dailey, 24 December 1978; available at http://news.xinhuanet.com/ziliao/2003–01/20/content_697755.htm (accessed 22 July 2022).

[42]   This top-down approach required the Party's endorsement for corporate gov- ernance related plans and proposals, before being introduced as enforceable regula- tion by the National People's Congress (NPC) or its Standing Committee. Conversely, a bottom-up approach would be one based on free choice in a market economy.

China and its determined desire to build a socialist market economy.[43] More than 4,000 SOEs were selected for a pilot scheme that saw them subject to reforms including emphasis on SOE autonomy and profiting sharing.[44] SOEs started to have certain rights to plan and manage as well as to retain a portion of profits. The government introduced an economic accountability system in 1981 which offered more autonomous power to enterprises to allow them to become independent economic units, responsible, and accountable for their own profits and losses.[45] The reforms were carried out without contravening the original framework of a planned economy.[46] The main purpose of the changes introduced in this period offered companies control rights over their corporate decisions and operation of firms and gave employees and directors (factory heads) incentives and the right to make profits for enterprises to improve output and ensure revenue growth.[47]

Generally speaking, China initiated an overall economic turnaround towards a market-based paradigm led by the Party-State.[48] This economic policy shift was inventively justified by the accompanying ideological development emphasising another aspect of Marxist theory, i.e., economic determinism describing the correlation between the material '*base*' and the ideological structure of a society that embraces all political, legal, and cultural institutions.[49] Since the opening up and reform in 1978 (or the second 30 years,

---

[43]   J. Fu, *Corporate Disclosure and Corporate Governance in China* (Alphen ann den Rijin: Kluwer Law International 2010) 6.

[44]   This was introduced by the State Council through 'The Regulations on the Expansion of Operational Management Autonomy for State-Owned Industrial Enterprises' and 'the Regulations on Retention of Profits by State-Owned Enterprises'; in 1979. See Regulations on the expansion of the state-owned enterprise management autonomy [关于扩大国营企业经营管理自主改革若干规定].

[45]   State-owned enterprises on the provisions of retained earnings[关于国营企业实行利润留成的规定].

[46]   Regulations such as the 'Interim Regulation on the Employee's Congress of SOEs' was enacted in 1982 and the 'Interim Regulation on SOEs' was enacted in 1983.

[47]   S. Hong and Z. Nong, *China's State-Owned Enterprise: Nature Performance and Reform*, (Danvers: World Science Publishing 2013) 3.

[48]   C. Wang, 'A Great Transformation from the State-Planned Economy to Socialist Market Economy [从计划经济到社会主义市场经济的伟大变革] [2008] 11 *Xinxiang Review* 1, available at http://cpc.people.com.cn/GB/68742/127229/127250/8344596 .html (accessed 22 July 2022). At the Plenary Session of the Communist Party Central Committee in 1984, the central committee indicated that the ownership and management of state-owned enterprises may be appropriately separated. This was codified in 1988, in the Law on Industrial Enterprises Owned by the Whole People. See Robert C. Art and Minkang Gu, 'China Incorporated: The First Corporation Law of the People's Republic of China' (1995) 20 *Yale Journal of International Law* 273, 278–9.

[49]   R. Wacks, *Understanding Jurisprudence: An Introduction to Legal Theory*, (Oxford: Oxford University Press, 3rd ed. 2012) 179.

as it was described by the Chinese press), socio-economic development in China has exhibited an interesting trend. While many elements of the Chinese economy, including the acceptance of foreign investment, the corporatisation of SOEs and the proliferation of the private economy, are endeavouring to resemble the US market-oriented regime, at least in form, in ideology these business features initiated and developed in capitalist countries are still justified under the basic tenet of the Communist Party of China, namely Party-State-led socialism.[50] The state still structures and leads the process of growth, channels capital, and guides the activities of private actors.[51]

3.3.3　　1987 to 1992

In 1987, the 13th National Congress of the Communist Party of China proposed the introduction of the joint-stock system. As a result, the property rights of small SOEs could be transferred to collectives or individuals. Since the late 1980s the emergence and increasing acceptance of a basic economic and legal entity was accompanied by a series of financial reforms that replaced state budgetary grants. Stock markets were established, with the two official stock exchanges being equipped for operation by creating a new government body – the CSRC – to regulate them. A major step in the evolution of the economy was the government policy of 'separating control from ownership' which, in certain ways, represented the end of the planned economy in China and the start of economic restructuring.[52] The provision of a two-track system can be also observed in legislation.[53] It is clear that the relevant authorities still retained residual power as far as important decision-making was concerned,[54]

---

[50]　R. Peerenboom, 'Judicial Independence in China: Common Myths and Unfounded Assumptions', in R. Peerenboom (ed.) *Judicial Independence in China— Lessons for Global Rule of Law Promotion*, (Cambridge: Cambridge University Press 2009) 91:

> China's reforms have been successful due in large part to the government's pragmatic approach and willingness to resist, selectively adopt, and adapt as needed the ideologically driven prescriptions offered by Western states and international donor agencies.

[51]　T. Ginsburg, 'Does Law Matter for Economic Development? Evidence from East Asia' (2000) 34(3) *Law & Society Review* 829.

[52]　J.P.H. Fan, T.J. Wong and T. Zhang, 'The Emergence of Corporate Pyramids in China' (2006) 52(2) *CESifo Economic Studies* 415; see also S. Claessens, S. Djankov and L.H.P. Lang, 'The Separation of Ownership in East Asian Corporations' (2000) 58(1–2) *Journal of Financial Economics* 81.

[53]　Enterprise Law was introduced in 1988 as the first codified law for SOEs.

[54]　Such as issuing a unified mandatory plan, appointing and approving the appointment of the factory head (directors) and management Article 55 Law of Industrial Enterprises Owned by the Whole People, 1988.

but it prohibited the state and its organs from encroaching on the autonomy of SOEs in their organisation of production and the managing of the business.[55] In addition, policies, rules and regulations for protecting the non-state owned sector[56] provide a legal guarantee for the development of the non-state owned sector. Despite these reforms introduced in the regulation of SOEs and steps being taken to gradually subject SOEs to market forces, the ownership pattern remained largely unchanged during that period.[57] However, it is fair to say that a hybrid system, including both administrative and market-based corporate governance, was under development in China at this stage.

3.3.4 Modern Enterprise System after 1992

In November 1993 following Deng's southern tour,[58] the Third Plenary Session of the 14th National Congress of the Community Party of China passed the 'Decision on Several Issues for Establishing a Socialist Market Economy System by the Central Committee of the CPC', which stated that the 'market was to play a fundamental role concerning the resources under macro control by the State'. After 1992, we see the emergence of a modern enterprise structure via legal reform, with the introduction of the first company and securities law in 1993 which confirmed the legal bases for non-SOEs and set out the rights and responsibilities of companies as separate legal entities, boards of directors, and shareholders' general meetings. After the enforcement of these two pieces of legislation, three periods followed which marked the start of the evolution of a modern corporate governance system. The first one focused on incorporatisation and securitisation reform (1992–1999), the second one on capital market development, and the third on implementing best corporate governance practices.[59] An important 'decision' was adopted

---

[55] Art. 58 Law of Industrial Enterprises Owned by the Whole People, 1988.

[56] Such as the Interim Regulations for the Administration of Urban and Rural Individual Industrial and Commercial Businesses, the Law of Foreign Invested Enterprises and the Provisional Regulations of Private Enterprises were successively promulgated.

[57] W. Shen, Q. Zhou and C. Lau, 'Empirical Research on Corporate Governance in China: A Review and New Directions for Future' (2016) 12(1) *Management and Organization Review* 41, 43.

[58] On his Southern tour in 1992, Deng Xiaoping gave a series of speeches that are regarded as keynote addresses that signal the beginning of the marketisation of China's economy.

[59] J. Fu, *Corporate Disclosure and Corporate Governance in China*, (Alphen ann den Rijin: Kluwer Law International 2010) 12.

in 1999,[60] identifying corporate governance as the core element of the modern enterprise system. During this period the market-oriented economy started to play an increasingly important role with 75 per cent of industrial output being contributed by private sectors and by 1999 these sectors employed more than 70 per cent of non-agricultural employees.[61]

The initial two stages of China's so-called Socialist Market Economic Reform was implemented in this period.[62] The first stage started in 1993, the central theme being the establishment of a market economy while preserving the dominating socialist theme.[63] In this general climate, the major goal of the first Company Law, passed in 1993, was to oil the wheels of the state-owned sector and enable struggling state-owned firms to raise capital from the general public, rather than to encourage the growth of private economy.[64] The second stage of China's economic development began in 2003, with the central policy imperative evolving to become the so-called Improvement of the Socialist Market Economy.[65] The position of private business improved markedly during this stage, formally legitimised as part of the Socialist Market Economy that China was heading towards.[66] Accompanying the subtle shift in policy attitude from repressing to encouraging the private economy sector, company law in China was modified accordingly, from primarily emphasising the governing function towards increasing reception of the market-based ideology and advocating the enabling role of company law. It is thus no coincidence that the 2005 company law reform was triggered and implemented immediately after

---

[60]   See the Fourth Plenum of the Chinese Communist Party's 15th Central Committee in September 1999.

[61]   F. Allen, J. Qian and M.J. Qian, 'Law, Finance, and Economic Growth in China' (2005) 77(1) *Journal of Financial Economics* 57.

[62]   *China's Socialist Market Economic Reform and Its Strong Theoretical Consciousness and Confidence,* People's Daily Online, Oct. 17, 2012, available at http://english.peopledaily.com.cn/100668/102793/7980397.html (accessed 22 July 2022).

[63]   *The Decision of the CPC Central Committee on Issues Concerning the Establishment of the Socialist Market Economy [*中共中央关于建立社会主义市场经济体制若干问题的决定*]*, adopted at the Third Plenary Session of the 14th Central Committee of the CPC on 14 November 1993, available at http://www.people.com.cn/item/20years/newfiles/b1080.html (accessed 29 July 2022).

[64]   Z. Chen, 'Capital Markets and Legal Development: The China Case' (2003)14(4) *China Economic Review* 451, 451.

[65]   *The Decision of the CPC Central Committee on Issues Concerning the Improvement of the Socialist Market Economy [*中共中央关于完善社会主义市场经济体制若干问题的决定*]*, adopted at the Third Plenary Session of the 16th Central Committee of the CPC on 14 Oct. 2003, available at http://news.xinhuanet.com/zhengfu/2003–10/22/content_1136008.htm (accessed 22 July 2022).

[66]   Ibid.

the 2003 economic policy shift,[67] symbolising the country's commitment to encouraging private entrepreneurship in the market economy.

Since the advent of the new Chinese Company Law 2005 and its amendment in 2013, corporate governance developments in China have entered a new phase where effective corporate governance mechanisms and practices have become a necessary condition to achieving sustainable and enduring prosperity in the context of a globally competitive market economy.[68] All in all, despite the fact that a wide range of modern corporate governance mechanisms and practices have been adopted and adapted in China, aiming to keep corporate governance and law development consistent with its rapid economic trans-formation and development, such as independent directors,[69] supervisory boards,[70] CSR,[71] there remain inherent systemic problems that hinder the effectiveness and efficiency of a sound corporate governance framework. In particular, the latest corporate law reform, involving the abolition of minimal capital,[72] suggested that the Chinese were ready for a bigger dose of market liberalism as this meant the abolition of regulations that impeded the entry of new firms or restrict competition. Echoing the powerful rhetoric of aligning Chinese corporate law more closely with that of other developed economies, much scholarly ink has been spilled in China commending this legislative change as the '*legal cornerstone underpinning China's future economic development*'[73] and advocating its effectiveness in prompting the growth of the private economy. Furthermore, portrayed as being borrowed from the Anglo-American derivative action regime, many also see this legislative change as an infusion of Anglo-American liberal market values.[74] These issues have their roots in administrative involvement or overly strong administrative

---

[67] N.C. Howson, *Judicial Independence and the Company Law in the Shanghai Courts in* R. Peerenboom (ed.) *Judicial Independence in China: Lessons for Global Rule of Law Promotion*, (Cambridge: Cambridge University Press 2010) 134, 136.

[68] O.K. Tam and C.P. Yu, 'China Corporate Governance Development' in C.A. Mallin, *Handbook on International Corporate Governance: Country Analyses*, (Cheltenham: Edward Elgar, 2nd ed. 2011) 223, 223.

[69] See art. 122, Chinese Company Law 2018.

[70] See arts 51–55, Chinese Company Law 2018.

[71] See art. 5, Chinese Company Law 2018.

[72] See the codified Company Law 2006 in 2013 (updated art. 26 and deletion of original 27(3) and 29).

[73] J. Liu, *The New Company Law 2013 is the Legal Cornerstone of China's Economic Development* [2013年新公司法是打造中国经济"升级版"的法律基石], (May 12, 2014), available at: http://www.ccpit-ah.com/news/detail/id/5629.html (accessed 29 July 2022).

[74] Ibid.; J. Liu, *A Proposal to Reform the Company Law and Securities Act Simultaneously* [建议《公司法》与《证券法》联动修改] [2013] 4 *Legal Forum*[法学论坛] 5.

power in the Chinese corporate governance system, including: negative consequences emanating from the dominance of state ownership of many listed
companies, the role of big state-owned banks and their influence on companies, poor discourse and monitoring processes due to the relationship between
boards of directors and government officials, and the weak enforcement of
laws. These issues require us to reconsider the function and drawbacks of
administrative corporate governance, and challenges that exist, including the
role played by the government and Party organisations, and issues of multiple
regulators, corporate culture and corporate objectives.[75]

As with previous reforms, the primary aim of the 2014 reform identified
by the Chinese government was still economically connected, i.e., '*to foster
economic development*' by way of stimulating the private sector.[76] Undeniably,
the rate of economic growth in China in the past decades has been incredible
– starting from scratch, the Chinese economy has managed an average 10.06
per cent annual growth since the economic opening-up in 1978,[77] and even
during and after the 2007–09 financial crisis that led to the worst worldwide
economic recession in seven decades, China's economy still managed above
7 per cent annual growth.[78] In the meantime, the unsustainability of the
state-investment-led, export-oriented model and an urgent need for economic
structural reforms was openly acknowledged by the Chinese leadership as
early as 2007.[79] This heavy reliance on exports has always been a '*chronic*

---

[75]   Addressing these issues takes place in relation to the emerging Chinese
economy which was the world's largest goods economy by 2014 (BBC, 'China 'overtakes' US as world's largest goods trader', available at http://www.bbc.co.uk/news/
business–25678415 (accessed 22 July 2022)), the second largest consumer economy
by 2013, possessed the largest foreign reserves by 2009 (*The Economist*, 'The World's
Second Biggest Consumer' 18 February 2014 available at https://www.economist.com/
analects/2014/02/18/the-worlds-second-biggest-consumer (accessed 29 July 2022)),
and the second largest world economy overall by 2011 with annual GDP growth rates
of 9–10 per cent for 30 years *The Guardian*, ('China Overtakes Japan as World's
Second-Largest Economy', available at http://www.theguardian.com/business/2011/
feb/14/china–second–largest–economy (accessed 22 July 2022).

[76]   State Council, *Notice of the State Council on the Issuance of the Reform Plan
to Amend the Registered Capital Registration System* [国务院关于印发注册资本登
记制度改革方案的通知*]*, Guofa (2014) No. 7, available at http://www.gov.cn/zwgk/
2014–02/18/content_2611545.htm (accessed 22 July 2022).

[77]   See World Bank Data with authors' calculation, available at http://data.worldbank
.org/indicator/NY.GDP.MKTP.KD.ZG?locations=CN (accessed 22 July 2022).

[78]   Statistics   China,   available   at   http://www.tradingeconomics.com/china/
gdp–growth–annual (accessed 22 July 2022).

[79]   'A country that appears peaceful and stable may encounter unexpected crises.
There are structural problems in China's economy which cause unsteady, unbalanced, uncoordinated and unsustainable development.' Remarks from Premier Wen

illness',[80] but its harmful impact began to be really felt around the end of the last decade after the worldwide crisis, when the general economic decline in world markets led to a significant fall in export demands and a rise of labour costs in China. Although steps were taken during the Hu-Wen administration, the first and foremost task facing the new generation leaders, led by Xi Jinping as the new Communist Party and military chief since March 2013, remained an engineered structural shift toward new modes of development, based less on exports and more on domestic growth and markets.[81] The desired shift entails a move away from largely state-run heavy industry to more entrepreneurial and services-led growth, which are mainly provided by the private sector.[82] Taking as a given rather than as an assumption that start-ups and small- and medium-sized enterprises (SMEs) are powerful economic drivers, the Chinese government has concluded that this cannot be achieved without more private capital investment. Inextricable from the microeconomic ideal that 'every small business is a potential Microsoft',[83] the abolition of market entry requirements by way of modifying capital provision rules is thus portrayed by the new Chinese leaders as apposite at this point of time, to encourage investment in start-up companies and further prompt the growth of the private economy. This motive has been repeatedly asserted by China's recent official discourse, in which the words 'small start-up businesses' and 'competitive and innovative' are frequently linked together.[84]

It is worth emphasising that corporate governance in China is moving towards a modernised model following the principles formulated by the OECD and the introduction of regulatory changes and new rules that affect corporate

---

Jiabao's Press Conference of 17 March, 2007. Full text is available at http://www .chinaconsulatesf.org/eng/xw/t304313.htm (accessed 22 July 2022).

[80] X. Ding, *Watch Out for the Chronic Illness of the China Model [*警惕中国模式 的 "慢性病"*]* (9 December 2010) *Southern Weekly [*南方周末*]*.

[81] 'To solve the long–term challenges of economic development in China, we must implement structural reform, even though we may let our economy grow at a lower rate.' Remarks made by President Xi Jinping at the first session of the G20 leaders' summit in 2013, after he assumed power in March. See J. Fu, J. Wu and S. Xie, *Xi Vows Economic Reform*, *China Daily*, 6 September 2013, available at https://www.chinadaily .com.cn/kindle/2013-09/06/content_16949683.htm (accessed 22 July 2022).

[82] Kevin Yao, *China Needs the Private Sector to Step Up*, *Reuters*, 16 May 2016 available at http://www.reuters.com/article/us–china–economy–investment–idUSKCN0Y60V4 (accessed 22 July 2022).

[83] I. Ramsay, 'Commentary: The Politics of Commercial Law' [2001] *Wisconsin Law Review* 565, 572.

[84] X. Yangge and P. Liu, *State Council Announce Significant Company Registration System Reform*, 14 November 2013, available at http://www.mondaq.com/ x/274880/Insolvency+Bankruptcy/State+Council+Announce+Significant+Company+ Registration+System+Reform (accessed 22 July 2022).

governance practices in China. The reform policy is to reduce the role of government planning and make sure the market plays a more important and active role, hoping that it will cure China's enduring problems of administrative interference and multiple lines of command over economic activities. The corporate law legislation has been reviewed and amended in order to ensure that companies are regarded as separate legal entities. The main goal of the transition is to build a governance system that is able to provide motivation for investment, adequate restraint and monitoring of management, and promote the optimal use of resources for wealth creation.[85] Against the backdrop of the Law and Development Movement which has dominated in past decades, seeking to promote an international order of economic and social institutions similar to those in more advanced economies,[86] some scholars suggest that the first and foremost purpose of such burgeoning borrowing activities in China is to prepare for the international unification of law amid globalisation.[87] The transition process entails changing the corporate objective and the management team appointment process, identifying new capital sources, reallocation of resources and a shift from state monopoly control to mixed and shared control in order to facilitate fairness, predictability and business confidence.[88] Despite the fact that policymakers may have favoured an economic model in principle at the beginning of the planned reform,[89] the reality has been the evolution of a dynamic hybrid model that changes in line with economic advancement, and legal and cultural development in Chinese society as a whole.

---

[85] J. Chen, *Corporate Governance in China*, (London and New York: Routledge Curzon 2005) 25.

[86] T. Ginsburg, 'Does Law Matter for Economic Development? Evidence from East Asia' (2000) 34(3) *Law & Society Review* 829; B.Z. Tamanaha, 'The Lessons of Law-and-Development Studies' (1995) 89(2) *American Journal of International Law* 470, 471.

[87] O. Kahn-Freund has identified three prime purposes of legal transplantation, namely:

> first, with the object of preparing the international unification of the law, secondly, with the object of giving adequate legal effect to a social change shared by the foreign country with one's own country, and thirdly, with the object of promoting at home a social change which foreign law is designed either to express or to produce.

O. Kahn-Freund, 'On Uses and Misuses of Comparative Law' (1974) 37(1) *Modern Law Review* 1, 2.

[88] R. Tomasic, 'Company Law Implementation in the PRC: The Rule of Law in the Shadow of the State' (2015) 15(2) *Journal of Corporate Law Studies* 285, 285.

[89] J. Chen, *Corporate Governance in China*, (London and New York: Routledge Curzon 2005) 61.

3.4   REASONS FOR TRANSITION

As China enters a more advanced phase with a transformed corporate governance system following the introduction of adjustments and the provision of
corporate governance reforms, it not only faces opportunities for development
as the result of external pressure and globalisation, but also with challenges to
the preservation and strengthening of its reform policies. The reasons for the
transformation are based on the following elements.

3.4.1   Corporatisation

China's corporate governance reform is aimed at transforming the traditional
SOEs into modern competitive firms operating on a market basis, which
has been regarded as the core element of continuing economic liberalisation
and structural reforms.[90] Early attempts at the reform of SOEs did not solve
the inefficiency problems of Chinese corporate governance because of their
limited focus on managerial incentives and autonomous expansion, without
addressing or challenging fundamental ownership concerns. The corporatisation process in China took place in multiple stages in the 1990s, 2000 and
2014.[91] It is regarded as a part of economic reform in which stock markets
are seen as an alternative to bank lending to provide new sources of capital to
the state sector. With the endorsement of the 14th National Congress of the
Party in 1993, there was diversification of forms of ownership by the state,
the entry of private and foreign investors, and an introduction of a framework
for modern corporate governance for SOEs. Thousands of poorly performing
national and regional SOEs were privatised or liquidated.[92]

The corporatisation reform is regarded as a complicated and interactive
process in which official ideologies, national policies and the interests of the
involved parties have become intertwined in a dynamic manner.[93] This process
manifests the transformation of corporate governance, especially in terms of
the government and administrative involvement. With the first serious attempt

---

[90]   J. Leng, *Corporate Governance and Financial Reform in China's Transition
Economy*, (Hong Kong: Hong Kong University Press 2009) 2.

[91]   See G. Wildau, 'China Kicks off Second Round of Corporatisation' *The
Financial Times*, 10 August 2014; available at http://www.ft.com/cms/s/0/
ec28674c–13ac–11e4–84b7–00144feabdc0.html#axzz3DOzmmx3b (accessed 22 July
2022).

[92]   Ibid.

[93]   C. Xi, 'Book Review of Yong Zhang, Large Chinese State-Owned Enterprises:
Corporatization and Strategic Development, Basingstoke and New York: Palgrave
Macmillan 2008' (2009)197 *The China Quarterly* 217, 218.

at SOE reform, commenced in the early 1990s, the government tackled
ownership reform in the SOE sector and aimed to diversify the ownership
structure of SOEs by transforming them into companies limited by shares with
an economic corporate governance structure. The most direct way of corporatisation was the split-share structure that granted legitimate trading rights to
the state-owned shares of listed SOEs.[94] This was a process where a certain
percentage of shares were held by the government but it enabled the SOEs to
go public by issuing minority tradable shares to investors and opened up China
for corporatisation. The reason for reorganising the shareholding structure in
split-share structure was to retain government control over companies, but at
the same time allowing for market mechanisms to influence and discipline
companies.[95] This split also maintained certain degrees of government and
administrative involvement in listed SOEs after reform. There was mixed
share ownership in tradable and non-tradable shares co-existing in listed
companies and increased involvement of market power in the capitalisation of
companies. The launch of the Shanghai and Shenzhen Stock Markets made the
trading of shares possible for listed companies. The launch also represented
a significant step towards market-oriented corporate governance reform and
corporatisation in China, as it represented one of the main events that marked
the transformation from a purely administrative model to a hybrid one. In this
hybrid model, the government aimed to boost SOEs output, profits and more
efficient employment patterns with the involvement of market power and
participation of private and foreign investments. The stock markets served as
a conduit to channel the investment of domestic citizens and passive foreign
investors into the ailing SOEs.[96] The reform adopted market mechanisms that

---

[94]   L. Liao, B. Liu and H. Wang, 'China's Secondary Privatization: Perspectives
from the Split-Share Structure Reform' (2014) 113(3) *Journal of Financial Economics*
500, 500.

[95]   H. Berkman, R.A. Cole and L.J. Fu, 'Improving Corporate Governance where
the State is the Controlling Block Holder: Evidence from China' (2014) 20(7–9) *The
European Journal of Finance* 752; see also Q. Sun and W.H.S. Tong, 'China Share
Issues Privatization: the Extent of its Success' (2003) 70(2) *Journal of Financial
Economics* 183, 188; M.A. Firth, 'Does One Size Fit All? A Study of the Simultaneous
Relations among Ownership, Corporate Governance Mechanisms and the Financial
Performance of Firms in China', in S. Boubaker, B.D. Nguyen and D.K. Nguyen
(eds), *Corporate Governance: Recent Development and New Trends*, (Heidelberg
and London: Springer 2012) 29; K. Xu, L. Tihanyi and M.A. Hitt, 'Firm Resources,
Government Power and Privatization' (2017) 43(4) *Journal of Management* 998; Y.S.
Kang and B.Y. Kim, 'Ownership Structure and Firm Performance: Evidence from
Chinese Corporate Reform' (2012) 23(2) *China Economic Review* 471.

[96]   D.A. Caragliano, 'Administrative Governance as Corporate Governance:
A Partial Explanation for the Growth of China's Stock Markets' (2009) 30(4) *Michigan
Journal of International Law* 1278, 1293.

played an innovative role in aligning the interests of the government and public investors. The corporatisation process mitigated the role played by the state by reducing its ownership and opening up the securities market to enable investors to share the risk and profit of enterprises that had hitherto been controlled by and responsible to the state.

3.4.2 Foreign Investment and Entering the World Trade Organization

According to figures from the United Nations Conference of Trade and Industry, foreign companies invested $128.5bn in making China the top destination for foreign direct investment in 2014.[97] The dramatic increase of foreign investment is regarded as an external push for the development of corporate governance towards a position where there is less government interference and administration in order to make it a fit for the internationalised equity market. In this sense, Chinese corporate governance may have benefited from the potential impact of foreign investment on governance and performance. Foreign investors have been allowed, in increasing numbers, by regulators and the government to take up substantial shareholdings, and this is considered desirable because of the investors' experience, sophistication and the potentially positive influence that they may bring to Chinese corporate governance.[98] China's accession to the WTO is a key aspect of its integration into the world economy and constitutes both an economic and symbolic policy success.[99] It was suggested by James Wolfensohn[100] that China needed to improve its corporate governance in order to attract more foreign investment and survive international competition following its WTO entry and to address 'special problems as a country with a huge number of State-owned enterprises'.[101] Trade liberalisation in the context of WTO entry created pressure to

---

[97] 'China Overtakes US for Foreign Direct Investment', *BBC*, 30 January 2015, available at http://www.bbc.co.uk/news/business–31052566 (accessed 22 July 2022); China is also at the top of the 2014–2015 list of the companies most attractive to multinational companies.

[98] S.A. Beatson and J. Chen 'Foreign Investment, Corporate Governance and Performance in the Chinese Listed A Share Companies' (2018) 16(1) *Journal of Chinese Economic and Business Studies* 59.

[99] R. Sally and R. Sen, 'Whither Trade Policies in Southeast Asia? The Wider Aisan and Global Context' (2005) 22(1) *ASEAN Economic Bulletin* 92. After an arduous negotiation process lasting more than 15 years, China became a member of the WTO, a body that probably constitutes the most remarkable achievement of economic globalisation in recent years.

[100] Former president of the World Bank group.

[101] WB President: Urgent to Improve Corporate Governance in Post-WTO China, *People's Daily*, 27 May 2002; available at http://www.china.org.cn/english/33352.htm (accessed 22 July 2022).

reallocate productive resources according to China's comparative advantages, which was regarded as the exercise of external pressure for a transition to a market economy. It was thought that corporate governance arrangements would decide the way that companies and other economic agents responded to these pressures.[102] The foreign investment and accession to the WTO can be regarded as external pressure for Chinese government to adopt international guidelines and for Chinese companies to be more familiar with westernised corporate governance practices.

3.4.3   Corporate Governance Guidelines and Internationally Recognised Guidelines

Apart from the government legislation for company law, the CSRC has played an active role in improving corporate governance. In January 2001 the CSRC issued its *Code of Corporate Governance for Listed Companies* (the Code) in China. The Code was revised in 2018.[103] The Code, like many other codes elsewhere in the world, contains broad and vague language describing guiding principles, rather than explicit regulation. The Code contains considerable evidence of convergence with international corporate governance guidelines, since the draft largely relied on the *OECD Corporate Governance Principles*[104] and almost all the provisions contained in it have parallel provisions in the law or the codes of corporate governance of the UK and the US. Despite the fact that there are many doubts about whether the *OECD Principles* are appropriate in an emerging economy like China,[105] the Code does propose good practices of corporate governance including the requirement for an active board of directors, independent outside directors as a majority of the board, and protecting the interests of minority shareholders and stakeholders which all require strong free markets and economic governance with minimum government interference.

---

[102]   S. Tenev and C. Zhang with L. Breford, *Corporate Governance and Enterprise Reform in China: Building the Institutions of Modern Markets*, (Washington, DC: The World Bank and the International Finance Corporation, 2002) 2; WTO membership has been seen as the most important government push for SOE reform, characterised by the acceleration of decentralised corporatisation and the emphasis of corporate governance primacy, with corresponding financial reforms in the banking and securities sectors.

[103]   See Sections 7–11 on Shareholders' Right.

[104]   OECD, *OECD Principles of Corporate Governance* 1999 (this is the version that has been followed by the Code). The Principles have now been updated in 2015; see V.Z. Chen, J. Li and D.M. Shaprio, 'Are OECD-prescribed "Good Corporate Governance Practices" Really Good in an Emerging Economy' (2011) 28(3) *Asia Pacific Journal of Management* 115.

[105]   See Chen, Li and Shaprio, ibid.

The International CSR standards have been regarded as examples of external pressure for the development of corporate governance in China. The most popular standard for manufacturers in China is SA8000.[106] However, adopting SA8000 is a controversial issue in China, where there are varied opinions about the role of CSR standards in the global supply chain. It is argued that with modernised awareness and attitudes towards CSR from Chinese authorities, who now recognise CSR as a way to improve the competitiveness of companies, the impact of SA8000 on Chinese industry and export-oriented firms has been taken on board.[107] ISO 26000, the Guidance on Social Responsibility, was introduced by the International Integrated Reporting Council in 2010 as a new approach to corporate reporting, and it has had a significant impact worldwide. A Chinese version of ISO 26000 was published[108] and provides 'a solid start' as a new way of conducting business.[109] These internationally recognised CSR standards make a self-regulatory framework increasingly important for Chinese companies in order to promote their corporate image and sustainability, and it addresses social and environmental problems, which were regarded as government problems that may only be settled through government policies and economic strategies in SOEs under administrative governance.

---

[106] See SA8000 is now internationally recognised and widely accepted as the most viable and comprehensive workplace management system for ethical issues. The system requires ongoing compliance and continual improvement of ethical standards of corporations, with involvement from stakeholders including participation by all key sectors in the SA8000 system, including employees, trade unions, companies, socially responsible investors, nongovernmental organisations, the government and the public; for more information see Social Accountability Accreditation Services (SAAS) website via http://www.saasaccreditation.org (accessed 22 July 2022).

[107] L. Zu, *Corporate Social Responsibility, Corporate Restructuring and Firm's Performance*, (Berlin: Springer-Verlag 2009) 45.

[108] The Chinese version was translated by the Standardisation Administration of the People's Republic of China under the authorisation of the International Organisation for Standardisation

[109] C. Wang, 'ISO 26000 in China: A New Way of Doing Business' (2012) *ISO Focus+* 46.

3.4.4   Cross-listing in China?

Figures from 2012[110] inform us that 84 Chinese listed companies cross-listed their stocks.[111] Cross-listing securities is an efficient way to access international financial markets, and is always related to improved corporate governance practices in a stronger investment environment and higher requirements for information disclosure and corporate governance rules.[112] It may also help companies to improve their corporate governance by voluntarily embracing both stronger regulatory regimes and soft laws, including regulations for stock exchanges and corporate governance codes required by the host exchange.[113] As far as companies in emerging markets are concerned, cross-listing through American Depository Receipts programmes is associated with more cross-border flows and greater integration in globalised capital markets.[114] A good example of enhanced cross-listing is South Korea, where listed companies are given the option to cross-list in nine foreign stock markets,[115] as part of the country's modernisation, globalisation and convergent corporate governance practice. The percentage of firms cross-listed in the US by China increased from 6 per cent (ranked fifth) to 29 per cent (ranked first) at the end of 2000 and 2010.[116] As of 31 March 2022, there were 261 Chinese companies listed on the US exchanges with a total market capitalisation of $1.4 trillion.[117]

---

[110]   84 Chinese listed companies are cross-listed on another stock exchange, including 80 on the Hong Kong Stock Exchange, ten on both the Hong Kong and New York Stock Exchanges, one on the Singapore Stock Exchange and two on both the Hong Kong and London Stock Exchanges. One is on three exchanges, namely the Hong Kong, New York and London Stock Exchanges.

[111]   There are 70 firms listed on the Hong Kong Stock Exchange, ten are listed on both the Hong Kong and New York Stock Exchanges, one company is listed on the Singapore Stock exchange, and two are listed on both the Hong Kong and London Stock Exchanges; see F. Jiang and K.A. Kim, 'Corporate Governance in China: A Modern Perspective' (2015) 32(6) *Journal of Corporate Finance* 190, 203–204.

[112]   J.C.J. Coffee, 'Do Norms Matter? A Cross-country Evaluation' (2001) 149(6) *University of Pennsylvania Law Review* 2151.

[113]   A.N. Licht, 'Legal Plug-Ins: Culture Distance, Cross-Listing, and Corporate Governance Reform' (2004) 22(1) *Berkeley International Law Journal* 195, 201–202.

[114]   A. Karolyi, 'The Role of ADRs in the Development and Integration of Emerging Equity Markets' (2004) 86 *The Review of Economics and Statistics* 670.

[115]   The cross-listing stock exchanges include NYSE, NASDAQ, AMEX, and stock markets in London, Frankfurt, Paris, Tokyo, Hong Kong and Singapore.

[116]   The data is adapted from Citibank Universal Insurance Guide (data refers to the NSDAQ and NYSE) (2011).

[117]   US–China Economic and Security Review Commission, Chinese Companies Listed on Major US Stock Exchanges, 31 March 2022, available at https://www.uscc.gov/research/chinese–companies–listed–major–us–stock–exchanges (accessed 22 July 2022).

Despite the fact that listing in stock exchanges in Hong Kong or Singapore may be comparatively more feasible and culturally friendly to Chinese corporations, these advantages have not dissuaded Chinese investors from listing in the US. China still has the highest percentage of cross-listing in the US. The high volume cross-listing will inevitably have an immense impact on the transformation of corporate governance model in China toward a more Anglo-American model. Aguilera and Cuervo-Cazurra also argued that cross-listing in a US-based exchange is likely to encourage the implantation of corporate governance code in order to enhance the efficiency of corporate governance in China.[118]

In detail, the accounting and reporting practices of cross-listing Chinese companies will, therefore, converge with those recruitments extant in the US. These requirements are normally designed to avoid market abuses and the enforcement of these regiments will reduce the involvement of administrative governance. It is argued that this cross-listing can facilitate competition among stock exchanges in terms of regulatory competition, with harmonisation and/or convergence as a result.[119] Listing companies in jurisdictions with more developed legal system and corporate governance model will subject the companies to a higher governance standard and a more sophisticated market discipline. On a different note, cross-listing will change the shareholding structure in China and reduce the concentrated ownership of the state. This will also lead to the greater internationalisation of Chinese companies.

3.5 CHARACTERISTICS AND IMPACT OF ADMINISTRATIVE GOVERNANCE IN THE TRANSFORMATION PROCESS

In this section, the characteristics and impact of administrative corporate governance will be examined to illuminate the uniqueness of corporate governance in China. The nature of administrative governance and government interference in companies will be discussed as important elements in the transformation process.

---

[118] R.V. Aguilera and A. Cuervo-Cazurra, 'Code of Good Governance Worldwide: What is the Trigger' (2004) 25(3) *Organization Studies* 415.

[119] H.J. Kim, 'Cross-Listing of Korean Companies on Foreign Exchange: Law and Policy' (2003) 3(1) *Journal of Korean Law* 1, 13.

3.5.1   Administrative Power and Corporate Governance in China

The long-term coexistence of administrative and economic corporate governance is a unique aspect in China. The impact from administrative power on corporate governance in China lies in the 'administrativisation' of resource allocation, corporate objectives, the appointment and removal of senior executives, and imposition of administrative liability for breaching the directors' duties.[120] The political involvement in corporate governance is seen as one of the primary manifestations of administrative corporate governance.[121] China launched a major economic reform and liberalisation strategy in the 1980s when two important strategies introduced during this period were the separation of state ownership and control and the separation of enterprise from government administration.[122] Instead of having no independent decision-making powers, the companies' role changed fundamentally.[123] The Chinese stock market was originally organised by the government as a vehicle for SOEs to raise capital and improve operating performance.[124] The Chinese government also tried to develop a unique corporate governance system that possessed specific characteristics including clearly defined property rights, designated authorities and responsibilities, separate functions between government and enterprise, and scientific management.[125] Notwithstanding the fact that the first

---

[120] Administrative penalties as the result of breach of the duties include warnings, fines, confiscation of illegal income or property, and administrative detention. According to the CSRC 2020 annual report, CSRC processed 501 requests for administrative reconsideration (including 43 carried over from previous years), closing 469 in 2020. The disciplinary inspection commissions of subordinate institutions imposed 114 disciplinary sanctions and 363 organisational punishments.

[121] W. Li, A. Qiu and Z. Gu, 'Dual Corporate Governance Environment, Political Connections Preference and Firm Performance – Study on Governance Transition of China's Private Listed Firms [双重公司治理环境_政治联系偏好与公司绩效_基于中国民营上市公司治理转型的研究]' (2010) 6 *China Industrial Economics* 85, 94.

[122] The decision of the Central Committee on Economic Structure Reform was announced in 1983, indicating the start of enterprise reform in order to improve inefficient SOEs. The committee was trying to transform the companies into legal entities with the goal of making profits, but also making them responsible for their losses.

[123] O.K. Tam, 'Capital Market Development in China' (1991) 19(5) *World Development* 511. The policy of autonomy allowed corporations to retain a certain portion of their profits for future strategic development.

[124] S. Green, *China's Stock Market: A Guide to its Progress, Players and Prospects: The Players, the Institutions and the Future*, (London: Profile Books Ltd. 2003).

[125] This is due to the reason that the Chinese government allowed productive enterprises to become separate legal persons in 1987. Article 41, The General Civic Law of the People's Republic of China (enforced on1 January 1987); see also O.K. Tam, 'Ethical Issues in Evolution of Corporate Governance in China' (2002) 37(3) *Journal of Business Ethics* 303, 307.

Chinese company law enshrined many classic features of corporate governance that were consistent with the Anglo-American model,[126] regulations were
drafted in such a way as to favour SOEs or companies with close ties to the
government.[127] Therefore, it is clear that consideration of both the transition in
corporate governance and the dynamic role played by administrative power
can contribute significantly to determine how the corporate governance model
in China is going to be shaped and structured in the future. The developments
in corporate governance that were initiated in the early days were labelled as
producing 'modern' companies, and reflected the intention behind the transition to a market-oriented economy, but with Chinese characteristics. Deng
Xiaoping clarified that 'planned' and 'market' were merely economic means
to achieve ends, and socialism can have a market too. Leaving aside arguments
over whether the theory of the socialist market comes from orthodox Marxist
economic theory, it seems that for the foreseeable future, the ownership
structure will not be substantially changed so that the country can 'keep to the
socialist road'.[128]

Along with the development of a socialist country, a market economy
and a market-oriented corporate governance system have been introduced
with unique Chinese characteristics.[129] However, the unbalanced progress
in the development of complementary, social, political, legal and economic
infrastructure, as well as the high percentage of control and ownership of the
shares by the state, makes it impossible for corporate governance to develop
a model-based solely on successful Western experiences, and it is probably
unreasonable and unnecessary for China to develop its corporate governance
in what would be, for China, an extreme direction. While SOEs have undoubt-
edly become the dominant force implementing this strategy, evidenced by their

---

[126] See arts 1, 5, 6, 14; see also O.K. Tam, *The Development of Corporate
Governance in China*, (Cheltenham: Edward Elgar 1999) Chapter 6–7.

[127] Q. Liu and Z. Lu, 'Corporate Governance and Earrings Management in the
Chinese Listed Companies: A Tunnelling Perspective' (2007) 13(5) *Journal of
Corporate Finance* 881, 884.

[128] L. Song, 'Emerging Private Enterprise in China: Transition Path and Implications'
in R. Garnaut and L. Song, *China's Third Economic Transformation: The Rise of the
Private Economy* (Abington: Routledge 2005) 29, 44–45; see also D. Morris, 'The
Reform of State-Owned Enterprises in China: The Art of the Possible' (1995) 11(4)
Oxford Review of Economic Policy 54; D. Su and X. He, 'Ownership Structure,
Corporate Governance and Productive Efficiency in China' (2012) 38(3) *Journal of
Productivity Analysis* 303.

[129] See Y. Qian and B.R. Weigast, 'China's Transition to Markets: Market-preserving
Federalism, Chinese Style' (1996) 1(2) *The Journal of Policy Reform* 149; J. Hong, C.
Wang and M. Kafouros, 'The Role of the State in Explaining the Internationalization of
Emerging Market Enterprise' (2015) 26(1) *British Journal of Management* 45.

control over $690bn in assets abroad, with 47 centrally-owned firms ranked in Fortune Global 500 in 2015,[130] four Chinese centrally-owned banks holding the top 14 spots in the 2021 Forbes Global 2000,[131] the role of government as shareholders, the administrative governance on SOEs, and political and social mission of SOEs make administrative corporate governance indispensable and SOEs, as the 'the eldest son of the Party-State', still denote their long-lasting and unbreakable ties with the Party-State administrative power.

3.5.2   Government Interference and Influence in China

Government decisions now only have a partial impact on the internal governance of Chinese listed companies, even those that the government controls.[132] This implies a 'dynamic interplay' between external and internal government mechanisms.[133] The transition that has taken place thus far has led to a corporate governance model characterised by gradualism, dualism, systematisation and path dependency.[134] It has been a systematic reform brought about by developments in legislation and legal enforcement, as well as changes in the nature of the shareholding ownership structure, but all of these are subject to the influence of other factors such as Chinese traditions, history, values and culture. The state's large shareholdings and its resultant control of companies is a solid reason for government involvement in the corporate governance. This indicates that government policy placed increasing importance on establishing a market economy and shifted towards a rule-based framework, however, always in the shadow of the still dominant SOE sector.[135]

The hybrid and transformative model discussed in this chapter makes the role of the CSRC unpredictable and unsystematic. CSRC is a ministerial-level public institution directly under the State Council and it is designed to perform a unified regulatory function in order to maintain a legitimate and orderly secu-

---

[130] Wendy Leutert, China's State Enterprise Reform: Bigger, Yes, but Better? 23 April 2015.

[131] See https://www.forbes.com/global2000/list/#country:China (accessed 22 July 2022).

[132] W. Li and D. Yan, 'Transition from Administrative to Economic Model of Corporate Governance: A New Analytical Framework for Research on China's Corporate Governance' (2013) 11(4) *Nankai Business Review International* 6.

[133] W. Li, 'Corporate Governance Code in China and its Interpretation [中国公司治理原则及其解说]' [2001] 1 *Nankai Business Review [南开管理评论]* 9, 10–11.

[134] W. Li and D. Yan, 'Transition from Administrative to Economic Model of Corporate Governance: A New Analytical Framework for Research on China's Corporate Governance' (2013) 11(4) *Nankai Business Review International* 4.

[135] M.J. Whincop, *Corporate Governance in Government Corporations,* (Hants: Ashgate 2005) 52.

rities market and capital market. For example, from the early 1990s when the Shanghai and Shenzhen Stock Exchanges were launched, the CSRC has been responsible for approving initial public offerings (IPOs), and the government tightly controlled the IPO process.[136] This situation changed during the late 1990s as the investment banks gradually took a greater role in the IPO process and assumed heavier responsibilities for identifying and developing candidates for listing.[137] The current official role of the CSRC in the IPO process is to ensure that issuers comply with the rules. However, while the foregoing seems to suggest a major move towards economic governance, the reality is that the CSRC still controls the IPO process tightly, while the CSRC has the power of financial approval regarding which firms can go public.[138] The CSRC plays a key role in administrative governance by exercising a supervisory role over the domestic securities and stock regulatory institutions, which consequently enables it to control the securities and stock markets. Stock markets in China have grown very rapidly since they were established in the early 1990s and have done so with weak or modest legal and corporate governance structures.[139] The weak legal system and immature corporate governance system make the government role distinct, necessary and direct.

The reforms that have been introduced came as a result of the fact that administrative corporate governance was heavily criticised due to its lack of efficiency and fairness. The main response to these criticisms has been a focus on the corporatisation of SOEs, as discussed in the reasons for transformation, with thousands of poorly performing national and regional SOEs being either

---

[136] Y.L.Cheung, Z. Ouyang and W. Tan, 'How Regulatory Changes after IPO Under-pricing in China' (2009) 20(4) *China Economic Review* 372; J. Aharony, J. Wang and H. Yuan, 'Tunnelling as an Incentive for Earnings Management during the IPO process in China' (2010) 29(1) *Journal of Accounting and Public Policy* 1; J.D. Piotroski and T. Zhang, 'Politicians and the IPO Decision: The Impact of Impending Political Portions on IPO Activities in China' (2014) 111(1) *Journal of Financial Economics* 111.

[137] See also E. Curran, 'Chinese Investment Banks on the Rise: China Renaissance Securities Is the Top Adviser on Chinese IPOs in New York This Year', *The Wall Street Journal* (June 20, 2014) available at https://www.wsj.com/articles/chinese-investment -banks-on-the-rise-1402981038 (accessed 29 July 2022); B.B. Francis, I Hasan and X. Sun, 'Political Connections and the Process of Going Public: Evidence from China' (2009) 28(4) *Journal of International Money and Finance* 696.

[138] F. Jiang and K.A. Kim, 'Corporate Governance in China: A Modern Perspective' (2015) 32(6) *Journal of Corporate Finance* 190, 191.

[139] G. Chen, M. Firth, D.N. Gao and O.M. Rui, 'Is China's Securities Regulatory Agency a Toothless Tiger? Evidence from Enforcement Actions (2005) 24(6) *Journal of Accounting and Public Policy* 451, 479–480.

privatised or liquidated.[140] Since 1980 the SOEs have gradually lost some of their primacy and advantage with the introduction of the Chinese government's policy on the separation of government functions and business operations. The transformation from the economic reform and opening up which started with Deng's policy to an unprecedented opportunity for market actors to influence policy decision-making under Jiang's leadership (ending in 2002) and which enabled two important changes to occur, namely a slow withdrawal from economic reform primarily dependent on SOEs' reconstruction and a transformation of state role from an active agent in the economy to a regulator.[141] Under Hu's leadership (2002–12), the process of corporatisation slowed down in order to deal with social problems, such as unemployment, in keeping with the Chinese value of establishing a harmonious society. Since 2013 under Xi's leadership, the internationalisation of SOEs has entered into a 'new era', marked by the robust initiation of China's 'One Belt, One Road' (OBOR) Intercontinental trade and infrastructure initiative, and the recent issuing of Guidance on Deepening SOE Reforms, which signals the finalisation of the SOE reform plan at the central leadership level. Central-government-owned enterprises have since been undertaking major projects in implementing the OBOR initiative, such as the Khorgos 'dry port' on the Kazakh-Chinese border and a railway link connecting Kazakhstan with Iran,[142] which have profound implications for regional collaboration, as well as provision for economic impact. SOEs investing abroad financed by the Chinese-controlled Asia Infrastructure Investment Bank seems to be one of the chief instruments used by China to realise its geopolitical goals and its more muscular foreign policies, at least in the near future. These changes precipitated the transformation of corporate governance from a purely administrative model to a hybrid

---

[140] See G. Wildau, 'China Kicks off Second Round of Corporatisation' *The Financial Times*, 10 August 2014; available at http://www.ft.com/cms/s/0/ec28674c–13ac–11e4–84b7–00144feabdc0.html#axzz3DOzmmx3b (accessed 22 July 2022).

[141] J.C. Teets, S. Rosen and P.H. Gries, 'Introduction: Political Change, Contestation and Pluralization in China Today' in P.H. Gries and S. Rosen, *Chinese Politics: State, Society and the Market*, (Abington: Routledge 2010) 1, 15.

[142] The OBOR Initiative focuses on connectivity and cooperation among countries between China and the rest of Eurasia, consisting of both the land-based 'Silk Road Economic Belt' and the ocean-based 'Maritime Silk Road'. It is estimated to cover 65 per cent of the world's population, about one-third of the world's GDP, and about a quarter of all the goods and services the world moves. See J. Farchy, J. Kynge, C. Campbell and D. Blood, 'One Belt, One Road, Financial Times Special Reports' available at https://ig.ft.com/sites/special–reports/one–belt–one–road/ (accessed 22 July 2022); China's One Belt, One Road: Will It Reshape Global Trade? McKinsey & Company Comments, available at http://www.mckinsey.com/global–themes/china/chinas–one–belt–one–road–will–it–reshape–global–trade (accessed 22 July 2022).

one. This hybrid model will be retained if there is no substantial change of the political system and while the state owns and controls companies engaged in the country's main industries.

This administrative corporate governance has less impact on non-SOE companies because their shareholders and directors do not have such a strong relationship with the government, and while the government can provide for mechanisms that permit it to interfere, it does not do so as frequently as with SOEs. Therefore, the upshot is that despite the fact that these companies are subject to administrative regulation from central government, provincial governments and stock exchanges, they are comparatively more independent and are able to take greater advantage of market forces. These companies are open to private investment and more flexible and willing to adopt westernised corporate governance and investment philosophy. These companies have employment relationships and supply chains that rely heavily on market power rather than central administrative allocation and appointments. It is worth mentioning that the government interference is not just a potential problem in China, but it is also the case in many other jurisdictions with emerging markets.[143] It is characterised by a high level of state ownership and weak market-oriented apparatus, and governments therefore often act as a functional substitute for control failure.[144]

3.5.3 Are Administrative Factors Hindering the Development of Efficient Chinese Corporate Governance?

It may be argued that the involvement of administrative factors could have a negative impact on sound corporate governance that fits into a competitive and globalised Chinese economy. The corporate governance model in China builds on a strong authoritarian national leadership and an elite state bureaucracy pursuing development oriented policies, including the direct means of

---

[143] J. Zhao, 'Promoting a More Efficient Corporate Governance Model in Emerging Markets through Corporate Law' (2016) 15(3) *Washington University Global Studies Law Review* 447, 457–463; J.P.H. Fan, K.C.J. Wei and X. Xu, 'Corporate Finance and Governance in Emerging Markets: A Selective Review and An Agenda for Future Research' (2011) 17(2) *Journal of Corporate Finance* 207; M.N. Young, M.W. Peng, D. Ahlstrom, G.D. Bruton and Y. Jiang, 'Corporate Governance in Emerging Economies: A Review of the Principal–Principal Perspective' (2008) 45(1) *Journal of Management Studies* 196; S. Claessens and B. Yurtoglu, 'Corporate Governance in Emerging Markets: A Survey' (2013)15(C)(1–33) *Emerging Markets Review* 1.

[144] J. Hong, C. Wang and M. Kafouros, 'The Role of the State in Explaining the Internationalization of Emerging Market Enterprise' (2015) 26(1) *British Journal of Management* 45, 45–46.

governing the market.[145] The economic success in the last two decades is the result of combative policies, sometimes ones that are inconsistent with government control, interference and administrative involvement. These include liberalisation of the product and labour markets, entry into the WTO, and corporatisation. These factors that are seemingly in opposition to the administrative approach and may, in the following ways, hinder the development of corporate governance and be regarded as barriers to the further improvement of corporate governance in China.

First, corruption as the result of administrative interference could be a primary concern that China faces in promoting more efficient corporate governance.[146] Despite the fact that China's anti-corruption campaign has led to the fall of hundreds of government officials, including board members of SOEs, one of the most frequent problems emanating from administrative involvement in the corporate governance is the possibility of excessive corruption as the result of abuse of power perpetrated by directors, and something known as state executive corruptions (*gaoguan fubai* 高管腐败).[147] It constitutes 60 per cent of the cases involving the acceptance of bribes, according to the China Entrepreneur Report on Crime.[148] Administrative governance increases the opportunity for corruption in the management team and it derives from shareholding ownership and involvement of the state and the Party in SOEs. According to the Chinese Company Law, decisions on matters concern-

---

[145]   R. Wade, *Governing the Market: Economic Theory and the Role of Government in East Asian Industrialization*, (Princeton, Princeton University Press 1990) 26.

[146]   See Q. Liu, T. Luo and G. Tian, 'Political Connections with Corrupt Government Bureaucrats and Corporate M&A Decisions: A Natural Experiment from the Anti-Corruption Cases in China' (2016) 37 *Pacific-Basin Finance Journal* 52; X. Wu, 'Corporate Governance and Corruption: A Cross Country Analysis' (2005) 18(2) *Governance* 151; C. Jia, S. Ding, Y. Li and Z. Wu, 'Fraud, Enforcement Action, and the Role of Corporate Governance: Evidence from China' (2009) 90(4) *Journal of Business Ethics* 561.

[147]   X. Lu, T. Wu and D. Long, 'Executives of State-owned Enterprises Corruption, Incentive Failure or Constraint Missing? – Analysis Based on The "Gujing Scandal"' (2015) 12 *Human Resources Development of China* 61; see also J. Xia, 'Study and Evaluation Method of SOEs Manager's Performance for Inhibiting Corruption' (2015) 6(10) *Modern Economy* 1051; J. Anderlini, 'China Corruption Purge Snares 115 SOE 'Tigers': A Fifth of Those 'Toppled from Their Horses' Come from the Energy' *The Financial Times*, 18 May 2015; available at https://www.ft.com/content/ad997d5c–fd3c–11e4–9e96–00144feabdc0 (accessed 22 July 2022); it is worth noting that China Ranks 83rd globally on corruption based on perceived corruption scores based on the 'Transparency International' in 2015; see Transparency International: The Global Coalition against Corruption, Corruption perceptions Index 2015, available at http://www.transparency.org/cpi2015 (accessed 22 July 2022).

[148]   'State Executive Crime Hits New High' *Shenzhen Evening News*, 11 February 2015, A21.

ing electing and replacing directors and supervisors and the remuneration of directors and supervisors is entirely determined by the shareholders' general meeting,[149] therefore, the fact that the state is the controlling shareholder places it in the absolute dominant position in many SOEs. Apart from the influence of the state via shareholders' meetings, the influence could also come from the Party. It is stated in the Company Law 2018 that 'an organization of the CCP [the Party] shall be established to carry out the activities of the Party in accordance with the charter of the CCP and the company shall provide the necessary conditions for the activities of the party organization'.[150]

Another awkward feature in Chinese SOEs is administrative rankings that are given to the chairmen and the senior executives by the government as they are an important factor and reflect the political connections that these senior officials have with political power.[151] These senior officers can be exchanged directly with officials in provisional or central government.[152] The administrative ranking is closely related to the culture of *guanxi* (relationship), *mianzi* (giving face), promotion and demotion with strong possibility of misuse of these rankings to foster corrupt purposes.[153]

Secondly, administrative power may hinder the efficiency of corporate governance. One of the main issues that exist in Chinese corporate governance is the conflicting roles of the government between the establishment of a functional corporate governance environment in connection with the market economy and the incomparable arbitrary and politically motivated government control. The administrative power somehow hinders the efficiency of corporate governance in terms of time scale and the strategic direction of the decision-making process. Many uncertainties are about the implementation of governance. Two of these are the fact that judicial decisions are ignored by agencies and corporate decisions that involve interference by government through the vast administrative bureaucracy within the hierarchy.[154] In addi-

---

[149] Art. 37(2), Chinese Company Law 2018.

[150] Ibid.

[151] For details of administrative levels in China see art.16, Civil Servant Law of the People's Republic of China 2005.

[152] J. Liu, 'Political Connection of State-Owned Enterprise: An Analysis Base on the Listed Companies of Shanghai and Shenzhen Stock Markets' in E. Qi, J. Shen and R. Dou, *The 19th International Conference on Industrial Engineering and Engineering Management* (Heidelberg: Springer 2013) 1009, 1012–2013.

[153] See D. Smith, '*Guanxi, Mianzi,* and Business: The Impact of Culture on Corporate Governance in China' (2012) 26 *Private Sector Opinion* 1; U. Braendle, T. Casser and J. Noll, 'Corporate Governance in China – Is Economic Growth Potential Hindered by *Guanxi*?' (2005) 110(4) *Business and Society Review* 389.

[154] P.B. Potter, 'The Future of China's Legal Regime' in D. Shambaugh, *Charting China's Future: Domestic and International Challenges*, (Abingdon: Routledge) 67, 69–70.

tion to the national representative bodies, including the executive, judicial, and administrative functions of the government, state-owned property and governance of this property is still closely regulated and supervised by the Chinese government, which involves a range of issues including accounting, investment, deposition, debt repayment, transfer and auditing of state-owned properties.[155]

Furthermore, the administrative involvement through various channels at different levels may also make the corporate governance rules uncertain and unpredictable. Due to the administrative power related to the drafting and implementing of corporate governance-related rules at different levels, including in relation to the state, government agencies such as the State-owned Assets Supervision and Administration Commission of the State Council and stock exchanges, and government at the provincial and city level, it may make foreign investors feel that the legislative framework they are subject to, when investing in China, is unstable and unpredictable which may hinder further investment and could impede the development of corporate governance. Besides, the administrative power may also deter foreign investors because of the layers of bureaucracy which add additional transaction costs and make doing business unnecessarily complicated due to ambiguity and unpredictability in the Chinese bureaucracy.

3.5.4   No Universal Path for Transition

It is suggested, based on the dynamic theory of corporate governance,[156] that there is no universal path for the development of corporate governance,[157] and

---

[155]   J. Shi, 'Consideration on the Relationship between Government and Market from the Legal Perspective [政府与市场关系的法治思考]' (2014) 18 *Journal of the Party of the Central Committee of the C.P.C* [中共中央党校学报]10, 14; see also G. Jefferson, 'State-Owned Enterprise in China: Reform, Performance and Prospects' in Brandeis University Working Paper Series 109 (2016).

[156]   See S. Toms, 'The Life Cycle of Corporate Governance' in M. Wright, D.S. Siegel, K. Keasey and I. Filatotchev (eds), *The Oxford Handbook of Corporate Governance*, (Oxford: Oxford University Press 2013) 365, 381; see also J. Leng, *Corporate Governance and Financial Reform in China's Transition Economy*, (Hong Kong: Hong Kong University Press 2009); M. Bratnicki, A. Fraczkiewicz and R. Kozlowski, 'The Dialectics of Entrepreneurial Leadership. Toward a Dynamic Theory of Corporate Governance' (2007) 18 *Proceedings Eighteenth Annual Meeting of the International Association* 333.

[157]   J. Zhao, 'Promoting a More Efficient Corporate Governance Model in Emerging Markets through Corporate Law' (2016) 15(3) *Washington University Global Studies Law Review* 447; see also T. Clarke, 'The Continuing Diversity of Corporate Governance: Theories of Convergence and Variety' (2016) 16(1) *Ephemera Theory & Politics in Organization* 19; M.A. Firth and O.M. Rui, 'Does One Size Fit All? A Study

this is true for Chinese corporate governance development and transformation. The development of Chinese corporate governance advances due to many factors that are related to government policies, culture, the legal system, board structure, the country's economic development, and the structure of the shareholding of its companies. Unlike classic corporate governance models, the governance model adopted by Chinese listed firms can best be described as a control-based system, in which the controlling shareholders, predominantly the state or state officials, 'tightly control listed companies through concentrated ownership and management-friendly boards'.[158] This hybrid model can be explained based on a political model of corporate governance provided by Mark Roe, who argued that path dependence can largely explain particular corporate governance models in different jurisdictions.[159] Any transition in style of corporate governance can only be achieved during a long process, and during this time both administrative and economic elements of corporate governance will co-exist in a Chinese model. This transformation is a systematic one and the corporate governance model in China is certainly undergoing continuous change. This is particularly the case in a country with an emerging and transitional capital market and where there are imperfect market regulatory mechanisms, immature investors and a unique shareholding structure.[160]

---

of the Simultaneous Relations Among Ownership, Corporate Governance Mechanisms and the Financial Performance of Firms in China' in S. Boubaker, B.D. Nguyen and D.K. Nguyen (eds) *Corporate Governance: Recent Developments and New Trends*, (Heiderlberg: Springer 2012) 29.

[158] Q. Liu, 'Corporate Governance in China: Current Practices, Economic Effects and Institutional Determinants' (2006) 52(2) *CESifo Economic Studies* 415, 429; see also N.W. Leung and M. Cheng, 'Corporate Governance and Firm Value: Evidence from Chinese State-Controlled Listed Firms' (2013) 6(2) *China Journal of Accounting Research* 89.

[159] M.J. Roe, *Strong Managers, Weak Owners: The Political Roots of American Corporate Finance* (Princeton University Press, 1994); see also M.J. Roe, *Political Determinants of Corporate Governance: Political Context, Corporate Impact* (Oxford: Oxford University Press 2002). The control-based model is a hybrid due to the gradual transition process that has been occurring over the past three decades during the transformation of the Chinese economy from a planned to a market model see W. Li, Y. Xu, J. Niu and A. Qiu, 'A Survey of Corporate Governance: International Trends and China's Mode' (2010) 13(6) *Nankai Business Review International* 4, 5–7; see also W. Li, X. Chen and Q. Yuan, *Chinese Corporate Governance: Road to Transition and Perfection* (*Zhongguo Gongsi Zhili: Zhuanxing yu Wanshan Zhilu*), (Beijing: China Machine Press 2012) 139–141.

[160] 'International Symposium on Securities Investors Protection Opened in Beijing', available at www.csrc.gov.cn/pub/newsite/bgt/xwdd/200911/t20091106_16722.htm (accessed 22 July 2022); see also R. Morck and B. Yeung, 'Corporate Governance in China' (2014) 26(3) *Journal of Applied Corporate Finance* 20; Y. Cheung, P. Jiang,

The existence of some elements of administrative corporate governance in China's present corporate governance model is seen as the result of continued government control over the decisions of companies, especially SOEs, in terms of resource allocation, strategic operational policy and objectives, and senior management appointments.[161] Within the administrative corporate governance model directors of SOEs are appointed directly by the Chinese government, and directors always retain certain administrative roles within the government while also acting as directors. The transformation of corporate governance is driven by internal and external forces which have legal, political, cultural and social impact through revised corporate objectives, amended mechanisms for appointing members of directors and stronger reliance on market forces. The process of transformation of Chinese corporate governance can be demonstrated by Figure 3.1 below, which shows the driving forces that lead to the economic result.

On this uncertain journey of corporate governance transition, both profit motives and the political motives of government officials under the administrative corporate governance model have the potential to distort policy objectives significantly.[162] For example, the political targets of SOEs are not compatible with the economic development of corporate governance, and are in conflict with economic targets of profit-making or maximisation. The government lacks adequate means to pursue corporate goals purely from the perspective that looking at companies as vehicles of doing business, and 'meta-agency' problems in government-controlled and owned companies, leads to the government failing to seek to maximise the welfare of their principals, which is the public;[163] rather government officers may well prefer to maximise their own welfare or pursue other politically-oriented missions.

The corporate governance transformation is characterised, looking at the general trends, by the weakening of administrative governance and the strengthening of economic governance. However, this dual corporate govern-

---

P. Limpaphayom and T. Lu, 'Corporate Governance in China: A Step Forward' (2010) 16(1) *European Financial Management* 94.

[161] See F. Gang and N.C. Hope, "The Role of State-Owned Enterprises in the Chinese Economy," China–United States Exchange Foundation, *China–US 2022, Economic Relations in the Next 10 Years* (2013), Chapter 16, 5, available at http://www.chinausfocus.com/2022/wp–content/uploads/Part+02–Chapter+16.pdf (accessed 22 July 2022).

[162] J. Leng, *Corporate Governance and Financial Reform in China's Transition Economy,* (Hong Kong: Hong Kong University Press 2009) 49; see also W. Li and R. Zhang, M. Kafouro, 'The Role of the State in Explaining the Internationalization of Emerging Market Enterprises' (2010) 26(1) *British Journal of Management* 45.

[163] M. Trebilcock and E, Kacobucci, 'Public Values in an Era of Privatization: Privatization and Accountability' (2003) 116(5) *Harvard Law Review* 1422, 1443.

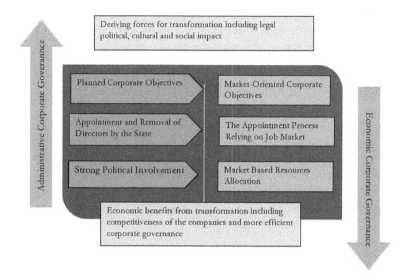

*Figure 3.1   Transformation from Administrative Corporate Governance
to Economic Corporate Governance in China*

ance model does retain many administrative characteristics, and it continues
to be subject to strong government interference and reliance on government
support and direction. It is also shaped by top-down bureaucratic intervention
and government control through the government's controlling power over
corporate management, via agents appointed by the state who were previously
government officials.[164] The reforms and developments, such as corporatisation and the convergence of corporate governance, have encountered serious
challenges in China's immature legal and institutional environment. The
legal mechanisms that are traditionally seen as important in reducing agency
costs are all very immature in China, especially in SOEs, such as executive
compensation contracts, the risk of takeover and takeover mechanisms, the
value of managerial reputations and a well-functioning competitive market.[165]

---

[164] M.N. Young, M.W. Peng, D. Ahlstrom, G.D. Bruton and Y. Jiang, 'Corporate
Governance in Emerging Economies: A Review of the Principal-Principal Perspective'
(2008) 45(1) *Journal of Management Studies* 196, 211.

[165] See H.G. Manne, 'Mergers and the Market for Corporate Control' (1965) 73(2)
Journal of Political Economy 110; E.F. Fama, 'Agency Problems and the Theory of
the Firm' (1980) 88(2) *Journal of Political Economy* 288; O.D. Hart, The Market
Mechanism as an Incentive Scheme' (1983) 14(2) *The Bell Journal of Economics*
366; other scholars indeed would throw some doubts on whether legal mechanisms

Therefore, administrative governance could be necessary and functional due to underdevelopment of the legal infrastructure, loose law enforcement and a problematic court system without a fully independent judiciary. Nevertheless, it has its own advantages at particular periods of time in different jurisdictions.

3.6   ADVANTAGES OF ADMINISTRATIVE ASPECTS OF CORPORATE GOVERNANCE

The problems that administrative governance can cause are deeply rooted in the Chinese political system, culture and shareholding ownership scheme. Government involvement and administrative governance will be elements of Chinese corporate governance as long as the Party is the sole political party in China and state ownership and control exists, and the Party's participation constitutes the primary way to secure political support to ensure that it remains in power. The market transition in China from a poor agrarian economy based in state socialism to a dynamic capitalist engine has riveted attention on the role played by government and administrative power in promoting transformative economic development.[166] It is submitted that both administrative and economic governance will co-exist in China for a long time with no likely possibility of convergence to any extreme models, and thus it is worth discussing how administrative governance can be taken advantage of in order to enhance fairness, efficiency and accountability in corporate governance and to provide a more sound and sustainable response to the globalisation of the Chinese market and economy. These positive effects may also be of relevance to other jurisdictions in emerging and/or mature markets.

3.6.1   A Critical but Accepting Attitudes towards Administrative Governance

For the pure economic corporate purpose of maximising firm value there should be no state control and ownership concentration in China. Administrative governance can be explained by politically-oriented reasons such as retaining the ability of the state to impose on companies aims other than shareholder value maximisation, such as retaining employees, enhancing societal harmony, ensuring employment across both urban and rural areas, maintaining control

---

do reduce agency cost: see, e.g., R.H. Sitkoff, 'An Agency Cost Theory of Trust Law' (2004) 89(3) *Cornell Law Review* 621; A. Anand, F. Milne and L. Purda, 'Monitoring to Reduce Agency Costs: Examining the Behaviour of Independent and Non-Independent Boards' (2014) 33(4) *Seattle University Law Review* 809.

[166]   V. Nee, S. Opper and S. Wong, 'Developmental State and Corporate Governance in China' (2007) 3(1) *Management and Organization Review* 19, 19.

of certain industries and the provision of social safety net services.[167] It was argued by Premier Li that if government is the organiser for reform, it is also the promoter of, and the object for, economic reform. Therefore, consideration needs to be given to how to enhance the positive role played by administrative governance in this transition.[168] Looking at the future, *The Economist* predicted that China will emerge as the largest economy in the world by 2040. We maintain that heathy and sound corporate governance will play a vital role in China's self-sustaining momentum, and administrative power and interference are unavoidable and critical.[169]

In the liberal political economy proposed by Adam Smith in his seminal work, *Wealth of Nations*,[170] the government monitors and enforces the regulatory environment in which companies compete for profit, but it should not directly be involved in a company's decisions and transactions. Since this was posited, many reasons have been advanced arguing that state control over commercial transactions will lead to benefits for business organisations. It is argued that, based on the efficiency of corporate form, direct involvement of state officials will impose on the companies multiple political interests which will dilute marketing motives when social objectives collide with shareholders' wealth maximisation. Informational asymmetry and uncertainty will constrain the effectiveness of coordination and interference from government. The willingness of the government to share the risk might both weakens the motivation of companies to make more profits and leads to soft budgetary constraints with a subsequent attenuation of a firm's efficiency. However, the effectiveness and necessity of government interference in business organisations have been questioned and discussed in various dimensions, especially after the financial crisis of 2008. Instead of having a direct role in facilitating and shaping the dynamic growth played by the state, it is posited that the state's ability in creating and maintaining a supportive climate of growth is key for an emerging market to achieve good levels of economic development

---

[167] J. Leng, *Corporate Governance and Financial Reform in China's Transition Economy*, (Hong Kong: Hong Kong University Press 2009) 226; e.g., it is argued that the most important political reason for maintaining state ownership is to defend the ruling position of the Party under the current political regime in terms of economic ownership and control of resource allocation, which is regarded as an important basis for the authority and legitimacy of government.

[168] Xinhua, 'Chinese Premier Stresses Importance of Reform, Opening-Up to Unleash Market Vitality' (2021) available at http://www.news.cn/english/2021-11/23/c_1310326401.htm (accessed 29 July 2022).

[169] 'The New Titans: A Survey of the World Economy', *The Economist*, 16 September 2006, 5.

[170] A. Smith, *An Inquiry into the Nature and Causes of the Wealth of Nations*, (Chicago: University of Chicago Press 2012).

and stability.[171] However, it is important for administrative involvement to be effective and only applicable when necessary. Positive attempts have been made to modernise the administrative governance system and reduce transaction costs, including the abolition of both the minimum registered capital[172] and the current paid-in capital registration system.[173] These legislative reforms aim to abolish excessive administrative burdens, reduce both bureaucratic procedures and the cost of market entry in order to stimulate investment and make administrative governance flexible and fit with inevitable developments.

3.6.2   Long-term Strategic Planning and Multiple Goals of SOEs

It is argued that government intervention, the most often-seen aspect of administrative governance, may inevitably change the corporate objective of SOEs in the direction that is preferred or designed by the government.[174] This distortion of the corporate objective may lead to investment inefficiency. SOEs may miss profitable investment opportunities due to the resources expended in executing the plans and policies of the government, and SOEs may find it difficult to terminate unprofitable projects or reduce their investment in these projects due to potential conflicts with government agenda and policies.[175] However, to see this as totally negative ignores the fact that a various supports could be offered to companies subject to administrative governance by giving boards of directors the right to consider the long-term interests of companies and make recommendations on the long-term strategic development plans and major investment decisions of the company as provided for in the corporate governance code. Within allowances made by government, administrative governance enables the company to employ corporate profit for further internal and external investment, expansion and sustainable corporate strategic

---

[171] G. Bertucci and A. Alberti, 'Globalization and the Role of the State: Challenges and Perspectives' paper presented at United Nations World Public Sector Report 2001 on 'Globalization and the State' (2001).

[172] Under the unrevised Law, the minimum registered capital was RMB5 million (about US$800,000) for a company limited by shares, and RMB30 000 (about US$5,000) for a company with limited liability. (Unrevised arts 26 and 81 of Chinese Company Law 2018)

[173] Unrevised arts 26, 30, 81 and 84 of Chinese Company Law 2018; which requires companies to file details of both their registered capital and paid-in capital with the State Administration for Industry and Commerce or its relevant branch. Furthermore, and removing the requirement for minimum cash contributions making up 30 per cent of the registered capital based on Unrevised Company Law art. 27.

[174] J.Y. Lin, F. Cai and Z. Li, 'Competition, Policy Burdens, and State-owned Enterprise Reform' (1998) 88(2) *American Economic Review* 422.

[175] Ibid., 425–427.

development. It has also laid the foundation for government supervision in order to mitigate the problems resulting from unstable financial markets in China. Furthermore, at the international level, SOEs are at the forefront of negotiations and business relationship with foreign governments, multinational corporations and international institutional investors who are willing to interact with the Chinese government and Chinese companies. State presence in SOEs is significant for the long-term healthy growth of the global economy and the sustainability of business and civil society as a whole.

An excessive concentration on short-term considerations is one reason that is often given for the rapid financial growth globally in the last decade and the ongoing worldwide crisis.[176] A lack of long-term goals and investment in human and social capital has been regarded as a patent problem for Anglo-American corporations, which leads to competitive disadvantages.[177] Short-term motivation has led to the pursuit of short-term reckless business strategies and insufficient risk management. The political economy literature has observed that government and administrative agencies are typically serving multiple goals, which could, in the short term, impede corporations from pursuing long-term interests.[178] Administrative governance with government interference may ease the pressure of companies pursuing shareholder value in the short term and put the emphasis on the long-term value of companies and national goals. Administrative governance could be used as an additional

---

[176] S. Bair, 'Lessons of the Financial Crisis: The Dangers of Short-Termism' Posted by the Harvard Law School Forum on Corporate Governance and Financial Regulation, on Monday (July 4, 2011), available at https://corpgov.law.harvard.edu/2011/07/04/lessons-of-the-financial-crisis-the-dangers-of-short-termism/ (accessed 23 July 2022); J.C. Coffee, 'What Went Wrong? An Initial Inquiry into the Causes of the 2008 Financial Crisis' (2009) 9(1) *Journal of Corporate Law Studies* 1; W. Lazonick, 'In the Name of Shareholder Value: How Executive Pay and Stock Buy-backs are Damaging the US Economy' In T. Clarke and D. Branson (eds), *The Sage Handbook of Corporate Governance*, (London: Sage 2012) 476; E. Avgouleas, 'The Global Financial Crisis, Behavioural Finance and Financial Regulation: In Search of a New Orthodoxy' (2009) 9(1) *Journal of Corporate Law Studies* 23; S. Frencha, A. Leyshona and N. Thrift, 'A Very Geographical Crisis: the Making and Breaking of the 2007–2008 Financial Crisis' (2009) 2(2) *Cambridge Journal of Regions, Economy and Society* 287; T. Clarke, 'The Impact of Financialisation on International Corporate Governance: The Role of Agency Theory and Maximising Shareholder Value' (2014) 8(1) *Law and Financial Markets Review* 39; T. Clarke, 'Dangerous Frontiers in Corporate Governance' (2014) 20(3) *Journal of Management & Organization* 268.

[177] For instance, see M.E. Porter, 'Capital Choices: Changing the Way American Invests in Industry', in D.H. Chew (ed.), *Studies in International Corporate Finance and Governance Systems: A Comparison of the U.S., Japan, and Europe*, (Oxford: Oxford University Press 1997) 5–8.

[178] D.E. Sappington and J.E. Stiglitz, 'Privatization, Information, and Incentives' (1987) 6(4) *Journal of Policy Analysis and Management* 567.

governance mechanism to mitigate conflicts such as those that exist in the case of companies trading across community boundaries, secondary policies in public procurement, and redundancies and reemployment to secure broader social consensus. Thus, administrative governance could facilitate and shape dynamic economic growth by establishing supportive business environments and introducing legislation that enables rather than hinders investors to establish companies as vehicles to do business.

Following the financial crisis of 2008 both government policies and academic literature has sought to develop a long-term approach in corporate life.[179] This long-term strategic planning is critical for China. The fact that it has a population of 1.357 billion means that there are many potential social and environmental problems such as the need for employment, fiscal health, regional development and social stability.[180] Positively, the World Bank reported that transformative economic growth in China resulted in 170 million people moving out of absolute poverty, thus accounting for more than a 75 per cent poverty reduction in the developing world from 1990 to 2000.[181] At the national level, SOEs can be regarded as important vehicles that may have an impact on elements of entire markets and enable the government to intervene in resource allocation and prices in the economy or settle social problems like unemployment in order to achieve long-term government strategy.[182]

Under the corporate governance regime with which government could identify, and the ability to monitor companies and enforce their interests as owners, government officials could replace entrepreneurs as the actors driving

---

[179] G. Cox, 'Overcoming Short-termism within British Business: The Key to Sustained Economic Growth: An independent review by Sir George Cox commissioned by the Labour Party' p.4, available at https://www.yourbritain.org.uk/uploads/editor/files/Overcoming_Short-termism.pdf (accessed 29 July 2022); Y. Liang, 'China's Short-Term and Long-Term Development After the 2007 Global Financial Crisis: Some Critical Reflection' (2012) 45 *The China Economy* 3; M. Moore, 'A Fresh Look at Stock Market Short-termism' (2014) 41(3) *Journal of Law and Society* 416; A. Johnston and P. Morrow, 'Towards Long-Termism in Corporate Governance: the Shareholder Rights Directive and Beyond' in S. Vitols, *Long-term Investment and the Sustainable Company: A Stakeholder Perspective* Vol. III, (Brussels: European Trade Union Institute 2015) 19 P. Habbard, 'Shifting to the Long-term: The Road Ahead' in S. Vitols, ibid., 93.

[180] S. Chen, Z. Sun, S, Tang and D. Wu, 'Government Intervention and Investment Efficiency: Evidence from China' (2011) 17(2) *Journal of Corporate Finance* 259, 260.

[181] World Bank, *World Development Indicators*, World Bank, Washington D.C (2004).

[182] Z. Wang, 'Corporate Governance under State Control: The Chinese Experience' (2012) 13(2) *Theoretical Enquires in Law* 487, 491.

the economic performance of companies, especially SOEs.[183] Despite the fact that economic literature suggests that the direct involvement of state officials who impose on companies multiple political interests may dilute profit-making as the primary goal of corporations and inhibit economic reforms in China, administrative involvement does have a function in long-term strategic planning because it is free from the pressure of pursuing immediate returns for demanding shareholders. Chinese SOEs have social responsibility as an additional goal and they serve as key vehicles to enable the state to achieve economic stability, development and sustainability.[184] SOEs are used to serve political and social objectives, which may have a negative impact on firms' economic performance based on the 'grabbing hand theory'.[185] However, it is argued as 'overly simplistic',[186] that the 'helping hand theory' may help government generate a positive effect on companies' performance in securing limited resources and use them in a more organised and strategic manner in a quasi-market economy so as to mitigate agency problems in a transformative corporate governance model.[187] Therefore, SOEs are able to achieve a combined objective of national goals and corporate performance, setting a model for compliance with the law as well as undertaking social responsibility.

Government officials are regarded as market-oriented agencies and they could use superior information and monitoring capacity to achieve long-term planning.[188] Like most other countries, one of the main roles and missions of SOEs is to promote social welfare and companies can curry favour with government by engaging in CSR activities.[189] It is argued by advocates of free markets that governments should have minimum interference in the business operation due to the fact that this could prompt decisions that threaten a com-

---

[183] V. Nee, S. Opper and S. Wong, 'Developmental State and Corporate Governance in China' (2007) 3(1) *Management and Organization Review* 19, 20.

[184] Z. Wang, 'Corporate Governance under State Control: The Chinese Experience' (2012) 13(2) *Theoretical Enquires in Law* 487, 488.

[185] Y. Qian, 'Enterprise Reform in China: Agency Problems and Political Control' (1996) 4(2) *Economics of Transition* 427; see also R. McGregor, 'The Little Red Book of Business in China', *The Financial Times*, 8 July 2001.

[186] J. Wang, *Company Law in China: Regulation of Business Organizations in a Socialist Market Economy*, (Cheltenham: Edward Elgar 2014) 152.

[187] E.C. Chang and S.M.L. Wong, 'Political Control and Performance in China's Listed Companies' (2004) 32(4) *Journal of Comparative Economics* 617, 618.

[188] With this function of the government, the long-term strategy also enables companies, especially SOEs, to address economic, political, social and environmental goals of government.

[189] F. Jiang and K.A. Kim, 'Corporate Governance in China: A Modern Perspective' (2015) 32(6) *Journal of Corporate Finance* 190, 195, 213.

pany's financial goals.[190] However, arguably administrative power will provide more political power for companies and the board of directors are under less pressure from their shareholders to pursue short-term interests. It will be comparatively easier for them to take advantage of, for example, scientific technology to maintain a sustainable and effective business environment in order to achieve strategic goals in the longer term.[191] China is undergoing a considerable corporate governance evolution but has yet to establish a unifying system that balances social-economic forces with the needs of the economy.

Government action could have an impact on both companies in which the state has controlling shares and those in which the state only owns part of the shares. It is argued by Musacchio et al. that the government has improved the corporate governance practices of SOEs.[192] In companies where the government outsources management to the private sector for reasons of privatisation and international investment, the state still has veto power over key strategic decisions.[193] A variety of state capitalism exists, including situations where the state acts as majority shareholder or minority shareholder, and in each type of case, the state is able to offer strategic support through policies stimulating companies' capabilities and long-term planning to achieve sustainable corporate goals. As the result of the administrative reforms carried out in the 1980s, government regulations, policies and procedural guidelines have become increasingly more precise and transparent and it has had a positive impact on the predictability of bureaucratic decisions in order to reduce the uncertainty

---

[190] A. Cuervo and B. Villalonga, 'Explaining the Variance in the Performance Effects of Privatization' (2000) 25(3) *Academy of Management* 581; see also J. Zysman, *Governments, Markets and Growth: Financial Systems and the Politics of Industrial Change*, (Cambridge: Cambridge University Press 1983).

[191] Petronas, a SOE in Malaysia is a good example of success as industrial top quartile which began an operational excellence campaign focusing on technical capabilities and more effective working cultural. See the 2009 sustainability report of Petronas available at https://www.petronas.com/sustainability/reporting (accessed 29 July 2022).

[192] A. Musacchio, S.G. Lazzarini and R.V. Aguilera, 'New Varieties of State Capitalism: Strategic and Governance Implications' (2015) 29(1) *The Academy of Management Perspectives* 115, 115. Taking Sinopec (China's national oil companies) as an example, so far as aspects of listing companies on stock exchanges, recruiting independent board members and enhancing financial reporting and these reforms have reduced agency conflicts and attracted minority private investors.

[193] A. Musacchio, S.G. Lazzarini and R.V. Aguilera, 'New Varieties of State Capitalism: Strategic and Governance Implications' (2015) 29(1) *The Academy of Management Perspectives* 115, 116; for a case study of Leviathan see C.F.K.V. Inoue, S.G, Lazzarini and A. Musacchio, 'Leviathan as a Minority Shareholder: Firm-level Performance Implications of Equity Purchases by the Government' (2013) 56(6) *Academy of Management Journal* 1775.

of government economic policies and strategic planning to encourage more active international investment for long-term, sustainable and quality growth in China.[194]

3.6.3 Effectiveness of Government Interference

The policies, rules and legislation introduced to further transformation can be categorised in two ways: globalisation and devolution, and the government plays a key role in both.[195] The transformation of corporate governance can also be regarded as the process by which we see the globalisation of the Chinese corporate governance model and the central government power devolution in order to give companies and boards of directors more autonomy to control companies and this includes SOEs. These transformations will also lead to economic globalisation, deepen China's market economy and intensify market competition. Therefore, the government will act as the main facilitator of economic development and adjust the market so that it can direct the route of transformation.[196] The government plays a triple role in the enforcement of the law, namely as a regulator in overseeing markets and corporations, as a supervisor and promoter of corporations, as well as having a role in the adaption and utilisation of international rules on corporate governance.[197] The government could use mandatory administration and legal means to remedy market failures so as to promote economic growth and industrialisation. In a country that lacks an independent and effective judicial system and a sufficient number of qualified legal professionals,[198] the administrative power that is derived from government interference is functional in responding to the inadequacies of efficient markets, and the existence of a unique market economy with Chinese

---

[194] V. Nee, S. Opper and S. Wong, 'Developmental State and Corporate Governance in China' (2007) 3(1) *Management and Organization Review* 19, 24; see also D. Headey, R. Kanbur and X. Zhang, 'China's Growth Strategies' in R. Kanbur and X. Zhang (eds), *Governing Growth in China: Equity and Institutions* (Abington: Routledge 2008) 1; for the discussion on government policy and Chinese stock market see N. Groenewold, Y. Wu, S.H.K. Tang and X.M. Fan, *The Chinese Stock Market: Efficiency, Predictability and Profitability*, (Cheltenham: Edward Elgar 2004).

[195] D.F. Kettl, 'The Transformation of Governance: Globalization, Devolution and the Role of Government' (2000) 60(6) *Public Administration Review* 488.

[196] M. Chen, 'Transformation of Chinese Government's Economic Function under Globalization' Proceeding for International Conference on Public Management: International Integration for Regional Public Management: New Challenges and Opportunities (2014).

[197] For example, adapting and adopting the new G20/OECD corporate governance principle.

[198] See F. Allen, J. Qian, and M. Qian, 'Law, Finance, and Economic Growth in China' (2005) 77(1) *Journal of Financial Economics* 57.

characteristics.[199] Administrative governance is introduced with multiple aims including investor protection, information disclosure and addressing systemic risks in order to maintain fair, efficient and transparent markets.

As for the market regulator, CSRC, is a ministerial-level public institution directly under the auspices of the State Council, performing a unified regulatory function.[200] Thus it needs to be emphasised that the CSRC is not independent. A good example of the government role in having a quick and swift market interference is CSRC's policy to bail out the stock market in July 2015. In order to slow down the stock market plunge, CSRC took the drastic step of banning shareholders holding more than 5 per cent from selling shares for six months in an effort to halt a plunge in stock prices.[201] This was done in order to maintain the stability of the capital market and effectively protect investors' lawful rights and interests in responding to an irrational slump that the Chinese securities market had experienced.[202] The CSRC used the halt in trading and other measures to control downward pressure amid volatility.[203] Another mechanism implemented by the CSRC was the 'circuit breaker' mechanism.[204] The mechanisms were introduced to give markets a cooling-off period so as to enable the markets and investors time to digest the market information and to enhance the stability of the Chinese stock market but were suspended after seven days.[205] This demonstrates the fact the government is capable of making

---

[199]   It might be argued that the role of the state in this way means that judicial effectiveness may never develop.

[200]   CSRC, 'Introducing the CSRC' available at http://www.csrc.gov.cn/pub/csrc_en/about/ (accessed 23 July 2022).

[201]   'China Bans Major Shareholders from Selling Their Stakes for Next Six Months' *The Guardian*, 9 July 2015, available at http://www.theguardian.com/world/2015/jul/09/china–bans–major–shareholders–from–selling–their–stakes–for–next–six–months (accessed 23 July 2022).

[202]   Announcement of the China Securities Regulatory Commission No. 18 [2015]. The prohibition applied to foreign investors who held stakes in Shanghai- or Shenzhen-listed companies, although most of their holdings are below 5 per cent.

[203]   However, some observers felt the system as designed could have increased investor concerns about the health of the market.

[204]   Circuit breaker mechanism is the measure approved by the SEC originally in 1987 in order to curb panic-selling on U.S. stock exchanges and excessive volatility. This was introduced on New Year's Day 2016, to prevent sharp falls and contain wild swings in the markets in late 2015. The mechanism is closely attached to CSI300 Index (the Index tracks the largest listed companies in Shanghai and Shenzhen). According to the circuit breaker mechanism, a move of five per cent, either up or down, from the index's previous close will led to a half-an-hour trade suspension across equity indexes of China if the move occurs before 2:30 pm local time. After that, a five per cent move will freeze trading until the market close at 3.00 pm.

[205]   The CSRC said that "the circuit breaker mechanism was not the main reason for the market slump. It just didn't work as anticipated. The negative effect of the mecha-

instant responses to the market with immediate effect through administrative governance. Despite the fact that these administrative interferences may have a negative impact on the predictability of rules and legislation, the efficient response from the government is effective and inevitable for the Chinese stock market. In the transformative journey in corporate governance the government's responses to problems, such as immature market failure, temporary market conditions and the abolition of ineffective legislative approaches, are crucial for China, a country with a massive number of individual market participants.

3.7 THE GOALS OF DERIVATIVE ACTION: ACHIEVING BOARD ACCOUNTABILITY THROUGH PRIVATE ENFORCEMENT

The derivative action gives the shareholders right to sue the parties on behalf of the company. The parties here include controlling shareholders and directors. The mechanism is designed to deter and combat mismanagement from the controlling power holders. The system also balances the interests of minority shareholders and controlling shareholders. It promotes sound corporate governance and fairness through company law mechanisms, which is the most popular 'export' of common law.[206] Throughout the decades, many jurisdictions from all legal families have instituted and adopted their own version of the shareholders' remedy in line with the logic and value of derivative action.

Accountability is a 'buzzword of modern governance'[207] and 'a golden concept that no one can be against'.[208] The notion has been used as a core value to pursue in the wake of the financial crisis 2008 and in the mid of the pandemic 2020, as the most influential global crisis in modern times. In response to the global financial crisis 2008–09, ex-US President Obama launched his Recovery Act with the goal to 'foster unprecedented levels of

---

nism outweighed its positive effect." See K. Allen and G. Wearden, 'China Suspends Circuit Breaker Aimed at Ending Stock Market Turmoil', *The Guardian*, 7 January 2016.

[206] G. Zouridakis and T. Papadopoulos, 'A Comparative Analysis of Derivative Action in Cypriot Company Law: Comparison with English Company Law and The Prospect of Statutory Reform' (2022) 29(1) *Maastricht Journal of European and Comparative Law* 62, 63.

[207] M. Bovens, T. Schillemans and R. E. Goodin, 'Public Accountability' 'Public accountability' in Mark Bovens, Robert E. Goodin and Thomas Schillemans (eds.), *The Oxford Handbook of Public Accountability*, (Oxford University Press 2016) 1.

[208] M. Bovens, 'Analysing and Assessing Accountability: A Conceptual Framework' (2007) 13(4) *European Law Journal* 447, 448.

accountability and transparency in government spending'.[209] In response to the COVID-19 pandemic, the Director General of the World Health Organization Tedros Adhanom Ghebreyesus also claimed that 'we want accountability more than anyone' at the annual ministerial assembly on 19 May 2020.[210] Corporate accountability refers to the obligation of the corporations, usually the board members, to give an explanation or reason for the company's actions and conduct. is a key element of effective and corporate governance. South Africa's King Report (King IV) defined accountability as 'the obligation to answer for the execution for responsibilities'. It is clarified that 'accountability cannot be delegated, whereas responsibility can be delegated'. Accountability operates overtly and implicitly in the field of corporate governance.[211] G20/OECD's Principles of Corporate Governance make it plain[212] that accountability is a critical element in corporate governance. It has been suggested that good corporate governance can best be achieved by holding directors accountable for their behaviour and decisions,[213] and this means that the issue of the accountability of the board of directors in a company is the most important aspect of accountability. It has been argued that the accountability of directors has been said to be at the heart of good corporate governance.[214]

It is envisaged that there are four stages involved in the accountability of boards,[215] all of which contribute to the connotation of the word. The first stage is the board providing accurate information concerning its decisions and actions. This stage will be archived by transparency through information

---

[209] Treasury Inspector General for Tax Administration Office of Inspections and Evaluations, *Review of the Internal Revenue Service's American Recovery and Reinvestment Act Fund Expenditures During the Period April 1, 2010 through September 30, 2010* (February 7, 2013), available at https://www.treasury.gov/tigta/iereports/2013reports/2013IER003fr.html (accessed 23 July 2022).

[210] WHO, *WHO Director–General's closing remarks at the World Health Assembly* (19 May 2020), available at https://www.who.int/dg/speeches/detail/who–director–general–s–closing–remarks–at–the–world–health–assembly (accessed 23 July 2022).

[211] E. Rubin, 'The Myth of Accountability and the Anti–Administrative Impulse' (2005) 103 *Michigan Law Review* 2073, 2073; A. Belcher, 'Codes of Conduct and Accountability for NHS boards' (1995) *Public Law* 288, 291.

[212] G20/OECD, Principles of Corporate Governance 2015, 51, available at http://www.oecd.org/daf/ca/Corporate–Governance–Principles–ENG.pdf (accessed 23 July 2022).

[213] E. Makuta, 'Towards Good Corporate Governance in State-Owned Industries: The Accountability of Directors' (2009) 3(1) *Malawi Law Journal* 55, 56.

[214] A. Belcher, *Directors' Decisions and the Law*, (Abingdon, Routledge 2014) 183.

[215] A. Keay and J. Loughrey, 'The Framework for Board Accountability in Corporate Governance' (2015) 35(2) *Legal Studies* 252.

disclosure and reports that explain the decisions of the board.[216] The second stage involves a board explaining and justifying the things for which it is responsible, including what it has done and what it has failed to do. Often this is seen as the predominant aspect of accountability, involving the board being answerable for what it has done, and it is the stage that is often focused on by elements of the accountability literature dealing with other areas of society and law. This stage requires the board to justify and explain what it has done (or not done), and why. The third stage is constituted by the questioning and evaluating of the board's reasons given for what has been done. Fourth, the final stage is that there is the possibility, but not the requirement, of the imposition of consequences. The derivative action plays a crucial role in investor protection and promoting accountability mechanisms to create and maintain confidence in the financial market.

3.8   CONCLUSION

The chapter offers a systemic, historical and rigorous study of Chinese corporate governance transformation, focusing on the development from an administrative model, one which relies on government and administrative power and imposes on corporations' controllers with administrative duties and objectives to a hybrid model which has both administrative and economic governance characteristics. This uniquely Chinese corporate governance consists of a set of customs, strategies and institutions which are designed to mitigate or even eliminate double agency problems[217] that arise as the result of the separation of ownership and control and separate government functions from enterprise management.

The role of market forces is still limited and restrained by political power and government interference in China. The existence and restrictions on state shareholders, state-controlled companies and SOEs hinder the development of the market for corporate control.[218] We perceive that the government/state continues to have a key role in corporate governance in China which makes administrative interference and power something that is embedded in corporate governance regimes through public and political policies, law enforcement, and strategic management policies of each corporation. Apart

---

[216]   J. Zhao and S. Wen, 'Corporate Social Accountability' (2022) 58(1) *Stanford Journal of International Law* 63.

[217]   S. Lin, *Derivative Actions in Chinese Company Law*, (Alphen aan den Rijn: Kluwer Law International 2015).

[218]   C.W. Calomiris, R. Fishman and Y.X. Wang, 'Profiting from Government Stakes in a Command Economy: Evidence from Chinese Asset Sales' (2010) 96(3) *Journal of Financial Economics* 399.

from being a dynamic and vibrant process that needs to react to business and political environmental variations, the transformation of corporate governance in China is one that involves a series of changes as a collective transformation including economic policies, and systems relating to leadership, labour, wages, social security, ownership as well as political policies.

Discussions on corporate governance transformation in a unique Chinese context give us new insights into the reconceptualisation of Chinese corporate governance, rather than just purely criticising the lack of effectiveness and efficiency of corporate governance because of administrative involvement. The administrative involvement might sacrifice efficiency, and effective market and corporate responses, however, it may bring comparative advantages for Chinese corporate governance in terms of support, long-term strategic planning and the setting of multiple goals for SOEs, with government interference producing immediate effect to prevent market failure.

The application of administrative power and administrative governance in the transformation of corporate governance might be seen, in many ways, as being justified, rational and fair in the context of China. Likewise, government and administrative interference may also be regarded as elements that enhance and establish a more sound corporate governance, or even as ways that provide remedies for market failure. For future research, it may be worth considering how administrative/government enhancement and judicial intervention on corporate governance could be balanced.[219] Moreover, to apply the discussion of the chapter in a wider context, the Chinese experience in administrative governance may provide some useful insights for both developing and transition economies seeking to establish capital markets and emerging markets in which the government interference plays a vital role in financial and securities market.

---

[219] For discussion on juridical intervention of corporate governance in China see Q. Yang, *Judicial Intervention in Corporate Governance* [公司治理的司法介入], (Beijing: Beijing University Press 2008).

4. Effectiveness and efficiency of derivative action under a unique Chinese corporate governance regime: Incentives, accessibility and eligibility

The derivative action mechanism was adopted to address one of six major defects in the company law of 1993,[1] functioning as part of a series of changes surrounding shareholder protection and shareholders' rights.[2] Notwithstanding the significance of derivative action in modern China, the ability and/or eligibility of shareholders to bring derivative actions have been largely overlooked by scholarly works in this fast-growing nation. Indeed, analyses in the following sections reveal that despite the fact that Article 151 is a relatively brief and seemingly straightforward provision, a detailed examination of its nature, designated scope, and relevant data from securities markets concerning its practical effects, exposes major problems hindering its application in JSLCs. This chapter focuses on the eligibility issue, by addressing two of these problems, namely the shareholding percentage requirement and the shareholding time period requirement. Research on the eligibility of claimants in derivative action is significant in terms of maintaining a proper balance between affording disgruntled shareholders an effective remedy to seek relief, and restraining

---

[1] Fourteenth Meeting of the Tenth National People's Congress from 25 to 28 February 2005; the six defects were summed up by Fan and Wang. see J. Fan and J. Wang, *Corporate Law* (Beijing: Law Press, 4th ed. 2015) 59; they were proposed to the Standing Committee of the National People's Congress in February 2005 including the registration of companies; corporate governance-related issues including the rights and liability of shareholding meetings, boards of directors and supervisory boards; the protection of minority shareholders and creditors including a more effective derivative action system; issuing, transferring and listing of shares; the supervision of listed companies; and fiduciary duties and related liability of board directors and supervisors.

[2] In detail, two distinct litigation techniques have been introduced for shareholders to vindicate their interests in the company on occasions where the directors' fiduciaries duties are breached by key members of the company, such as directors, supervisors, senior management executives and sometimes the controlling shareholders. The mechanisms include direct suits and derivative suits as shareholder remedies, enabling them to bring legal action against the controllers of the company in accordance with arts 151–152, Chinese Company Law 2018.

excessive numbers of shareholders from launching derivative suits against companies, which may lead to boards and management being overloaded with unnecessary lawsuits and becoming distracted/discouraged from managing the company's affairs, as well as the extra workload for the Chinese judicial system. Almost 11 years after the enforcement of Article 151, the virtually complete lack of reported cases in the field[3] suggests that it is time to conduct systematic research to revisit the eligibility of claimants in derivative actions in Chinese JSLCs, with particular regard to the fast growth of China's financial markets, the increasing diversification of its investors, and the now massive group of minority shareholders.

The chapter aims to explore whether the eligibility requirements in Article 151 hinder minority shareholders in JSLCs, especially listed companies, from initiating a derivative suit. The eligibility of shareholder claimants according to Article 151 of Chinese Company Law 2018 will be critically analysed in order to deliver a comprehensive picture of the rationale for the different treatment of LLCs and JSLCs, and to determine whether shareholders in JSLCs are truly eligible to bring derivative actions in China. After exposing the defects in current laws, the chapter will make suggestions for reforms to the current regime. As well as doctrinally clarifying the eligibility of shareholders in terms of raising derivative suits and filling the existing legal loopholes, the research is also important from an international business perspective, given the increasing number of foreign investors in China.[4] A legal mechanism providing more effective remedial means for investors will make China a more attractive place for investment, in the sense that foreign investors will be reassured that their rights will be more substantially protected.

The study will begin with an examination of the company law framework and legislative processes in China. Also, it plans to examine what other jurisdictions have sought to do in relation to shareholder eligibility to bring derivative actions, in order to find solutions to the problems that are encountered by JSLCs in China. This will involve comparative analyses of the legislation in jurisdictions such as Japan, Korea, the US, the UK, Germany and Taiwan, as well as empirical analyses of listed companies in China and their top ten shareholders. The empirical analysis of the publicly available data will assist

---

[3]   Considering the current situation, which is that only one case has been brought against JSLCs, including listed companies.

[4]   It was reported that China became the largest FDI recipient in the world in 2014; see United Nations Conference on Trade and Development (UNCTAD), World Investment Report 2015: United Nations, Reforming International Investment Governance, pp. 4–5. It was reported that foreign firms invested $128bn in China, and $86bn in the US.

researchers to work out a more sensible and internationally compatible threshold for derivative mechanism which fits Chinese shareholders.

The chapter is structured as follows. After the introduction, the rationale for different treatments of LLC and JSLCs in current Chinese company law and the importance of enhancing minority shareholder protection in JSLCs will be examined in Section 1, based upon which their eligibility issues will be discussed in detail. Two interrelated issues will be addressed to explore why JSLCs are treated differently in derivative action – on one hand, the mechanism threshold which avoids malicious litigation considering the number of shareholders in JSLCs in China, and on the other hand, the significance of Chinese reform for more user-friendly shareholder remedy mechanisms in JSLCs. Section 2 moves on to assess whether the shareholding percentage threshold requirement for JSLCs embedded in Article 151 of Chinese Company Law 2018 is appropriate, enforceable and effective. In Section 3, the nature and characteristics of anonymous shareholders in the unique Chinese context, and their implications for the limited use of derivative action schemes, will be discussed. In Section 4, consideration will be given to the validity and effectiveness of the shareholding period threshold requirement for JSLCs, also embedded in Article 151 of Chinese Company Law 2018. Section 5 goes on to present legislative experience from other jurisdictions, in hope of clarifying and promoting the necessity of reconsidering the issue in JSLCs in China. Finally, there are some concluding remarks.

4.1 JUSTIFICATION OF DIFFERENT TREATMENTS FOR LLCS AND JSLCS

Article 151 of Chinese Company Law 2018 provides a threshold requirement concerning the size of the shareholding and the period for which it must be held, but it only operates in relation to shareholders in JSLCs who wish to bring derivative actions, not to their counterparts in LLCs. Before discussing the threshold requirement in detail, it is important to analyse the rationale for offering different treatment to minority shareholders in JSLCs and LLCs in terms of bringing a derivative action. In addition, the reasons why the protection of shareholders in JSLCs is becoming increasingly significant will be investigated in the context of the transformation of Chinese corporate governance and the Chinese economy.

4.1.1 Enquiries about the Status Quo

Research concerning derivative action in China thus far can be roughly divided into two groups; before the 2006 legislative reform, research mainly focused on the rationality of transplanting a derivative action mechanism to the Chinese context and the preliminary construction of this regime. After the promulgation of Article 151 of Chinese Company Law 2018, the literature, based upon discussions of reported cases, tended to focus on the interpretation of the legislative wording and the functions of the regime.[5] One presumption behind most research was that Chinese shareholders, including minority shareholders, would not hesitate in opting to use derivative action if they feel mistreated. However, even a cursory look at relevant legal practices would cast doubt on this presumption. As reported by the China Securities Regulatory Commission's 2018 annual report, only 244 cases were closed, and 224 decisions were made to impose sanctions involving fines and disgorgement orders due to the misconduct of directors in listed companies in 2018. These included 80 disclosure violation cases, 86 involving insider trading cases and 31 market manipulation cases. Totals of 335 and 233 cases were concluded in 2017 and 2016 respectively.[6] In detail, these cases were for various reasons including a breach of duties owed by the directors, supervisors and senior managers because of the violation of laws, administrative regulations or the articles of association, losses caused to the company, and the controlling shareholder or actual controlling parties using their dominant position to control the company's assets and harm the interests of the company. Most of these cases could have easily become reasons for minority shareholders to bring lawsuits on behalf of the company. However, shareholders in JSLCs in China are not currently using derivative action as a mechanism, even though it is a system used in public companies in many other jurisdictions. In other words, there is a great untapped potential for derivative action to be used by shareholders in JSLCs.

The limited use of derivative action seems particularly acute in JSLCs.[7] Cases in which shareholder(s) have brought derivative actions on behalf of companies have been reported in the Chinalawinfo (*Beida Fabao*) search

---

[5]   For example, the interpretation of 'shareholders that have held in aggregate' has been interpreted by M. Hu and P. Zhang, 'Research on Legal Application of Derivative Action in China [股东代表诉讼的法律适用研究]' [2007] *People's Judicature [人民司法]* 79; on the function of the mechanism see X. Mi, 'Analysis Of Some Important Measures To Protect Minority Shareholders' Rights and Benefits In The New "Corporation Law"' [评新《公司法》对小股东权益保护的几项重要举措] [2006] 1 *Law Science Magazine [法学杂志]* 72.

[6]   CSRC, 2018 Annual Report p. 59.

[7]   In Chinese Company Law, the LLC and the JSLC are the functional equivalents of a private company and a public company under English law; see J. Wang, *Company Law in China: Regulation of Business Organizations in a Socialist Market Economy*, (Cheltenham: Edward Elgar 2014) 50–51; see also M. Gu, *Understanding Chinese Company Law*, (Hong Kong: Hong Kong University Press 2006) 22–23.

engine since the enforcement of the 2005 Chinese Company Law.[8] Purely judging from the number of cases identified by Huang, we agree that the derivative action mechanism has had a noticeable impact in China.[9] However, an in-depth investigation of the corporate contexts in which the actions occurred suggests otherwise. The claimants in these reported cases are shareholders in LLCs only. Since the implementation of Article 151, there have only been five lawsuits brought by shareholders of JSLCs and one of them as a listed company, which is unreported in *Beida Fabao* but was subsequently accepted by the Shandong Higher People's Court on 11 December 2009,[10] implying that shareholders in JSLCs were either extremely reluctant or encountered significant difficulties in bringing cases of litigation on behalf of their companies. As will be discussed, the latter seems to be the major reason: at the current time the derivative action legal mechanism functions as no more than window dressing or 'a big disappointment'[11] for shareholders in JSLCs in China.

4.1.2   Treating LLCs and JSLCs Differently

Article 2 of the Chinese Company Law 2018 provides that 'the term "companies" refers to LLCs and companies limited by shares established within the territory of China under the Law (namely JSLCs)'.[12] Regarding the investment of shareholders in China, a shareholder in a LLC can limit his liability to the equitable capital contribution, whereas the liability of the shareholder in a JSLC is limited to the full payment of shares for which he or she subscribed.[13] Despite the fact that LLCs are not exclusively SMEs, the LLC form is most attractive for SMEs in China.[14] Compared to LLCs, JSLCs are characterised

---

[8]   Chinalawinfo was launched by the Legal Information Centre of Peking University and Peking University IAC Technology Co., Ltd. jointly as a one-stop intelligent legal information retrieval platform: Law Info China.

[9]   H. Huang, 'Shareholder Derivative Litigation in China: Empirical Findings and Comparative Analysis' (2012) 27(4) *Banking and Finance Law Review* 619, 644.

[10]   The case involves an attempt by the plaintiffs, 78 shareholders of *Shanlian Shangshe*, to bring a derivative claim against the former controlling shareholder. See also Section 6.2 below.

[11]   H. Huang, 'Shareholder Derivative Litigation in China: Empirical Findings and Comparative Analysis' (2012) 27(4) *Banking and Finance Law Review* 619, 644.

[12]   Equivalent of private and public companies.

[13]   Art. 3, Chinese Company Law 2018.

[14]   R.C. Art and M. Gu, 'China Incorporated: The First Corporation Law of the People's Republic of China' (1995) 20 *Yale Journal of International Law* 273, 292. It is claimed that China only had 10,000 joint-stock companies and 2,800 listed companies among 77,469,000 registered companies up to January 2016.

by more dispersed ownership and larger sizes. There are four main differences between JSLCs and LLCs in China.

First, traditionally speaking, many listed companies within the scope of JSLCs in China still constitute 'listed SOEs', and the largest shareholder normally is the state, which dominates the shareholding in listed companies. It is reported that an average of 31.27 per cent of the shares in these companies are held by the government.[15] This ownership by the state may suggest concentrated shareholding as a characteristic of Chinese corporate governance in terms of shareholding structure, due to the dominance of state shares in China. However, a detailed investigation into the share ownership composition of listed companies would suggest diversity rather than concentration: individual and non-state institutional shareholders have increased dramatically in the last ten years with 91 million *gu min* (the shareholder population) in July 2015, and an incredible 80 per cent of urban Chinese households which are or were formerly investors in the equity market.[16] The dispersed share ownership makes it sensible to introduce eligibility provisions for JSLCs with the purpose of preventing boards of directors or the courts from being overloaded with lawsuits. Comparatively, LLCs must be invested in and established by no more than 50 shareholders.[17] Shareholders in LLCs are thus more likely to have a substantial share ownership percentage. Indeed, an investigation reveals that fellow shareholders in Chinese LLCs are usually family members, relatives, colleagues or close friends.[18] Shareholders in LLCs need compelling reasons to break these close ties and enforce their rights to bring a derivative action, considering the close *guanxi*[19] (either family *guanxi* or friend *guanxi*) between shareholders and directors in LLCs.

---

[15]   Y. Thanatawee,'Ownership Structure and Dividend Policy: Evidence from China' (2014) 6(8) *International Journal of Economics and Finance* 197,199 quoted by OECD, OECD Survey of Corporate Governance Frameworks in Asia 2017.

[16]   See the report of CSDC, available at http://www.chinaclear.cn/english/en_index .shtml (accessed 23 July 2022).

[17]   Art. 25 of Chinese Company Law 2018.

[18]   J. Liu, 'Experience of Internationalization of Chinese Corporate Law and Corporate Governance: How to Make the Hybrid of Civil Law and Common Law Work?' (2015) 26(1) *European Business Law Review* 107, 118–119; see also S.S. Tang, 'Corporate Avengers Needs not be Angels: Rethinking Good Faith in the Derivative Action' (2016) 16(2) *Journal of Corporate Law Studies* 471.

[19]   *Guanxi* means close relationship in Chinese. It is, in essence, a coalition-based network of stakeholders sharing resources for survival, and it plays an important role in achieving business success in China. See J.H. Pac and Y.H. Wong, 'A Model of Close Business Relationship in China (guanxi)' (2001) 35(1/2) *European Journal of Marketing* 51; S. Ruehle, 'Guanxi as Competitive Advantages during Economic Crises: Evidence from China during the Recent Global Financial Crisis', in X. Fu (ed.), *China's Role in Global Economic Recovery*, (Abingdon: Routledge 2012) 64; J.

Second, despite the fact that shareholders in JSLCs do enjoy freedom in terms of buying and selling shares, it is still important and necessary for them to have comprehensive and accessible remedies. It is clear that dissatisfied shareholders in JSLCs could very easily leave the company by selling their shares on the stock markets, whereas there is no liquid market for potential share transactions in LLCs. The disadvantaged position of shareholders in LLCs is exacerbated by the legal requirement of imposing a legal restriction on equity transfers in LLCs. A member must obtain the consent of at least half the other shareholders prior to the member selling their shares.[20] Therefore, the tie between the shareholders and the company in LLCs seems stronger, and it is less likely that shareholders will abuse the system and want to buy shares for the purpose of bringing a derivative action or using them to put pressure on board members in the interests of shareholders.

Third, although JSLCs are subject to more demanding reporting requirements, including promoter's agreements, minutes of general meetings, minutes of the meetings of the board of directors, minutes of the meetings of the board of supervisors, financial and accounting reports[21] and the information disclosure requirements embedded within the corporate governance code for listed companies, information asymmetry problems between minority shareholders and corporate controllers, either as the result of shareholders' limited access to information or their ignorance and/or lack of understanding of the available information, are still a significant issue in JSLCs. This places minority shareholders in a disadvantaged position in terms of triggering derivative action.[22] In terms of derivative action, shareholders are required to gather facts in order to evaluate whether an action should be commenced or to assess the strength of any potential action.[23] Therefore, information is an important precondition and incentive for successful litigation. Minority shareholders may not have effective access to the information; they are likely to be limited to the information already available to the public. This may be another reason why a more functional and effective shareholder remedy system should be promoted in China for JSLCs including listed ones. More effective and user-friendly mechanisms

---

Dunning and C. Kim, 'The Cultural Roots of Guanxi : An Exploratory Study' (2007) 30(2) *The World Economy* 329, 333; K. Xin and J. Pearce, 'Guanxi : Connections as Substitutes for Formal Institutional Support' (1996) 39(6) *Academy of Management Journal* 1641.

[20]   Art. 72 of Chinese Company Law 2018.

[21]   Arts 90, 96, 97 and 151 of Chinese Company Law 2018.

[22]   J. Oliver, W. Qu and V. Wise, 'Corporate Governance: A Discussion on Minority Shareholder Protection in China' (2014) 6(3) *International Journal of Economics and Finance* 11, 11.

[23]   See L. Field, M. Lowry and S. Shu, 'Does Disclosure Deter or Trigger Litigation?' (2005) 39(3) *Journal of Accounting & Economics* 487.

for derivative action will facilitate information exchanges between shareholders who are willing to bring litigation together, and will encourage those shareholders who 'lose hope' in derivative actions in terms of acquiring knowledge about the companies and becoming more concerned about the performance of the companies in a positive manner.

Lastly, different requirements for derivative actions in LLCs and JSLCs mitigate different problems stemming from various modes of ownership and control. JSLCs in China consist of SOEs and non-SOEs. In non-SOEs, ownership and control are becoming separated with the purpose of transformation from an administrative and planned economy to a more market-oriented economy – professional directors are appointed for corporations just as they are in countries with industrialised and developed markets, such as the US or the UK,[24] where there has been the encouragement of a more scattered and diversified shareholding structure and hence the legal systems have fostered better protection of minority shareholders.[25] In order to promote the corporate governance of JSLCs that are non-SOEs, effective shareholders' remedies in these companies, as one of the critical fairness goals for corporate governance, are key for the transformation of the economic model in China from a planned to a market economy, including the transformation of corporate governance from an administratively-oriented model to a more economic-oriented one as desired by the Chinese government.

In SOEs, the boards of directors, namely Bureau of State Asset Management officers, are trying to maximise the interests of the state, who is the biggest shareholder as well as their principal. They are civil servants employed by the government, whose remunerations are decided by the government and their administrative ranking, rather than relating to the performance of the corporations they manage. These directors will 'align their interests with the local government, whose political interests may be to preserve employment rather than increase the efficiency of the listed SOEs'.[26] These non-economic concerns could lead to the trend of diverting the company's profits or assets which may harm the economic interests of the company, and for that matter, the interests of the minority shareholders. Many listed companies, especially SOEs, do accommodate objectives other than profit maximisation, most commonly, administrative goals. Apart from making profits, such corporations

---

[24] A.A. Berle and G.C. Means, *The Modern Corporation and Private Property*, (New York: The Macmillan Corporation 1932).

[25] R. La Porta, F. Lopez-de-Silanes, A. Sheifer and R. Vishny, 'Law and Finance' (1998) 106(6) *The Journal of Political Economy* 1113.

[26] L.H. Tan and J.Y. Wang, 'Modeling an Efficient Corporate Governance System for China's Listed State-owned Enterprises: Issues and Challenges in a Transitional Economy' (2007) 7(1) *Journal of Corporate Law Studies* 143, 149.

have other more immediate administrative missions such as the maintenance of urban employment, other social and environmental purposes or various administrative tasks required by the CSRC in order to regulate China's stock market. Administrative interference aims to serve the state's interests and strategic plans by controlling or influencing multifarious issues of business operation.[27] The administrative approach stems from the government policy of maintaining a full or controlling ownership in corporations so as to achieve direct control of key industries such as energy, banking and telecommunications.[28] Furthermore, it may entail direct involvement in upstream industries due to their strategic importance in sustaining the growth of downstream industries.

Different corporate forms understandably entail different agency costs. As argued by Lin, two kinds of agency costs are particularly acute in China, namely vertical agency costs between shareholders and managers, and horizontal agency costs between majority shareholders and minority shareholders due to the vulnerability of minority shareholders and the exploration of blockers; the latter is common in jurisdictions with concentrated ownership jurisdictions, particularly those with widespread SOEs.[29] Generally speaking, the incentive for SOEs to maximise the interests of other non-state shareholders is less distinct and strongly relies on managers taking autonomous executive actions. Inversely, effective protection means offered to minority shareholders in state-owned JSLCs, would serve the dual purpose of mitigating the conflicts of interest between shareholders and boards of directors and between majority shareholders (i.e., the state) and minority shareholders.[30] They might be particularly helpful to those who invest in state-owned or -controlled JSLCs but have been mistreated in the process of corporations pursuing administrative goals set by the government.

---

[27] H.X. Wu, 'Accounting for the Sources of Growth in Chinese Industry 1980–2010' in L. Song, R. Garnaut and C. Fang (eds), *Depending Reform for China's Long-term Growth and Development*, (Canberra: The Australia National University Press 2014) 431, 432–433.

[28] Q. Liu and Z. Lu, 'Corporate Governance and Earnings Management in the Chinese Listed Companies: A Tunnelling Perspective' (2007) 13(5) *Journal of Corporate Finance* 881, 884; see also L.S.O. Wanderley, R. Lucian, F. Farache and J.M. de Sousa Filho, 'CSR Information Disclosure on the Web: A Context-Based Approach Analysing the Influence of Country of Origin and Industry Sector' (2008) 82(10) *Journal of Business Ethics* 369.

[29] S. Lin, 'Double Agency Costs in China: A Legal Perspective' (2012) 9 *The Asian Business Lawyer* 116, 116 and 129.

[30] See A. Shleifer and R. W. Vishny, 'A Survey of Corporate Governance' (1997) 52(2) *Journal of Finance* 737.

In stark contrast, in LLCs, ownership is only marginally separated from control. These kinds of companies typically have an ownership structure comprising several significant shareholders.[31] Instead of various information disclosure requirements, a dialogue mechanism is normally established between the board of directors and the shareholders owing to their close ties.[32] This dialogue will be comparatively easier with limited shareholder requirements and the overlap between shareholders and board members. In most circumstances, the board seats in a LLC are directly occupied by shareholders themselves.

Therefore, it can be shown that LLCs and JSLCs are treated differently in China due to their different shareholding structures, different levels of separation of ownership and control, different levels of information disclosure requirements, their shareholder volume, and their different practices for issuing shares. The variations in the treatment of LLCs and JSLCs are necessary to avoid both malicious litigation and increasing the workloads of boards of directors, supervisors and the courts. Furthermore, a balance should be maintained between giving boards discretion to manage companies in the way that they consider will promote the success of the company, and monitoring mechanisms and intervention in any proceedings from shareholders to which the company is a party at an appropriate level.

4.1.3   Importance of Effective Derivative Action as a Tool to Protect Companies' Interests for Shareholders in JSLCs

Derivative action is a critical mechanism, operating in the interests of companies and their shareholders to promote corporate governance goals such as fairness, accountability and effectiveness. After all, one issue that all corporate governance mechanisms attempt to address is opportunistic and abusive corporate behaviours by controllers of a company.[33] It is expected that improved shareholder remedy schemes will also promote the sustainable development of

---

[31]   See A. Gomes and W. Novaes, 'Multiple Large Shareholders in Corporate Governance', unpublished working paper, The Wharton School, Philadelphia, PA (1999); see also N. Attig, S.E. Ghoul and O. Guedhami, 'Do Multiple Large Shareholders Play a Corporate Governance Role? Evidence from East Asia' (2009) 32(4) *The Journal of Financial Research* 395.

[32]   It is also suggested by the European Confederation of Directors' Association (ecoDa) Corporate Governance guidance and Principles for Unlisted Companies in European 2015 Principle 7 that 'There should be a dialogue between the board and the shareholders based on the mutual understanding of objectives. The board should as a whole have responsibility for ensuring that a satisfactory dialogue with shareholders take place.'

[33]   S.S. Tang, 'Corporate Avengers Needs not be Angels: Rethinking Good Faith in the Derivative Action' (2016) 16(2) *Journal of Corporate Law Studies* 471, 473.

the capital market. It is positive to see that a number of mechanisms have been introduced in China for shareholder protection purposes, such as cumulative voting systems,[34] guidelines[35] and notifications.[36] However, there is still room to improve minority shareholder protection. The World Bank Doing Business Index provides objective measures of business regulations for local firms in 189 economies and selected cities at the sub-national level, and rankings are issued annually, with 'protecting minority investors' included as one of 11 sets of indicators; whether shareholders can sue derivatively is a key question (with follow-up questions) for the assessment of this indicator. Based on the 2017 report, China ranks 123rd in this indicator, in comparison with a position of 78th in the general ranking.[37] The indicator related to minority shareholder protection is noticeably weaker compared with other indicators evaluating how easy and safe it is to 'do business' in China.

A number of studies have been addressing the improvement of corporate governance in response to problems and troublesome practices in China, with many suggestions and recommendations to improve various values of corporate governance;[38] the protection of shareholders, including effective remedies for minority shareholders, have been a particularly important aspect.[39] Based on the empirical report by Protiviti/China and the Chinese Academy of Social Sciences, the 'conflict of interests between majority shareholders and minority shareholders remains a major issue in the corporate governance of Chinese

---

[34]   See art. 105, Chinese Company Law 2018; see also Y. Chen and J. Du, 'Regulatory Reform of Cumulative Voting in Corporate China: Who were Elected and its Impact' available at http://papers.ssrn.com/sol3/papers.cfm?abstract_id=2556157 (accessed 23 July 2022); see also C. Xi and Y. Chen, 'Does Cumulative Voting Matter? The Case of China: An Empirical Assessment' (2014) 15(4) *European Business Organization Law Review* 585.

[35]   For example, the modification of the 'Rules for General Meetings of Shareholders of Listed Companies and Guidelines on the Articles of Association of Listed Companies' which is expected to improve disclosure requirements and voting information for minority shareholders.

[36]   In 2014, CSRC and the People's Bank of China jointly released the Rules for Bonds Statistics and issued a notification of the *Hirisun* Case, where we also witnessed the first case to require majority shareholders to compensate minority shareholders for their losses caused by the misrepresentation of listed companies. This proved to be an effective way for shareholders to seek remedies, and a rewarding attempt at building up a compensation mechanism for minority shareholders in listed companies.

[37]   World Bank Group, *Doing Business 2017: Measuring Regulatory Quality and Efficiency* (World Bank Group, 14th ed. 2007).

[38]   See, e.g., A. Keay and J. Zhao, 'Transforming Corporate Governance in Chinese Corporations: A Journey Not A Destination' (2018) 38(2) *Northwestern Journal of International Law and Business* 187.

[39]   R. Tomasic and N. Andrews, 'Minority Shareholder Protection in China's Top 100 Listed Companies' (2007) 9(1) *Australian Journal of Asian Law* 88, 110.

listed companies', regarded as one of the important risk indicators.[40] Other things China currently lacks include 'a comprehensive set of legal rules that provide protection for outside investors' and 'the ability to implement effectively the existing laws that govern the operations of corporations and the securities market',[41] which both hinder the provision of better remedies for shareholders in China. An effective derivative action mechanism for JSLCs in China is thus crucial for enhancing shareholder value, cultivating the soundness of corporate governance, restoring the confidence of domestic and international investors and establishing the sustainable development of capital markets in China.[42]

On a broad spectrum, the importance of derivative action is further evidenced in light of the rapid development of the stock market in China. Chinese stock exchange markets, including the Shanghai and Shenzhen Stock Exchanges, have grown to become the largest in Asia and the second largest globally. A key characteristic of the Chinese capital markets[43] has been the extremely high percentage of small investors holding less than RMB 1 million (approximately 0.13 million Euro) in cash or share equivalent, accounting for 98.8 per cent and 99.3 per cent of the total number of share capital in the Shanghai and Shenzhen Stock Exchanges respectively.[44] With large numbers of individual shareholders, the average turnover rate is understandably high, coming at

---

[40]   Protiviti/China and Chinese Academy of Social Sciences, 'Corporate Governance Assessment Summary Report on the Top 100 Chinese Listed Companies for 2012' 1, 9.

[41]   T. Kato and C. Long, 'CEO Turnover, Firm Performance, and Enterprise Reform in China: Evidence from Micro Data' (2006) 34(4) *Journal of Comparative Economics* 796, 798; see also F. Allen, J. Qian and M. Qian, 'Law, Finance, and Economic Growth in China' (2005) 77(1) *Journal of Financial Economics* 57; F. Jiang and K.A. Kim, 'Corporate Governance in China: A Modern Perspective' (2015) 32(6) *Journal of Corporate Finance* 190; K. Pistor and C. Xu, 'Governing Stock Markets in Transition Economies: Lessons from China' (2005) 7(1) *American Law and Economic Review* 184; H. Zou, S. Wong, C. Shum, J. Xiong and J. Yan, 'Controlling-minority Shareholder Incentive Conflicts and Directors' and Officers' Liability Insurance: Evidence from China' (2008) 32(12) *Journal of Banking and Finance* 2636.

[42]   J. Liu, 'Experience of Internationalization of Chinese Corporate Law and Corporate Governance: How to Make the Hybrid of Civil Law and Common Law Work?' (2015) 26(1) *European Business Law Review* 107, 117; D.C. Clarke, 'Corporate Governance in China: An Overview' (2003) 14(9) *China Economic Review* 494, 502–503; S. Lin and D. Cabrelli, 'Legal Protection for Minority Shareholders in China' (2013) 8(2) *Frontiers of Law in China* 266.

[43]   Analyses surrounding the high percentage of small investors was based on a 2008 Report issued by the CSRC, which has not provided any updated reports since that date.

[44]   See China Securities Regulatory Commission, *China Capital Markets Development Report* 2008, 269–270.

201.3 in 2013 and 240.3 in 2014.[45] In the light of the booming capital market, with a daily turnover of more than RMB 1.25 trillion and a trading volume of 1,296 million corporate clients and 3,715 million individual clients,[46] packed with poorly informed and unsophisticated individual investors, the problems of inadequate shareholder protection are becoming increasingly acute for Chinese regulators.[47] The rapid growth of the Chinese stock markets does require a more effective and rigorously monitored shareholder remedies mechanism that is fit for purpose in the growing financial market and for effective supervision by market participants.

Corporate governance wise, derivative action has been introduced to China as a supplementary means of restricting corporate behaviour and the power of boards of directors. Indeed, during the 2005 Company Law legislation process, the professionalism and competitiveness of the directors on the boards were severely questioned. These problems were particularly acute among directors of SOEs, given that most of them either were or had connections with government officials. In the eyes of the legislators, derivative action as a potentially functional shareholder remedy to enforce directors' duties[48] would serve the purpose of enhancing corporate transparency and the accountability of boards of directors, so as to benefit companies and their shareholders in general.[49]

---

[45] The World Bank, Stocks Traded, Turnover Ratio of Domestic Shares (%), data available at http://data.worldbank.org/indicator/CM.MKT.TRNR (accessed 23 July 2022).

[46] CSRC, 2014 Annual Report p.14, 21.

[47] X. Huang, 'Shareholders Revolt: The Statutory Derivative Action in China' (2009) 49 *Comparative Research in Law & Political Economy* 1, 5.

[48] F.X. Hong, 'Director Regulation in China: The Sinonization Process' (2010) 19 *Michigan State Journal of International Law* 502, 536–542; see R. Lee, 'Fiduciary Duty without Equity: "Fiduciary Duties" of Directors under the Revised Company Law of the PRC' (2007) 47(4) *Virginia Journal of International Law* 897.

[49] See L. Chun, *The Governance Structure of Chinese Firms*, (Heidelberg and London, Springer 2009); J. Yang, J. Chi and M. Young, 'A Review of Corporate Governance in China' (2011) 25(1) *Asian–Pacific Economic Literature* 15; N. Rajagopalan and Y. Zhang, 'Corporate Governance Reform in China and India: Challenges and Opportunities' (2008) 51(1) *Business Horizons* 55; Y. Cheung, P. Jiang, P. Limpaphayom and T. Lu, 'Does Corporate Governance Matter in China' (2008) 19(3) *China Economic Review* 460; H. Sami, J. Wang and H. Zhou, 'Corporate Governance and Operating Performance of Chinese Listed Firms' (2011) 20(2) *Journal of International Accounting, Auditing and Taxation* 106; L. Miles and Z. Zhang, 'Improving Corporate Governance in State-Owned Corporations in China: Which Way Forward?' (2006) 6(1) *Journal of Corporate Law Studies* 213; S. Li, 'China's (Painful) Transition from Relation-based to Rule-based Governance: When and How, Not If and Why' (2013) 21(6) *Corporate Governance: An International Review* 567; G. Xu, T. Zhou, B. Zeng and J. Shi, 'Directors' Duties in China' (2013) 14(1) *European Business Organization Law Review* 57.

Using derivative action as a legal tool may be employed as a remedy of compensation, whereas successful lawsuits may confer monetary benefits to the company and impose financial penalties on wrongdoers.[50] On the basis of the above-stated concerns, the derivative action regime was introduced as a mechanism complementary to other structural as well as internal and external corporate governance devices, to better enforce directors' duties, ensure that directors pay attention to their legal duties,[51] and to achieve fairness in corporate governance between controlling shareholders and minority shareholders. As described by Huang, the adoption of this mechanism was 'a major development in Chinese company legislation' which was expected to have 'far-reaching implications for corporate governance' in China.[52] These implications might be said to include additional enhancement of minority shareholder protection, the provision of effective means against wrongdoing by managing officers and directors of companies, who may be predominantly majority shareholders, especially in SOEs,[53] and the resolution of power imbalances between directors and shareholders and between minority and majority shareholders, to name but a few.

4.2   SHAREHOLDING PERCENTAGE REQUIREMENT

After discussing the significance of a well-designed eligibility threshold, this section goes on to examine a few doctrinal deficiencies in terms of shareholders' eligibility to bring a derivative action in the Chinese Company Law, with a particular focus on the shareholding percentage requirement in JSLCs.

---

[50]   R. Kraakman, H. Park and S. Shavell, 'When are Shareholder Suits in Shareholder Interest?' (1993) Discussion Paper No. 133 Harvard Law School Cambridge, MA 02138.

[51]   A. Reisberg, *Derivative Actions and Corporate Governance: Theory and Operation* (Oxford, Oxford University Press 2007) 45, 52; see also A. Keay, 'The Ultimate Objective of the Company and the Enforcement of the Entity Maximisation and Sustainability Model' (2010) 10(1) *Journal of Corporate Law Studies* 35, 40–45; J. Zhao, 'A More Efficient Derivative Action System in China: Challenges and Opportunities through Corporate Governance Theory' (2013) 64(2) *Northern Ireland Legal Quarterly* 233.

[52]   H. Huang, 'The Statutory Derivative Action in China: Critical Analysis and Recommendations for Reform' (2007) 4(2) *Berkeley Business Law Journal* 227, 242.

[53]   See J.V. Feinerman, 'New Hope for Corporate Governance in China?' (2007) 191 *China Quarterly* 590, 605.

4.2.1 Rational and Legislative Experiences for Imposing a Percentage Requirement

The shareholding percentage is not required as one of the elements qualifying shareholders to bring a derivative action in public companies in common law countries.[54] This is probably because of the case law-based tradition of common law countries, which allows more flexibility in lawmaking and judicial control, to avoid abuse of the derivative action mechanism. For instance, in the UK CA 2006, court permission is required before a claim brought by a shareholder can even continue as a derivative claim, upon proving the existence of a '*prima facie*' case.[55] In the US, taking the most influential Delaware corporate law practice as an example, a two-step test was established in the Supreme Court case of *Zapata Corp v Maldonado*[56] in reviewing the decision of the special litigation committee: the court 'must inquire into the independence and good faith of the committee and the bases supporting its conclusions', and a company 'should have the burden of proving independence, good faith and a reasonable investigation'. Judicial control in common law countries purportedly restrains potential abusive usages of the derivative action mechanism, whereas civil law countries with great respect for legislation would normally use *ex ante* procedural safeguards to achieve the same purpose, shareholding percentage requirement being a typical example.[57]

In Germany, the current law allows one or more persons holding shares constituting at least 1 per cent of the company's capital, or having a nominal value of at least 100,000 Euro, to file a derivative action in companies limited by shares.[58] South Korean law stipulates that the shareholding threshold for filing a derivative suit is 0.01 per cent in the case of listed companies.[59] As for non-listed companies, any shareholder who holds no less than 1 per cent of the total outstanding shares may demand that the company file an action against the directors to enforce their liability.[60] In Taiwan, the derivative action mechanism is only available to companies limited by shares, and any shareholder(s)

---

[54]   For the UK law, see Sections 260–263 of the UK CA 2006. The UK makes no distinction between private and public companies in this regard.

[55]   Section 261(2) UK CA 2006; see also *Lesini v Westrip Holdings Ltd* [2011] 1 BCLC 498; *Abouraya v Signund* [2014] EWHC 277.

[56]   *Zapata Corp v Maldonado* 430 A. 2d 779, 788 (Delaware 1981).

[57]   A. Cahn and D.C. Donald, *Comparative Company Law: Text and Cases on the Law Governing Corporations in Germany, the UK and the USA*, (Cambridge: Cambridge University Press 2010) 602.

[58]   §148(1) Aktg 1965.

[59]   Korean Securities and Exchange Act 1962 (amended in 1976 and 2002) § 191–13(1).

[60]   Art. 403. Commercial Act (Republic of Korea) 1963.

who hold(s) 3 per cent or more of the shares may request the supervisors of the company to institute an action against a director(s).[61] This threshold is widely criticised by scholars as unnecessarily high and pragmatically prejudicial against minority shareholders who wish to bring a derivative action.[62] Japan is one of the first countries in the civil law group not to have a quantitative shareholding requirement.[63] Empirical research demonstrated that 119 derivative actions were brought in listed companies in Japan during the period from 1993 to 2009, significantly more than the number of lawsuits in China.[64]

4.2.2   Identifying the Differences in Application of Derivative Action between LLCs and JSLCs

In light of the requirements, reforms and criticisms in other jurisdictions, the 1 per cent shareholding threshold requirements enshrined in Article 151 of the Chinese Company Law 2018 seemingly constitute a barrier hindering the vast majority of shareholders, including individual and institutional shareholders,

---

[61]   Art. 214, Companies Act (Taiwan) 2009; L.Y. Liu, 'The Derivative Action' (2004) 64 *Taiwan Law Journal* 156.

[62]   W.R. Tseng and W.W.Y. Wang, 'Derivative Actions in Taiwan: Legal and Cultural Hurdles with A Glimmer of Hope for the Future, in D. Puchniak, H. Baum and M. Ewing-Chow (eds), *The Derivative Action in Asia: A Comparative and Functional Approach* (Cambridge: Cambridge University Press 2012) 215; L.Y. Liu, 'The Derivative Action' (2004) 64 *Taiwan Law Journal* 156; H. Wang, 'The Derivative Action in Taiwan Company Law and Reform Suggestions [公司法中的代表诉讼缺失与改进之道]' in *Commercial Monographs – Professor Lai Fiftieth Birthday Congratulations Proceedings [商法专论– 赖英映照教授五十岁生日祝贺论文集]* (Taipei: Yuanzhao Publishing 1995) 130.

[63]   Section 847 (1), (2) of Companies Act (Japan) 2005 replaced Section 267 (1) with the old Japanese Commercial Code. Both sections allow any shareholder who held at least one share continuously for six months to demand that a corporation act to enforce a directors' duties; M.M Siems, 'Private Enforcement of Directors' Duties: Derivative Action as a Global Phenomenon' in S. Wrbka, S. Van Uytsel and M. Siems, *Collective Actions: Enhancing Access to Justice and Reconciling Multilayer Interests?* (Cambridge: Cambridge University Press 2012) 93.

[64]   M. Nakahigashi and D.W. Punchniak, 'Land of the Rising Derivative Action: Revisiting Irrationality to Understand Japan's Unreluctant Shareholder Litigate' in D.W. Puchniak, H. Baum and M. Ewing-Chow (eds), *The Derivative Action in Asia: A Comparative and Functional Approach* (Cambridge: Cambridge University Press 2012) 128, 172–173. Other than the absence of a shareholding requirement, this may also be due to a number of other factors, of which low and fixed litigation costs are important. See M.D. West, 'Why Shareholders Sue: The Evidence from Japan' (2001) 30(2) *Journal of Legal Studies* 351; Z. Zhang, 'Making the Shareholder Derivative Action Happen in China: How should Lawsuits be Funded?' (2008) 38 *Hong Kong Law Journal* 523.

in JSLCs who wish to bring derivative actions as an effective remedy, proved by the drastic differences between derivative action cases in LLCs and JSLCs. The number of derivative action cases in LLCs in China is notably higher, or at least not considerably lower, than the number of derivative action cases in other jurisdictions.[65] In the meantime, the *Sanlian Shangshe* case in 2009 was the only case involving a shareholder in a JSLC bringing a derivative action. The question arises, therefore, why the mechanism has been scarcely used in JSLCs in China, considering that shareholders in LLCs in China seek to use the scheme much more often.

In a logical manner, doubts have been thrown on the threshold applicable to JSLCs. For example, the percentage requirement prescribed in Chinese Company Law has been heavily criticised by scholars thus far. The following sections contribute to this matter by way of an empirical analysis, and feasible alternatives are suggested as a result.[66]

4.2.3   Data from the Chinese Stock Market and Practical Difficulties in Meeting the 1 per cent Threshold

One should review the statistics in relation to the general scale and percentage of shareholding in China before commenting on whether the current 1 per cent shareholding percentage threshold is too high for shareholders in JSLCs. A report issued by the China Securities Investor Protection Fund Corporation

---

[65]   See Chapter 6; see also A. Keay, 'Assessing Rethinking the Statutory Scheme for Derivative Action under the Companies Act 2006' (2016) 16(1) *Journal of Corporate Law Studies* 39, 41 and 59–67. In Japan, according to Nakahigashi and Punchniak, 29 derivative actions were brought from 1993 to 2009 for unlisted companies; M. Nakahigashi and D.W. Punchniak, ibid.; 27 cases were bought on behalf of private companies among 31 cases from 2000–05 according to Ramsay and Saunders; see I.M. Ramsay and B.B. Sanders, 'Litigation by Shareholders and Directors: An Empirical Study of the Statutory Derivative Action' (2006) 6(2) *Journal of Corporate Law Studies* 397, 420.

[66]   S. Lin, *Derivative Actions in Chinese Company Law* (Alphen ann den Rijin: Kluwer Law International 2015); H. Huang, 'The Statutory Derivative Action in China: Critical Analysis and Recommendations for Reform' (2007) 4(2) *Berkeley Business Law Journal* 227; J. Deng, 'Building an Investor-Friendly Shareholder Derivative Lawsuit System in China' (2005) 46(2) *Harvard International Law Journal* 347; W. Cheng, 'Protection of Minority Shareholders after the New Company Law: 26 Case Studies' (2010) 52(4) *International Journal of Law and Management* 283; Z. Zhang, 'Shareholder Derivative Action and Good Corporate Governance in China: Why the Excitement is Actually for Nothing' (2011) 28(2) *UCLA Pacific Basin Law Journal* 174; J. Zhao, 'A More Efficient Derivative Action System in China: Challenges and Opportunities through Corporate Governance Theory' (2013) 64(2) *Northern Ireland Legal Quarterly* 233.

in 2012 indicated that 52.27 per cent of surveyed investors invested less than RMB 100,000 in stocks, and 85.2 per cent of them invested less than RMB 500,000.[67] This study was continued by the Feng Hua Finance and Economic Consulting Firm (丰华财经) for their report in 2013, finding that 45.36 per cent of the surveyed investors invested less than RMB 50,000 in stocks and 85.57 per cent invested less than RMB 500,000.[68] More recently, a report published by the Shenzhen Stock Exchange disclosed that 84.4 per cent of the investors had invested less than RMB 500,000.[69] Finally, a report from the China Securities Depository and Clearing Corporation Limited (CSDC) indicated that 76.73 per cent of the surveyed investors invested less than RMB 100,000 and 95.15 per cent of them invested less than RMB 500,000.[70] Considering the fact that most of the listed companies have a market value of RMB 1 billion,[71] RMB 500,000 is a long way from 1 per cent of the market value. Therefore, the holders of these stocks, more than 84 per cent of the shareholders in listed companies based on the data from 2012–15, do not have the right to bring a derivative action as an independent claimant under the current company law of China.

Furthermore, based on the shareholding distribution of A-shares[72] held by professional institutional shareholders in 2014, the breakdown of the shareholding percentage of seven groups of intuitional shareholders, including pension funds, QFIIs, insurance companies, trusts, corporate annuities, securities firms (proprietary accounts) and securities firms (asset management schemes) in listed companies in China, were 0.61 per cent, 1.17 per cent, 1.71 per cent, 3.87 per cent, 1.37 per cent, 0.14 per cent, 0.31 per cent and 0.23 per cent respectively. It is reported by the China Securities Depository and Clearing Corporation Limited that there are 289,900 institutional shareholders

---

[67] A Survey of Securities Investors 2012 [2012年中国证券投资者综合调查报告] p.43, available at http://www.sipf.com.cn/images/NewCH/zxdc/2013/03/01/EC3861DC3E3764896A8CB1DC5F4E94C7.pdf (accessed 23 July 2022).

[68] JFINFO, A Survey of Individual Investors 2013, available at http://www.jfinfo.com/special/2013report.pdf(2014) (accessed 23 July 2022) p.11.

[69] Shenzhen Stock Exchange, A Survey of Individual Shareholders of 2015 [2015年个人投资者状况调查报告], available at http://investor.szse.cn/institute/bookshelf/report/P020180703407700981075.pdf (accessed 29 July 2022).

[70] J. Coffee and D.E. Schwartz, 'The Survival of the Derivative Suit: An Evolution and a Proposal for Legislative Reform' (1981) 81 *Columbia Law Review* 261, 312.

[71] China Centre for Market Value Management, 'The A Share Annual Report of China 2012 and 2013' [2012 年中国A股市值年度报告 2013年中国A股市值年度报告].

[72] A-shares are denominated in Renminbi; comparatively, B-shares are denominated in foreign currency (US dollars in the Shanghai Stock Exchange and Hong Kong dollars in the Shenzhen Stock Exchange).

investing in 2,839 listed companies in China. [73] On average, more than 100 institutional shareholders, in various forms, are investing in an individual listed company. It is also likely that there will be more than one institutional shareholder investing in a company that belongs to one of the seven international shareholder groups mentioned above. Therefore, the likelihood is that a number of institutional shareholders will not qualify as a claimant for bringing derivative action either.

4.2.4   Empirical Observations

The author collected a set of original data in July 2016. This involved investigating the eligibility of the top ten biggest shareholders from a sample of 800 listed companies in China in terms of bringing a derivative action. [74] The samples consist of 400 listed companies on the Shenzhen Stock Exchange and 400 on the Shanghai Stock Exchange. This empirical research was carried out using purposive sampling, with controls placed on the types of companies chosen for the survey in terms of nature and size, and we specifically looked for representative samples to make sure the sample is correctly balanced. We identified the key index factors for JSLCs in terms of their key characteristics. As detailed below, we selected these samples on the basis of various criteria: was it a SOE or not; the number of shareholders; total capitalisation; and industrial classification. The aim was to deliver a set of legitimate and comprehensive data that genuinely reflects the pattern of listed companies in China, and lay a solid base for research on the shareholding percentage of the top ten shareholders. [75] The top ten shareholders were selected because the publicly available data on shareholding percentage was limited to this information.

The sample of 800 selected companies was composed of 396 listed SOEs and 404 listed non-SOEs (see Figure 4.1), aiming to deliver a balanced view of the unique shareholding structure of SOEs in China and its implications for derivative action. As JSLCs in China consist of SOEs and non-SOEs, the

---

[73]   China Securities Depository and Clearing Corporation Limited (CSDC), CSDC Monthly Report, February 2016 http://www.chinaclear.cn/zdjs/editor_file/20160314173907448.pdf (accessed 23 July 2022) p.2.

[74]   The data was collected from 15 to 22 June 2016 and reflected the shareholding structures of sample companies as of these dates.

[75]   This sample-selection methodology is preferred instead of investigating all listed companies as: (1) the massive number of listed companies adds to the pragmatic difficulty of a thorough investigation; (2) the shareholding structure, the number of shareholders and the number of listed companies constantly change with time; (3) a random selection of samples would not reflect the industry attributes of listed companies and might lead to biased results on shareholding structures that are heavily influenced by the industries the companies engage in.

selection of data is important for our research on the importance of derivative actions in both SOEs and non-SOEs in China, and the distinct position of non-SOEs in the corporate governance transformation to a more economic and market-oriented model. Figure 4.2 aims to show a clear and balanced view of the unique shareholding structure of SOEs in China and its implications for derivative action. The figure works well with Figures 4.1–4.4 below to demonstrate that the sample selection method is convincing and coherent.

Non-SOE Listed Companies

SOE Listed Companies

Figure 4.1   Balance of SOE and Non-SOE Listed Companies from the sample of 800 Listed Companies

Second, the sample involves companies which are representative of the target companies, namely JSLCs, in terms of the number of shareholders and total share capital. In other words, the distribution of the number of the companies based on different industrial classifications should match those of the entire target population. These two aspects are investigated in order to ensure that the poll represents a balanced and representative sample. As for the former, the distribution of the number of shareholders in the sample of 800 listed companies collected by the authors, as demonstrated in Figure 4.2, is consistent with the distribution of all listed companies in terms of shareholder numbers, based on data collected by EastMoney (东方财富) on 30 June 2016[76] regarding the number of shareholders in listed companies in China. As for the latter, the pattern of the total share capital collected and organised by the authors, demon-

---

[76]   Obviously, the authors are aware there are limitations to this matching exercise since there is a small timescale gap here. Available at http://data.eastmoney.com/cmjzd/ (accessed 23 July 2022).

strated in Figure 4.3, is also consistent with the pattern based on the data for the total capitalisation of listed companies collected and produced by Hexun Data (和讯数据).[77]

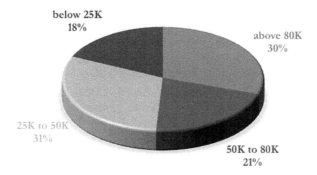

Figure 4.2   *The number of shareholders in the sample of 800 Listed Companies*

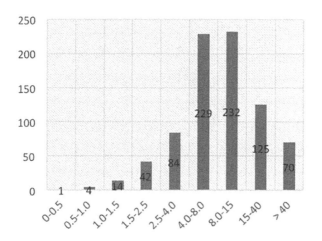

Note: Share Capital RMB 0.1 Billion

Figure 4.3   *The number of companies based on different shareholder capital ranges*

---

[77] Available at http://datainfo.stock.hexun.com/ssgs/jbsj/gbfb.aspx (accessed 23 July 2022).

Third, these samples, including both SOEs and non-SOEs, cover all industries with listed companies, including manufacturing, information technology and software, construction, scientific research and technical services, wholesale and retailing, transport warehousing and postal industries, mining, the financial industry, education, electricity, heat, gas and water protection and supply, and water conservation, environmental and public facilities management (Figures 4.4 and 4.5 below). The percentages of the sample companies in each industry are roughly consistent with the pattern of industry classification published by the National Equities Exchange and Quotations listed companies in the CSRC annual report.[78] We aimed to select a sample of 800 companies from all relevant types of industries to enhance the representativeness of our sample of all listed companies in a fair manner.

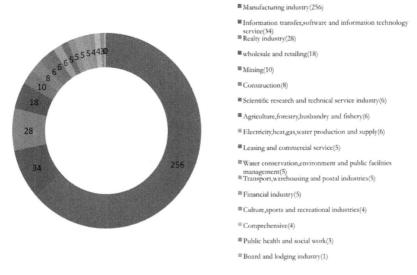

■ Manufacturing industry(256)

■ Information transfer,software and information technology service(34)
■ Realty industry(28)

■ wholesale and retailing(18)

■ Mining(10)

■ Construction(8)

■ Scientific research and technical service industry(6)

■ Agriculture,forestry,husbandry and fishery(6)

■ Electricity,heat,gas,water production and supply(6)

■ Leasing and commercial service(5)

■ Water conservation,environment and public facilities management(5)
■ Transport,warehousing and postal industries(5)

■ Financial industry(5)

■ Culture,sports and recreational industries(4)

■ Comprehensive(4)

■ Public health and social work(3)

■ Board and lodging industry(1)

Figure 4.4   Industrial classifications of non-SOEs

The hypothesis was that if the current shareholding threshold prescribed in Chinese Company Law does not hinder the use of the derivative action mechanism by minority shareholders in listed companies, which we assume to have a dispersed ownership structure, the top ten shareholders, or at least the majority of them, should be not barred by the shareholding threshold from bringing

---

[78]   CSRC, 2014 Annual Report p.13.

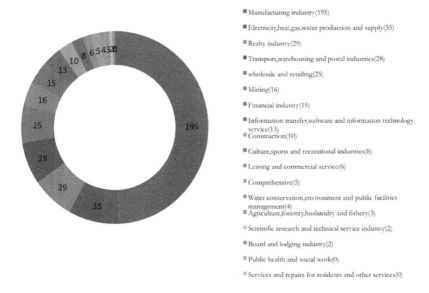

Figure 4.5   Industrial classifications of SOEs

derivative actions due to their shareholding percentage.[79] A few questions were raised in order to investigate the soundness of the hypothesis, as well as the possibility of law reform: how many shareholders among the top ten are entitled to bring derivative action, if they were to bring a lawsuit on their own? What is the average percentage shareholding? What if the percentage requirement were to be lowered to 0.5 per cent? And what if the percentage requirement was lowered to 0.1 per cent?

The result of this quantitative research informs us that on average (as demonstrated in Figure 4.6 below), 52.10 per cent of the shareholders could bring a derivative action if the standing requirement was 1 per cent, 75.44 per cent if the standing requirement was 0.5 per cent, and 99.44 per cent if the standing requirement was 0.1 per cent.[80] Drawing from this empirical study, it is logical to propose a lower shareholding percentage requirement for listed companies, to enable more minority shareholders to use the derivative action regime to protect their interests. More user-friendly eligibility criteria could

---

[79]   Data on the top ten shareholders' shareholding percentage is on file and available on request.

[80]   Data available on request.

significantly improve the enforcement of company law, and thus contribute to good corporate governance.[81]

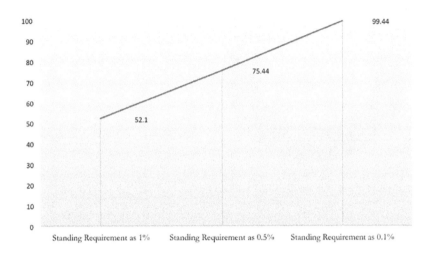

Note: Data based on a sample of 800 listed companies

Figure 4.6   The percentage of top ten shareholders' eligibility to bring a derivative action and different standing in Company Law

4.2.5   Difficulties in Collective Action

Some might argue that it is possible for two or more shareholders to bring a derivative action in a collective manner since the law does allow 'shareholders that hold an aggregate 1% or more' to bring such derivative actions.[82] However, it is not practically feasible to call for collective action among shareholders in JSLCs, especially listed ones, at least in China, where most minority shareholders are individual shareholders.[83] Organising a number of individual shareholders who are willing to bring a collective derivative action

---

[81]   J.V. Feinerman, 'New Hope for Corporate Governance in China?' (2007) 191 *The China Quarterly* 590, 600–601.

[82]   Art. 151 of Chinese Company Law 2018.

[83]   F.X. Hong and S.H. Goo, 'Derivative Action in China: Problems and Prospectus' [2009] 4 *Journal of Business Law* 376, 388.

can be a very difficult process. In principle, individual shareholders of listed companies who propose to commence or intervene in a lawsuit may consult the central securities registry and the clearance agency to obtain details of other shareholders who may want to bring this litigation jointly. However, in practice it is very hard for them to acquire contact information because of privacy considerations. As a result, these shareholders almost invariably rely on the 'last resort' of soliciting other shareholders publicly, which will damage the confidence of public investors in the company and could affect the reputation of the company.[84] Information asymmetry has proved in practice to be a major obstacle for joint derivative action claimants, who need to acquire sufficient information about their follow shareholders. Therefore, it is clear that joint litigation is either impractical or harmful (or at least very difficult), which is against the purpose of the derivative action mechanism to protect the interests of the company.

4.2.6 Proposals for Changes and Difficulties in Transplanting Common Law Principles: UK Law as an Example

In light of the above-stated difficulties, Zhu and Chen proposed a legislative change, intending to replace the current shareholding percentage threshold with a share sum requirement with a focus on the value of the shares.[85] Presumably, the value of the shares here refers to market value rather than nominal value, an arbitrary figure bearing no relevance to the business reality. However, the fact that the market value of the shares floats with the market is likely to bring a lot of uncertainties and difficulties in enforcement, should this proposal be adopted. No alternative suggestion has yet been offered to address this potentially serious matter.

From a practical point of view, it is noted by Zhang, for instance, that a 1 per cent shareholding is a 'substantial figure' in listed companies, and this figure

---

[84] J. Liu, 'Experience of Internationalization of Chinese Corporate Law and Corporate Governance: How to Make the Hybrid of Civil Law and Common Law Work?' (2015) 26(1) *European Business Law Review* 107, 119; this also happens in cases in which shareholders try to protect themselves through direct litigation; see, e.g., *Yinguansha Shareholders Claims* December [银广夏小股东维权] 2011; and more recently *MingYao Investment v FAW Automotive* [明曜投资董事长曾昭股东维权抗 两家一汽系] 2016.

[85] H.C. Zhu and G.Q. Chen, 'China Introduces Statutory Derivative Action' *International Financial Law Review*, 1 July 2005, available at http://www.iflr.com/ Article/1984802/China–introduces–statutory–derivative–action.html (accessed 23 July 2022).

is reached mostly by big block-holders in China,[86] many of whom are SOEs or other government-controlled entities which were brought into corporate shareholding structures during the period of restructuring traditional SOEs for listing, and are in a strong rather than vulnerable position in comparison to directors, who are often appointed by government entities.[87] In order to address the concern that the shareholding percentage requirement may be a hurdle for shareholders in JSLCs, some scholars have suggested that China follow the common law route and abolish the shareholding percentage requirement, claiming that any fixed minimum percentage or monetary value of shareholding is arbitrary, as the quantity of ownership does not reflect the potential ability of minority shareholders to make valid and legitimate decisions and judgements.[88]

Derivative action in most common law jurisdictions is provided for in codified statutes. The courts' decisions to grant applications are always decisions made according to statutory criteria. Criteria need to be met before the court can authorise the initiation of a derivative action. Taking the UK as an example, derivative claims were delivered at common law for years until a statutory derivative proceedings scheme was introduced in the UK CA 2006, following the approach extant in many Commonwealth countries[89] in order to promote simplification and modernisation of the law to improve its accessibility.[90] Keay argued that the primary characteristic of statutory shareholder derivative action is that the 'courts are required to perform a gatekeeper role in order to exclude frivolous or unmeritorious cases'.[91] Permission can be only granted if the shareholders who propose to bring a derivative action pass two stages successfully. These two stages are designed to enable the court to make decisions in an efficient manner about whether to give permission to proceed with the action in absence of involvement from the company.[92] First, they have

---

[86]   Z. Zhang, 'The Shareholder Derivative Action and Good Corporate Governance in China: Why the Excitement is Actually for Nothing' (2011) 28(2) *UCLA Pacific Basin Law Journal* 174, 194.

[87]   Ibid.

[88]   The 'rationale underpinning the minimum shareholding strategy is flawed', Z. Zhang, 'The Shareholder Derivative Action and Good Corporate Governance in China: Why the Excitement is actually for Nothing' (2011) 28(2) *UCLA Pacific Basin Law Journal* 174, 197.

[89]   Such as Canada, Australia, New Zealand and Singapore.

[90]   Law Commission, 'Shareholder Remedies: Report on a Reference under s. 3(1) (e) of the Law Commissions Act 1965' (1997) 7 and para 6.4.

[91]   A. Keay, 'Assessing Rethinking the Statutory Scheme for Derivative Action under the Companies Act 2006' (2016) 16(1) *Journal of Corporate Law Studies* 39, 40.

[92]   These first two have been merged by the courts in some cases, such as *Bridge v Daley* [2015] EWHC 2121 (Ch); *Stimpson v Southern Private Landlords Association* [2009] EWHC 2072.

to establish a *prima facie* case on merit.[93] This stage of the permission process is designed to assess whether the company and the respondent should be put to the expense and inconvenience of considering and contesting the application for permission.[94] The court will therefore filter out cases that stand little or no chance of success and dismiss the frivolous claim without company involvement at the earliest possible opportunity.[95]

If this stage proves successful, the case may proceed towards a second stage.[96] Here, the court must decide whether to grant permission by taking into account three criteria listed in section 263(2), including, for example, whether 'a person acting in accordance with Section 172 (duty to promote the success of the company) would not seek to continue the claim'.[97] Although no discretion should be given to the courts at this point, the court subsequently has the discretion to decide whether to allow the claim to proceed if none of the criteria in section 263(2) apply. In the process of exercising this discretion, the court must take into account factors that are embedded in sections 263(3) and (4).[98]

The court as the 'gatekeeper' and the discretion vested in the court regarding whether or not to proceed are seen as central issues under the new statutory procedures. However, we do have reservations in adopting this two-staged threshold in China, based on the following four reasons. First, commentators do not completely agree about the effectiveness of this approach. The criterion that the applicant has to act in good faith in bringing a derivative claim,[99] for example, is criticised as 'uncertain and unworkable'.[100] It is argued that the court needs to decide whether the benefit from proposed litigation would be outweighed by the harm that it would potentially cause to the company,

---

[93]   See s. 261(2) UK CA 2006; see also *Iesini and Others v Westrip Holdings Ltd. and Others* [2009] EWHC 2526 (Ch), [2011] 1 BCLC 498, [2010] BCC 420.

[94]   *Langley Ward Ltd. v Trevor* [2011] EWHC 1893 (Ch), [62].

[95]   HL Deb 9 May 2006, vol 681, col 883 (Lord Goldsmith).

[96]   See A. Keay and J. Loughrey, 'Derivative Proceedings in a Brave New World for Company Management and Shareholders' [2010] 3 *Journal of Business Law* 151.

[97]   Section 261(2) UK CA 2006.

[98]   Davies and Worthington, however, think this is a third stage, where a number of factors are laid down which the court must take into account in deciding whether to give permission, such as whether the shareholder seeking to bring the claim is acting in good faith, possibilities of ratification, and the likelihood of company pursuing the claim. See ss 263(3) and 268(2) UK CA 2006; P.L. Davies and S. Worthington, *Gower Principles of Modern Company Law* (Sweet Maxwell, 10th ed. 2016) 601–602.

[99]   See *Stimpson v Southern Landlords Association* [2009] EWHC 2072; [2010] BCC 387; s. 263(3) a, UK CA 2006.

[100]   A. Reisberg, 'Theoretical Reflections on Derivative Action in English Law: The Representative Problem' (2006) 3(1) *European Company and Financial law Review* 69, 101 and 103.

without full evidence verified by cross-examination.[101] The transplant should therefore be subject to a more rigorous assessment of its fitness with comprehensive consideration of other path dependence factors, including a number of issues such as overburdened court systems, limited judicial resources, judges' skills and knowledge,[102] the limited knowledge of shareholders as natural persons, and information asymmetries between minority shareholders and institutional shareholders. As a matter of fact, only 56 per cent of Chinese judges hold degrees,[103] and many civil servants who are described as judges and work in administrative roles.[104]

Second, the *prima facie* test has been made familiar by lawyers in the UK and some other common law countries, and was seen as the primary test in applications for interim injunctions in most cases during the twentieth century.[105] However, the test is not widely known and applied in China in relation to company law.

Third, the codified restatement of directors' duties, which reflect common law and equitable principles, is key for the understanding and enforcement of directive action in the UK and other common law countries.[106] It is indeed the fact that the concept of fiduciary duties, including the duty of loyalty and the duty of care, are explicitly stipulated in Chinese company law,[107] with the codification of a number of misconducts in terms of the violation of duties by directors.[108] However, the successful application and enforcement of the approach are heavily dependent on judicial discretion about when this inclusive and flexible principle may be applied to individual cases, so the

---

[101] Contribution of Zhang Zhong quoted in J. Loughrey, 'Directors' Duties and Shareholder Litigation: The Practical Perspective' in J. Loughrey (ed), *Directors' Duties and Shareholder Ligation in the Wake of the Financial Crisis* (Cheltenham: Edward Elgar 2013) 229, 245.

[102] See T. Gong, 'Dependent Judiciary and Unaccountable Judges: Judicial Corruption in Contemporary China' (2004) 4(2) *China Review* 33; W. Gu, 'The Judiciary in Economic and Political Transformation: Quo Vadis Chinese Courts?' (2013) 1(2) *The Chinese Journal of Comparative Law* 303.

[103] J. Zhu (ed), *China Legal Development Report [*中国法律发展报告：数据库和指标体系*]* (Beijing: Renmin University Press 2007) 34.

[104] 'Legal Reform Judging Judges' *The Economist*, 24 September 2015.

[105] See *Hoffman-La Roche (F) & Co. v Secretary of State for Trade & Industry* [1975] AC 295 at 338 and 380; see also C. Gray, 'Interlocutory Injunctions since Cyanamid' (1981) 40(2) *Cambridge Law Journal* 307; P. Carlson, 'Granting an Interlocutory Injunction: What is the Test' (1982–1983) 12 *Manitoba Law Journal* 109.

[106] S. Watkins, 'The Common Law Derivative Acton: An Outmoded Relic' (1999) 30 *Cambrian Law Review* 40; J.L. Yap, 'Whither the Common Law Derivative Action' (2009) 38 *Common Law World Review* 197.

[107] Art. 147 of Chinese Company Law 2018.

[108] Art. 148 of Chinese Company Law 2018.

nature and scope of the duty may be constantly refined and enriched by the precedential ruling by judges.[109] This makes it problematic to transplant this common law approach to jurisdictions with a civil law background, with difficulties in making the principle a workable one in judicial practice.[110] This is demonstrated by the empirical research of Xu et al. and historical evidence from Japanese transplantation.[111]

Fourth, the use of derivative action in the UK also depends on its relationship with the remedy of unfair prejudice, embedded in section 994 of the UK CA 2006 without court authorisation. The notion of 'unfair prejudice' does not have an equivalent in Chinese company law in terms of shareholder rights in bringing a lawsuit.[112]

The imposition of a fixed and lowered threshold figure for listed companies seems necessary at least at the current time in China, for its effect in avoiding excessive litigations or malicious lawsuits. Given that the above-discussed empirical study results indicate that a modification from a 1 per cent threshold to a 0.1 per cent threshold would render roughly 99 per cent of the top ten shareholders in listed companies (ranked in terms of their shareholding percentage) eligible to bring derivative actions, the authors suggest lowering the current shareholding requirement to at least 0.1 per cent of the total shareholding of the company, to enable an adequate number of minority shareholders in listed companies to use the mechanism to protect their interests, to use their collective powers in the company's best interests, and most importantly, to mitigate the potential risk of frivolous lawsuits.

4.2.7   0.1 per cent Proposal and the Balance Between Voices and Exits

Another legitimate question that needs addressing is whether a shareholder who owns 0.1 per cent of the company share in a JSLC would have incentive to sue in the interests of the company in his own name. It is crucial to point out that even under the proposed new threshold of 0.1 per cent of shareholding, those shareholders who are eligible in JSLCs are not small shareholders or

---

[109]   G. Xu, T. Zhou, B. Zeng and J. Shi, 'Directors' Duties in China' (2013) 14(1) *European Business Organization Law Review* 57, 87.

[110]   Ibid.

[111]   The loyalty duty has not been applied separate by Japanese courts; see H. Kanda and C.J. Milhaupt, 'Re-examining Legal Transplants: The Director's Fiduciary Duty in Japanese Corporate Law' (2003) 51(4) *American Journal of Comparative Law* 887.

[112]   M.M. Siems, 'Private Enforcement of Directors' Duties: Derivative Action as a Global Phenomenon' in S. Wrbka, S. Van Uytsel and M. Siems, *Collective Actions: Enhancing Access to Justice and Reconciling Multilayer Interests?* (Cambridge: Cambridge University Press 2012) 93, 101.

minority shareholders. Based on our empirical data, 7.65 per cent of the top ten shareholders fall within the shareholding percentage range of 0.1–0.2 per cent. As we mentioned earlier, the CSDC concluded that 76.73 per cent of the surveyed investors had invested less than RMB 100,000. It would be difficult to imagine that these shareholders would have incentives to bring a derivative action. However, considering the 91 million *gu min* (data from July 2015), it is highly unlikely that these shareholders would fall in the category suggested by us based on a threshold shareholding percentage of 0.1 per cent. Moreover, regarding individual shareholders, only a small portion of shares in listed companies are held by them, with average ownership equalling 2.38 per cent for all individual shareholders, and it is very unlikely that they will hold 0.1 per cent of the shares in any company.[113] We are convinced that shareholders(s) who own(s) 0.1 per cent have sufficient self-interest in the outcome of litigation to conduct a truly adversarial lawsuit.

Furthermore, it is important to clarify the rationale for giving adequate standing to members while dissatisfied shareholders in a listed company could use the 'exit strategy' by leaving the company. It is clear that derivative actions may entail possible benefits in two ways. First, Reisberg summarised two main purposes of derivative action, including deterrence of mismanagement and compensating the company and its shareholders for harm caused.[114] The recovery involved *ex post* liability and it may only be made after the derivative action is brought. Therefore, despite the fact the shareholders could choose to sell their shares, the damage has taken place and the interests of the company and the shareholders have been harmed, and they are entitled to the financial benefit of compensation. Lin argued that the selling of shares in this scenario does not mean that they are not affected by the alleged wrongdoing, since the value of shares may have been affected by this wrongdoing and thus the value of the shares, as the property of the shareholders, has reduced.[115] Selling the shares, in this sense, would lead to immediate loss without having their voice heard for remedy and compensation.

Second, while the 'shareholder engagement', 'long-term economic interests' and 'long-term investment culture' have been emphasised post-financial crisis 2008,[116] it may not always be rational to use an 'exit strategy' as an

---

[113] OECD, OECD Survey of Corporate Governance Frameworks in Asia 2017, 5.

[114] A. Reisberg, *Derivative Actions and Corporate Governance: Theory and Operation*, (Oxford: Oxford University Press 2007) 51.

[115] S. Lin, 'A New Perspective on China's Derivative Actions: Who is Best Suited to Assessing Derivative Actions?' (2016) 27 *International Company and Commercial Law Review* 1, 3.

[116] See, e.g., Financial Reporting Council, The UK Stewardship Code, and September 2012; Association of British Insurers, 'Improving Corporate Governance and

option. Despite the fact that it is difficult to find an optional mix of exit and voice, Hirschman famously argued that 'exit' and 'voice' work best together, and voice plays a crucial role in understanding how organisations actually work.[117] This may also apply to shareholders when they are faced with the option of getting their voice heard by bringing derivative actions when they perceive that firms are demonstrating a decrease in quality, or such actions would benefit the company (and their members).

4.2.8 Accessibility and Incentives for Institutional Investors to Bring Derivative Actions

Existing research has supported the argument that altering the shareholding threshold will likely improve the accessibility of the derivative action mechanism for shareholders, which is the major legislative aim of Chinese law drafters.[118] Therefore, a proposal for a lower threshold in relation to the shareholding percentage and period will be made to make derivative action in China more effective, and to ensure that the regime is utilised more systematically in JSLCs instead of being mere window-dressing. Moreover, since China has chosen to adopt a statutory derivative action mechanism in current legislation, it is necessary for the mechanism to be user-friendly for shareholders who are genuinely willing to initiate law suits on behalf of companies. It is particularly relevant for institutional shareholders in China with strong motivation to engage in corporate governance.[119]

Compared with countries with mature financial markets, it may seem worrying that institutional shareholders in China have demonstrated a less

---

Shareholder Engagement'; The Investment Association, Supporting UK Productivity with Long-Term Investment: The Investment Association's Productivity Action Plan, March 2016; New York Stock Exchange Commission on Corporate Governance 2010.

[117] A.O. Hirschman, *Exit, Voice and Loyalty: Responses to Decline in Firms, Organization and State*, (Cambridge: Harvard University Press 1970); see also J. Fox, 'Exit, Voice, and Albert O. Hirschman' *Harvard Business Review*, 12 December 2012.

[118] H. Huang, 'Shareholder Derivative Litigation in China: Empirical Findings and Comparative Analysis' (2012) 27(4) *Banking and Finance Law Review* 619; S. Lin, *Derivative Actions in Chinese Company Law*, (Alphen ann den Rijin: Kluwer Law International 2015).

[119] See F. Jiang and K.A. Kim, 'Corporate Governance in China: A Modern Perspective' (2015) 32(6) *Journal of Corporate Finance* 190; B. Gong, *Understanding Institutional Shareholder Activism: A Comparative Study of the UK and China* (London: Routledge 2014); Z. Chen, B. Ke and Z. Yang, 'Minority Shareholders' Control Rights and the Quality of Corporate Decisions in Weak Investor Protection Countries: A Natural Experiment from China' (2013) 88(4) *The Accounting Review* 1211.

active level of involvement in corporate governance[120] to promote private enforcement. It is undeniable that there are means other than derivative action for institutional shareholders to monitor and evaluate directors' performance, ranging from the threat of diverting their shares, to the active use of their voting power in board elections and proxy contest.[121] They are becoming increasingly active in governing their portfolio companies;[122] this is particularly the case for securities investment funds. In particular, the existing literature seems to suggest that in general they prefer behind-the-scenes private engagements such as voting;[123] presenting proposals at shareholders' meetings and ongoing dialogues in public, activist engagements and courtroom confrontations are regarded as the very last resort.[124] Our empirical research specifically identified some characteristics of institutional investors' derivative action. As discussed above, since the implementation of the Chinese Company Law 2005 till end of 2020, 466 cases have been accepted by the People's Court when shareholder(s) brought derivative actions either individually or collectively. Among these derivative action cases we identified, there were 160 in which institutional shareholders acted as claimants. We further found that only 39 out of these 160 cases were allowed (including those that were fully or partly accepted), while the rest were rejected for reasons such as shareholders failing to make a request to the supervisor first (*Hunan Xianchu, Nantong Hengxiang, UNISON, Pumuyuan*), alleging both direct action and derivative action in one case (*Chongqing Li Hao*), claimants with conflicts of interests (*Yiwu Harvest, Pumuyuan and UNISON*), directors acting within the authorisation specified by the articles of association (*Yiwu Harvest; Siyang*), directors fulfilling their duty of care (*Siyang*), or failing to prove damages (*Pinghai, Nantong East*

---

[120] B. Gong, 'The Limits of Institutional Shareholder Activism in China and the United Kingdom: Some Comparisons' in R. Tomasic (ed.) *Routledge Handbook of Corporate Law*, (London: Routledge 2017)163.

[121] W. Wu, S.A. Johan and O.M. Rui, 'Institutional Investors, Political Connections, and the Incidence of Regulatory Enforcement Against Corporate Fraud' (2016) 134(4) *Journal of Business Ethics* 709, 712.

[122] C. Xi, 'Institutional Shareholder Activism in China: Law and Practice (Part 1)' (2006) 17 *International Company and Commercial Law Review* 251, 251.

[123] Y. Zeng, Q. Yuan and J. Zhang, 'Dark Side of Institutional Shareholder Activism in Emerging Markets: Evidence from China's Split Share Structure Reform' (2011) 40(2) *Asia–Pacific Journal of Financial Studies* 240, 259.

[124] C. Xi, 'Institutional Shareholder Activism in China: Law and Practice (Part 1)' (2006) 17(10) *International Company and Commercial Law Review* 251,253; see also S. Estrin and M. Prevezer, 'The Role of Informal Institutions in Corporate Governance: Brazil, Russia, India, and China Compared' (2011) 28(1) *Asia Pacific Journal of Management* 41.

River). The status of derivative actions in China litigated by institutional share-holders is dominated in the following Figure 4.7.

■ Non-institutional investors' litigations

■ Institutional investors' litigations that have been allowed

■ Institutional investors' litigations that have been rejected

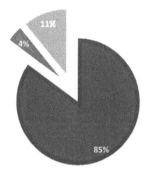

Figure 4.7   Status of institutional investors derivative action

Looking at the causes of these 19 actions, they include matters such as appropriating the company's funds (*Hunan Xianchu, Nantong Hengxiang, Nantong East River, Beijing YiJin, UNISON*), taking loans from the company (*Xinjiang WujiaquXinbao, Shanxi Pharmaceutical*), exclusion from man-agement (*UNISON, Nantong Hengxiang*), taking over the company stamp or financial accounts (*Chongqing Li Hao, Nantong Hengxiang, Shanghai Huayuan*), failing to pay capital contributions (*Pinghai, Pumuyuan*), failing to fulfil obligations under the shareholders' agreement (*Zhoushan Aviation*), undervalued transfers (*Siyang*) and unfair competition (*Beijing YiJin*). It is worth highlighting that most actions (with three exceptions) aimed to settle a deadlock between two shareholders or two 'camps' of shareholders, and the actions were usually brought by minority shareholders against majority share-holders or directors appointed by majority shareholders.[125]

It may also be observed that the derivative action mechanism has not been widely used for institutional shareholders to bring lawsuits against directors,

---

[125] One case was filed by the majority against a minority shareholder, where the majority was a foreign investor excluded from the management (*UNISON*); one case was filed by the majority shareholder against the director (*Siyang*); and the other case was filed by the supervisory board against the directors who allegedly have competed with the company and diverted the company's funds (*Beijing YiJin*).

supervisors or senior officers. The cases have all happened in LLCs where no shareholding period and percentage threshold are required.

The lack of cases and incentives for institutional shareholders to initiate derivative proceedings may be the result of various intuitional, legal and reputational constraints. For instance, constraints may rest on traditional Chinese culture, which did not encourage litigations, since the strong and deeply rooted system of conventional Confucian ethics declared that 'the most important thing was to avoid litigation' for the cultivation of personal virtue in promoting good and humane governance.[126] The reluctance of institutional shareholders to intervene may also be partly attributable to the regulatory threshold, with shareholding percentages and periods required for eligibility to bring derivative actions, as well as other legal constraints. Another important issue relates to the incentives for initiating such actions and the potential reputation costs related to this litigation. In the following section, we will address why derivative action should be further developed and encouraged on Chinese soil despite the existence of these constraints.

The first institutional constraint may rest on the belief that cultural values deeply affect the choices of dispute resolution means in Chinese society. The Confucian injunction to maintain long-term relationships between people and harmony with others may discourage litigations, with the law used as a vehicle for promulgating policies for the common good rather than resolving disputes among private parties.[127] Following this philosophy may undermine the use of shareholder litigation, like other litigations, to avoid conflicts and maintain Confucian virtues. Instead, the mediation of disputes would be encouraged.

However, contemporary arguments in the context of the economic and legal framework in China suggest a different trajectory. For example, the legalists believe that a nation's cohesion can be secured by the application of strict legislation, together with harsh and legitimate punishment.[128] Adopting strict laws has contributed substantially to social stability and the settlement of disputes in China.[129] With the emergence and development of the rule of law in China as a self-sustaining principle in line with the goals for market-led economic

---

[126] Confucius, Analects 12.13 and 13.3. see also L. Miles, 'The Application of Anglo-American Corporate Practices in Societies Influenced by Confucian Values' (2006) 111(3) *Business and Society Review* 305.

[127] H.W. Liu, 'An Analysis of Chinese Clan Rules: Confucian Theories in Action' in A.F. Wright, *Confucianism and Chinese Civilization* (Stanford: Stanford University Press) 16, 29–30.

[128] C. Wang and N.H. Madson, *Inside China's Legal System* (Oxford: CP Chandos Publishing 2013) 35.

[129] S. Lin, 'Private Enforcement of Chinese Company Law: Shareholder Litigation and Judicial Discretion' (2016) 4 *China Legal Science* 73, 80.

growth,[130] it is no longer unusual to resolve disputes through litigation in the current commercial and economic climate. As pointed out by Lin, there is an interaction between culture and derivative action, and the commercial culture promoted by Chinese recent economic development indicates that shareholders, especially institutional shareholders, would not hesitate to bring an action if it is necessary to do so.[131]

The second institutional constraint arguably rests on the inability of the underdeveloped judiciary system in China to accommodate the increasing volume of litigations. Issues such as overburdened court systems, limited judicial resources, judges' skills and knowledge[132] could all be potential worries and obstacles here. In fact, Chinese judges still lack experience and knowledge,[133] and many civil servants are known as judges and work in administrative roles.[134] Problems such as this lack of expertise and the absence of case law to help judges make decisions make derivative actions in China far from useful, compared with ordinary suits. These factors may discourage shareholders from bringing derivative actions.

Whilst acknowledging the judicial difficulties, it is also worth pointing out that China has been making considerable strides in building a more competent and professional judiciary with the enactment of Judge Law and the rigorous National Bar Exam[135] to gather the most talented people (*rencai*) for the legal profession.[136] Many improvements have been made including diminished local protectionism, increased professionalism and the improved enforcement of commercial cases, due to multiple factors such as the increasingly diversified

---

[130] D. Chen, S. Deakin, M. Siems and B. Wang, 'Law, Trust and Institutional Change in China: Evidence from Qualitative Fieldwork' (2017) 17(2) *Journal of Corporate Law Studies* 257, 287.

[131] S. Lin, *Derivative Actions in Chinese Company Law*, (Alphen ann den Rijin: Kluwer Law International 2015) 138–139.

[132] See T. Gong, 'Dependent Judiciary and Unaccountable Judges: Judicial Corruption in Contemporary China' (2004) 4(2) *China Review* 33; W. Gu, 'The Judiciary in Economic and Political Transformation: Quo Vadis Chinese Courts?' (2013) 1(2) *The Chinese Journal of Comparative Law* 303.

[133] J. Zhu (ed), *China Legal Development Report [*中国法律发展报告：数据库和指标体系*]* (Beijing: Renmin University Press 2007) 34.

[134] 'Legal Reform Judging Judges' *The Economist*, 24 September 2015.

[135] M. Jia, 'Chinese Common Law? Guiding Cases and Judicial Reform' (2016) 129(8) *Harvard Law Review* 2213, 2213–2214.

[136] J. Pan, 'On the Relationship between Undergraduate Legal Education and the Judicial Exam [论司法考试与大学本科法学教育的关系]' [2003] 21 *Law Review [*法学评论*]* 147; see also J. Huang, 'Cultivating High-quality Qualified and Talented People with Moral integrity and ability [培养德才兼备的高素质法治人才]' 2 September 2017, available at http://theory.people.com.cn/n1/2017/0809/c40531–29459887.html (accessed 23 July 2022).

economy, streamlined court procedures, the improved judicial system and adequate funding.[137] These positive aspects may encourage qualified shareholders in JSLCs to bring actions, giving them more confidence in the fairness of judgments and the efficiency of enforcement measures. If there is an increased number of derivative actions as the result of the proposed more relaxed 'unnecessary'[138] threshold in this chapter, it may be confidently claimed that 'there are sufficient judicial resources to deal with this increase in shareholder litigation', partly indicated by a healthy and comparatively higher ratio of one judge to every 48,000 people.[139] The attitude of the Chinese courts towards shareholder litigation has become increasingly friendly towards shareholders since the SPC issued its Second Circular to lift the restriction on accepting cases in 2002.[140]

Additionally, the guiding case system was introduced as a novel attempt to benefit from the advantages of both the common law and civil systems. The SPC has converted 92 judicial opinions into what are intended to be *de facto* binding decisions, which local courts at all levels may reference when making decisions on similar cases since January 2012.[141] This will potentially bring benefits by enhancing faith in the judiciary in China.[142] Although no cases have been converted to authoritative judicial opinions concerning derivative action, partly due to the shortage of cases involving JSLCs as the result of the high threshold and litigation fee, Chinese judges are practically accustomed to searching similar cases reported in *Beida Fabao* and 'China Judgements Online'[143] for reference before making judgments, which has been helpful in terms of ensuring judicial consistency in China.

One of the biggest legal constraints for shareholders, including institutional shareholders, in bringing derivative actions is the litigation fee.[144] The

---

[137] X. He, 'Rule of Law in China: Chinese law and Business: The Enforcement of Commercial Judgments in China' The Foundation for Law, Justice and Society in collaboration with The Centre for Socio-Legal Studies, University of Oxford (2008)

[138] S. Lin, *Derivative Actions in Chinese Company Law*, (Alphen ann den Rijin: Kluwer Law International 2015) 139.

[139] Ibid.

[140] R. H. Huang, 'Private Enforcement of Securities Law in China: Past, Present and Future' in R.H. Huang and N. C. Howson, *Enforcement of Corporate and Securities Law: China and the World*, (Cambridge: Cambridge University Press 2017) 138, 141.

[141] See The Supreme People's Court of China's Guiding cases; available at http://www.court.gov.cn/fabu–gengduo–77.html (accessed 23 July 2022).

[142] R. Li, 'Case-law Adopted by China?' available at https://ukconstitutionallaw.org/2012/01/26/ruiyi–li–case–law–adopted–by–china/ (accessed 23 July 2022).

[143] China Judgements Online [中国裁判文书网] http://wenshu.court.gov.cn/ (accessed 23 July 2022).

[144] J. Zhao, 'A More Efficient Derivative Action System in China: Challenges and Opportunities through Corporate Governance Theory' (2013) 64(2) *Northern Ireland Legal Quarterly* 233, 243.

legislative legal basis of the costs of derivative action in China rests on Civil Procedure Law 1992, Measures for the Administration of Attorneys' Fee 2006. The usual rule is that the losing party will be ordered by the court to pay the winning party's 'case acceptance fee', the fee charged by the court that tries the case, while each party pays its own attorney's fees and other expenses.[145] From September 2017, in order to make sure that litigation costs are tailored to a level that does not further discourage shareholders from bringing these actions so that the scheme can 'reach its full potential',[146] Provision IV were introduced to address the question of whether the claimant shareholder may be reimbursed for their expenses. It is stipulated that the courts should support the indemnity claims of shareholders who successfully bring a lawsuit on behalf of a company, allowing them to claim for attorneys' fees, investigation fees, assessment fees, notary fees and other reasonable costs incurred during the litigation.[147] Since the 'dearth of public company derivative suits can be mainly attributed to the restrictive standing requirement and the prohibitive litigation costs issues',[148] the most significant problem for derivative actions among JSLCs would be the shareholding percentage and period threshold if Article 26 of Provision IV can be effectively enforced in China. Furthermore, Huang made it clear through empirical study that the availability of 'the risk agency fee has facilitated the bringing of securities civil suits and has led to the emergence of many entrepreneurial lawyers in China'.[149] Referencing experience in the US,[150] the increase and popularity of entrepreneurial lawyers may also lead to an increase in derivative action in China with the enforcement of Provision IV, leaving the shareholding period and percentage as an unnecessary thresh-

---

[145] Art. 29, Measure on Payment of Litigation [诉讼费用交纳办法] 2007.

[146] H. Huang, 'The Statutory Derivative Action in China: Critical Analysis and Recommendations for Reform' (2007) 4(2) *Berkeley Business Law Journal* 227, 248.

[147] Art. 26, Provisions of the Supreme People's Court on Some Issues about the Application of the Company Law of the People's Republic of China (IV). [最高人民法院关于适用《中华人民共和国公司法》若干问题的规定（四）].

[148] H. Huang, 'Shareholder Derivative Litigation in China: Empirical Findings and Comparative Analysis' (2012) 27(4) *Banking and Finance Law Review* 619, 654.

[149] R.H. Huang, 'Private Enforcement of Securities Law in China: Past, Present and Future' in R.H. Huang and N. C. Howson, *Enforcement of Corporate and Securities Law: China and the World* (Cambridge: Cambridge University Press 2017) 138, 146.

[150] J.R. Macey and G.P. Miller, 'The Claimants' Attorney's Role in Class Action and Derivative Litigation: Economic Analysis and Recommendations for Reform' (1991) 58(1) *The University of Chicago Law Review* 3, 4; J.C. Coffee, 'The Regulation of Entrepreneurial Litigation: Balancing Fairness and Efficiency in the Large Class Action' (1987) 54(3) *University of Chicago* 887; M. Gilles and G.B. Friedman, 'Exploding the Class Action Agency Costs Myth: The Social Utility of Entrepreneurial Lawyers' (2006) 155(1) *University of Pennsylvania Law Review* 103.

old awaiting urgent attention to encourage eligible shareholders to resolve disputes through this mechanism.

The reputational constraint has also been referred to when discussing the inactivity of institutional investors. While private engagement approaches such as voting and resolutions normally target the misconduct or performance of the board of directors as a collective body, derivative actions involve a 'personal attack on specific directors'.[151] This may lead to a negative impact on the '*guanxi*' between the attacked directors and the institutional shareholders,[152] and may put companies' reputations at risk by sending a signal to the public that they have been poorly managed. As a result, some argued that intuitional shareholders may be cautious about using the derivative action mechanism as an activism strategy.[153]

However, one is tempted to argue that this may be an arbitrary conclusion without a detailed analysis of the compensation and deterrence functions of derivative action.[154] The procedural rule of demand surrounding derivative actions has been adopted to strike a balance between improving shareholder remedies and preventing vexatious suits, which is particularly relevant for public companies.[155] Shareholders are not entitled to file a lawsuit directly to the court to remedy alleged harm without first making a written demand to the (board of) directors or the (board of) supervisors.[156]

When assessing the importance and possibilities of continuing a claim the supervisor, the supervisory board, the board of directors or the executive director should consider issues such as the cost of the proceedings and potential damage to the company's reputation before making a decision as to whether or not to pursue actions in court. In other words, this procedural requirement is 'a nod to the principle of exhaustion of intra-corporate remedies',[157] emphasising that an opportunity should be given to the company before the intervention of the court because the company is the party that has suffered directly. If

---

[151] B. Gong, *Understanding Institutional Shareholder Activism: A Comparative Study of the UK and China*, (London: Routledge 2014) 164.

[152] A. Keay and J. Zhao, 'Accountability in Corporate Governance in China and the Impact of *Guanxi* as a Double-Edge Sword' (2017) 11(2) *Brooklyn Journal of Corporate, Financial & Commercial Law* 377.

[153] B. Gong, *Understanding Institutional Shareholder Activism: A Comparative Study of the UK and China*, (London: Routledge 2014) 165.

[154] See J.D. Cox, 'Compensation, Deterrence, and the Market as Boundaries for Derivative Suit Procedures' (1983) 52 *George Washing Law Review* 745.

[155] H. Huang, 'Shareholder Derivative Litigation in China: Empirical Findings and Comparative Analysis' (2012) 27(4) *Banking and Finance Law Review* 619, 652.

[156] Art. 151 Chinese Company Law 2018.

[157] S. Lin, *Derivative Actions in Chinese Company Law* (Alphen ann den Rijin: Kluwer Law International 2015) 114.

a company has other possible approaches to solve the problem, there is no need to resort to judicial resources if the wrong may be corrected by itself; this may also benefit the company.[158] The demand rule is helpful for companies and their shareholders to make sure that they initially exhaust internal remedies. Therefore, concerns for corporate reputation have been mitigated. Considering the screening process carried out by the director, the supervisor, the board of directors or the supervisory board, who have access to the resources of the company as well as information about the directors' conduct and decisions,[159] it is questionable to stipulate the shareholding percentage and period requirements at an exorbitantly harsh level.

Although the fundamental interests of shareholders, especially those of institutional shareholders, would be successful and profitable investments rather than becoming mired in litigation, it could be argued that shareholders' incentives to engage in litigation would likely increase with the dynamic cultural, judiciary, and legal framework transformation in China. With clarification of litigation fee-related issues through the Provision IV, the trajectory of the popularity of derivative actions may rise; this was the Japanese experience, another jurisdiction that was also influenced by cultural constraints such as Confucian philosophy, with fundamental change starting from the *Nikko Securities* case[160] decisions by the Tokyo High Court. This change in Japan came as an unexpected shock,[161] and this could also occur in China.

4.3   THE CASE OF ANONYMOUS SHAREHOLDERS

The issues of shareholders' eligibility are even more complicated in JSLCs because of the existence and power of anonymous shareholders. An anonymous shareholder will normally undertake investment liabilities and collect investment returns. Apart from registered shareholders, the existence of anonymous (undisclosed) shareholders has become a widespread phenomenon in

---

[158]   D.A. Demott, 'Shareholder Litigation in Australia and the United States: Common Problems, Uncommon Solutions' (1986) 11 *Sydney Law Review* 259, 262.

[159]   D.R. Fischel, 'The Demand and Standing Requirements in Stockholder Derivative Actions' (1976) 44 *University of Chicago Law Review* 168, 171.

[160]   *Asai v.Iwasaki, Tokyo District Court*, 797 Hanrei Times 382 (1992), rev'd, Tokyo High Court, 823 Hanrei Times 131 (1993).

[161]   T. Fujita, 'Transformation of the Management Liability Regime in Japan in the Wake of the 1993 Revision' in H. Kanda (ed.) *Transforming Corporate Governances in East Asia*, (London: Routledge 2008) 13, 17; see also M. Nakahigashi and D.W. Puchniak, 'Land of the Rising Derivative Action: Revisiting Irrationality to Understand Japan's Reluctant Shareholder Litigate' in D.W. Puchniak, H. Baum and M. Ewing-Chow (eds), *The Derivative Action in Asia: A Comparative and Functional Approach*, (Cambridge: Cambridge University Press 2012) 128.

China. Over the past three decades of the Chinese economic transformation, it has been normal for government officials and certain investors with sensitive identities to maintain anonymity when investing, in order to hide their wealth and avoid resentment or potential violation of Party rules.[162] Although some of these arrangements are for lawful purposes, such as the protection of privacy, they are generally regarded as grey areas used to overcome legal barriers, including the requirement that prohibits government officials from purchasing shares in certain business entities. A few characteristics are shared by all anonymous shareholders: first, these are actual investors who subscribe for shares in a company, but who are not recorded as such in official documents like the company's articles of association, the register of shareholders and business registration material; second, the purpose of such arrangements may be legitimate or illegitimate; and third, anonymous shareholders lack the formative requirement of being shareholders under current Chinese company law.

It is stipulated in Article 33 of Chinese Company Law 2018 that 'the shareholders on the register of shareholders may claim and exercise shareholders' rights on the basis of the register of shareholders'. This implies that the shareholders' rights only become valid after official registration. It is further stipulated in Article 32 that if there 'is a change in the registered items, change registration shall be carried out. Anyone that fails to complete registration or change registration may not resist the claims of a third person'.[163] This provision is designed to protect innocent third parties and refute the identity of anonymous shareholders in order to maintain transaction safety and sustainable economic ordering. It is further required under Chinese Company Law 2018 that the articles of association of LLC companies shall disclose information including 'the name and domiciles of the shareholders',[164] and 'shareholders shall sign and affix their seals on the company's articles of association',[165] ostensibly suggesting that the identities of all shareholders shall be disclosed.[166] The anonymity of some shareholders gives rise to potential legal violations that generate practical problems for registered companies, and third parties such as creditors.[167]

---

[162] J. Wang, *Company Law in China: Regulation of Business Organizations in a Socialist Market Economy*, (Cheltenham: Edward Elgar 2014) 138–139.

[163] Art. 32, Chinese Company Law 2018.

[164] Art. 25(4) Chinese Company Law 2018.

[165] Art. 25 Chinese Company Law 2018.

[166] J. Wang, *Company Law in China: Regulation of Business Organizations in a Socialist Market Economy*, (Cheltenham: Edward Elgar 2014) 139.

[167] L. Gu, 'Legal Problems of Anonymous Shareholder of Limited Liability Companies有限责任公司隐名股东法律问题研究' [2011] 36 *Legal System and Society [法制与社会]* 97, 97–98.

Appreciating the existence of anonymous shareholders, the Supreme People's Court of China provides guidance concerning their investor identities in the Company Law Interpretation III of 5 December 2010, stipulating that the courts should uphold the validity of the contract between an actual investor and a nominal investor in a LLC.[168] The courts should also support the actual investor against the nominal investor if the actual investor has performed his or her capital contribution obligation, if a dispute arises between them over the vesting of the investment rights and interests.[169] This judicial interpretation confirms the validity of the legal status of anonymous shareholders based on the freedom of contract:[170] the arrangement between a nominal and an actual investor should be treated as a binding one that is legitimate internally between the two parties.[171] In the meantime, the doctrine of privity of contract[172] indicates that this internal arrangement between these two investors cannot have a legal impact on a third party. Shareholders' rights, including the right to bring a derivative action, may still have to be legitimately exercised by nominal shareholders before the title could be legally transferred to actual investors.[173] A negative answer thus becomes inevitable to the question of whether an anonymous shareholder (whose name does not appear on the companies' register of shareholders) could exercise the right to sue on behalf of the company in a derivative action based on the wrongdoer being in control, on basis of traditional contract law principles: the contract between the actual and nominal shareholders is an internal one which does not have a legal impact on third parties; the derivative action is an action brought on behalf of the

---

[168] Art. 25(1), Provisions of the Supreme People's Court on Some Issues about the Application of the Company Law of the People's Republic of China (III).

[169] Art. 25(2), Provisions of the Supreme People's Court on Some Issues about the Application of the Company Law of the People's Republic of China (III).

[170] See S. Williston, 'Freedom of Contract' (1920) 6 *The Cornell Law Quarterly* 365; P.S. Atiyah, *The Rise and Fall of Freedom of Contract*, (Oxford, Oxford University Press 1985); L.A. Bebchuk, 'Limiting Contractual Freedom in Corporate Law: The Desirable Constrains on Charter Amendments' (1989) 102(8) *Harvard Law Review* 1820.

[171] X. Hua, 'Validation of Anonymous Shareholders' Identity in Limited Liability Companies' (2008) 99 *Journal of Gansu Institute of Optical Science and Law* 115, 116–117.

[172] The principle provides that a contract cannot confer rights or impose obligations arising under it on any person or agent except the parties to it; see *Tweddle v Atkinson* (1831) 1 B&S 393; *Dunlop Pneumatic Tyre Co. Ltd. v Selfridges & Co. Ltd.* [1915] AC 847; *Beswick v Beswick* [1968] AC 58.

[173] Civil Division II Supreme People's Court, *Understanding and Application of Provisions of the Supreme People's Court on Some Issues about the Application of the Company Law of the People's Republic of China*, Beijing: The People's Court (2011) 371.

company against the controlling parties of the company, primarily managing directors or supervisors; and the company, directors and supervisors are all regarded as third parties in the contractual relationship between the nominal and actual investors.

However, a consideration given to international practices in the field suggests that a one-size-fits-all approach to deny the right of anonymous shareholders to bring derivative action might be too arbitrary, considering the application of law, commercial practice, and the harmonisation of law and taking into account the international integration of financial markets in China. Looking at the US Model Business Corporation Act, shareholders entitled to bring derivative proceedings are clearly defined as those who 'include[s] a beneficial owner whose shares are held in a voting trust or held by a nominee on the beneficial owner's behalf'.[174] In terms of state law, it is stated in the California Corporation Code that 'the plaintiff alleges in the complaint that the plaintiff was a shareholder, of record or beneficially, or the holder of voting trust certificates at the time of the transaction'.[175] New York state law states that a derivative action may be brought 'by a holder of shares or of voting trust certificates of the corporation or of a beneficial interest in such shares or certificates'.[176] Likewise, there are also challenges to the traditional privity of contract doctrine in other common law jurisdictions, when it comes to anonymous shareholders' right to bring a derivative action. In a Cayman Court of Appeal case *Schultz v Reynolds*,[177] it was held that a beneficial owner may not bring a derivative action due to the fact that the company was not obliged to recognise the existence of the trust over its shareholders.[178] In another Cayman case, *Svanstrom v Jonasson,*[179] the court gave a negative answer to the question of whether the unregistered shareholders could bring a derivative action on

---

[174] § 7.40. Sub-chapter Definitions (2), US Model Business Corporation Act 2002. However, there has not been a consensus on the opinion on eligibility of anonymous shareholders globally. Japanese law, e.g., only allows such actions to be brought by registered shareholders. See *Batchelder v Kawamoto*, 147 F.3d 915 (9th Cir. 1998) in which it is held that based on a clause in the agreement, Japanese law must apply to shareholder action, and such action can also only be brought by registered shareholders in Japan. This requirement is also followed by ten states in the US. For a discussion and list of the ten states see J. Coffee and D.E. Schwartz, 'The Survival of the Derivative Suit: An Evolution and a Proposal for Legislative Reform' (1981) 81 *Columbia Law Review* 261, 311.

[175] Section 800 (b) (1), California Corporation Code.

[176] Section 626 (a), New York Business Corporation Law.

[177] *Schultz v Reynolds* [1992] 3 CIL 59.

[178] Ibid., at 64; see also T. Lowe, 'Vindicating Shareholder Rights under Nominee and Custodian Agreements' (2015) 30 *Butterworths Journal of International Banking and Financial Law* 331.

[179] *Svanstrom v Jonasson* [1977] CILR 19.

behalf of the company, referring to the judgment in *Schultz* as the strongest authority.[180] In the English law case *Jafari-Fini v Skillglass*,[181] it was claimed that the term 'member' should include 'beneficial owner with standing to bring such action', i.e., to file a derivative action,[182] and 'to deny the beneficial owner the standing to bring a derivative action may frustrate at least the efficient and expeditious bringing of the company's grievance to court'.[183] The Court of Appeal dismissed the appeal and it was held that the judge identified the point on beneficial owners correctly.[184]

A more flexible approach was proposed in a recent case in the Court of Appeal of the Supreme Court of Queensland, *Zabusky v Virgtel*, in the hope of offering a test for each case, to better reflect the diverse interests of anonymous shareholders.[185] The test adopted a rule that would 'take account of the circumstance that a derivative action is exceptional and should not be allowed to proceed unless the plaintiffs demonstrate in their pleading, perhaps supported by affidavit, that the suit is a proper one'. That means that more incomplete proofs, compared with the register, would be regarded as undeniable proofs for the title of beneficial owners, who would therefore be allowed to bring a derivative suit.

While the flexible approach drawn from *Zabusky* has merit, it does not seem to be the proper way forward for China as a civil law country since it will be extremely difficult for Chinese judges to apply a test at the level of each individual case due to the legal system itself and the qualification of judges.[186] Judges would find it extremely difficult to adopt a flexible approach in civil law contexts and maintain the essential judicial consistency, if the written law is inadequate and further interpretations are needed depending on each individual scenario.[187] Adopting this approach is pragmatically thorny, and it may be simply too demanding for Chinese judges and make the legal principles in the area even more complicated and unclear.

---

[180] T. Lowe, 'Vindicating Shareholder Rights under Nominee and Custodian Agreements' (2015) 30 *Butterworths Journal of International Banking and Financial Law* 331, 331.

[181] *Jafari-Fini v Skillglass* [2004] EWHC 3353 (Ch) 2004 WL 3520124.

[182] Ibid., at para. 22.

[183] Ibid., at para. 42.

[184] *Jafari-Fini v Skillglass* [2005] EWCA Civ 356; [2005] B.C.C. 842 para. 38.

[185] *Zabusky v Virgtel* [2012] QCA 107.

[186] Y. Zang, 'The Quality of Training of Judges in the Context of Comprehensive Rule by Law in China[全面依法治国背景下法官素质的培养]' [2015] 10 *Legal System and Society [法制与社会]* 239.

[187] J. Dainow, 'The Civil Law and the Common Law: Some Points of Comparison' (1967) 15(3) *American Journal of Comparative Law* 419, 433.

Because current Chinese legislation does not explicitly allow anonymous shareholders to bring derivative actions or prohibit them from doing so, many anonymous shareholders may have 'wasted' their legislative rights in protecting their and the company's interests. It would be very useful for Chinese Company Law to adopt and accommodate the term of 'beneficial owner', not only for the legal identity of anonymous shareholders but also for their eligibility to bring derivative suits. After adopting the notion of 'beneficial owner', it may be the way forward for Chinese law to reference the English approach to make the law on the eligibility of anonymous shareholders clear, clean, efficient and, from an international perspective, compatible with international practice. It would be clear that anonymous shareholders should not be banned from bringing derivative suits since they do fairly and adequately represent the interests of the shareholders, in the same way that is positioned in enforcing shareholders' right according to the contract between shareholders and the company, namely the article association. This also fits into practice when it was discussed, as early as 1981, that the exclusion of beneficial holders in bringing derivative actions seems 'pointless and inconsistent with contemporary commercial practice' since securities are increasingly held in 'street names' for customers according to proxy rules, not to mention the added judicial complications in China.[188] Furthermore, it would be unfair and illogical for courts in China to deny the suitability of the beneficiary owner (the shareholder) if nominal shareholders fail to take action when moral hazards against the beneficiary take place.

4.4   THE CASE OF HOLDERS OF STATE SHARES (*GUOJIA GU*) AND FOREIGN CAPITAL SHARES (*WAIZI GU*)

Another issue that is common and in need of clarification in China is the case of owners of state shares and foreign capital shares. This unique situation is due to two facts: first, China has gone through a major reform with a focus on the privatisation of SOEs, as a tool to depoliticise SOEs and provide incentives

---

[188]   J. Coffee and D.E. Schwartz, 'The Survival of the Derivative Suit: An Evolution and a Proposal for Legislative Reform' (1981) 81 *Columbia Law Review* 261, 331; see also L. Zhu, 'Concerns of Chinese Lawyers: Stock ownership Issues to be Clarified' *21st Century Economic Report*, 22 November 2014, available http://m.21jingji.com/article/20141122/2a8d50ba9c069c6c0c43710b282fa357.html (accessed 24 July 2022); Y. Zhang, 'On Legal Issues Concerning China's Securities Lending and Borrowing' (2012) 9 *Shanghai Finance* 9.

for economic restructuring since 1980.[189] This has involved action to 'Separate Government Functions from Enterprise Management' (*zhengqifengkai*政企分开) and 'Separate Government Functions from Corporate Financing' (*zhenzifengkai*政资分开), on the assumption that administrative power hinders the efficiency of corporate governance in terms of timescale and the strategic direction of the decision-making process. The most direct method of corporatisation was the split-share structure, a legacy of China's initial share issue privatisation that granted legitimate trading rights over the state-owned shares of listed SOEs.[190] State shares are regarded as a 'special phenomenon' that occurs in conjunction with the disappearance of SOEs.[191] In response to this economic reform, the composition of shareholders became diversified to include artificial bodies, including central government agencies, local government and authorised institutions, who hold shares on behalf of the state. These shares are generally categorised into three classes: those which originally were the net assets of SOEs and subsequently have been converted into shares of JSLCs via processes of privatisation; shares which were originally issued by companies and later bought by central or local government departments to invest on behalf of the state; and shares originally issued by companies and bought by investment companies, asset management companies and economic entities

---

[189] J. Kornai, *The Socialist System: The Political Economy of Communism*, (New York: Oxford University Press) 67–70; it is discussed that from 1950 to 1984, companies in China were established and classified as traditional SOEs in which the state wholly owns the companies and the government exerts management control over them; see C.A. Schipani and J. Liu, 'Corporate Governance in China: Then and Now' (2002) *Columbia Business Law Review* 1, 5.

[190] L. Liao, B. Liu and H. Wang, 'China's Secondary Privatization: Perspectives from the Split-Share Structure Reform' (2014) 113(3) *Journal of Financial Economics* 500,500; based on empirical research conducted by Du and Liu, the number of fully SOEs decreased sharply from 34,078 in 1998 to 5,755 in 2008: see J. Du and X. Liu, 'Selection, Stating, and Sequencing in the Recent Chinese Privatization' (2015) 58(3) *Journal of Law and Economics* 657.

[191] L. Fang, 'China's Corporatization Experiment' (1995) 5(2) *Duke Journal of Comparative & International Law* 149, 202–203; see also C. Guo, L. Yu and C. Ke, 'Understanding the Chinese Stock Market' (2007) 18(6) *Journal of Corporate Accounting & Finance* 13; C. Shi, *Political Determinants of Corporates Governances in China* (Abingdon: Routledge 2012) 130–139; J. Hassard, J. Sheehan, M. Zhou, J. Terpstra-Tong and J. Morris, *China's State Enterprise Reform: From Marx to the Market*, (London: Routledge 2007) see pp. 1–82; E. Xu and H. Zhang, 'The Impact of State Shares on Corporate Innovation Strategy and Performance in China' (2008) 25(3) *Asia Pacific Journal of Management* 473; H. Liang, B. Ren and S.L. Sun, 'An Anatomy of State Control in Globalisation of State-owned Enterprise' (2015) 46(2) *Journal of International Business Studies* 223.

authorised to make investments on behalf of the state.[192] In terms of the eligibility to bring a derivative action, it may be confusing as to how the state, as a shareholder, could do this. It needs to be clarified that via the corporatisation of SOEs that commenced in 1979 and restarted in 2014[193] and through the legal and political governance of SOEs,[194] the holders of state shares are now trading on exchanges and holding shareholders in the form of legal persons. Therefore, it is logical to say that the holders of state shares, just like institutional shareholders, should have the right to bring derivative actions. However, they are bringing actions as the legal person who owns state shares, not as the state.

Second, in response to the accession to the WTO, since 2012 the purchase of state shares and legal person shares has been possible for foreign investors.[195] Furthermore, Qualified Foreign Institutional Investors (QFIIs)[196] were also allowed to have limited holdings of individual A-shares.[197] Foreign capital shares are officially termed 'domestically listed foreign capital shares (*Jingnei Shangshi Waizi Gu*)' or B-shares. These are shares in Chinese listed companies, listed on the Shenzhen Stock Exchange, issued to foreign shareholders

---

[192]   See L. Fang, 'China's Corporatization Experiment' (1995) 5(2) *Duke Journal of Comparative & International Law* 149, 203; see also The State Asset Bureau, 'Interim Measures for Administering the Rights of State Shares in Joint Stock Limited Liability Companies (股份有限公司国有股权管理暂行办法*Gufen youxian gongsi guoyou guquan guanli zanxing banfa*)' November 3, 1994 State-owned Assets Supervision and Administration Commission of the State Council, available at http://www.flyzzx.com/article/73739.html (accessed 29 July 2022).

[193]   See L. Liao, B. Liu and H. Wang, 'China's Secondary Privatization: Perspectives from the Split-Share Structure Reform' (2014) 113(3) *Journal of Financial Economics* 500.

[194]   J. Wang, 'The Political Logic of Corporate Governance in China's State-owned Enterprises' (2014) 47(3) *Cornell Internal Law Journal* 631, 648–657.

[195]   See CSRC and Ministry of Foreign Trade and Economic Cooperation, 'Some Opinions Concerning Foreign Investment in Listed Companies [关于上市公司涉及外商投资有关问题的若干意见]' in November 2001; CSRC, 'Circular on the Transfer of State Shares and Legal Person Shares to Foreign Investors [关于向外商转让上市公司国有股和法人股有关问题的通知]' in November 2002, and Ministry of Finance and State Commission on Economy and Trade, 'Interim Provisions on Introducing Foreign Investment to Reorganize State-Owned Enterprises[利用外资改组国有企业暂行规定]' in November 2002; see also J. Wang, 'Dancing with Wolves: Regulation and Deregulation of Foreign Investment in China's Stock Market' (2004) 5(1) *Asian–Pacific Law and Policy Journal* 1, 22–29.

[196]   See D. Jin, H Wang, P. Wang and D. Yin, 'Social Trust and Foreign Ownership: Evidence from Qualified Foreign Institutional Investors in China' (2016) 23(C)(1) *Journal of Financial Stability* 1.

[197]   Based on the Article QFII Rule Article 18, this needs to be approved by the CSRC, and the investment amount must not exceed the quota granted by the State Administration of the Foreign Exchange.

and denominated in Chinese Renminbi but sold in US Dollars on the Shanghai Stock Exchange and in Hong Kong Dollars on the Shenzhen Stock Exchange respectively. To encourage more foreign investors to invest in China, a collective of rights should be offered to foreign shareholders. Understanding of the nature of the share is universal; a share does not confer on its owner a right to the physical procession of anything, but only confers a number of rights against the company.[198] These rights obviously include the right to file a lawsuit on behalf of the company when necessary to achieve a variety of benefits and remedies, including their own. Affording foreign shareholders the eligibility to bring derivative action also indicates the fair treatment of foreign shareholders, compared with domestic shareholders in light of the globalisation of corporate governance in China; this will also attract international investors and make China into an attractive place for investment, which was one of the goals of the company law reform to ensure sustained and increasing integration in the world economy.[199]

4.5 SHAREHOLDING PERIOD REQUIREMENT

Apart from the shareholding ownership percentage requirement, shareholders in JSLCs are also required to hold their shares for more than 180 consecutive days to be qualified as claimants for derivative action.[200] This 180-day rule was further clarified by the SPC in 2006, stating that 'the shareholding period of at least 180 days in succession specified in Article 151 of the Company Law shall have elapsed by the time the shareholder(s) institute(s) a suit in the people's court'.[201] This means the criteria of the shareholder must have held 1 per cent of the shares at the time the action is initiated. The Chinese Company Law does not require that the shareholders bringing the action must have been shareholders at the time the cause of action arose, and the US-origin 'contemporary

---

[198] See s. 541 of UK CA 2006.

[199] See X. Zhang, 'Company Law Reform in China' in J. Garrick, *Law and Policy for China's Market Socialism* (London: Routledge 2012) 39; this becoming particularly important with the growth of foreign direct investment in China that increased from US\$ 74.8 billion to US\$ 119.6 billion in 2014, see Ministry of Commerce, 'Characters of Utilisation of Foreign Capital in China in 2014: Improving Steady and Reasonably Structured [2014年我国利用外资规模稳中有进,结构更趋合理]15 January 2015, http://www.mofcom.gov.cn/article/ae/ai/201501/20150100868311.shtml (accessed 24 July 2022).

[200] Art. 151, Chinese Company Law 2018.

[201] Art. 4 'Supreme People's Court Regulations on the Application of Company Law of the People's Republic of China 2006: First Volume'.

ownership rule'[202] was rejected. These requirements are very similar to those embedded in the old Japanese Commercial Code.[203] The provision is retained with an additional urgency requirement in the New Japanese Commercial Law, as an exception to bring derivative actions in urgent circumstances where failure to bring such a suit immediately could result in irreparable damage to the company's interests.[204] Chinese Company Law transplanted this Japanese approach. Additionally, it is the duty of a party to an action to provide evidence in support of his allegations according to Chinese Civil Procedure Law.[205] Thus, it is the duty of the claimant, namely the shareholder(s), to provide that he, she or they have held their shares uninterrupted for 180 consecutive days. This does not come as a surprise, given the fact that to a certain extent China's company law framework was modelled on that of its civil law neighbour countries and regions.

In terms of the function of the shareholding period requirement and its exceptions, Hong and Goo hold a double-edged view and describe these as requirements that are 'really helpful to deter unmeritorious suits given the heavy caseload in Chinese courts' from a positive side, but from the negative side they could 'cause further loss to the company because the plaintiff shareholders have to wait for six months to bring the action without any exceptions'.[206] They also think this transplant is 'disappointing due to the ineffectiveness and problems of the Japanese approach',[207] and the equivalent of the six-month shareholding period requirement in Japan has been criticised for its arbitrariness.[208]

The shareholding period requirement was introduced to avoid malicious litigation and unnecessary distractions for directors, supervisors and senior managers in dealing with claims. It will avoid shareholders purchasing shares to bring litigation. It will also mitigate the risk that claimants may abuse derivative actions to threaten the plaintiff for shareholders' own personal interests and illegitimate purposes. The emphasis here is on the length of the shareholding period, which has advantages in the clarity and convenience in

---

[202] *Hawes v City of Oakland*, 104 U.S. 450 (1881); see also Delaware General Corporation Law, s. 327.

[203] Art. 267 Japanese Commercial Code 1950 (continuous ownership of six months).

[204] Art. 847(5) Japanese Commercial Code amended 1993.

[205] Art. 64 Civil Procedure Law of the People's Republic of China 1991.

[206] F.X. Hong and S.H. Goo, 'Derivative Action in China: Problems and Prospectus' (2009) 4 *Journal of Business Law* 376, 388.

[207] Ibid.

[208] M.D. West, 'The Pricing of Shareholder Derivative Actions in Japan and the United States' (1994) 88 *Northwest University Law Review* 1436, 1447; see also S. Kawashima and S. Sakurai, 'Shareholder Derivative Litigation in Japan: Law, Practice, and Suggested Reforms' (1997) 33(1) *Stanford Journal of International Law* 9.

the application. However, it is a shame that there is no linkage between the shareholding period requirement and the timing of the directors' infringement. This may contradict the purpose of imposing a shareholding period requirement in terms of avoiding people buying shares to bring a suit. Commentators have therefore suggested transplanting the US contemporary ownership model to remedy this defect.[209]

As mentioned at the beginning of this section, the contemporary ownership rule was rejected in the revised Chinese company law enforced in 2006. The reasons for the rejection, according to the explanation of the highest court on 10 May 2006, are as follows. First, the complexity of corporate misconduct and difficulties in defining the start date of directors' infringements make it very costly for courts to apply the model in practice. Second, the mechanism should be compatible with corporations' institutional development and judicial understanding of the derivative action system as a shareholder remedy with an accumulation of cases. It was argued that the underdevelopment of derivative action makes stringent restrictions on such actions unnecessary, and a positive attitude should be adopted so that the mechanism may be conducted in a way that improves corporate governance and promotes shareholders' awareness of executing their rights.[210] However, after 11 years of enforcement, the number of cases involving JSLCs is rather disappointing and the application of the mechanism in LLCs has built experience in applying and referencing the tool in practice. Therefore, this may be a good opportunity to reconsider the feasibility and merits of adopting the rule.

The contemporary ownership model requires that the demanding party was a shareholder at the time the cause of action arose. It may function as a more shareholder-friendly threshold than the 180 uninterrupted days, and deals with issues such as impracticability and the unreasonable length of time for individual shareholders. The requirement could be applied in the courts for the 'prevention of strike suits and speculative litigation'.[211] On the other hand, the rule has also been criticised[212] for being unfair to shareholders who detect directors' misconduct giving rise to a lawsuit only after becoming

---

[209] N. Chen, *Research on Derivative Action* [派生诉讼制度研究], (Beijing: Intellectual Property Publishing 2013) 150–151.

[210] Press Conference on 'Provisions on Several Issues Concerning the Application of Company Law (I)' and the Explanation of the Principal of Civil Second Chamber of SPC, available at http://www.lawinfochina.com/display.aspx?lib=law&id=23812 (accessed 29 July 2022).

[211] J.D. Cox and T.L. Hazen, *Corporations*, (New York: Aspen Publisher, 2nd ed. 2003) 425–428.

[212] This argument is similar to Liu's criticism of the 180-day shareholder period threshold, which will be explored in the next paragraph.

shareholders.[213] However, linking the committing of the alleged wrong to share ownership seems more shareholder-friendly than the 180 days, while both mechanisms may not only avoid malicious litigation but also ensure that the plaintiff has sufficient self-interest in the outcome of the litigation to conduct a truly adversarial proceeding.[214] The change is consistent with the purpose of removing legal procedural hurdles and building an investor-friendly and enabling shareholder lawsuit system to protect 'its numerous unsophisticated public investors effectively'.[215]

From a practical point of view, this standard of 180 days, together with thresholds on shareholding ownership, may seriously hinder the initiation of derivative suits in JSLCs. The duration requirement hinders shareholders from using the mechanism 'in time' to stop the misconduct of directors and protect the interests of the company. Shareholders have to wait until the 180th day before they bring a lawsuit, even if they are convinced that the director has breached their duties. Liu discussed the irrationality of the shareholding period requirement in a hypothetical scenario. A shareholder purchases shares on the first day and detects evidence of the directors' misbehaviour on the second day.[216] Even if the shareholder holds more than 1 per cent of the shares, they still need to 'wait for' 178 days before they can bring a derivative action. During this 178-day period, they may witness additional misconducts from the board and reductions in the share price.[217] However, what they are able to do in response to these misbehaviours is limited to encouraging the supervisory board or independent directors to start an investigation, encouraging eligible shareholders to bring lawsuits, or using mass media to put directors under pressure.[218] These approaches are only likely to be successful if those share-holders who are not eligible are influential, and the whole process can also be rather time-consuming, which may even take longer than 180 days. Lin further argued that these appeals may be ignored, and not all shareholders are able to access or use the media under such scenarios to put pressure on management.[219]

---

[213]   J. Deng, 'Building an Investor-Friendly Shareholders Derivative Lawsuit System in China' (2005) 46(2) *Harvard International Law Journal* 347, 376.

[214]   W. Fletcher, *Cyclopedia of the Law of Private Corporations* (Eagan, MN: Thomson/West 1908) Sections 5908 and 5981.

[215]   J. Deng, 'Building an Investor-Friendly Shareholders Derivative Lawsuit System in China' (2005) 46(2) *Harvard International Law Journal* 347, 351.

[216]   The example provided here might be rare or extreme in daily life. However, it is entirely possible.

[217]   J. Liu, *Modern Corporation Law* [现代公司法], (Beijing: Law Press, 3rd ed. 2015) 408–409.

[218]   Ibid.

[219]   S. Lin, *Derivative Action in Chines Company Law*, (Alphen ann den Rijin: Kluwer Law International 2015) 109–111.

Obviously, arguments of 'exit remedies' may also be relevant here. In addition to the discussions presented in section 4.2.7, the exit strategy would not solve the fundamental problems to do with shareholders recovering damages and deterring directors from misbehaviour. Besides, some shareholders may simply wish to stay with the company in which they hold shares for a number of reasons, such as their belief in the company's prospects in the long term, and the fact that 'exit remedies' contradict shareholders' intentions to invest in good faith, their willingness to engage in sustainable investment and their need to have their voices heard by challenging wrongdoers in order to hold them accountable.

In relation to the secondary sources and with reference to recent data, Li argued that the consecutive 180-day requirement would constitute a barrier for healthy derivative actions due to the quick turnover in China,[220] which was demonstrated by Jin's survey in which the average shareholding period in Chinese listed companies is four months.[221] Peng claimed that 180 days is too long for individual shareholders in JSLCs, especially for listed ones, since the majority of individual shareholders invest for the profit available by selling their shares rather than for claiming dividends.[222] She contended that the 'harsh' shareholding period threshold would not benefit the effectiveness of the derivative action mechanism at its very early stage in China.[223] It has been reported by the CSRC, taking the survey in 2015 as an example, that the average holding period is approximately 44 days for individual shareholders in listed companies.[224] Looking at data for the Shenzhen Stock Exchange only, in 2012 the average holding period was approximately 39.1 days for individual shareholders in listed companies.[225] From these two sets of data, the 180-day requirement apparently excludes the majority of the individual shareholders in

---

[220] X. Li, *Shareholder's Derivative Action from the Company Law Perspective: A Comparative Study of England, US, Germany and China [*公司法视角下的股东代表诉讼: 对英国, 美国, 德国和中国的比较研究*]*, (Beijing: Law Press 2009) 281.

[221] X. Jin, *Shareholding Structure and Corporate Governance in Chinese Listed Companies [*上市公司股权结构与公司治理*]*, (Beijing: China Finance Publishing House 2005).

[222] X. Peng, 'Study on China's Shareholder Derivative Action System [我国股东派生诉讼制度研究]' [2011] 5 *Hebei Law Science [*河北法学*]* 150, 151.

[223] Ibid.

[224] B. Zhu, 'CSRC Claimed that the Profit of Institutional Shareholders Increase with Shareholding Period [证监会就机构股东的持股时间的研究]', *Securities Daily*, 20 June 2016.

[225] X. Hu, 'Characteristic of Investors Structural and Behavioural Changes Shenzhen' Shows the Average Shareholding Period: Individual and Institutions Shareholders Own Their Shares for 190.3 days 39.1 Days Respectively 《深市投资者结构和行为变化特征》显示投资者平均持股: 个人39.1天 机构190.3天' *Securities Times [*证券时报*]* 8 May 2013.

listed companies. Therefore, the 180-day threshold creates an artificial barrier for individual shareholders.

Indeed, for individual shareholders, the investment incentives of a large proportion of shareholders have been shown to be short term and oriented by statistics. These investors, who have the goal of immediate returns, are normally ignorant about the details and strategies of the companies and vote with their feet.[226] With limited information and insufficient incentives, it is extremely unlikely that these short-term trading shareholders would bring a derivative lawsuit against boards of directors and challenge their decisions.[227] Furthermore, the concept of 'avoiding litigation' is deeply rooted in people's minds based on the belief of 'turning big problems into small ones and small problems into no problems at all'.[228] In a social relationship like this, people sometimes choose to tolerate problems even if their interests are jeopardised. Therefore, under the current investment and legal environment, it is very hard for individual Chinese shareholders to file a lawsuit for the interests of the company and other shareholders. Even if they could, there remains the problem of their incentive to do so.

However, even in light of the fact that minority shareholders are unlikely to bring a derivative action in China, the legislation itself should not put individual shareholders in an even more disadvantaged position by making it hard or impossible for individual shareholders to use the tool to question decisions of the board. Individual shareholders currently encounter particular difficulties when they seek redress against JSLCs. With limited information and incentives, the tool has only been used once in the last 11 years, but scandals such as Wanke and Geli demonstrated the strong necessity of shareholder litigation and supervision in listed companies in China; this is particularly important for those who are non-controlling shareholders.[229] At the same time, the lack of cases in JSLCs is partly due to the availability of information and difficulties in applying shareholder remedy mechanisms such as derivative action in practice. It is clear that the 'burden' of self-regulation, the investigatory power of the

---

[226] See X. Jia and R. Tomasic, *Corporate Governance and Resource Security in China: The Transformation of China's Global Resources Companies*, (Abington: Routledge 2010) 63.

[227] It is not just the case in China that small shareholders in listed companies are very unlikely to abuse the mechanism of derivative action, see R.B. Thompson and R.S. Thompson, 'The Public and Private Faces of Derivative Lawsuits' (2004) 57(5) *Vanderbilt Law Review* 1747, 1784–1785.

[228] 大事化小, 小事化无

[229] Z, Liu, 'If Baoneng could Successfully Remove the Directors of Wanke, Geli will Unfortunately Face the Same Destiny [若宝能罢免万科董事成功 格力也会遭遇同样命运]' available at http://finance.sina.com.cn/stock/s/2016–06–28/doc–ifxtmweh2639028.shtml (accessed 24 July 2022).

CSRC and indeed criminal and administrative law are insufficient to cope with fraud or mismanagement that may occur in JSLCs. A logical response here would thus be the necessity of proposing changes in the current company law in order to make derivative action more accessible for individual shareholders, focusing on less demanding shareholding period requirements for JSLCs.

With the emphasis on shareholder protection, especially on the lack of voice, information and bargaining power, derivative action, as a system for shareholder remedy, should be designed in an enabling rather than hindering manner, and should give access to shareholders who sincerely care about corporate performance and directors' decisions and behaviour. Derivative action is one of the most ingenious accountability mechanisms for larger formal organisations, and supervisors and accountees should include share-holders beyond powerful and well-informed ones. From the perspective of the sustainable development of derivative action in China, Wang argued that the shareholding period requirement should be abolished considering its very intermittent usage for shareholders in JSLCs after the enforcement of Chinese Company Law 2005.[230] He argued that a shorter or no shareholding period threshold would not only allow more shareholders to join the ranks to supervise directors, but also reaffirm shareholders in remedies, which is particularly important in China with its immature corporate governance and unbalanced structural shareholding ownership.[231] Reformers have made some agreements according to which a different timeframe should be introduced in listed companies and JSLCs, with three months for shareholders in non-listed JSLCs and an even shorter period for listed companies.[232] The reason for the different treatment rests on the incentives for investment. It is claimed that the investment purpose for minority shareholders in JSLCs, especially listed companies, is to make a profit through stock market transactions. They tend to stay in the market for shorter periods of time to get an immediate return on their investment. Although the authors agree with the reason for shortening the shareholding period requirement, the 'half-price' approach, proposing a three-month period instead of six months, seems random with little theoret-ical and empirical support. As discussed above, this standard seems arbitrary, and it is difficult to set an exact bar for the shareholding period. A shorter or abolished shareholding period regimen seems to be the way forward.

---

[230] G. Wang, 'Derivative Action Mechanism in China and Some Reform Proposals [试论我国股东派生诉讼制度及其完善]' (2015) available at http://www.66law.cn/lawarticle/12767.aspx (accessed 24 July 2022).

[231] Ibid.

[232] X. Wang, "Plaintiff Standing in Shareholder Derivative Actions [股东代表诉讼的原告资格问题] *People's Court Daily [人民法院报]* (28 January 2004), p. 4; avail-able at http://rdbk1.ynlib.cn:6251/Qk/Paper/248488 (accessed 29 July 2022).

A comparatively new legislative approach in Germany, a civil law country, may give us some insightful suggestions, considering that China drafted its corporate law in a hybrid manner, employing rules and institutions borrowed from Germany and the US.[233] The approach adopted in German corporate law in the new § 148 of the AktG in 2005 by the *Gesetz zur Unternehmensintegrität und Modernisierung des Anfechtungsrechts* in Germany sets the threshold for shareholders in JSLCs at only a shareholding percentage or quantity requirement for JSLCs (0.1 per cent shareholding percentage in China as proposed in Section 2 above), with no requirement in terms of the shareholding period.[234] In addition, if the legislators in China are convinced of this approach for Chinese JSLCs, the rule that requires the shareholders to have held the shares before they learned about the alleged breaches of duty or alleged damage from a publication should be also adopted to avoid malicious litigation, as justified in Section 3.[235]

4.6   EXPERIENCES FROM OTHER JURISDICTIONS

The imbalance in derivative actions between LLCs and JSLCs in China has not been evident in every jurisdiction. More well-adjusted figures in other jurisdictions could be regarded as the result of multiple factors. Therefore, the figures for derivative actions in public companies in other jurisdictions should not be exclusively regarded as the result of an absence of or lower shareholding period/percentage. However, considering the sharp difference in the figures between LLCs and JSLCs in China, the relatively high shareholding percentage requirement may have a causal link with the unpopular application of derivative action in JSLCs in China. In this section, factors such as mitigated thresholds through legal reforms, litigation costs and court permission as thresholds will be discussed in a few jurisdictions' context to offer the reader a more comprehensive view of the hurdles and incentives for initiating derivative actions. It is not feasible and not the theme of the chapter for the authors to illuminate every reason for the comparative popularity of this mechanism in

---

[233]   See J. Wang, *Company Law in China: Regulation of Business Organizations in a Socialist Market Economy*, (Cheltenham: Edward Elgar 2014) 26; see also M.M. Siems, 'Legal Origins: Reconciling Law and Finance and Comparative Law' (2007) 52(1) *McGill Law Journal* 55; T. Ruskola, 'Conceptualizing Corporations and Kinship: Comparative Law and Development Theory in a Chinese Perspective' (2000) 52(6) *Stanford Law Review* 1599.

[234]   It is required in § 148 (1) sentence 1 AktG that a shareholder or shareholders who together hold 1 per cent of the statutory capital or shares with a par value of EUR 100,000 may file a petition for the right to assert the claims of the company for damages mentioned in § 147(1) sentence 1 in their own name.

[235]   § 148 (1) 1 AktG.

other jurisdictions. The mechanism of derivative action is designed, in public companies, to work with securities markets, under conditions of media scrutiny and public enforcement to protect the interests of companies through the empowerment of shareholder voices.[236] If a jurisdiction chooses to introduce the mechanism, efforts should be made to make it work effectively in both LLCs and JSLCs.

In Korea, a shareholder requirement of 0.01 per cent is regarded as 'low enough' to ensure that derivative suits are feasible.[237] It has been reported that over half of the 55 derivative actions filed in Korea between 1997 and 2010 involved public companies.[238]

In common law countries, directors of public companies may be involved as defendants in derivative actions. Provisions for the creation and procedures of statutory derivative action have been enacted in these countries. Many reasons could contribute to the numbers of derivative action cases. In the US many cases involve public companies, based on the empirical research of Tompson and Thomas.[239] Derivative actions against listed firms have been regarded as a common issue historically, based on research on a sample of 535 public corporations.[240] The high percentage of settlement in the US due to the structure of indemnification rights and insurance coverage is another reason for the popularity of derivative suits in the US. Furthermore, derivative action in the US is argued as a lawyer-driven (litigation market-oriented) mechanism. They do not normally have any shares in the company, and therefore it is irra-

---

[236] K.B. Davies, 'The Forgotten Derivative Suit' (2008) 61(2) *Vanderbilt Law Review* 388, 450.

[237] B.S. Black, B.R Cheffins and M. Klausner, 'Shareholder Suits against Korea Directors' in H.J. Kim (ed.) *Korean Business Law*, (Cheltenham: Edward Elgar 2012) 27, 41.

[238] H.J. Rho and K.S. Kim, 'Invigorating Shareholder Derivative Actions in South Korea' in D.W. Puchniak, H. Baum and M. Ewing-Chow (eds), *The Derivative Action in Asia: A Comparative and Functional Approach* (Cambridge: Cambridge University Press 2012)186; internationally, 0.01 per cent is still considered a major impediment to derivative litigation – see K. Kim and M. Choi, 'Declining Relevance of Lawsuits on the Validity of Shareholder Resolution in Korea' in Tübingen:Mohr Siebeck; H. Fleischer, H. Kanda, K.S. Kim and P. Mülbert (eds), *German and Asian Perspectives on Company Law*, (Mohr Siebeck 2016) 218, 241.

[239] R. Thompson and R. Thomas, 'The Public and the Private Faces of Derivate Lawsuits' (2004) 57(5) *Vanderbilt Law Review* 1747; see *Caremark International Inc. Derivative Litigation*, 698 A.2d 959 (Del. Ch. 1996); *Re The Walt Disney Company Derivative Litigation*, 825 A.2d 275 (Del. Ch. 2003); *Re Oracle Corp. Derivative Litigation*, 824 A.2d 917 (Del. Ch. 2003); *Re The Walt Disney Company Derivative Litigation*, 906 A.2d. 27, 62–67 (Del. 2006).

[240] R. Romano, 'The Shareholder Suit: Litigation without Foundation?' (1991) 7(1) *Journal of Law, Economics, and Organization* 55.

tional to have lawyers initiating actions based on financial incentives.[241] The general rule in the US is that each party is responsible for his own attorney's fees. Irrespective of the result of the action, both parties bear their own legal costs under the US Rules of Civil Procedure.[242] Moreover, the *'contingency fee arrangement'* is regarded as common practice, where the fees are fixed at a percentage no higher than 30 per cent of the amount of the damages claimed as the result of a successful litigation.[243]

In the limited evidence from the UK, three cases, namely *Bridge v Daley*,[244] *Eckerle v Wickeder Westfalenstahl GmbH*[245] and *BNP Paribas SA v Open Joint Stock Company Russian Machines*,[246] have involved public companies. The relatively healthy ratio with public companies may also have a connection with many factors, such as litigation costs. The *'indemnity order'* established that a company should indemnify a shareholder defendant in a derivative suit since the shareholder acts on behalf of the company and the company is the direct beneficiary, even, in fact especially, where the litigation is ultimately unsuccessful.[247] The decision is reflected in the Civil Procedure Rules where the court has the power at a permission hearing to order the company to indemnify the successful shareholder in relation to his or her costs.[248] The cost of a proposed action is regarded, in the UK, as a practical hurdle and a major disincentive to launching a derivative action.[249] The Law Commission also asserted that the inclusion of the power to provide for an indemnity was a significant incentive to shareholders to initiate proceedings.[250] In Australia, four of the 31 concerned companies were publicly held companies during the

---

[241] J.C. Coffee, 'Rescuing the Private Attorney General: Why the Model of the Lawyer as Bounty Hunter is Not Working' (1983) 42 *Maryland Law Review* 215, 233; see also J.R. Macey and G.P. Miller, 'The Plaintiffs' Attorney's Role in Class Action and Derivative Litigation: Economic Analysis and Recommendations for Reform' (1991) 58(1) *The University of Chicago Law Review* 1, 45.

[242] See *Alyeska Pipeline Service Co. v. Wilderness Society*, 421 U.S. 240 (1975). See also 42 U.S.C. § 1988 (1982).

[243] Arts 11–13, Measures for the Administration of Attorneys' Fee 2006.

[244] *Bridge v Daley* [2015] EWHC 2121 (Ch).

[245] *Eckerle v Wickeder Westfalenstahl GmbH* [2013] 3 WLR 1316 [2014] BCC 1.

[246] *BNP Paribas SA v Open Joint Stock Company Russian Machines* [2011] EWHC 308 (Comm); in this case, the first defendant, Open Joint Stock Company Russian Machines, and the second defendant, Joint Stock Asset Management Company Ingosstrakh–Investments, are both Russian companies.

[247] *Wallersteiner v Moir (No. 2)* [1975] QB 373 AT 392.

[248] Civil Procedure Rules 19.9E.

[249] A. Dignam and J. Lowry, *Company Law*, (Oxford: Oxford Univeristy Press, 9th ed. 2016) 196–197.

[250] *Shareholder Remedies,* Consultation Paper No 142, 1996, para. 18.1.

period from March 2000 (the introduction of Part 2E1A) to 12 August 2005.[251] Again, many issues could be also involved here, including, for example, the broader range of applicants; former members and officers of the company are allowed to bring derivative proceedings as well as members.[252]

4.7   CONCLUSION

The mechanism of the derivative action is one of the most important legal tools, working side by side with statutory oppression remedies,[253] and it has been a staple of corporate law in most common law jurisdictions.[254] Overall, the Chinese Company Law 2005 introduced the derivative regime into China as a notable improvement to the previous version of company law, hoping that it would contribute to corporate governance and establish an investor-friendly legal and business environment.[255] However, this regime is far from perfect, and this chapter attempts to point out its inaccessibility by clarifying some thorny issues regarding the eligibility of shareholder claimants. The stand-

---

[251]   I.M Ramsay and B.B. Saunders, 'Litigation by Shareholders and Directors: An Empirical Study of the Australian Statutory Derivative Action' (2006) 6(2) *Journal of Corporate Law Studies* 396, 420.

[252]   Section 236 of the Australian Corporations Act 2001.

[253]   Art. 20, Chinese Company Law 2018. When the first company law was introduced in China in 1993 as a result of the economic reconstruction that placed the reform of SOEs at the top of the agenda, Western concepts were introduced including private ownership, the ownership of shares and the diversification of enterprise ownership; see O.K. Tam, *The Development of Corporate Governance in China*, (Cheltenham: Edward Elgar 1999) 1.

[254]   C. Hawes, 'The Chinese "Oppression" Remedy: Creative Interpretations of Company Law by Chinese Court' (2015) 63(3) *American Journal of Comparative Law* 559, 559; see, e.g., UK CA 2006, s. 994 (the wording of the UK oppression remedy was broadened, in the 1990s, to encompass unfair prejudice); B. Hannigan, 'Drawing Boundaries Between Derivative Claims and Unfairly Prejudicial Petitions' [2009] 6 *Journal of Business Law* 606; J. Payne, 'Shareholders' Remedies Reassessed' (2004) 67(3) *Modern Law Review* 500; J. Payne, 'Section 459–461 Companies Act 1985 in Flux: The Future of Shareholder Protection' (2005) 64(3) *Cambridge Law Journal* 647; H. McVea, 'Section 994 of the Companies Act 2006 and the Primacy of Contract' (2012) 75(6) *Modern Law Review* 11123; *Re CMB Holdings Ltd.; Hamilton v Brown* [2016] EWHC 191 (Ch); *Re Migration Solutions Holdings Ltd.* [2016] EWHC 523 (Ch); *Flanagan v Liontrust Investment Partners LLP* [2016] EWHC 446 (Ch); *Apex Global Management Ltd. v FI Call Lt* [2015] EWHC 3269 (Ch); *Re Charterhouse Capital Ltd.* [2015] EWCA Civ 536; [2015] BCC 574; [2015] 2 BCLC 627; *Graham v Every* [2014] EWCA Civ 191; [2014] BCC 376; [2015] 1 BCLC 41; *Re Coroin Ltd.* [2013] EWCA Civ 781; [2014] B.C.C. 14; [2013] 2 BCLC 583; *Baker v Potter* [2004] EWHC 1422 (Ch); [2005] B.C.C. 855.

[255]   J.V. Feinerman, 'New Hope for Corporate Governance in China?' (2007) 191 *The China Quarterly* 590.

ing requirements applying exclusively to JSLCs are, from our research, a double-edged sword as they deter meritorious litigation even as they also prevent vexatious suits. The most important element of the standing requirement is to locate an appropriate level that makes derivative action effective, applicable and functional. This differential treatment was based upon the consideration that the 'plight of minority shareholders in the limited liability company is generally graver than that of their counterparts in the joint stock limited liability company'.[256] After all, the derivative action scheme was originally introduced to be an effective weapon to deter misconduct among management personnel, rather than just being window dressing for JSLCs or a useful mechanism for LLCs alone.

Thus far the limited use of the mechanism in JSLCs requires us to reconsider the sense and appropriateness of this bar on the qualification of a claimant in JSLCs. Analyses reveal that most of the derivative lawsuits to date have involved private companies. In the meantime, it is hard for shareholders to invoke this action in JSLCs, especially in listed ones. While some doubt the willingness of institutional investors to initiate derivative action in JSLCs, our analysis has shown that conventional institutional, legal, and cultural barriers for institutional investors to actively engage in litigations are diminishing, and their incentives to engage in derivative action would likely increase in the future with the dynamic cultural, judiciary, and legal framework transformation in China. Our empirical analysis further discovered that the shareholding percentage threshold imposed by Article 151 of Chinese Company Law 2018 has been a big barrier in this regard, pragmatically and problematically excluding a large proportion of even the top ten shareholders. Modifications of the shareholding ownership percentage and the shareholding period in China are proposed with the aim of making the derivative action mechanism more effective, by making the threshold more rational and consistent considering the current securities market structure in China.[257]

A proposal of at least 0.1 per cent shareholding percentage and a revised or even abolished shareholding period requirement with a contemporary ownership rule is suggested in order to make derivative action in China more effective, and to ensure that the regime is utilised more systematically in JSLCs instead of being mere window dressing. The goals of this proposed enlarged provenance of shareholder claimants for derivative action are consistent with the initial legislative purpose of imposing thresholds for shareholders in JSLCs. The proposed changes to the qualification requirements will

---

[256] H. Huang, 'The Statutory Derivative Action in China: Critical Analysis and Recommendations for Reform' (2007) 4(2) *Berkeley Business Law Journal* 227, 237.

[257] Chapter 2 of G20/OECD, Principles of Corporate Governance 2015.

entitle and encourage more participation from shareholders to challenge and inspect directors' (mis)conducts and decisions, and they will be more likely to be responsible and act in a fiduciary manner.[258] As a result, the boards are expected to be more accountable to their companies. It is believed that these suggested reforms will not only promote the suitability and enabling character of Chinese Company Law, but also enhance corporate governance values such as fairness, accountability and effectiveness. The eligibility-related problems identified and discussed in this chapter are timely, important, and urgently need to be addressed by legislators in order to make derivative actions into a useful and functional mechanism for shareholders in JSLCs. The pragmatic impact of lowered thresholds would merit more empirical research, particularly if the reform suggestions in this chapter are adopted by the government.

Based on other jurisdictions' experiences and empirical analyses on the situation in China, one sees the goal of the proposed reform of derivative action as to maintain a suitable balance between improving shareholder remedies and preventing vexatious suits, particularly in relation to public companies.[259] A rational and balanced threshold (lower than current levels, as we will suggest in this chapter) will deter immoral malfeasance by directors and hold them accountable for corporate decisions. A more effective and enabling derivative action mechanism will also put less pressure on the CSRC, which uses its regulatory powers to facilitate the settling of compensation issues out of court through administrative sanctions.[260] Coupled with proposed changes in law, it might also be helpful to set up a 'China's Investor's Association' to provide investor education and support investor litigation, financed by a public fund to ensure its independence and impartiality, so that the shareholders in China will be better equipped with knowledge and information concerning how and why to bring such actions.[261]

---

[258] It needs to be reaffirmed that the authors agree that overly-relaxed *locus standi* requirements will generate malicious litigation and unnecessary distractions for the board and senior officers.

[259] H. Huang, 'Shareholder Derivative Litigation in China: Empirical Findings and Comparative Analysis' (2012) 27(4) *Banking and Finance Law Review* 619, 652.

[260] See R.H. Huang, 'Rethinking the Relationship between Public Regulation and Private Litigation: Evidence from Securities Class Action in China' (2018) 19(1) *Theoretical Inquiries in Law* 333, 353–357.

[261] J. Liu, 'Improving Investor-Friendly Legal Environment in Chinese Capital Market' in R.H. Huang and N.C. Howson, *Enforcement of Corporate and Securities Law: China and the World*, (Cambridge: Cambridge University Press 2017) 162, 175.

5. Funding derivative actions and incentives to commence litigation

This chapter focuses on the cost element of such actions in China, which may deter the commencement of proceedings. The rule in *Foss v Harbottle* is said to be 'essentially an issue of funding'.[1] Prospective claimants may consider a few issues, including the size of the litigation fee at stake, the legal costs and the likelihood of success, in deciding whether to put forward a lawsuit.[2] Logically speaking, litigation would only be rational where the sums recoverable and the chances of success exceeded the costs of legal expenses and the probability of losing the action. Since the implementation of the Chinese Company Law, shareholders in JSLCs are either extremely reluctant or encountered significant difficulties in bringing cases of litigation on behalf of their companies. The derivative action legal mechanism has been criticised as no more than window dressing for shareholders in JSLCs in China.[3]

In terms of difficulties, issues such as the appropriateness of thresholds, including shareholding periods and shareholding ownership percentage requirements, have been discussed in the previous chapter. As for the shareholders' incentives in bringing derivative actions, the unique nature of derivative action means the incentives for bringing these actions are challenging, since the mechanism allows shareholders to bring lawsuits as nominal claimants while the company is the actual claimant in terms of the fundamental interests of successful litigation.[4] In other words, the claimant as a shareholder could benefit from a slice of the success of a derivative action, based on the fact that the value of his or her shares may grow *pro rota* as the assets of the company increase leading to hypothetical benefits, but nevertheless disproportionate and inappropriate litigation fees may affect the popularity of derivative actions, especially among those who own a relatively low percentages of

---

[1]   D.D. Prentice, 'Wallersteiner v Moir: The Demise of the Rule in Foss v Harbottle?' (1976) 41 *Conveyancer and Property Lawyer* 58.

[2]   W.M. Lands, 'An Economic Analysis of the Courts' (1971) 14(1) *Journal of Law and Economics* 61.

[3]   H. Huang, 'Shareholder Derivative Litigation in China: Empirical Findings and Comparative Analysis' (2012) 27(4) *Banking and Finance Law Review* 619, 644.

[4]   S. Lin, *Derivative Action in Chinese Company Law*, (Alphen ann den Rijin: Kluwer Law International 2015) 175.

shares and who may have limited resources, information and voice in the company as a result.[5] Therefore, these fee-related issues are strong disincentives for claimant shareholders to launch derivative actions.

Unlike in common law countries such as the UK, where inadequacies may be alleviated by case law[6] and corresponding procedure rules,[7] the legislative legal basis of the legal costs of derivative action in China rests on the Civil Procedure Law 1992, Measures for the Administration of Attorneys' Fee 2006, supplemented by the Provision IV. The usual rule is that the losing party will be ordered by the court to pay the winning party's 'case acceptance fee', the fee charged by the court that tries the case, while each party pays its own attorney's fees and other expenses.[8] The question of whether the claimant shareholder may be reimbursed their expenses if the claim is successful is addressed by the Provision IV, where it is stipulated that the courts should support the indemnity claims of shareholders who successfully bring a lawsuit on behalf of a company for attorneys' fees, investigation fees, assessment fees, notary fees and other reasonable costs incurred during the litigation.[9]

It is crucial to make sure that litigation costs are tailored to a level that does not further discourage shareholders from bringing these actions so that the scheme could 'reach its full potential'.[10] Constructive and feasible proposals are in urgent need to address problems of fee-related issues. This chapter aims to address three inter-related and incremental questions: are current fee-oriented stipulations in China hindering the effectiveness and enforcement of derivative action in China? If so, could Chinese Company Law learn from the legislative experiences of the UK, the US and Japan so as to address the problem of insufficient incentives for minority shareholders to bring derivative actions? Should China directly transplant a proven successful legislative exercise, or should a unique approach be adopted in China considering its unique

---

[5]   See L. Benjamin, 'Class Action Litigation in China' (1998) 111(6) *Harvard Law Review* 1534; W. Cheng, 'Protection of Minority Shareholders after the New Company Law – Twenty Six Case Studies' (2010) 52(4) *The International Journal of Law and Management* 291.

[6]   See *Wallersteiner v Moir (No. 2)* [1975] QB 371 at 391; *Carlisle & Cumbria United Independent Supporters' Society Ltd. v CUFC Holdings Ltd.* [2010] EWCA Civ 463; [2011] BCC 855; *Stainer v Lee* [2010] EWHC 1539 (Ch). [2010] EWHC 1539 (Ch).

[7]   Rule 19.9E of the Civil Procedure Rules.

[8]   Art. 29, Measure on Payment of Litigation[诉讼费用交纳办法] 2007.

[9]   Art. 35, Provisions of the Supreme People's Court on Some Issues about the Application of the Company Law of the People's Republic of China (IV). [最高人民法院关于适用＜中华人民共和国公司法＞若干问题的规定（四）].

[10]   H. Huang, 'The Statutory Derivative Action in China: Critical Analysis and Recommendations for Reform' (2007) 4(2) *Berkeley Business Law Journal* 227, 248.

shareholding structure, corporate law, juridical system, culture, history, legal profession, political, and social institutions, and professional ethics of lawyers and judges? A complex interplay between the transplant and socio-cultural forces may well cause the transplant process to be far from straightforward. This chapter aims to establish a balanced and effective approach, through theoretical and comparative analysis, in order to eliminate the obstacles that hinder the smooth operation of derivative action and protect the interests of the company and shareholders.

This original comparative attempt may enhance our knowledge and understanding of the topic and enable derivative action to be more practically used in China at both the national and domestic levels.[11] The research is important in putting forward proposals to alter the situation whereby a shareholder 'has nothing to gain but much to lose'[12] in the scenario of derivative action. The research is significant in terms of enabling healthy numbers of shareholders to launch derivative suits against companies, especially among minority shareholders in JSLCs. These questions should be an essential primer for legal practitioners, in-house counsel who have to deal with shareholder claims issues on a regular basis, shareholders, members of supervisory boards, and legal theorists who are working in the field, not only in China but also globally. Since the initiation of China's OBOR intercontinental trade and infrastructure initiative in 2013 under the leadership of President Xi, shareholder protection, including foreign investors, has become a significant issue beyond the domestic market, with international implications and impact.[13]

5.1   THE IMPORTANCE OF THE FEE ISSUE TO PROMOTE THE EFFECTIVENESS OF DERIVATIVE ACTION

The critical issue in relation to corporate governance in China rests on how to enhance legal deterrence.[14] With the inherently weak public enforcement

---

[11]   For more discussions on three purposes of comparative law see M. Siems, *Comparative Law*, (Cambridge: Cambridge university Press 2014) pp. 3–4.

[12]   *Wallersteiner v Moir (No. 2)* [1975] QB 373, 395, per Lord Denning.

[13]   It is reported that foreign corporations invested $128.5bn, making China the top destination for foreign direct investment in 2014. 'China Overtakes US for Foreign Direct Investment', *BBC*, 20 January 2015, available at http://www.bbc.co.uk/news/business–31052566 (accessed 24 July 2022); China is also at the top of the 2014–15 list of the corporations most attractive to multinational corporations.

[14]   Z. Zhang, 'Legal Deterrence: The Foundation of Corporate Governance—Evidence from China' (2007) 15(5) *Corporate Governance: An International Review* 741.

of law in China[15] and the incomplete picture of private enforcement mechanisms such as securities fraud class action, derivative action is a mechanism which carries high expectations from both government and shareholders in order to enhance corporate governance in China. Derivative action, as a legal deterrent, should be given a prominent position. A unique feature of this deterrent is that the claimant does not enjoy relief and compensation from the litigation directly. Instead, recoveries from the action will go to the company.[16] Furthermore, derivative action may add additional burdens to companies, which may feel that they 'might be killed by kindness'.[17] Companies may suffer from collateral harm, including monetary and non-monetary harms such as unwanted publicity disclosure and negative long-term reputation damage, which could outweigh any gains from the litigation.[18]

In addition to these obstacles, funding issues are central to encouraging eligible and sincere shareholders to bring legitimate actions, in order to promote the long-term interests of the company. The mechanism's effectiveness in constraining managerial misconduct is highly doubtful if these obstacles could not be removed. These unique lawsuits brought by claimants will encounter obstacles to the initiation of a derivative action if we could not position appropriate and reasonable rules to settle funding issues in derivative actions.

The cost of litigation is not just a problem for derivative action in China. It is an issue in a number of jurisdictions due to the nature of the litigation, and related rules will have a direct impact on the popularity of this type of action. For example, private shareholder actions have been regarded as a major feature of corporate governance in the US, but this is not the case in the UK because the rule on litigation costs promotes the launching of lawsuits in the US but discourages the same in the UK.[19]

The UK, the US and Japan are chosen to act as examples here due to the fact that these three jurisdictions represent three main approaches in practice[20] to

---

[15]   Q. Liu, 'Corporate Governance in China: Current Practices, Economic Effects, and Institutional Determinants' (2006) 52(2) *CESifo Economic Studies* 415.

[16]   See *Spokes v The Grosvenor & W End Ry. Terminus Hotel Co. Ltd.* (1897) 2 Q.B. 124; *Prudential Assurance Co. Ltd. v Newman Industries Ltd. (No. 2)* [1982] Ch 204.

[17]   *Prudential Assurance Co. Ltd. v Newman Industries Ltd. (No. 2)* [1982] Ch 204 at 221.

[18]   A. Reisberg, *Derivative Actions and Corporate Governance: Theory and Operation*, (Oxford: Oxford University Press 2007) 47–48.

[19]   J. Armour, B. Black, B. Cheffins and R. Nolan, 'Private Enforcement of Corporate Law: An Eremitical Comparison of the US and UK' Preliminary Draft of Law and Economic Working Paper No. 89, University of Texas School of Law (2007).

[20]   J. Zhao, 'A More Efficient Derivative Action System in China: Challenges and Opportunities through Corporate Governance Theory' (2013) 64(2) *Northern Ireland Legal Quarterly* 233, 243.

deal with issues surrounding funding derivative actions. Another reason that these three jurisdictions have been selected is that derivative actions are relatively popular in terms of the number of public companies in these countries, which is a major concern in China. However, it should be noted that more well-adjusted figures in other jurisdictions could be regarded as the result of multiple factors, such as mitigated thresholds through legal reforms, litigation costs and court permission as a threshold.

In Japan, where the shareholding percentage is not a requirement for bringing a derivative action, derivative actions involving publicly held companies have exceeded those involving closed companies since 1993.[21] It is reported that 119 derivative actions were brought against listed companies in Japan from 1993 to 2009.[22] In the US, many cases involve public companies. The empirical research conducted by Tompson and Thomas showed that the percentage of derivative suits against public companies is as high as 80 per cent in the US.[23] Derivative actions against listed firms have been regarded as a common issue historically, based on research on a sample of 535 public corporations.[24] In the limited evidence from the UK, three cases, namely *Bridge v Daley*,[25] *Eckerle v Wickeder Westfalenstahl GmbH*[26] and *BNP Paribas SA v Open Joint Stock Company Russian Machines*,[27] have involved public companies.

---

[21]   S. Kawashima and S. Sakurai, 'Shareholder Derivative Litigation in Japan, Law, Practice and Suggested Reforms' (1997) 33(1) *Stanford Journal of International Law* 9, 37.

[22]   M. Nakahigashi and D.W. Punchniak, 'Land of the Rising Derivative Action: Revisiting Irrationality to Understand Japan's Unreluctant Shareholder Litigate' in D.W. Puchniak, H. Baum and M. Ewing-Chow (eds), *The Derivative Action in Asia: A Comparative and Functional Approach*, (Cambridge: Cambridge University Press 2012) 128, 171–173.

[23]   R. Thompson and R. Thomas, 'The Public and the Private Faces of Derivate Lawsuits' (2004) 57(5) *Vanderbilt Law Review* 1747; see *Caremark International Inc. Derivative Litigation*, 698 A.2d 959 (Del. Ch. 1996); *Re The Walt Disney Company Derivative Litigation*, 825 A.2d 275 (Del. Ch. 2003); *Re Oracle Corp. Derivative Litigation*, 824 A.2d 917 (Del. Ch. 2003); *Re The Walt Disney Company Derivative Litigation*, 906 A.2d. 27, 62–67 (Del. 2006).

[24]   R. Romano, 'The Shareholder Suit: Litigation without Foundation?' (1991) 7(1) *Journal of Law, Economics, and Organization* 55.

[25]   *Bridge v Daley* [2015] EWHC 2121 (Ch).

[26]   *Eckerle v Wickeder Westfalenstahl GmbH* [2013] 3 WLR 1316 [2014] BCC 1.

[27]   *BNP Paribas SA v Open Joint Stock Company Russian Machines* [2011] EWHC 308 (Comm); in this case, the first defendant, Open Joint Stock Company Russian Machines, and the second defendant, Joint Stock Asset Management Company Ingosstrakh–Investments, are both Russian companies.

5.2 THE CURRENT LAW FOR FILING FEES FOR DERIVATIVE ACTION IN CHINA AND THE JAPANESE EXPERIENCE: CHALLENGES AND OPPORTUNITIES

The Chinese civil procedure has not been directly transplanted from any mainstream legislative approach, including the approaches used in the UK, the US, Japan or in Taiwan, which has a quasi-public foundation with the function of bringing such actions.[28] The fundamental rule currently applied in the Chinese civil procedure is that the loser pays the costs of litigation and the court fees, whereas the attorneys' fees are borne by their respective parties.[29] In the sample study by Clarke and Howson of 50 cases in China, court fees are generally allocated to the loser, while the issue of how attorneys' fees are allotted between the parties has not been revealed.[30]

The current Chinese law and regulations on both civil litigation filing fees and attorneys' fees have been factors that deter shareholders from bringing derivative claims on behalf of companies.[31] As far as court fees are concerned, the rule on these fees is regulated by the Measure on Payment of Litigation (*Susong Fei Jiaona Banfa*) 2007. Court fees consist of filing fees, application fees and court expenses. In detail, filing fees (case acceptance fees) are the fees that every claimant needs to pay within seven days upon a notification issued by the court.[32] Application fees comprise the expenses of applying for the enforcement of judgment and mediation by the People's Court, taking preservation measures; a payment warrant, a public summons, insolvency, etc.[33] Court expenses include 'the travel expenses, accommodation expenses, living expenses, and subsidies for missed work, which are incurred by witnesses,

---

[28] See W.R. Tseng and W.W.Y. Wang, 'Derivative Action in Taiwan: Legal and Culture Hurdles with a Glimmer of Hope for the Future' in D.W. Puchniak, H. Baum and M. Ewing-Chow (eds), *The Derivative Action in Asia: A Comparative and Functional Approach*, (Cambridge: Cambridge University Press 2012) 215.

[29] Sections 6 and 29, Measure on Payment of Litigation [诉讼费用交纳办法] 2007.

[30] D. Clarke and N.C. Howson, 'Pathway to Minority Shareholder Protection: Derivative Action in THE People's Republic of China' in D.W. Puchniak, H. Baum and M. Ewing-Chow (eds), *The Derivative Action in Asia: A Comparative and Functional Approach*, (Cambridge: Cambridge University Press 2012) 243, 291.

[31] F.P. Meng, 'Funding Derivative Action in China: Lessons from *Wallersteiner v Moir* (No. 2) for the Court' (2010)31(1) *Company Lawyer* 29, 29.

[32] Section 22, Measure on Payment of Litigation [诉讼费用交纳办法] 2007.

[33] Section 10, Measure on Payment of Litigation [诉讼费用交纳办法] 2007.

authenticators, interpreters and adjustment makers for their appearance in the People's Court on designated dates'.[34]

In practice, application fees and court expenses are charged based on the amounts that are incurred, such fees are generally low and they are not the concern of this chapter.[35] However, according to Article 29 of the Measure, a major part of the cost of the litigation is the case filing fee, which is based on the 'loser pays' rule. The filing fee is calculated in two ways according to the nature of the case, namely if the case is a litigation against a property claim.[36] Where the nature of the claim is property-oriented, a sliding scale will be adopted, whereas a fixed fee will be charged for non-property claims. Derivative actions are regarded as litigations brought by shareholders on behalf of companies for *damages* against misconduct by the Board of Directors or majority shareholders. The property nature was delimited for derivative actions, and therefore a sliding scale is adopted.

The approach is similar to the litigation calculation rules adopted in Japan before the 1993 Commercial Code, where a sliding scale system was adopted. This means that the litigation fee is charged in proportion to the amount of damage the defendants seek to claim. According to Article 13(1) of the Measure, RMB 50 shall be paid for each case for damages of no more than RMB 10,000. After the initial RMB 10,000, different percentages (starting at 2.5 per cent) of the damages sought (starting from amounts between RMB 10,000 and 100,000) will be charged for different damage amounts. The lowest percentage of 0.5 per cent will be charged for damages of more than RMB 20 million. In derivative actions, the claimants may have to pay huge amounts in litigation fees if the claimed damages are high. This is particularly likely to be the case for listed companies due to their size, capitalisation and the seriousness of potential damages caused by directors' misconduct.

Despite a lack of a clear legal basis for derivative actions, there were such cases before 2006, when the new Company Law came into force. These derivative actions were based on the SPC's Court's reply to a Jiangsu court enquiry,[37] setting out that shareholders should be permitted to take an action to redress a wrong done to a company where the company itself was unable to do so.[38] For example, in the case of *Zhejiang Hexin Electricity Power*

---

[34]   Section 6(3), Measure on Payment of Litigation [诉讼费用交纳办法] 2007

[35]   S. Lin, *Derivative Action in Chinese Company Law*, (Alphen ann den Rijin: Kluwer Law International 2015) 29–30.

[36]   Section 13, Measure on Payment of Litigation [诉讼费用交纳办法] 2007.

[37]   The first enquiry was made in 1993 from High Court of Jiangsu Province in the case of *Zhangjiakang Dilunchang v Jixiong Ltd Hong Kong* 1993.

[38]   See the Supreme Court's reply to the enquiry of the High Court of Jiangsu Province [关于中外合资经营企业对外发生经济合同纠纷，控制合营企业的外方

Development Ltd (浙江和信电力开发有限公司),[39] the shareholders claimed RMB 3.52 billion, involving total court fees of RMB 1.1 million. In another example, although it was fortunate that the two shareholders were financially strong, in the case of *Zhongqi qihuo jingji youxian gongsi* (中期期货经纪有限公司) the litigation fee was charged at the rate of RMB 830,000 with a claim of more than RMB 0.16 billion.[40] Clearly, this would be extremely difficult for shareholders if they were not financially solvent.

Liu also reported another controversial case in terms of the inappropriateness of the litigation cost, namely *Hongshi Shiye youxian zeren gongsi* (红石实业有限责任公司).[41] In this case three individual litigant shareholders (Gang Wang, Guanxue Xie and Jun Yao) found it difficult to pay RMB 500,000 for the filling fee (based on their monetary compensation claim of RMB 100.5 million after consultation with the high court). However, the estimated compensation claim prior to the consultation was more than RMB 1 billion.[42] Despite the fact that this case was settled outside court, it is important and perhaps ironic to mention that, from the facts of the case, the final value of the claimant's claim was reduced to one-tenth of the original claim partly because the claimant could not afford the litigation cost, which emphasises the necessity of reassessing the reasonableness of litigation costs. In the *Sanlian Shangshe* (三联商社) case of 2009, the only case involving a shareholder in a JSLC bringing a derivative action, the litigation cost was also astonishingly high at RMB 191,800. Although the case acceptance fee is in principle coverable when the derivative action is successful,[43] the need to pay in advance without knowledge of the result of the case could be a considerable hurdle in the way of bringing such actions.

与卖方有利害关系，合营企业的中方应以谁的名义向人民法院起诉问题的复函 1994]; see also Opinions of the Supreme People's Court on Several Issues Concerning the Trial of Cases of Corporate Disputes (1) 2003 [最高人民法院关于审理公司纠纷案件 若干问规定（一）].

[39]   *Zhejiang Hexin Electricity Power Development Ltd. Co. et al v Tonghe Zhiye Investment Ltd. Co. et al*, Min 2nd Zhong Zi No 123 (2008) (Supreme Court).

[40]   J. Zhao, G. Wu and edited by P. Jiang, China *Lawyer Today: Derivative Actions[* 中国律师办案全程实录: 股东代表诉讼*]*, (Beijing: Law Press 2007) 27–260.

[41]   D. Liu, *Study on Shareholders' Derivative Actions in China [*我国股东派生诉讼制度研究*]* (Beijing: People' Press 2011) 103.

[42]   'Real Estate Big Names Encountered Astronomical Claims Pan Shiyi Billion Lawsuits Trap' [地产大腕遭遇天价索赔 潘石屹亿元官司陷胶着*]*, *Global Times*, 25 November 2004.

[43]   Art. 29, Measures for the Administration of Attorneys' Fee 2006.

Looking at the legislative experience in Japan, the sliding scale system has historically proven to be a barrier to shareholder derivative claims in Japan,[44] constituting 'the real determining factor'.[45] The story in Japan may be traced back to the earlier period before the reform of 1993, which provided the impetus for a palpable increase in derivative suits.[46] Prior to 1993, shareholders needed to purchase an *inshi* (revenue stamp) before filing a derivative action. The claims were divided into two kinds based on the nature of the claims, being categorised as 'calculable' and 'incalculable' claims. In the former case the stamp fee was calculated based on a sliding scale dependent on the amount of claimed damages, and a normal fixed flat rate was charged in the latter case.[47] The actual effect of the pre-1993 Japanese litigation fee principles was to discourage all suits due to the high litigation fees, which were not recoverable unless the shareholders eventually won the case.[48] Statistics show that there were fewer than 20 derivative action suits between 1950 and 1990, but there was a dramatic increase after 1993 to hundreds of lawsuits each year.[49] It was reported that 119 derivative actions were brought against listed companies in Japan from 1993 to 2009,[50] and it is claimed that Japan has now started to imitate the litigious US where derivative actions are actively used.[51] This

---

[44]   M. Blomstrom and S. La Croix, *Institutional Change in Japan*, (Oxford: Routledge 2006) 241; see also M. West, 'The Pricing of Shareholder Derivative Action in Japan and United States' (1994) 88 *Northwestern University Law Review* 1436.

[45]   T. Fujita, 'Transformation of the Management Liability Regime in Japan in the Wake of the 1993 Revision' in H. Kanda (eds) *Transforming Corporate Governances in East Asia*, (London: Routledge 2008) 13, 16.

[46]   S. Kawashima and S. Sakurai, 'Shareholder Derivative Litigation in Japan: Law, Practice and Suggested Reforms' (1997) 33(1) *Stanford Journal of International Law* 9, 11.

[47]   See art. 847(6), Company Law 2005; and art. 4(2), Law on the Fee of Civil Lawsuits.

[48]   C.J. Milhaupt and M.D. West, *Economic Organizations and Corporate Governance in Japan: The Impact of Formal and Informal Rule*, (Oxford: Oxford University Press 2004) 21.

[49]   M.D. West, 'Why Shareholders Sue: The Evidence from Japan' (2001) 30(2) *Journal of Legal Studies* 351, 352.

[50]   M. Nakahigashi and D.W. Punchniak, 'Land of the Rising Derivative Action: Revisiting Irrationality to Understand Japan's Reluctant Shareholder Litigate' in D.W. Puchniak, H. Baum and M. Ewing-Chow (eds), *The Derivative Action in Asia: A Comparative and Functional Approach*, (Cambridge: Cambridge University Press 2012) 128, 171–173.

[51]   G. Goto, 'Growing Securities Litigation against Issuers in Japan: Its Background and Reality' (12 January 2016); available at SSRN: https://ssrn.com/abstract=2714252 or http://dx.doi.org/10.2139/ssrn.2714252 (accessed 24 July 2022).

increase could be a consequence of multiple reasons, but the fee issue is widely discussed and accepted as a very important one.[52]

This fundamental change, which came as an unexpected shock,[53] started from the *Nikko Securities* case decisions by the Tokyo High Court, where the court supported the shareholders' argument that the stamp fee for bringing a derivative action should be tailored to a normal fixed rate, because the economic benefit of shareholders from derivative actions is in practice 'incalculable'.[54] The principle was subsequently confirmed by national legislation embedded in the amended Article 267 of the Commercial Code, in order to confirm that all derivative actions 'shall be deemed to be lawsuits with respect to non-property claims for the calculation of the amount of the claim'.[55] As the result, filing a derivative action, as non-property non-calculable claims, was reduced to a flat fixed fee at 8,200 Japanese Yen if the target of the litigation did not exceed 950,000 Yen (in 2003, the filing fee was changed to a flat rate of 13,000 Yen for the target of the litigation does not exceed 1.6 million Yen).[56] This amended fee is obviously likely to be lower the stamp fee, and this is regarded as one of the most influential events in Japanese corporate governance history.[57] It is argued that the reform will improve the performance of Japanese firms in the long run and enhance the law's disciplinary effects on management misconduct.[58]

In China, it was concluded that, through historical evidence related to case numbers, the current sliding system served as 'a robust disincentive to prospec-

[52]   H. Oda, 'Shareholder's Derivative Action in Japan' (2011) 8(3) *European Company and Financial Law Review* 334; M.D. West, 'Why Shareholders Sue: The Evidence from Japan' (2001) 30(2) *Journal of Legal Studies* 351; S. Kawashima and S. Sakurai, 'Shareholder Derivative Litigation in Japan: Law, Practice and Suggested Reforms' (1997) 33(1) *Stanford Journal of International Law* 9.

[53]   T. Fujita, 'Transformation of the Management Liability Regime in Japan in the Wake of the 1993 Revision' in H. Kanda (ed.) *Transforming Corporate Governances in East Asia* (London: Routledge 2008) 13, 17.

[54]   *Shiryou–ban Shouji–Houmu* 70 (Tokyo High Court, 30 March, 1993); see also H. Oda, 'Shareholder's Derivative Action in Japan' (2011) 8(3) *European Company and Financial Law Review* 334.

[55]   Art. 267 (4) Japanese Commercial Code.

[56]   Art. 4(2) Law on the Fee of Civil Lawsuits of Japan.

[57]   T. Fujita, 'Transformation of the Management Liability Regime in Japan in the Wake of the 1993 Revision' in H. Kanda (ed.) *Transforming Corporate Governances in East Asia*, (London: Routledge 2008) 13, 15–16.

[58]   S. Hirose and N. Yanagawa, 'The Impact of Reform on Derivative Action to the Firm Value [デリバティブ行為に対する改革の企業価値への影響] (2002 unpublished).

tive shareholders suing derivatively on behalf of the company'.[59] Therefore, it is worth considering partially transplanting the Japanese approach in China, in order to encourage shareholders in JSLCs to use derivative actions as effective shareholder remedies to safeguard the interests of companies. This is relevant due to the fact that the sliding scale system was first adopted following the approach in Japan. The transplant of the fee rules is necessary and urgent to promote board accountability in China[60] and open boards up to the supervision and scrutiny of shareholders, since the only way to make monitoring effective is to provide sufficient financial rewards to compensate for mounting costs.[61] Proposals have already been made to transplant the Japanese rule for filing costs.[62] Within these proposals, the focus has been on proposals in transplanting the fixed fee. However, there has been lack of discussion of the rationale for these proposals, which should be closely linked to the nature of claims and remedies of derivative action.

The nature of derivative action mechanisms is related to the filing fee in two interlocking ways. First, it is important to clarify that what shareholders are claiming for is remedies and recoveries by taking legal action on behalf of their companies. Companies which will benefit directly from the successful litigation. The company is the 'functional claimant' as 'the real party of interest'.[63] In the derivative action regime, companies are the aggrieved party, and the claimants enforce the right of the companies to take legal action.[64] Therefore, the compensation claim is an indirect one. Second, the relief from successful litigation rests upon various factors, including some that are long-term or short-term, tangible or intangible, and directly or indirectly linked to the suspension or deterrence of directors' misconduct. Like derivative action in any jurisdiction, it is virtually impossible to assess the benefits of the deterrence of corporate wrongdoing or the net recovery from the litigation. A shareholder, under the scheme, will institute an action on behalf of the company for the harm suffered by the company, in circumstances where the boards of directors

---

[59] F. Meng, 'Funding Derivative Action in China: Lessons from Wallersteiner v Moir (No.2) for the Court' (2010)31(1) *Company Lawyer* 29, 29.

[60] See A. Keay and J. Zhao, 'Ascertaining the Notion of Board Accountability in Chinese Listed Companies' (2016) 46 *Hong Kong Law Journal* 671.

[61] J. Tirole and B. Holmstrom, 'Market Liquidity and Performance Monitoring' (1993) 101(4) *Journal of Political Economy* 678.

[62] J. Liu, *Modern Corporation Law [现代公司法]* (Beijing: Law Press, 3rd ed. 2015) 408; D. Wang, 'The Analysis of Establishing Adequate Funding Incentive of Shareholder Derivative Litigation [派生诉讼资金激励问题研究]' [2015] *Research on Comparative Law [比较法律研究]* 165.

[63] J. Erickson, 'Corporate Governance in the Courtroom: An Empirical Analysis' (2010) 51(5) *William & Mary Law Review* 1749, 1756.

[64] *Famham v Fingold* (1972) 3 OR 688.

are reluctant or incompetent to enforce their rights. The benefit that the share-holders could obtain from increased share prices and higher dividends as the result of any deterrence of misconduct cannot be calculated. The shareholders will thereby ensure the management of company affairs in a manner whereby they stand to acquire maximum returns on their investments through divi-dends, if declared.[65] A derivative action is an action to rectify a wrong,[66] but the result of this wrongdoing may be impossible to calculate. It may be a long-term outcome, affected by a range of factors that have an impact on share price and company performance, including strategic management policies, corporate governance, a better business environment or government policies, etc. The shareholder, as the direct claimant, shares the success of the litigation partially and proportionately with other shareholders, and indirectly at the discretion of the board, in cases where rewards from successful derivative actions are achieved through the payment of dividends.

All in all, learning from Japanese historical, empirical and legislative experiences, it is clear that filing fees can have an immense impact on the pop-ularity of derivative actions. If derivative action is to be used as an effective tool to promote corporate governance and protect shareholders by improving the soundness and effectiveness of boards' decisions, the barrier of the filing fee needs to be removed. This is particularly relevant and urgent for the case of JSLCs, where professional directors are appointed to ensure a separation of ownership and control, as a central feature of a modern corporate governance mechanism for public companies. The derivative action mechanism not only has a supervision function towards boards' behaviour; it also has a deterrence function in terms of the misconduct of boards and majority shareholders. Unreasonable fees based on a sliding scale should be replaced by fixed and affordable fees. The filing fee is one of the most significant barriers for JSLCs to pursue derivative actions.[67] However, due to the dispersed shareholding ownership of JSLCs in China, a reasonable fixed filing fee, in combination with an appropriately revised shareholding percentage and period, would be a way forward in order to achieve a good balance between giving adequate incentives to shareholders to use derivative action and the avoidance of issues

---

[65] S. B. Carol, 'Juggling Shareholder Rights and Strike Suits in Derivative Litigation: The ALI Drops the Ball' (1993) 77 *Minnesota Law Review* 1339, 1344–1345.

[66] K.P. Thomas, 'Shareholder Derivative Suits: Demand and Futility where the Board Fails to Stop Wrongdoers' (1994) 78 *The Marquette Law Review* 172, 172.

[67] Other barriers include the prescribed shareholding threshold, constituting a requirement to hold 1 per cent or more of the company's shares for 180 consecutive days, and the difficulties in pre-payment (with the possibility of getting indemnified).

such as malicious litigation, an unnecessary distraction for directors, supervisors and senior managers, and excessive workloads for the courts,.

5.3   THE CURRENT LAW CONCERNING LAWYERS' (ATTORNEYS') FEES FOR DERIVATIVE ACTION IN CHINA: CHALLENGES AND THE US EXPERIENCE

Another key litigation cost that has a direct impact on the incentives of attorneys and claimant shareholders to bring derivative lawsuits is lawyers' fees. There is no legislation in China directly regulating lawyers' fees, because the relationship between the lawyer and claimant shareholders is seen as a private business relationship. The 'American rule' has been adopted in China to address the issue of lawyers' fees: the claimant and defendant will pay their own attorney's fee irrespective of the outcome of the lawsuit.[68]

In terms of the value of the attorneys' fee, two options are available according to the Measures for the Administration of Attorneys' Fees 2006: the fees may be fixed at a percentage no higher than 30 per cent of the amount of the damages claimed as the result of successful litigation, and a *'reasonable fee arrangement'* may be adopted, whereby fees are charged on the basis of the subject matter of the case or of the time taken.[69] In the approach based on a fixed percentage of the amount of damage, a claimant shareholder could conclude an agreement and the attorney's fee would be charged contingent on the amount of the claimed damages in a successfully litigated or settled case, which is similar to the approach adopted in the US based on a contingency fee arrangement.[70] However, a deeper and closer look at the approach does generate some concerns about making this relatively successful method equally efficacious in China.

5.3.1   Contingency Fee Agreement

A 'contingency fee arrangement' has been adopted and was regarded as an approach that provides a 'significantly lower disincentive to prospective claimants', compared with the approaches adopted in other jurisdictions such

---

[68]   J.M. Zimmerman, *China Law Deskbook: A Legal Guide for Foreign–Invested Enterprises* (ABA Section of International Law and Defending Liberty Pursing Justice, 3rd ed. 2010) see chapter 3.

[69]   F.P. Meng, 'Funding Derivative Action in China: Lessons from Wallersteiner v Moir (No. 2) for the Court' (2010) 31(1) *Company Lawyer* 29.

[70]   Z. Zhang, *The Derivative Action and Good Corporate Governance in China*, (Saarbrücken: Lambert Academic Publishing 2011) 212.

as the UK.[71] However, a question arises as to whether this positive effect will also be applicable in China, where the claimant shareholder could reach an agreement with the attorney by agreeing the attorney's fee if the damages claims are monetary. This fee may only be payable contingent on the result of the derivative action, thereby providing incentives for shareholders to employ the arguably under-used derivative action mechanism.[72]

The pervasiveness of 'contingency fee agreements' in the US largely settled the problem of a lack of compensatory incentives for shareholders.[73] According to this rule, claimant shareholders are not supposed to pay attorneys' fees unless and until the attorney recovers compensation for the shareholders by acquiring a settlement or by attaining a favourable trial judgement. In another word, the shareholders and attorney agree that the latter will shoulder the financial cost of pursuing the litigation, and will be compensated according to a fixed percentage for successful litigation or settlement.

However, at the first glance the contingency fee arrangement has already shown potential unreasonableness and deficiencies for China as a fair approach for shareholders, or gives them sufficient incentives to bring a derivative action. If the litigation is successful, the benefits will be awarded to the company and indirectly to the shareholders. The claimant shareholder would have to fund the initial attorneys' fee because the service contract is between the shareholder and the attorney. Consequently, claimant shareholders will receive only a small *pro rata* benefit, and the rest of the shareholders will enjoy a free ride on the backs of claimant shareholders.

Under this contingency fee approach, the shareholder would personally have to pay up to thirty percent of the damages recovered up-front, if the litigation is successful for monetary claims. The fees go to attorneys only if the derivative action generates monetary income and tangible relief, which is not always possible in derivative actions. Some of the damages related to directors' misconduct may be measurable, while some may be hard to assess in terms of their long-term damaging impact on the company, such as reputational damage. Positively, it is stipulated by the SPC in China that courts should support the indemnity claims of shareholders who successfully bring lawsuits on behalf of

---

[71] A. Reisberg, *Derivative Actions and Corporate Governance: Theory and Operation*, (Oxford: Oxford University Press 2007) 226.

[72] See Y. Zhu, 'The Realisation of Derivative Action[论股东派生诉讼的实现]' [2012] 6 *Tsinghua Law Journal [清华法学]* 107; J. Liu, *Modern Corporation Law [现代公司法]* (Beijing: Law Press, 3rd ed. 2015) 408; W. Chen, *A Comparative Study of Funding Shareholder Litigation*, (London: Springer 2017) 18–31.

[73] C. Milhaupt, 'Nonprofit Organizations as Investor Protection: Economic Theory and Evidence from East Asia' (2004) 29(1) *Yale Journal of International Law* 169, 184–185.

the company, and they should be indemnified for attorneys' fees, investigation fees, assessment fees, notary fees and other reasonable costs incurred from the litigation.[74] However, it is not completely clear that the attorneys' fee will be fully recoverable. Ironically, if the litigation is not successful the shareholder might be in a more optimistic position in terms of the litigation costs, being free from responsibility for attorneys' fees based on the contingency fee arrangement.

Before 2006, the 'no win, no fee' agreement was very common in China for cases of derivative action, despite the fact that the mechanism itself had not been adopted in national legislation. However, under the current regulation in China the contingency fee approach has been prohibited in specified classes of cases, such as critical, administrative, state compensation suits and multi-claimant lawsuits.[75] In relation to litigation in derivative actions, the rule applies to multi-claimant lawsuits. Despite the fact that this limits the application scope of the contingency fee arrangement, which we gave a mixed review, this could be problematic in terms of derivative action, particularly in JSLCs, due to difficulties in reaching the holding threshold of 1 per cent or more of the company's shares for 180 consecutive days. There may be a need for collective litigation in order to satisfy the 1 per cent requirement.[76]

Furthermore, the approach adopted in China, which is similar to the contingency fee arrangement, may not work in the same way as in the US for a number of reasons. Primarily, in China the contingency fee arrangement is not supported by a 'common fund' (this concept will be discussed in the next section) which would allow the payment of attorneys' fees out of the fund recovered from successful actions. A claimant shareholder needs to pay the attorney's fee for a successful lawsuit, despite the fact that the relief and rewards from successful derivative lawsuits go to the company. It is rather irrational and discouraging that claimant shareholders do not pay attorneys' fees for unsuccessful claims based on the contingency fee agreement, whereas they have to pay if the lawsuits are successful. The cost for claimants actually increases, and shareholders may seek remedies other than bringing an action on behalf of the company in a derivative manner. All in all, it is worth revisiting the case of multi-claimant (collective) litigation, including clarification

---

[74]   Art. 35, Provisions of the Supreme People's Court on Some Issues about the Application of the Company Law of the People's Republic of China (IV). [最高人民法院关于适用＜中华人民共和国公司法＞若干问题的规定（四）].

[75]   Arts 11–12, Measures on services fee of lawyers 2006 律师服务受理费管理办法 2006.

[76]   Art. 151 Chinese Company Law 2018; however, organising a number of individual shareholders who are willing to bring a collective derivative action can be a very difficult process.

regarding whether constraints apply to collective derivative action litigation where more than one shareholder brings the lawsuit in order to satisfy the 1 per cent shareholding ownership requirement. Additionally, it is also significant to explore the possibility of introducing the common fund arrangement and the notion of 'entrepreneurial attorneys' in China, although this may be quite difficult and involve a long period of transformation.

5.3.2   Common Fund Arrangement

The 'common fund' is set up in a scenario where an attorney in a derivative action helps to set up, accumulate or maintain a fund from which the attorneys themselves may receive fees and claim expenses directly.[77] This approach is designed to encourage more attorneys to take on cases of derivative actions.[78] All monetary awards to companies or settlements resulting from derivative actions have to be paid into the common fund, and the contingency fee of the attorney based on the agreement between the claimant shareholders and the attorney is treated as a first charge on the common fund.[79] The attorneys will get a certain percentage of the common fund as their tangible fee (from 20 to 30 per cent, depending on the contract between the attorney and the claimant shareholders). The common fund principle and supplementary mechanisms as adopted in the US shift the financial risk of pursuing a derivative action from the claimant shareholders to the attorneys.[80] Therefore, shareholders may be willing to proceed with the lawsuit even if they are not confident about the litigation, considering that there are fewer downside risks.[81]

Additionally, the common fund principle for US attorneys, as controllers of the conduct of litigation on behalf of the claimant shareholders, is closely related to the nature of litigation as entrepreneurial activities with the purpose of maximising profit. Attorneys are commonly regarded as 'entrepreneurs' who could conduct litigation nearly independently without being monitored by shareholders, in the case of derivative actions. The shareholders are merely

---

[77]   See *Boeing Co. v Van Gemert* 444 U.S. 472, 478 (1980).

[78]   See H. Kritzer, *Risk, Reputation and Rewards: Contingency Fee Legal Practice in the United States*, (Stanford University Press 2004) 177.

[79]   See C. Hammett, 'Attorneys' Fees in Shareholder Derivative Suits: the Substantial Benefit Rule Re-Examined' (1972) 60(1) *California Law Review* 164.

[80]   H. Baum and D.W. Puchniak, 'The Derivative Action: an Economic, Historical and Practice-oriented Approach' in D.W. Puchniak, H. Baum and M. Ewing-Chow (eds), *The Derivative Action in Asia: A Comparative and Functional Approach*, (Cambridge: Cambridge University Press 2012) 1, 21.

[81]   Ibid.

used as the key to the courtroom door.[82] This type of entrepreneurial litigation is regarded as a process by which adversaries reach an agreement on the litigation odds and subsequently settle the case out of court so as to avoid additional transaction costs.[83] Different from the two-way fee shifting in English law, the attorney in the US model is seen as being in a joint venture with the litigant shareholders. Attorneys and their clients seem to be in the same boat, sharing the gains and the fruits of victory in the litigation. However, without involvement, supervision and monitoring by their clients, the attorneys, who are typically senior partners in the US,[84] may act largely according to their own interests, subject to the regulations imposed by 'bar disciplines, judicial oversight and their own sense of ethics and fiduciary responsibilities'.[85]

Applying the same notion in China, it is argued by Huang that 'there is no shortage of entrepreneurial lawyers in China, and they race to represent as many investor plaintiffs as possible in the area of securities cases'.[86] He observed through empirical research that 'China's securities civil actions are lawyer-driven'.[87] Coffee asserts that 'the size and scale of the Chinese securities market could soon encourage and support a sizable indigenous population of entrepreneurial litigators'.[88] These arguments imply that the environment for establishing a common fund arrangement does exist in China, entrepreneurial lawyers are not uncommon, and the situation may apply to derivative action cases. However, the legislative framework in areas such as bar discipline and legal ethics are under development in China, and the enforcement of legislative frameworks in these areas is worrying and far from perfect.[89]

---

[82]   J.C. Coffee, 'The Regulation of Entrepreneurial Litigation: Balancing Fairness and Efficiency in the Large Class Action' (1987) 54(3) *University of Chicago* 887.

[83]   J.P. Gould, 'The Economics of Legal Conflicts' (1973) 2(2) *Journal of Legal Studies* 279, 288–91, 296.

[84]   D.E. Rosenthal, *Lawyer and Client: Who's in Charge?* (New York: Russel Sage Foundation 1974).

[85]   J.R. Macey and G.P. Miller, 'The Claimants' Attorney's Role in Class Action and Derivative Litigation: Economic Analysis and Recommendations for Reform' (1991) 58(1) *The University of Chicago Law Review* 3, 4.

[86]   H. Huang, 'Private Enforcement of Securities Law in China: A Ten-Year Retrospective and Empirical Assessment' (2013) 61(4) *American Journal of Comparative Law* 757, 768.

[87]   Ibid., 798.

[88]   J.C. Coffee, 'The Globalization of Entrepreneurial Litigation: Law, Culture, and Incentives', available at https://papers.ssrn.com/sol3/papers.cfm?abstract_id=2857258 (accessed 24 July 2022); see also J.C. Coffee, *Entrepreneurial Litigation: Its Rise Fall and Future*, (Harvard University Press 2015) Chapter 10.

[89]   See E. Wald, 'Notes from Tsinghua: Law and Legal Ethics in Contemporary China' (2008) 23 *Connecticut Journal of International Law* 369; C. Arup, 'Lawyers for China: The Impact of Membership of the World Trade Organization on Legal Services

A few additional concerns may require policy makers and the government to think carefully before introducing such an approach in China with some potential challenges. First, the current emphasis on economic development in China and the companies' priorities in putting profit maximisation at the front of the queue make it very hard for companies to set aside money to establish a common fund for litigations against their board members or controlling shareholders at the request of minority shareholders. Traditionally, many listed companies within the scope of JSLCs in China still constitute 'state-owned enterprises (SOEs)', and the largest shareholder is normally the state.[90] It may be even harder for SOEs to establish a common fund for derivative actions where the claimants in these cases are civil servants (as directors) and the state is the majority shareholder. It is hard for the board of directors to authorise such a common fund, considering the close *guanxi* between executive board members, supervisors, and controlling shareholders. Moreover, it is problematic to envisage that Chinese lawyers would be willing to take on the big risks of pursuing derivative actions if the initiation of the case comes from minority shareholders, who may have limited voice and information that could be made available for attorneys to believe in the success of the cases. The attorneys may be also aware of difficulties in convincing the supervisor or supervisory board to pursue derivative actions, particularly if they are aware of difficulties in concluding a successful derivative lawsuit considering the *guanxi* between the two boards, independent directors and the controlling power of majority shareholders and the directors.

Furthermore, as a strong theoretical basis for the common fund principle, classic Anglo-American derivative actions are, *de facto*, double suits at equity, one of which is a claim by the company as the 'real party claimant' against alleged wrongdoers, while the other is the claim by the shareholder.[91] In China, conventionally a company in a derivative lawsuit could be regarded as either

---

and Law in China' (2001) 4 *The Journal of World Intellectual Property* 741; S. Liu, 'Lawyers, State Officials and Significant Others: Symbiotic Exchange in the Chinese Legal Services Market' (2011) 206 *The China Quarterly* 276.

[90]   It is reported that an average of 31.27 per cent of the shares in these companies are held by the government. Y. Thanatawee, 'Ownership Structure and Dividend Policy: Evidence from China' (2014) 6 *International Journal of Economics and Finance* 197, 199 quoted by OECD, OECD Survey of Corporate Governance Frameworks in Asia 2017.

[91]   D. Clarke and N.C. Howson, 'Pathway to Minority Shareholder Protection: Derivative Action in the People's Republic of China' in D.W. Puchniak, H. Baum and M. Ewing-Chow (eds), *The Derivative Action in Asia: A Comparative and Functional Approach*, (Cambridge: Cambridge University Press 2012) 243, 291; see also M. Koessler, 'The Stockholder's Suit: A Comparative View' (1946) 44(5) *Columbia Law Review* 238.

a second claimant, after the shareholders who initiate the derivative action, or a third party, allowed under the Civil Procedure rules on a voluntary basis if the company considers that it has the independent right to claim the subject matter of the action or join the litigation without independent rights.[92]

It is also possible the company is not regarded as a party.[93] In practice, companies are often classified as *the third party*.[94] Consistent with common practice, the statutes of companies and shareholders in derivative actions have been explicitly confirmed after the enactment of the Provision IV,[95] where it is specified that the company will be regarded as the *claimant* in direct litigation (through the shareholders' requests in writing)[96] where the board of supervisors, or the supervisors, in the case of a LLCs without a board of supervisors, are regarded as litigation representatives. In cases of derivative action,[97] the shareholders will be classified as *claimant* whereas the company will be regarded as *the third party*. Therefore, recognition and a clear classification of the role played the company will be important before the common fund principle may be established in China. If the company is defined as the *de facto* claimant in derivative action, it would make cost allocation appropriate and rational, which in turn makes the potential transplant of the 'common fund principle' possible and legitimate.

5.3.3   American Rule and Substantial Benefit Test

In addition to and in conjunction with the contingent rule and the common fund approach, a few more rules and tests are applied in the US courts in order to give attorneys enough incentive to take on derivative actions. These include the 'American rule' and the 'substantial benefit test'. The 'American rule' provides that each party in the litigation is responsible for paying their own attorney's fee, irrespective of the result of the litigation.[98] Functioning

---

[92]   See art. 56(1), Civil Procedure Law of the People's Republic of China 2013.

[93]   See D. Clarke and N.C. Howson, 'Pathway to Minority Shareholder Protection: Derivative Action in the People's Republic of China' in D.W. Puchniak, H. Baum and M. Ewing-Chow (eds), *The Derivative Action in Asia: A Comparative and Functional Approach*, (Cambridge: Cambridge University Press 2012) 243, 291.

[94]   Y. Qian, 'The Position of the Company in the Derivative Action [论股东代表诉讼中公司的地位]' (2011) 5 *Tsinghua Law Journal [清华法学]* 88.

[95]   Art. 30, Provisions of the Supreme People's Court on Some Issues about the Application of the Company Law of the People's Republic of China (IV). [最高人民法院关于适用＜中华人民共和国公司法＞若干问题的规定（四）].

[96]   Art. 152 of Chinese Company Law 2018.

[97]   Art. 152 of Chinese Company Law 2018.

[98]   See *Alyeska Pipeline Service Co. v Wilderness Society*, 421 U.S. 240, 247 (1975); for criticism of the rule see Report of the Third Circuit Task Force, Court Awarded Attorney Fees, 108 F.R.D. 237, 241 (1985).

on the basis of the principle of 'no win, no fee',[99] the 'American rule' makes the claimant in derivative actions less concerned about attorneys' fees, since attorneys will be paid by the company out of that recovered from the action for successful cases, whereas they will not be eligible for any payment if cases are lost. However, these benefits only apply to cases when there is a tangible benefit to the company.

As for intangible or therapeutic relief, the 'substantial benefit test' makes economic incentives for claimant attorneys possible and enforceable[100] by allowing them to receive a contingency fee through the 'lodestar method'. [101] Based on this method, the attorneys are paid for their work by multiplying the number of hours they reasonably spent on the case by a reasonable hourly rate.[102] If a successful derivative action brings about a substantial benefit for the company, the lodestar will be adjusted by a multiplier to reflect a number of additional factors including, most significantly, the risk of the litigation. The 'substantial benefit' doctrine is regarded as an exception to the contingency fee rule,[103] since the payment of contingency fees is limited to tangible relief. It is necessary and functional for fee-oriented issues due to the unique nature of the derivative action mechanism. This was further affirmed by the practical implication of the rule demonstrated by an empirical study, which concluded that derivative actions in the US always result in non-monetary relief.[104]

It can be observed that the contingency fee system, enriched by common funds and the substantial benefit doctrine, gives attorneys and shareholders adequate incentives to use the derivative action approach. However, the lodestar method, which is used in the majority of courts in the US for awarding fees out of the fund, has various problems and drawbacks such as 'enormously burdensome calculation costs'; it may also give attorneys an incentive to exag-

---

[99] Rule 1.5(d) of the Model Rules of Professional Conduct of the American Bar Association.

[100] J. Cox and T. Hazen, *Corporations*, (Springfield: Aspen Publisher, 2nd ed. 2003).

[101] See *Mills v Electric Auto–Lite Co.* 396 U.S. 375 at 392 (1970).

[102] *Friedrich v Fidelity Nat. Bank*, 545 S.E. 2d 107 – Ga: Court of Appeals 2001; *Lindy Bros. Builders v American Radiator & Standard Sanitary Corp.*, 487 F.2d 161 (3d Cir. 1973). See also R.T. Mowrey, 'Attorney Fees in Securities Class Action and Derivative Suits' (1977) 3 *The Journal of Corporation Law* 267, 334–48.

[103] See *Vincent v Hughes Air West, Inc.*, 557 F.2d 759, 768 n.7 (9th Cir. 1977); *Alyeska Pipeline Serv. Co. v Wilderness Society*, 421 U.S. 240, 264–67 n.39 (1975); see also A. Reisberg, 'Funding Derivative Actions: A Re–Examination of Costs and Fees as Incentives to Commence Litigation' (2004) 4(2) *Journal of Corporate Law Studies* 345.

[104] R. Romanno, 'The Shareholder Suit: Litigation without Foundation?' (1991) 7(1) *Journal of Law, Economics, and Organization* 55, 61.

gerate their hours, delay the litigation needlessly, or overstate the number of the hours for a higher fee.[105] It also fails to give claimants' attorneys a proper incentive to reach a settlement agreement, which may maximise recovery for the claimant, since it assures the recipient of the fees of the attorneys if successful.[106]

These problems could be equally if not more significant in China, considering problems such as a lack of a comprehensive legal system regulating attorneys' behaviour, and the information asymmetry that affects minority shareholders. This may lead to blind trust in the attorney's advice and proposed solutions, which will be discussed in detail in Chapter 6. Furthermore, it is widely acknowledged that Chinese communities suffer from low trust and China has been in a credibility-and-trust crisis since the 1960s, mainly as a result of the Cultural Revolution. This has been extended to companies with the global impact of corporate scandals such as the San Lu baby milk powder scandal in 2008 and the Hogwash cooking oil scandal in 2010.[107] Furthermore, the lack of an effective and rigorous public complaints mechanism, a unified industry assessment supervision mechanism and commonly recognised average market prices are further reasons making the effective enforcement of the lodestar method doubtful and difficult.

5.4   THE APPROACH IN THE UK: POPULARITY AND ENFORCEABILITY

The approach in the UK has been followed by most Commonwealth jurisdictions, as the traditional approach in order to address the obstacle of funding in a derivative action.[108] The logic and reason for the approach of the '*indemnity order*' rests on the principle of equity.[109] The rationale is that the rights being vindicated are those of the company and recovery flows to it, and therefore the company should be responsible for the repayment of the costs.[110]

---

[105]   J.R. Macey and G.P. Miller, 'The Plaintiffs' Attorney's Role in Class Action and Derivative Litigation: Economic Analysis and Recommendations for Reform' (1991) 58(1) *The University of Chicago Law Review* 3, 22.

[106]   Ibid., 4.

[107]   W. Zhang and R. Ke, 'Trust in China: A Cross–Regional Analysis [信任及其解释: 来自中国的跨省调查分析]' [2002] 10 *Economic Research Journal [经济研究]* 59; Q. Yang and W. Tang, 'Exploring the Sources of Institutional Trust in China: Culture, Mobilization, or Performance?' (2010) 2(3) *Asian Politics & Policy* 415.

[108]   See *Foyster v Foyster Holdings Pty Ltd.* [2003] NSWSC 135; s. 166 Companies Act 1993 (New Zealand); s. 236 Australian Corporations Act 2001.

[109]   *Wallersteiner v Moir (No. 2)* [1975] QB 373, 391.

[110]   See J.D. Wilson, 'Attorney Fees and the Decisions to Commerce Litigation: Analysis, Comparison and an Application to the Shareholders' Derivative Action' (1985) 5 *Windsor Yearbook of Access to Justice* 142, 177.

The '*indemnity order*' was enforced in the UK in order to address issues of disincentives for claimants in taking derivative actions.[111] The rule was first made legitimate in *Wallersteiner v Moir (No. 2)*,[112] where Lord Denning in the Court of Appeal asserted that a company should indemnify a shareholder defendant in a derivative suit since the shareholder was acting on behalf of the company and the company was the direct beneficiary.[113]

The difficulties of Mr. Moir received sympathy from the Court of Appeal, particularly from Lord Denning.[114] In the judgment, shareholders who bring a claim should be treated as trustees or agents who act on behalf of the bene-ficiary or the principal, namely the company. Lord Denning suggested a more reasonable procedural rule[115] and the test in deciding whether to make such an order was held to be whether it would have been reasonable for an independent board of directors to bring such actions in the company's name.[116] The result of a derivative action is irrelevant to the order of indemnity. That means that even if an action fails, the claimant is also entitled to be indemnified since the lawsuit is an action of the company and hence the risk of losing the case should be borne by the company. It is non-arguable that if the derivative action is successful the recoveries accrue to the company as a whole, with the share-holder who brought the claim receiving only a small percentage of the benefit. The fact that other shareholders may have a 'free ride' and directly benefit from derivative claims brought by the defendant shareholder, who did all the

---

[111] Z. Zhang, 'Making Shareholder Derivative Action Happen in China: How Should Lawsuits be Funded' (2010) 38 *Hong Kong Law Journal* 523, 530.

[112] *Wallersteiner v Moir (No. 2)* [1975] QB 373; see also *Masri v Consolidated Contractors International Co SAL* [2011] EWHC 1024; *Air Canada v Secretly of State for Trade (No. 2)* [1983] W.L.R. 494.

[113] This was demonstrated by what Lord Denning MR stated in the celebrated case of *Wallersteiner v Moir (No. 2)* ([1975] QB 371 at 391):
> The minority shareholder, being an agent acting on behalf of the company, is entitled to be indemnified by the company against all costs and expenses rea-sonably incurred by him in the course of the agency... Seeing that, if the action succeeds the whole benefit will go to the company, it is only just that the minority shareholder should be indemnified against the costs he incurs on its behalf....

[114] At the time, Mr. Moir had exhausted all his financial resources during the ten-year litigation.

[115] Lord Denning gave consideration to Mr. Moir's plight (at 392):
> The minority shareholder should apply ex parte to the master for directions, supported by an opinion of counsel as to whether there is a reasonable case or not. The master may then, if he thinks fit, straightaway approve the continuance of the proceeding until close of pleadings, or until after discovery or until trial ... The master need not, however, decide it ex parte ... The master should simply ask himself: is there a reasonable case for the minority shareholder to bring at the expense (eventually) of the company? If there is, let's go ahead.

[116] Ibid., at 404, per Buckley LJ.

hard work, will make defendant shareholders less willing and give them less incentive to bring such actions in the future.

The principle has been followed in both case law and statutes in the UK. Hoffmann LJ in *McDonald v Horn*[117] (with whom Hirst and Balcombe LJJ agreed) referred to the principles which apply when trustees and other fiduciaries apply for an indemnity out of the relevant fund; Roth J claimed in *Stainer v Lee*[118] that a shareholder who has passed the stages for derivative action 'should normally be indemnified as to his reasonable costs by the company ...'.[119] Arden LJ asserted in *Carlisle & Cumbria United Independent Supporters' Society Ltd. v CUFC Holdings Ltd.*[120] that 'as the action was a derivative action on behalf of the club, the trust had an expectation of receiving its proper costs from the companies on an indemnity basis ...'.[121] However, the court needs to exercise considerable care in deciding whether to give a pre-emptive indemnity order.[122] The circumstances under which an order is to be made are rather obscure,[123] with many uncertainties dependent on judicial discretion.[124] This considerable discretion may create uncertainties and cause great distress for shareholders, and result in no positive impact on encouraging derivative actions. This could be a major flaw that may hinder transplanting the regime into Chinese law.

Furthermore, variations in understanding of nature of indemnity orders make it harder for China to learn from common law principles with uncertainties and ambiguity. For example, it was established in *Wallersteiner* that an indemnity order by the court should be one that is 'simple and inexpensive' without being allowed to 'escalate into a minor trial'.[125] However, Walton J took a restrictive view of the jurisdiction to make an indemnity order, and found that the order

---

[117] [1995] ICR 685.

[118] [2010] EWHC 1539 (Ch).

[119] Ibid., para. 56.

[120] [2010] EWCA Civ 463; [2011] BCC 855.

[121] Ibid., para. 8.

[122] *Bhullar v Bhullar* [2015] EWHC 1943 (Ch).

[123] C.A. Paul, 'Derivative Actions under England and German Law – Shareholder Participation between the Tension Filled Areas of Corporate Governance and Malicious Shareholder Interference' (2010) 7(1) *European Company and Financial Law Review* 81, 96; see also *Smith v Croft* [1986] 1 WLR 580; *Jaybird Group Ltd. v Greenwood* [1986] BCLC 319.

[124] A. Hargovan, 'Under Judicial and Legislative Attack: The Rule in *Foss v Harbottle*' (1996) 113 *South African Law Journal* 631, 648.

[125] *Wallersteiner v Moir (No. 2)* [1975] QB 373 at 394.

would be 'palpably unjust'.[126] There are also concerns that the very possibility of obtaining an order could conceivably encourage vexatious claims.[127]

Furthermore, a 'financial need test' was proposed for the application of an indemnity order in *Smith v Croft*,[128] where Walton J dealt with funding issues in a cautious manner due to the fact that making an indemnity order 'may turn out to have imposed on the company a liability which ought never to have been imposed upon it'.[129] It was held that an indemnity order would have been oppressive and unfair and should not be made *ex parte*.[130] Following this logic, shareholders should only pursue funding through 'an order for interim payment' if they do not have sufficient resources to fund the action or can demonstrate that they genuinely require funding support.[131] It is held that the precise amount of the order will depend upon the 'pecuniary situation' and 'the individual circumstances of each case'.[132] Additionally, the test of whether an independent board of directors would consider taking action in the same circumstances to clarify the availability of an indemnity order was introduced by Walton, which may further complicate the application of the *Wallersteiner* principle. Also, the independent judgement and board independence are vague definitions.[133] The dual-proceedings rule applies to the indemnity order, and the independent judgement test[134] further muddies the waters.

The approach derived from the *Wallersteiner* has been criticised for contradicting the nature of derivative action, where shareholders are the 'representatives' and the financial situations of shareholders should not be relevant to decisions of the court on granting an indemnity order.[135] The approach also increases the discretion of the court, not only on whether to grant the order, but also on how much should be granted if the application were successful. This increased discretion makes it harder for civil law countries with limited

---

[126] *Smith v Croft (No. 1)* [1986] 1 WLR 580 at 589.

[127] See 679 HL Official Report (5h Series) col G 13, (27 February 2006).

[128] *Smith v Croft (No. 1)* [1986] 1 WLR 580; (1986) 2 BCC 99010; see also *Intercontinental Precious Metals Inc. v Cooke* [1994] WWR 66 (Canadian case); *Farrow v Register of Buildings Society* [1991] 2 VR 589 (Australian case).

[129] *Smith v Croft*, ibid., at 597.

[130] Ibid.

[131] Ibid.

[132] Ibid., at 598; see also *Kiani v Cooper* [2010] 1BCLC 427 at [48]–[49].

[133] See S. Bhagat and B. Black, 'The Non–Correlation between Board Independence and Long–Term Firm Performance' (2002) 27 *The Journal of Corporation Law* 231, 232.

[134] *Smith v Croft (No. 1)* [1986] 1 WLR 580.

[135] A. Reisberg, *Derivative Actions and Corporate Governance: Theory and Operation*, (Oxford: Oxford University Press 2007) 238.

judicial resources and worrying judicial ability to use discretion in reaching legitimate and justifiable decisions on a case-by-case basis.

The principle derived from *Wallersteiner* has been embedded in statutes.[136] It is stipulated that 'the court may order the company... for the benefit of which a derivative claim is brought to indemnify the claimant against liability for costs incurred in the permission application or in the derivative claim or both'.[137] However, it has not promoted the enforcement and frequency of application of this mechanism. In general terms, it is argued by Keay that in only two of the eight cases in which the shareholder has been successful under the statutory regime has the court granted costs with limits.[138] He proposed a more relaxed attitude in terms of awarding an indemnity in relation to the costs of shareholders who successfully obtain permission to continue a derivative action, and criticised the current scheme for being overly 'harsh'.[139]

The question then arises of whether the '*indemnity cost order*' should be adopted in China. Meng looks at the indemnity order in a positive manner and thinks it is a 'feasible scheme for funding shareholders in China', and this could 'fairly conveniently achieved' by order of the court without introducing new reforms to the current legal structure.[140] It is argued that two aspects need to be considered, including whether a case is 'a reasonable case for the minority shareholder to bring at the expense (eventually) of the company', and whether the court is convinced that the claimant has any real prospect of success.[141] Without additional or detailed guidelines for the claimant and court to follow, the application of the rule needs to be sought at the discretion of the judge. Current legislation or rules of court fail to give any clear and enforceable instruction to the shareholder as to what they should do, or the criteria for their litigation being funded by the company. The transplant of the principle in China seems irrational and difficult.

The transplant should also be subject to a more rigorous assessment of its fitness with a comprehensive consideration of other path dependence factors, including a number of issues such as overburdened court systems, limited judicial resources, judges' skills and knowledge,[142] the limited knowledge of share-

---

[136] This includes Order 15, R 12A of the Rule of Supreme Court, 162–163 of Schedule 1 of the Civil Procedure Rule 1998, and Civil Procedure Rule 2000.

[137] R 19.9E Civil Procedure Rule 2000.

[138] A. Keay, 'Assessing Rethinking the Statutory Scheme for Derivative Action under the Companies Act 2006' (2016) 16(1) *Journal of Corporate Law Studies* 39, 57.

[139] Ibid., 57–58.

[140] F.P. Meng, 'Funding Derivative Action in China: Lessons from *Wallersteiner v Moir* (No. 2) for the Court' (2010) 31(1) *Company Lawyer* 29, 29–30.

[141] Ibid., 30.

[142] See T. Gong, 'Dependent Judiciary and Unaccountable Judges: Judicial Corruption in Contemporary China' (2004) 4(2) *China Review* 33; W. Gu, 'The

holders as natural persons, and information asymmetries between minority and institutional shareholders. As a matter of fact, only 56 per cent of Chinese judges hold degrees,[143] and many civil servants are described as judges and work in administrative roles.[144] Problems such as the lack of expertise and the absence of case law to help judges make decisions make derivative actions in China far from useful, compared with ordinary suits. The authors' hesitation extends to the scenario in Hong Kong, a jurisdiction with similar history, tradition, culture and geographical location to China. Courts have been very reluctant and did not approve a single order to indemnify an applicant in relation to the costs incurred in a statutory derivative action substantive litigation.[145]

Additionally, the large extent of corruption in China's judicial system makes it of even greater concern that such a regime should be applied as the instrumental variable to assess the possibility of adoption. The guiding cases system was introduced as a novel attempt to benefit from the advantages of both the common law and civil systems. It has the potential to bring some benefits by enhancing the faith of the masses in the judiciary in China.[146] However, guiding cases are nothing more than administrative instructions presented in the form of cases,[147] and it is hard to obtain instruction in the case of litigation costs, which vary significantly for individual cases with heavy involvement of directors' discretion.

5.5 FINDING THE MOST SUITABLE APPROACH FOR CHINA: AN OPTION THAT SHOULD INCLUDE MULTI-DIMENSIONAL FACTORS

The new Company Law contains no provisions on funding issues related to derivative action. The provisions provide that the court should support the indemnity claims of a shareholder who successfully brings a lawsuit on behalf of a company, providing that they should be indemnified for attorneys' fees, investigation fees, assessment fees, notary fees and other reasonable costs

---

Judiciary in Economic and Political Transformation: Quo Vadis Chinese Courts?' (2013) 1(2) *The Chinese Journal of Comparative Law* 303.

[143] J. Zhu (ed.), *China Legal Development Report [*中国法律发展报告：数据库和指标体系*]* (Beijing: Renmin University Press 2007) 34.

[144] 'Legal Reform Judging Judges', *The Economist*, 24 September 2015.

[145] F.E. Mezzanotte, 'The Unconvincing Rise of the Statutory Derivative Action in Hong Kong: Evidence from its First 10 Years of Enforcement' (2017) 17(2) *Journal of Corporate Law Studies* 469, 472.

[146] R. Li, 'Case–law adopted by China?' available at https://ukconstitutionallaw.org/2012/01/26/ruiyi–li–case–law–adopted–by–china/ (accessed 24 July 2022).

[147] J. Deng, 'The Guiding Case System in Mainland China' (2015) 10(3) *Frontiers Law China* 449, 450.

incurred from the litigation.[148] Considering the fundamentally disadvantaged position of shareholders, especially minority shareholders in JSLCs who suffer from information asymmetry and weak bargaining power, incentives should be given to shareholders to bring derivative actions. As suggestions for how to make derivative action possible and effective while not instigating nuisance lawsuits, different proposals have been put forward for the reform of litigation fees and attorneys' fees in relation to derivative action. Issues related to costs are largely responsible for the relative unpopularity of statutory derivative actions. Reform suggestions should be considered carefully in relation to the nature of derivative action as a lawsuit instigated by shareholders on behalf of the company with indirect and uncertain benefits for claimant shareholders.

Commentators have approached this problem from different backgrounds and have made different proposals, which are largely based on legal transplants,[149] as 'a smart way of choosing a foreign legal model that has proven to work well'.[150] From our discussions of the importance of legal costs in relation to derivative actions in the context of the legislative experiences of the US, the UK and Japan, it seems that a simple transplant should not be the way forward. Just like companies' decisions on whether to 'make or buy' certain raw materials,[151] it may be more efficient and rational to adopt a hybrid approach,

---

[148]   Art. 35, Provisions of the Supreme People's Court on Some Issues about the Application of the Company Law of the People's Republic of China (IV). [最高人民法院关于适用＜中华人民共和国公司法＞若干问题的规定（四）].

[149]   Clarke and Howson claim that it is the losing party who should be responsible for the attorneys' fee D. Clarke and N.C. Howson, 'Pathway to Minority Shareholder Protection: Derivative Action in the People's Republic of China' in D.W. Puchniak, H. Baum and M. Ewing-Chow (eds), *The Derivative Action in Asia: A Comparative and Functional Approach*, (Cambridge: Cambridge University Press 2012) 243, 291. Huang proposes that the US model is more suitable for China due to the effectiveness of the contingency fee arrangement in encouraging derivative action in JSLCs, and the unfitness of '*indemnity order*' since the leave of the court is not required in China; see H. Huang, 'Statutory Derivative Action in China: Empirical Findings and Comparative Analysis' (2012) 27(4) *Banking and Finance Law Review* 619,653. Mao proposed the adoption of the Japanese model in order to achieve multiple goals, including encouraging minority shareholders to bring derivative actions on behalf of companies and mitigating litigation risks and costs. W. Mao, *A Study on Shareholder Representative Action from an Equilibrium Perspective [均衡视角下的股东 代表诉讼研究]*, (Beijing: China Modern Economic Publishing House) 157; see also H. Zhou, Z. Liu and T. Li, 'Research on Cost and Compensation Problems of Derivative Action 股东派生诉讼诉讼费用补偿问题研究' [2013] *Legality Vision[法制博览]* 269, 269.

[150]   M. Siems, *Comparative Law*, (Cambridge: Cambridge University Press 2014) 137.

[151]   R. Michael, 'Make or Buy – A New Look at Legal Transplants' in H. Eidenmuller (ed.), *Regulatory Competition in Contract Law and Dispute* (Munich: Minich Beck 2013) 27; R. Michael, 'One Size Can Fit All' – Some Heretical Thoughts on the

adopting a model in China that is partly imported from other jurisdictions and then made to fit the Chinese context.

The legal cost issue should be regulated through a mechanism including stipulations on litigation costs that include court fees, which be further divided into filing fees and other litigation costs, and also attorneys' fees. The selection of the most appropriate model should rest on the *status quo* of the judicial system, together with the weakness and reform necessity of the derivative action mechanism in China. Moreover, it is important to embed such elements as the nature of the claimants and the current situation of the legal profession in China.

As for filing fees, as a cost that the litigant needs to pay in advance, a reform should also be adopted in China to address the key problem of the lack of incentive behind the reluctance of shareholders in JSLCs to bring derivative actions. This could be done by introducing a fixed charge as the litigation cost. This is due to two reasons including first, the number of damages to be paid to the suing shareholder is normally difficult to determine; second, a fixed charge is predictable and shareholder friendly. The number of derivative actions in Japan[152] could be echoed in China with the aim of enhancing the popularity and effectiveness of the derivative action system.

Despite the fact that successful shareholders may be indemnified for investigation fees, assessment fees, notary fees and other reasonable costs incurred from the litigation,[153] it is unclear whether shareholders who are successful in lawsuits may claim filing fees from the company. Furthermore, the result of such an action is unpredictable, and Provision IV may not play a positive role in encouraging more shareholders to bring lawsuits where they are uncertain about the result. Moreover, it is key for courts to acknowledge the nature of derivative actions, which are different from other commercial litigations. The shareholders' attorneys could play a central role in orchestrating the whole procedure and not being paid until the derivative action is settled successfully,

---

Mass Production of Legal Transplant' in G. Frankenberg (ed.), *Order from Transfer: Comparative Constitutional Design and Legal Culture*, (Cheltenham: Edward Elgar 2013) 56.

[152] M. Nakahigashi and D.W. Puchniak, 'Land of the Rising Derivative Action: Revisiting Irrationality to Understand Japan's Reluctant Shareholder Litigate' in D.W. Puchniak, H. Baum and M. Ewing-Chow (eds), *The Derivative Action in Asia: A Comparative and Functional Approach*, (Cambridge: Cambridge University Press 2012) 128, 171–173; S. Kawashima and S. Sakurai, 'Shareholder Derivative Litigation in Japan, Law, Practice and Suggested Reforms' (1997) 33(1) *Stanford Journal of International Law* 9, 37.

[153] Art. 35, Provisions of the Supreme People's Court on Some Issues about the Application of the Company Law of the People's Republic of China (IV). [最高人民法院关于适用＜中华人民共和国公司法＞若干问题的规定（四）].

which could be a rather long process.[154] This does lead to difficulties whereby shareholders may have to wait a long time before being eligible for indemnity. The scope of the Provision IV, namely investigation fees, assessment fees and notary fees, appears much narrower than the court fees stipulated in the Measures on Payment of Litigation 2007.[155] Furthermore, the big 'burden' and serious concern about filing fees have not been explicitly stipulated here.

We are reluctant to offer an exact figure, which may sound arbitrary without empirical support.[156] Nevertheless, the introduction of a fixed fee will achieve dual goals – first, encouraging sincere and legitimate shareholders to bring healthy derivative actions for the interests of companies. Just as West argued in the context of Japan, the change in nature of derivative action to involve a nominal fixed stamp fee (a reduction in most cases) explains 'much of the increase in filed cases [derivative actions]'.[157] Second, it would support claims that shareholders' benefits from derivative actions are truly 'incalculable'. It is accurate, rational and consistent with respect to the nature of the derivative action mechanism itself, since shareholders are only entitled to the benefits of successful litigation in percentage terms, indirectly, and with very vague causal links between the benefit to shareholders and the claims of the lawsuits. The *pro rota* benefits that the shareholders may enjoy are too difficult to quantify and enumerate. The American Law Institute validates the derivative action mechanism as an outstanding mechanism of shareholder remedy with virtually incalculable, or at least no readily quantifiable, deterrent effect.[158] In the author's opinion, it is of fundamental importance to clarify the nature of

---

[154] H.-J. Rho and K.-S, Kim, 'Invigorating Shareholder Derivative Actions in South Korea' in D.W. Puchniak, H. Baum and M. Ewing-Chow (eds), *The Derivative Action in Asia: A Comparative and Functional Approach*, (Cambridge: Cambridge University Press 2012) 186, 205.

[155] Particularly see Sections 6 and 13.

[156] A bold attempt at reform could be a fee of RMB 780 Yuan (equivalent to 13,000 Yen) should be charged for LLCs, although a higher fee should probably be used for JSLCs or claims with a very high target (capped at probably 0.1 million Yuan which is equivalent to 1.6 million Yen) since the monetary claims are likely to be much higher in value due to the size of the companies and the destructive nature of directors' dereliction of duty and complicity in these cases, with substantially higher costs as a result. Due to the threshold of 1 per cent ownership for 180 days in JSLCs, a higher fee than RMB 780 Yuan should not put companies under any pressure.

[157] M.D. West, 'Why Shareholders Sue: The Evidence from Japan' (2001) 30(2) *Journal of Legal Studies* 351, 352–353.

[158] American Law Institute, *American Law Institute Principles of Corporate Governance: Analysis and Recommendations*, (Philadelphia: American Law Institute Publishers, 1994); see also M.A. Eisenberg, 'An Overview of the Principles of Corporate Governance' (1992) 48 *The Business Lawyer* 1272.

derivative action claims, specifying that all derivative actions are defined as 'incalculable' claims in the national company law legislation.

In terms of attorneys' fees, it would be feasible but complicated to introduce the US model, with the 'exceptional nature of the economic incentives'[159] provided within the derivative action regime, in China, due to the fact that attorneys are regarded as entrepreneurs and derivative suits are seen as entrepreneurial litigation. It is argued that there are two important but rather difficult prerequisites for the contingency fee arrangement to work effectively in China: a common fund principle and a substantial benefit test. A well-understood and reformed approach needs to be introduced in China gradually, and it is always quicker to test ideas at the regional level. As a starting point, it may be valuable to explore the possibilities of introducing localised regulatory measures to deal with the issues surrounding litigation fees. Areas that are popular for listed companies and individual investment culture would be a good start, such as Shanghai City, Guangdong Province (where Shenzhen City is located), Beijing City, Zhejiang Province and Jiangsu Province, which has more than 1 trillion yuan in deposit balance.[160] Such a localised approach may give local authorities flexibility in designing or making attempts to develop a workable approach to funding in derivative actions. Local courts have always seemed to be more proactive in awarding legal fee reimbursement for successful claimants.

In fact, the juridical opinions promulgated by local courts always contain rules to the effect of contingent fees. For example, it is suggested by the Civil Division of the High People's Court of Shanghai that a shareholder who successfully brings a lawsuit on behalf of a company should be indemnified for reasonable litigation costs (予以适当补偿).[161] The provincial higher court of Jiangsu province, for another example, has issued rules to make indemnifying the claimants possible if they wish to bring derivative litigation. The fee-oriented requirement issued by Jiangsu court was designed to be more protective, and the rule provided that:

> if the court supports the claimant's derivative claims, litigation costs should be borne by the claimant and other reasonable litigation fees such as the attorney fees and travel costs should be borne by the company; if the court does not support the

---

[159] D. Puchniak, 'The Derivative Action in Asia: A Complex Reality' (2012) 9 *Berkeley Business Law Journal* 1, 18.

[160] Askci, *The Richest Region in China is the Most Money: Deposit Balance Ranking 31 National Provinces and Cities in 2016 [*中国哪个省最有钱？*2016*全国 *31*省市存款余额排名一览*]*, available at http://www.sohu.com/a/113866159_378843 (accessed 29 July 2022).

[161] Art. 5(2) Subsection 4, *Opinions on Adjudicating Cases in Relation to Litigation Regarding Companies 2003* [2003关于审理涉及公司诉讼案件若干问题的处理意见 （一）] (Civil Division of the High People' Court of Shanghai).

derivative claims, the litigation cost should be paid by claimant shareholders; while the court partly supports the claims, the claimant shareholders and the company should bear the cost *pro rata*.[162]

Of course, these flexibilities would also bring uncertainties, which may not resolve issues of the lack of incentives for derivative action in China. Furthermore, detailed rules on the nature of 'benefits', the triggering point at which a claimant is eligible for compensation and how to satisfy a 'reasonable' or right '*pro rata*' still need further discussion.

5.6   CONCLUSION

The mechanism of derivative claims has been a focus of interest in China with the development of corporate governance, particularly in relation to the corporate reform of SOEs and the stock markets development in China. A more sensible fee arrangement is important for a more enforceable mechanism and better corporate governance. Derivative actions are lawsuits brought by shareholders on behalf of companies, asserting claims that corporations have not pursued on their own.[163] The mechanism was adopted to address one of six defects in the Company Law of 1993.[164] Notwithstanding the significance of derivative action in modern China, the litigation-related cost of derivative action has been largely overlooked by scholarly work in this fast-growing nation.

The existing research recognises the need for a continuous process of adaptation and development, learning appropriately from experience and responding sensitively to local conditions. To date, the development of the financial system in China has had uniquely Chinese characteristics, and it has been suggested that this pathway to growth will continue. The omission of legal issues on how derivative actions should be funded is a critical failure for the new Company Law, considering the lack of incentives for shareholders to bring derivative actions, particularly those who are investors in JSLCs. Fee-related issues have been addressed in the recent Provision IV, but this provision failed to address three important aspects, including fee-related issues for shareholders who lose their case, funds that could be made available for

---

[162] Art. 79, *Opinions on Several Issues in relation to Adjudicating Corporate Disputes*   [江苏省高级人民法院关于审理适用使用公司法案件若干问题的意见] (the High People's Court of Jiangsu Province).

[163] D.A. Demott, *Shareholder Derivative Actions: Law and Practice* (Eagan: Clark Boardman Callaghan 2015) § 1.01.

[164] Fourteenth Meeting of the Tenth National People's Congress from 25–28 February 2005; the six defects were summed up by Fan and Wang.

shareholders when they bring litigation rather than paying up-front and hoping to be indemnified, and the clear scope of the fund that could be indemnified. The scope in the Provision IV seems much narrower than the court fees stipulated in the Measures on Payment of Litigation 2007. We discussed the legal approaches in Japan, the US and the UK as three classic approaches practiced globally. We conclude that a fixed fee (as in Japan) and a contingency fee supported by a common fund and substantial tests should be the way forward. The approach adopted in the UK is neither feasible nor desirable for China. It is also suggested that the introduction of any reform is obviously hindered by multiple path dependence factors such as Chinese history, culture, the quality and ethics of the legal professions, existing legislation, and the positions and information available to shareholders, especially minority shareholders in JSLCs.

6. Trends and developments in Chinese Company Law: The application of the derivative action scheme in the past 15 years

Looking at the existing research concerning derivative action in China thus far, studies can be roughly divided into two groups: before the 2006 legislative reform, research mainly focused on the rationality of transplanting the derivative action mechanism to the Chinese context and the preliminary construction of this regime.[1] After the promulgation of the Chinese Company Law, the literature, based upon discussions of limited reported cases, tended to focus on the interpretation of the legislative wording and the problems of the regime.[2] There is a gap when it comes to ascertaining trends of law in practice, the trajectory of legislative direction, and identifying problems in the application of the mechanism. This can be only achieved through a comprehensive study of all reported cases, regardless of location, result and size of the company and shareholding percentage since it is impossible and unnecessary to identify a valuable, consistent and representative sample against a number of criteria and variations. Focusing on law in practice, this chapter tries to fill this gap by focusing on complications surrounding the consistency and accuracy in terms of case judgements of derivative action in different courts, litigated by different kinds of shareholders in China.

The chapter aims to look through all reported cases from 2006 to 2020 and address the question of whether the mechanism been consistently and confidently used by shareholders, particularly in terms of promoting accessi-

---

1   For example, on the function of the mechanism see J. Deng, 'Building an Investor-Friendly Shareholder Derivative Lawsuit System in China'(2005) 46(2) *Harvard International Law Journal* 347.

2   For example, the interpretation of 'shareholders that have held in aggregate' has been interpreted by M. Hu and P. Zhang, 'Research on Legal Application of Derivative Action in China [股东代表诉讼的法律适用研究]' [2007] 3 *People's Judicature [人民司法]* 79; X. Mi, 'Analysis Of Some Important Measures To Protect Minority Shareholders' Rights and Benefits In The New "Corporation Law"' [评新《公司法》对小股东权益保护的几项重要举措]' (2006) 1 *Law Science Magazine [法学杂志]* 72.

bility, effectiveness and balancing function. Assessing the targeted period post enactment of Chinese Company Law, we will ascertain if the new statutory mechanism achieves its legislative goals such as redressing the wrongs done to the company, improving the position of shareholders, deterring directors from breaching their duties and punishing breaches where they do occur.[3]

Compared with previous work, this chapter makes an original contribution to the literature as it is the most complete case study to date, covering all available cases from 2006 to 2020.[4] It is challenging to provide a complete picture of all derivative actions, as there is no single, comprehensive source of data on the issue. Hence, this chapter uses different means to piece together a full picture of China's derivative actions. It looks at cases in two databases, *Beida Fabao* and *China Judgments online*, and it also uses direct online searches using Chinese search engines and the websites of various courts.[5]

This research should provide an essential primer for legal practitioners and in-house counsel who deal with shareholder litigation and corporate governance issues on a regular basis, and legal and business theorists on corporate law and governance. The research outcome will also be helpful for legislators and policy makers to understand potential problems for the application of the law and directions for reform. Also, it will enable practitioners to comprehend and prepare for the inconsistency and complications that will arise when different courts interpret and apply the law in a different way.

The chapter proceeds as follows. Section 6.1 explains our methodology and the selection of 466 cases for our study, in order to clarify why our cohort of cases is the most complete and comprehensive to date. Sections 6.2–6.9 presents eight key findings of our empirical analysis, with follow-up reflections and reform proposals.

---

[3] J. Coffee and D.E. Schwartz, 'The Survival of the Derivative Suit: An Evolution and a Proposal for Legislative Reform' (1981) 81 *Columbia Law Review* 261, 302–309.

[4] We are not going to explore cases before 2006 as they have been discussed elsewhere in detail; see S. Lin, *Derivative Actions in Chinese Company Law* (Alphen ann den Rijin: Kluwer Law International 2015).

[5] Previous empirical research has only examined cases from *Beida Fabao* since *China Judgments online*, the official website for case reports in China, was established fairly recently in 2014; see H. Huang, 'Shareholder Derivative Litigation in China: Empirical Findings and Comparative Analysis' (2012) 27(4) *Banking and Finance Law Review* 619; S. Lin, 'Derivative Actions in China: Case Analysis' (2014) 44 *Hong Kong Law Journal* 621.

6.1　CASE ANALYSIS IN CHINA, AND OUR SAMPLE

In this section, a brief introduction to the Chinese case report system will be presented, together with a narrative for our methodology in establishing a complete sample of derivative action cases.

The case report system started at national and local levels in early 2000. The SPC started a pilot programme for the reporting of court decisions as early as 2000 at the national level, and courts at all levels have been required to publish their decisions since 2009. However, a national official database for judicial decisions was not established until recently.[6] From 2014 onwards the SPC has issued regulations that require all judicial decisions to be published online.[7] Subsequently, an electronic database – *China Judgments online* – was established to publish all judicial decisions in the country. The total number of cases contained in the database had reached over 55 million as of November 2018.[8]

This enhanced reporting system for judicial decisions is part of the SPC's efforts to strengthen the judiciary and improve the quality and accountability of judicial decisions.[9] An open database also facilitates consistency and predictability in judgments. The judges will be able to refer to the previous decisions both horizontally based on the level of the courts and vertically based on the timing of the judgments. In addition, access to judgments online may stimulate legal research and scholarly discussions. With more transparency and consistency in judicial decisions, it is practicable and meaningful to conduct empirical research to evaluate judicial decisions and examine the trajectory of legislation.

We identified 466 cases of derivative action to constitute our full sample. Efforts have been made to ensure the best possible completeness of the sample through two streams: searching by the key phrase 'representative action *daibiao susong* (代表诉讼)' in the category of corporate-related disputes,[10] as

---

[6]　B. Ahl and D. Sprick, 'Towards Judicial Transparency in China: The New Public Access Database for Court Decisions' (2017) 32(1) *China Information* 3.

[7]　The SPC's provisions on the publication of the People's Courts' judicial decisions on the internet [最高人民法院关于人民法院在互联网公布裁判文书的规定] (published in 2013, amended in 2016).

[8]　See Jun Xu, The Total Number of Visits to the China Judging Online exceeded 20 Billion [中国裁判文书网总访问量突破两百亿] 14 November 2018, http://ip.people.com.cn/n1/2018/1114/c179663–30400147.html (accessed 24 July 2022).

[9]　B. Ahl and D. Sprick, 'Towards Judicial Transparency in China: The New Public Access Database for Court Decisions' (2017) 32(1) *China Information* 3.

[10]　'Corporate-related disputes [与公司有关的纠纷]' is a sub-category under the category of 'civil disputes related to corporation, securities, insurance and bills [与公司、证券、保险、票据等有关的民事纠纷]' in all law databases in China. We are aware that the use of the term 'representative action' may be not an accurate descrip-

well as the relevant provisions.[11] It is the common practice of Chinese courts to use the term 'representative action'.[12] After we had collected all relevant cases, we carefully analysed each one and confirmed that the litigations in the cases were derivative actions. We eliminated cases that only dealt with jurisdiction, as well as cases that were easily confused with derivative actions, including cases that were classified as shareholders' direct actions and companies' actions.

In order to differentiate derivative actions, direct actions and company actions systematically, we reference Articles 23–26 of the Provision IV.[13] Provision IV clarified that Article 151 provides for two different types of litigation – the 'company's direct action' (*gongsi zhijie susong* 公司直接诉讼)[14] and the derivative action. To be specific, Provision IV states that at the request of shareholders, the board of directors/executive director or the board of supervisors/supervisors can bring actions against wrongdoers. Such actions are viewed as company actions brought directly by the company itself, and the company will be treated as the claimant in such actions.[15]

In practice, a strict approach has been adopted in Chinese courts to segregate the direct/derivative dichotomy. Cases that are brought as direct actions but contain a legal basis for derivative action are usually rejected by the courts on basis of making the wrong claim. We have eliminated such cases from our sample, as their merits were not considered by the courts. Under Chinese law,

---

tion. Although derivative action is commonly referred to as representative action not only in judgment but also in secondary literatures in the Chinese language, strictly speaking the concept of 'representative action' may be broader than 'derivative action', and refers to a lawsuit where one party acts on behalf of others. It can include class actions or actions brought by governmental authorities or consumer associations on behalf of private parties. A derivative action is a representative action brought by shareholders on behalf of and in the name of the company.

[11] This includes art. 151 (art. 152 before 2013) that provides for derivative action, arts 147–150 (directors' duties) and Arts 20–22 that might form the cause of action for a derivative action.

[12] See the SPC's guidance book on adjudicating corporate litigations, which refers to derivative action as representative action. W. Du (ed.), *SPC Guidance Book on Adjudicating Company Cases [*最高人民法院商事审判指导丛书：公司案件审判指导*]*, (Beijing: Law Press 2018).

[13] Lack of Interpretation IV may be a reason why previous studies have not fully considered the distinctive features of derivative action under Chinese law.

[14] A 'company's direct action' refers to actions brought by internal authorities of the company (e.g., board of supervisors/directors) and regarded as actions brought directly by the company. It is frequently used in academic discussions to contrast with a derivative action. See, e.g., J. Zhang and M. He, 'Institutional Design of Derivative Action in China [中国股东代位诉讼制度设计：法理探讨与经济分析]' (2005) 5 *Journal of East China University of Political Science and Law [*华东政法大学学报*]* 5.

[15] Provision IV, art. 23.

shareholders' direct actions can be brought under Articles 20, 22 and 152.[16] In our opinion, this strict approach is not necessarily the most efficient. We identified a number of cases where direct actions were brought but the claims were rejected because the courts thought that claimants should have initiated the cases as derivative actions, although the courts could have trailed the cases as derivative actions so that these cases could be settled more efficiently. These cases always involved scenarios where wrongs were found to cause loss to the company, including signing or terminating a contract to the detriment of the company,[17] siphoning corporate assets,[18] undervaluing transfers,[19] using related party transactions to sign false contracts,[20] not being vigilant in provid-

---

[16]   For a general discussion of 'oppression' in China, see C. Hawes, K.A. Lau and A. Young, 'The Chinese "Oppression" Remedy: Creative Interpretations of Company Law by Chinese Courts' (2015) 63 *The American Journal of Comparative Law* 559. Arts 20, 22 and 152 of Chinese Company Law 2018 allow shareholders to raise direct actions against other shareholders, the company and directors respectively. Also see the Guiding Case No. 10 (*Li Jianjun v Shanghai Jiapower Environment Protection Science and Technology Co. Ltd.*) issued by the SPC, available at https://cgc.law.stanford.edu/ guiding–cases/guiding–case–10/ (accessed 24 July 2022). Art. 152 is usually cited when there is a breach of directors' duties.

[17]   *Chen Zhixiong v Chen Zhiwen* (2014 GanMinErZhong No. 13) [陈志雄与陈志文损害股东利益责任纠纷案(2014)赣民二终字第13号]; *Mo Haijun v Hu Haibo et al.* (2013 GuishiMinerZhongZi No. 183) [莫海军与胡海波等损害股东利益责任纠纷上诉案(2013) 桂市民二终字第183号.

Mo Haijun v Hu Haibo et al. (2013 GuishiMinerZhongZi No. 183) [莫海军与胡海波等损害股东利益责任纠纷上诉案(2013)桂市民二终字第183号.

[18]   *Chen Guorong v Huang Qing Shao* (2014 ZhuZhongfaliMinzhonZi No. 234) [陈国荣等诉黄庆韶等损害股东利益责任纠纷案 (2014)珠中法立民终字第234号].

[19]   *Zhang Ding v Zhang Yong* (2016 Lu 01 Minzhong No. 5133) [张丁诉张勇等损害股东利益纠纷案(2016)鲁01民终5133号]; *Li Jian v Hao Gui Dong* (2016 Supreme People's Court Minshen No. 84) [李健诉郝贵东等损害股东利益责任纠纷案(2016)最高法民申84号]; *Tan Lixing v Li Jingwei* (2014 Supreme People's Court MinshenZi No. 693) [谭利兴等诉黎经炜等董事、高级管理人员损害股东利益赔偿纠纷案(2014)民申字第693号]; *Bi Jianhua and Wang Hao Civil Judgment* (2020 Lu 01 Min Zhong No. 7407) [毕建华与王灏损害公司利益责任纠纷2020鲁01民终7407号民事判决书].

[20]   *Beijing Brain Think Tank Education Technology Co. Ltd. v Lin Shixun and the third party Beijing Knight Medal Education Technology Co. Ltd.* (2018) Jing 04 Min Chu No. 382 [北京大脑智库教育科技有限公司与林士勋和第三人北京骑士勋章教育科技有限公司公司关联交易损害责任纠纷一案(2018)京04民初382号].

ing relevant information requested by supervisors[21] and unauthorised disposal of the company's property.[22]

The courts have strictly distinguished between losses to the company and personal losses to shareholders, and found that shareholders may not make a personal claim where their loss is only incurred indirectly as a result of the loss to the company.[23] We have not included these cases in our sample because the courts rejected the cases without considering their merits. To our knowledge, no claimants have initiated follow-up derivative actions. The following sections present seven key research findings of our empirical analysis, and some reflections.

6.2 NUMBER OF CASES BY YEAR AND PATTERN OF CASES IN JSLCS AND LLCS

The number of cases is a straightforward statistic with meaningful implications. The following figures indicate the flow of cases every year since the enforcement of the Chinese Company Law revised in 2005 on 1 January 2006. The data indicate that the mechanism has been reasonably applied used by shareholders for the deterrence of mismanagement, and for compensating companies and their shareholders for harm caused. We found 466 derivative actions during the period from 2006(inclusive) to 2020(inclusive) – an average of 31 cases per year. The overall trend is rising, with the increasing popularity of derivative actions since 2014. This may be explained by an improved understanding of derivative actions, including among lawyers, judges and shareholders, particularly after the issuing of Provision IV in 2014, which offered guidance before it was formally enforced in September 2017.

---

[21]   *Beijing Yusen Equity Investment Co. Ltd. v Li Kechun et al.* (2020) Jing 04 Min Chu No. 348北京煜森股权投资有限公司与李克纯等损害公司利益责任纠纷一案 (2020)京04民初348号.

[22]   *Luo Xiaofeng v Wenzhou is Xu Film and Television Production Co. Ltd.* (2014 WenluShangchuZi No. 5108)[罗晓凤诉温州正栩影视制作有限公司等公司债权人利益责任纠纷案(2014)温鹿商初字第5108号].

[23]   For example, in *Li Jian v Hao Gui Dong* (2016 Supreme People's Court Minshen No. 84) [李健诉郝贵东等损害股东利益责任纠纷案(2016)最高法民申84号], the shareholder plaintiff claimed that the defendant, who was both the chairman of the board and the general manager of the company, had infringed his shareholder right by selling the coal products of the company at a low value. However, the court rejected his claim on the grounds that the losses caused by the transaction were directly accrued to the company, and the plaintiff only incurred indirect losses. The shareholder's property rights are separate from those of the company, and his entitlement to the company's property was limited to the right of distribution as provided by art. 34.

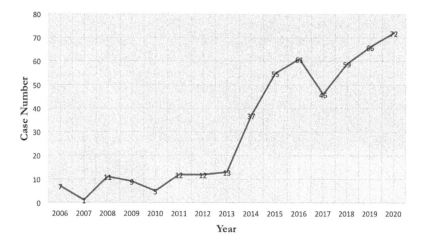

Figure 6.1   Number of cases for derivative actions (2006–2020)

'The biggest problem of derivative actions in China is not too many lawsuits, but too few of them.'[24] The lack of cases has been regarded as the result of the non-litigious culture or the civil law legal system.[25] We think it is meaningful to investigate the number of cases in other jurisdictions, in order to give a comparative view of the practical application of the mechanism purely based on the criterion of case numbers. We selected cases in Japan, another jurisdiction with a non-litigious culture, and the UK, a counter-example of a civil law system, to investigate the causal link between these reasons and the frequency of derivative action in China demonstrated by the number of cases.

Looking at the numbers of cases in Japan and the UK gives us some interesting insights: In Japan, it was reported that 119 derivative actions were brought against listed companies between 1993 and 2009.[26] This increase

---

[24]   This is the translation of the sentence我国当前面临的最大问题不是股东代表诉讼太多了，而是股东代表诉讼太少了 in J. Liu, *Modern Corporation Law [*现代公司法*]* (Beijing: Law Press, 3rd ed. 2015) 408.

[25]   L. Miles, "The Application of Anglo-American Corporate Practices in Societies Influenced by Confucian Values" (2006) 111(3) *Business and Society Review* 305; D.W. Puchniak, 'The Complexity of Derivative Actions in Asia' in D.W. Puchniak, H. Baum and M. Ewing-Chow (eds), *The Derivative Action in Asia: A Comparative and Functional Approach*, (Cambridge: Cambridge University Press 2012) 90.

[26]   M. Nakahigashi and D.W. Punchniak, 'Land of the Rising Derivative Action: Revisiting Irrationality to Understand Japan's Uneluctant Shareholder Litigate' in D.W. Puchniak, H Baum and M Ewing-Chow (eds), *The Derivative Action in Asia: A Comparative and Functional Approach*, (Cambridge: Cambridge University Press 2012) 128, 171–173.

could be a consequence of multiple reasons, such as the fixed litigation fee reform after the *Nikko Securities* decision by the Tokyo High Court, or a more relaxed standing requirement without a shareholding percentage threshold.[27] It is obvious that the mechanism has been much more frequently used in Japan than in China although both countries have a non-litigious culture. Therefore, it may not be tenable that the non-litigious culture is the main reason for the unpopularity of the mechanism in China.

Comparatively, in common law countries, which have better minority share-holder protection according to La Porta, Lopez-de-Silanes, Sheifer and Vishny (LLSV),[28] derivative actions are brought by shareholders in both private com-panies and public companies. In the UK the enforcement of the mechanism has not been very strong. It is claimed that statutory derivative action is unlikely to be more efficient or more cost-effective, even after the mechanism was codi-fied in the UK CA 2006.[29] Partly echoing this statement, Keay's study showed that since section 260 of the UK CA 2006 came into force on 1 October 2007, 22 derivative actions were instituted up to September 2015.[30] After September 2015 and up to end of 2021 there were only 15 reported cases;[31] 37 derivative actions have been instituted up to end of 2021, an average of 2.64 cases every year.[32] Indeed, the low popularity and lack of effectiveness of the derivative action mechanism in the UK is influenced by many factors. Unfair prejudice, based on section 994 of the UK CA 2006, has proved to be a much more popular mechanism in shareholder remedies, which may be a comprehensive

---

[27]   Art. 847 of the Japan Companies Act 2005.

[28]   R. La Porta, F. Lopez-de-Silanes, A. Sheifer and R. Vishny, 'Law and Finance' (1998) 106(6) *Journal of Political Economy* 1113–1155.

[29]   J. Lowry, 'Reconstructing Shareholder Actions: A Response to the Law Commission's Consultation Paper' (1997) 18(8) *Company Lawyer* 247, 249.

[30]   A. Keay, 'Assessing and rethinking the statutory scheme for derivative actions under the Companies Act 2006' (2016) 16(1) *Journal of Corporate Law Studies* 39, 57; the data were collected from a search of the Westlaw, Lexis and BAILII databases for three jurisdictions, namely England and Wales, Scotland, and Northern Ireland.

[31]   *SDI Retail Services Ltd. v King* [2017] EWHC 737 (Ch); *Wilton UK Ltd. v Shuttleworth* [2018] EWHC 911 (Ch); *Coyne (Suing on behalf of herself and all other shareholders in MFW Developments Limited other than the First Defendant) v Walsh* [2019] EWHC 3725 (Ch); *Saatchi v Gajjar* [2019] EWHC 3472 (Ch); *Homes for England v Nick Sellman (Holdings) Ltd.* [2020] EWHC 936 (Ch); *Boston Trust Co. Ltd. v Szerelmey Lt.d* [2020] EWHC 1136 (Ch); *Hughes v Burley* [2021] EWHC 104 (Ch); *Gill v Thind* [2020] EWHC 2983 (Ch); *Monaghan v Cunningham* [2021] NICh 14; *Percy v Merriman White (A Firm)* [2021] EWHC 22 (Ch); *Hut Group Ltd., Re* [2020] EWHC 5 (Ch); *Robert Glew and Denton and Co Trustees Ltd. v Matossian-Rogers* [2019] EWHC 3183 (Ch); *Dodoun v Collings* [2019] EWHC 2008 (Ch); *Zavahir v Shankleman* [2016] EWHC 2772 (Ch); *Brannigan v Style* [2016] EWHC 512 (CH).

[32]   This was calculated as 37 cases in the period of 14 years.

barrier to instituting a derivative claim. Therefore, it is difficult for us to gather sufficient evidence to build a causal link between the civil law system and the lack of derivative actions in China, as the problem exists in common law countries too. Scholars even argued that China is a counter-example for LLSV's famous assertions.[33]

This comparative analysis between Japan, the UK and China suggests that, although it is still at an early stage in its development, derivative action has made a noticeable impact in China. One distinct finding in relation to the number of cases in China is that most of the shareholders who are using this mechanism are shareholders in LLCs. Previous studies have found that most derivative cases in China are brought for LLCs, with only one (or none) for JSLCs.[34] Our study reaffirms the continuing shortage of cases brought on behalf of JSLCs. However, we have found five cases of derivative action brought by shareholders of JSLCs with only one of them as a listed company.

With the size of the stock market in China, how to encourage shareholders to use derivative actions more effectively and how to make the mechanism more accessible for shareholders in JSLCs is a significant issue. There are multiple reasons for the shortage of cases brought in JSLCs, such as thresholds on shareholding ownership percentage and period, prohibitive litigation fees, exit options for shareholders, and additional public enforcement measures for listed companies. Moreover, free riding is a problem caused by the nature of a derivative action, as the remedy will go to the company and shareholders as a whole, with the claimant only benefiting on a *pro rata* basis according to the value of his or her shares. If the case fails, the plaintiff shareholders bear all of the litigation costs.[35] This creates incentives for shareholders to free-ride, as they can reap benefits without bearing any risk if others are prepared to bring a derivative suit.[36] This free-riding problem is more serious in JSLCs because shareholders are scattered, difficult to organise and often wait for others to take action.[37]

---

[33]   F. Allen, J. Qian and M. Qian, 'Law, Finance, and Economic Growth in China' (2005) 77(1) *Journal of Financial Economics* 57.

[34]   S. Lin, 'Derivative Actions in China: Case Analysis' (2014) 44 *Hong Kong Law Journal* 621.

[35]   Wen-Yeu Wang, 'The IPC Model for Securities Law Enforcement in Taiwan', in R.H. Huang and N.C. Howson (eds) *Enforcement of Corporate and Securities Law: China and the World*, (Cambridge: Cambridge University Press 2017) 454, 466.

[36]   A. Keay, *Board Accountability in Corporate Governance*, (Abington: Routledge 2015) 220.

[37]   W. Wang, 'The IPC Model for Securities Law Enforcement in Taiwan, in R.H. Huang and N.C. Howson (eds) *Enforcement of Corporate and Securities Law: China and the World*, (Cambridge: Cambridge University Press 2017) 454, 466.

It is also possible that the rules on corporate governance formulated by the SPC (including those on derivative action) are more oriented towards LLCs, as the regulatory framework related to JSLCs has been heavily monopolised by the CSRC. Consequently, shareholders in JSLCs are more reliant on public enforcement by the CSRC than on private litigation.[38] Additionally, the fact that derivative actions in China almost exclusively concern LLCs indicates the lack of fully-fledged remedies for minority shareholders in LLCs.[39]

A detailed analysis will be offered on the cases brought for JSLCs in our sample. One case brought by a single shareholder was rejected by the court on the grounds that the shareholder did not meet the shareholding percentage requirement of 1 per cent; also the shareholder had not satisfied the procedural requirement of demanding that the company should take action first.[40] However, the court supported the rest of the cases brought by shareholders in JSLCs. In *Kaiming Construction et al. v Huang Dayin et al.*,[41] institutional shareholders were joined by individual shareholders (four plaintiffs in total),[42] and they sued the controlling shareholder for failing to repay a loan borrowed

---

[38] R.H. Huang, 'Private Enforcement of Securities Law in China: A Ten-Year Retrospective and Empirical Assessment' (2013) 61(4) *The American Journal of Comparative Law* 757. Further evidence is the fact that the guiding cases regarding corporate litigations issued by the SPC are all concerned with LLCs. These cases are: *Lin Fangqing v Changshu Kailai Industry Co. Ltd. et al.* (Guiding case No.8) [林方清诉常熟市凯莱实业有限公司、戴小明公司解散纠纷案]; *Shanghai Cunliang Trading Co. Ltd. v Jiang Zhidong et al.* (Guiding case No.9) [上海存亮贸易有限公司诉蒋志东、王卫明等买卖合同纠纷案]; *Li Jianjun v Shanghai Jiapower Environment Protection Science and Technology Co. Ltd.* (Guiding case No. 10) [李建军诉上海佳动力环保科技有限公司公司决议撤销纠纷案]; *XCMG Construction Machinery Co. Ltd. v Chengdu Chuanjiao Industry et al.* (Guiding case No. 15) [徐工集团工程机械股份有限公司诉成都川交工贸有限责任公司等买卖 合同纠纷案].

[39] C. Hawes, K. Alex Lau and A. Young, 'The Chinese "Oppression" Remedy: Creative Interpretations of Company Law by Chinese Courts' (2015) 63(3) *The American Journal of Comparative Law* 559.

[40] *Gu Shanhua v Hong Kong Shengxun Enterprise Co. Ltd. et al.* (SuMinZhong No. 217) [顾善华因诉香港盛迅企业有限公司、镇江八佰伴商贸 有限公司及第三人镇江百货股份有限公司损害公司利益案（2016）苏民终217号].

[41] *Kaiming Construction et al. v Huang Dayin et al.* (2017 Yu 0110 MinChu No. 9690) [原告凯明建筑等与被告黄达银等损害公司利益案 (2017) 渝0110民初9690号].

[42] The two institutional shareholders in this case are Chongqing Kaiming Construction Engineering Co. Ltd. and Sichuan Universal Real Estate Development Co. Ltd. Each of the four shareholders in this case satisfies the requirement that a shareholder should hold 1 per cent or more of the company's shares for 180 consecutive days in order to bring a derivative action.

from the company. In *Huang Congfu et al. v Huang Runguo et al.* [43] four individual shareholders collectively brought an action against third persons who defaulted on a contract with the company.[44] Interestingly, the individual plaintiffs were residents of the same village with the same family name, and the company involved was a 'village enterprise'. In the third case,[45] the institutional shareholder with 70 per cent of the ownership brought the case over liability for injuring the company's interests. In *Beijing Gold Exchange Center Co. Ltd. Yuan Bing*,[46] the act of the director on behalf of the company conforms to the legal characteristics of related party transactions and the director is in breach of the duty as company law prohibits company shareholders, actual controllers, directors, supervisors, senior managers, etc., from using affiliated relationships to harm the company's interests.

It is worth noting that all four cases discussed above involved non-listed JSLCs. Compared with listed JSLCs, shareholding in non-listed JSLCs is less dispersed, and it is easier to satisfy the 1 per cent shareholding threshold. A smaller group of shareholders could more comfortably overcome the collective action problem in shareholder litigation with lower costs.[47]

The case brought by villagers suggests the important role of mutual trust and social networks in initiating collective action. This is particularly relevant in China where *guanxi*, in this case the family *guanxi*, plays a significant role in reducing transaction and information costs and operational uncertainty. Social networks can encourage and promote trust and reciprocity among members of the network. With mutual trust, members are more likely to cooperate and take

---

[43]   *Huang Congfu et al. v Huang Runguo et al.* (2016, Xiang 1022 MinChu No. 711) [原告黄丛付等与被告黄润国等损害公司利益责任纠纷一 案 (2016) 湘1022民初711号].

[44]   The four defendants in this case had contracted the business of the company (chemical fertiliser) but failed to pay contracting fees to the company in time. The shareholders' claim was for the defendant to pay the contracting fees in arrears as well as the penalty.

[45]   *Guangzhou Shenggao Yangtao Hotel Co. Ltd. v Shenggao Chain Hotel Management Co. Ltd.* (2019) Yue 0106 Min Chu No. 15080 [原告广州市胜高杨桃酒店有限公司与胜高连锁酒店管理股份有限公司损害公司利益责任纠纷一案 (2019) 粤0106民初15080号].

[46]   *Beijing Gold Exchange Center Co. Ltd. Yuan Bing* (2020) Wan 08 Minzhong No.   1051北京黄金交易中心有限公司袁兵确认合同无效纠纷二审民事判决书 (2020) 皖08民终1051号.

[47]   M. Olson, *Logic of Collective Action: Public Goods and the Theory of Groups*, (Harvard: Harvard University Press 1965) 52:

[S]ize is one of the determining factors in deciding whether or not it is possible that the voluntary, rational pursuit of individual interest will bring forth group-oriented behaviour. Small groups will further their common interests better than large groups.

collective action.[48] Nevertheless, as a double-edged sword, *guanxi* may also lead to illicit strike suits and malicious litigation undertaken not in good faith.

This discussion has shed light on how to facilitate shareholders' collective action in JSLCs, especially the listed ones with dispersed share ownership and limited embedded social network. Since the size of the group matters, it might be desirable to form a collective action group for shareholders with a small number of members. Moreover, communication among group members should be improved to facilitate trust. It has been found that face-to-face communication before action can enhance mutual trust and facilitate cooperation.[49] Evidence has been found in other jurisdictions, such as Canada, that collective action can facilitate shareholder activism.[50]

We were unable to locate the first and only case brought in a listed JSLC[51] in the database, but it was well reported by the media. In 2010 the shareholders in the *Sanlian Shangshe* brought a derivative action against the *Sanlian* Group, the controlling shareholder, for infringing the trademark of the company. The controlling shareholder raised a jurisdictional issue and requested the case to be transferred from the Shandong Higher People's Court to the SPC.[52] However, this request was rejected by the SPC, and subsequently the Shandong Court suspended the case because the result of the case depended on the trial of another case.[53]

---

[48]   E. Ostrom, 'Collective Action and the Evolution of Social Norms' (2000) 14(3) *Journal of Economic Perspectives* 137; E.R. Smith and D.M. Mackie, *Social Psychology*, (New York: Psychology Press 2014) 547; OECD, *Providing Agri-environmental Public Goods through Collective Action* (OECD Publishing 2013) 103.

[49]   Smith and Mackie, ibid.

[50]   C. Doidge et al., Can Institutional Investors Improve Corporate Governance Through Collective Action? (Rotman School of Management Working Paper No. 2635662), https://papers.ssrn.com/sol3/papers.cfm?abstract_id=2635662 (accessed 24 July 2012).

[51]   D. Clarke and N. Calcina Howson, 'Pathway to Minority Shareholder Protection: Derivative Action in THE People's Republic of China' in D.W. Puchniak, H. Baum and M. Ewing-Chow (eds) *The Derivative Action in Asia: A Comparative and Functional Approach* (Cambridge: Cambridge University Press 2012) 243, 291.

[52]   *Huang Hongwei et al. v Shangdong Sanlian Group* (2010 MinsanZhongZi No. 5) [黄伟宏等诉山东三联集团有限责任公司侵犯商标专用权纠纷管辖权异议案（2010）民三终字第5号].

[53]   CSRC (Tianjin Securities Regulatory Bureau), *The Trajectory of Investors' Rights in the Last Ten Years: A Journey that is Steadily Moving Forward* (2012) [十年维权路漫漫 投资者权益保护稳步前行], http://www.csrc.gov.cn/tianjin/xxfw/tjjfxjy/201210/t20121010_215613.htm (accessed 24 July 2022).

6.3   CASE LOCATION

We have found that most cases, including derivative actions, are generally concentrated in economically developed areas such as Beijing, Shanghai, Zhejiang, Guangdong and Jiangsu. As the most developed regions in China with the highest GDP (see Table 6.1 below), these cities and provinces play an essential role in the economic growth of the country. Beijing is the capital city and political centre of China. Shanghai is the biggest city in China and lies at the centre of the Yangtze River Delta, as the most economically developed region in China with economic growth largely driven by Jiangsu and Zhejiang provinces. Zhejiang is home to 92 of the top 500 privately-owned companies, ranked highest among all provinces in China for consecutive 21 years.[54] The economic performance of Guangdong is not as strong as that of Zhejiang, but it was the original site of reform and opening up, and the Pearl River Delta, as a bustling region with massive manufacturing and trade, is located in this province. This is an area closely linked with Hong Kong and includes metropolises such as Shenzhen and Guangzhou. The two main stock exchanges in China are located in Shanghai and Shenzhen, and they have grown to become the second and fourth largest in Asia and the fourth and eighth largest globally, with 2,208 and 1,575 listed companies respectively and total free-floating market capitalisations of 8,515 trillion as of December 2019.[55] Due to the number of commercial transactions, these areas with high GDPs are, unsurprisingly, the areas where most cases are trialled. Tianjin City seems to be an exception, although this major northern port municipality has admitted to falsifying GDP data.

In total, cases in these five developed regions out of 23 provinces and four municipalities, apart from Tianjin, account for 59.21 per cent (216) of all derivative actions.[56] The result is not surprising as in large economies more conflicts will be generated between shareholders and controllers of companies. It may also reflect better awareness and understanding of derivative actions from shareholders and other claims and better professional knowledge among lawyers with more experience in corporate law cases. In China where most company laws are transplanted, economic development in a region is usually

---

[54]   See X. Nan, China's top 500 private enterprises announced, Zhejiang ranked first in 21 consecutive years [中国民营企业500强公布，浙江上榜数量连续21年第一], *Zhejiang Online*, 22 August 2019, http://js.zjol.com.cn/ycxw_zxtf/201908/t20190822_10859820.shtml (accessed 24 July 2022).

[55]   The WFE Statistics Team, *Market Statistics – January 2020* https://focus.world–exchanges.org/issue/january–2020/market–statistics (accessed 24 July 2022).

[56]   These cities and provinces have the highest GDP per capita in China. See http://www.xuetz.com/xuetz–info/64552.html (accessed 24 July 2022).

Table 6.1   *Court location*

Area	Number of Cases	Percentage	GDP per capita 2019 (thousand $)
Beijing	46	10%	2.38
Shanghai	51	11%	2.28
Jiangsu	57	12%	1.79
Zhejiang	51	11%	1.58
Guangdong	70	15%	1.38
Developed Regions	**275**	**59%**	
Others	191	41%	
Total	466	100%	

the foundation for effective enforcement of law and provides stimulation for more comprehensive legal practice.

6.4   DEFENDANT

As illustrated in Figure 6.2 below, we found that the largest group of defendants is shareholders (270), and the second largest is non-shareholder directors (85). Supervisors are the smallest group (19), and the number the defendants drops in the category of 'other people' is only slightly smaller than the number of directors (92). It should be noted that there are cases in which more than one defendant is sued, so the total number of defendants (466) is larger than the number of cases.

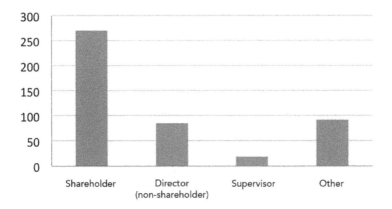

Figure 6.2   *Defendant's identity*

The fact that 59 per cent (270/466) of defendants are shareholders sheds light on two significant aspects of corporate governance problems in China. First, we have found that most of these cases were concerning LLCs (as discussed in section 6.2) with no clear separation between ownership and control, where the main agency problem arises between the controlling shareholder and the minority shareholders.[57] It is always the case that the defendants have the dual identity as shareholders and directors but, rather strangely, the file of the case record the defendant as shareholders, rather than directors. It also reveals the problem that the claimants may have a stronger recognition of the defendants' identity as controlling shareholders rather than the directors and direct litigation should have been a more appreciated channel. Second, it may indicate the claimants' knowledge and understanding of the nature of derivative actions (as litigation brought on behalf of the company) are immature.

In terms of the 'other people' defendants besides shareholders, directors and supervisors. Article 151(3) explicitly permits shareholders to bring a derivative action against 'other people' who infringe on the interests of the company and cause loss to the company. It is a catch-all phrase for both insiders and outsiders of the company. The number of outsider defendants is larger than the number of supervisor defendants, who might lack real power with limited opportunity to abuse it. According to Article 151(1), defendants in derivative actions include directors, supervisors and senior officers. The 'any other person' as a defendant embedded in Article 151(3) makes the law uncertain. The result of our sample places 'other people' in the following five categories:

(1)   companies connected with the controlling shareholder/director;[58]
(2)   family and relatives of the controlling shareholder, director or those with dual identity;[59]
(3)   assistants in fraud against the company;[60]

---

[57]   This is in contrast with public companies, where the separation of ownership and control results in severe agency problems between shareholders and directors.

[58]   *Gao Bingrui v Shunming Fujian Construction Engineering Co. Ltd.* (2012 SanminChuZi No. 118) [高炳瑞与顺明福建建设工程有限公司等损害公司利益责任纠纷 一案（2012）三民初字第 118 号].

[59]   *Zhang Baode v Li Heping, Cheng Qinghui* (2017 Shan 0303 Minchu No. 2421) [张宝德与李和平、成清慧损害公司利益案 (2017)陕 0303 民初 2421号].

[60]   *Sichuan Huqiang Equity Investment Fund Management Co. Ltd. et al. v Sichuan Shengyu New Rural Construction Co. Ltd.* (2015 ChenghuaMinChuZi No. 6212) [四川省互强股权投资基金管理有限公司等与四川圣禹新农村建设有限公司损害公司利益案 (2015)成华民初字第6212号]; *Deng Xiyan et al. v Guangzhou Jicaoyuan Cosmetics Co. Ltd.* (2014 HuiYunFaMinerChuZi No. 767) [邓喜艳等诉广州集草缘化妆品有限公司加工合同纠纷案 (2014)穗云法民二初字第767号].

(4)   third parties who have contractual or tortious relationships with the company;[61] and

(5)   government agencies that have infringed the interests of the company.[62]

However, the judicial practice is inconsistent. It has been concluded that derivative actions may not be brought against 'outsiders' of the company in some courts.[63]

Looking at the equivalence in the UK company law, 'the cause of action may be against the director or another person (or both)'.[64] It is claimed that 'another person' only applies to those persons who have assisted directors in the breach of their duties.[65] Chinese scholars also made some attempts to interpret the term. Liu argues that defendants in derivative actions may include directors, supervisors, senior managers, majority shareholders and third persons (监事、高管、大股东、第三人等人员对公司的侵害行为).[66] Rather than explicitly listing constituencies, we think it may be more reasonable to describe the scope of 'other people' as Cai interpreted that defendants should include parties against whom companies are not capable or not willing to institute a lawsuit (公司无意或无力起诉的人).[67] Together with the interpretation of the UK law, 'other people' include those persons who have assisted directors and supervisors in the breach of their duties but companies do not intend to or are not capable of bringing litigation against these parties. This interpretation ascertains the scope of the defendant and may enhance the accessibility and effectiveness of the law. Shareholders may gain access to the mechanism

---

[61]   *Zhang Lijuan v Dong Yongkang et al.* (SuZhongShangChuZi No. 00289) [原告张丽娟诉被告董永康损害公司利益案 (2014) 宿中商初字第 00289 号].

[62]   *Guo Mouhai et al. v Danzhou City Government* (2012 HainanErZhonghangZhongZi No. 13) [郭某海等诉儋州市人民政 府土地行政登记案（2012）海南二中行终字第 13号].

[63]   *Liang Chengjia v Bao Aiguo et al.* (2014, JinMiner(Shang)ChuZi No. 168) [梁成佳与包爱国、赵炜、陈芝荣 损害公司利益案 (2014) 金民二(商)初字第 168 号]; *Yang Guiping v Kaiyuan Zhongxin Toys Co. Ltd.* (2013 JuhouShangChuZi No. 0142) [杨桂平诉江苏开元众鑫玩具有限公司利益案 (2013)句后商初字第 0142 号]; *Deng Weiwei et al. v Foshan Chengzhiyuan Trading Co. Ltd.* (2017 Yue 1882 Minchu No. 305)[邓维维等与佛山市诚之远贸易有限公司损害公司利益案 (2017)粤1882 民初305 号].

[64]   Section 260(3), UK CA 2006.

[65]   D. Kershaw, *Company Law in Context: Text and Materials* (Oxford: Oxford University Press 2009) 556.

[66]   K. Liu, 'The Judicial Application and Legislative Perfection of Shareholder Representative Action [股东代表诉讼的司法适用与立法完善]' [2008] 4 *China Legal Science [中国法学]* 157.

[67]   L. Cai, 'The Scope of Defendant in Derivative Suit论股东派生诉讼中被告的范围' (2007) 1 *Contemporary Law Review* [当代法学] 153, 158.

Table 6.2   Plaintiff identity: Nature Person vs Institution

Number of plaintiffs	Number of cases	Percentage
Individual	160	66%
Institutional	306	34%
Total	466	100%

where companies are incapable of initiating litigation. The flexibility of this definition will also enhance the effectiveness of the mechanism to give courts guidance to evaluate the eligibility of defendants.

6.5   CLAIMANTS

6.5.1   Nature of Claimants – Individual vs Institutional Shareholders

As illustrated in Table 6.2 below, it is uncommon for institutional shareholders to bring derivative actions, with 34 per cent (160/466) of all claimants. This may come as a surprise, since institutional shareholders are regarded as important parties to monitoring companies' performance with a strong motivation to engage in corporate governance.[68] Furthermore, they also have access to information and resources which will make it easier for them to institute an action on behalf of companies.

Compared with countries with mature financial markets and a high level of shareholder activism such as the US, Japan the UK or Australia,[69] it may seem worrying that institutional shareholders in China have a less active involvement in corporate governance.[70] There are obvious means other than derivative actions by which institutional shareholders may monitor and evaluate directors' performance, ranging from the threat of diverting their shares to the active use of voting power in board elections and proxy contests.[71] The existing literature seems to suggest that in general, these shareholders prefer behind-the-scenes

---

[68]   See B. Gong, *Understanding Institutional Shareholder Activism: A Comparative Study of the UK and China*, (London: Routledge 2014).
[69]   Lazard's Shareholder Advisory Group, *2019 Review of Shareholder Activism* (January 2020).
[70]   B. Gong, 'The Limits of Institutional Shareholder Activism in China and the United Kingdom: Some Comparisons' in R. Tomasic (ed.) *Routledge Handbook of Corporate Law*, (London: Routledge 2017)163.
[71]   W. Wu, S.A. Johan and O.M. Rui, 'Institutional Investors, Political Connections, and the Incidence of Regulatory Enforcement Against Corporate Fraud' (2016) 134(4) *Journal of Business Ethics* 709, 712.

Table 6.3   *Nature of claimants – single vs collective*

Number of plaintiffs	Number of cases	Percentage
Collective	88	21%
Single	378	81%
Total	466	100%

private tactics.[72] Proposals at shareholders' meetings, dialogues in public, activist engagements and courtroom confrontations are regarded as the last resort.[73] The lack of cases and incentives for institutional shareholders to initiate derivative proceedings may be the result of reputational costs. These are in addition to the regulatory thresholds, with a minimum required shareholding percentages and periods, as discussed earlier in this chapter. Another reason why institutional shareholders are not actively involved might be that most derivative actions are litigated in LLCs with a limited number of institutional shareholders.

6.5.2   Nature of Claimants – Collective vs Individual Actions

As illustrated in Table 6.3 below, 81 per cent (378/466) of cases have single claimants, whereas only 19 per cent (88/466) of cases involve shareholders that have filed derivative actions collectively.

Collective litigation is not a common practice in China. This echoes our previous finding of the lack of claims in JSLCs, and difficulties for shareholders to bring a collective action to satisfy 'the aggregate 1 per cent or more' threshold.[74] It is difficult to initiate collective action among shareholders in JSLCs, especially the listed ones, at least in China where most minority shareholders are individual ones.[75] Organising a number of individual shareholders who are willing to bring a collective derivative action can be a very difficult and problematic process. These shareholders almost invariably rely on the 'last resort' of soliciting other shareholders publicly, which will damage the con-

---

[72]   Y. Zeng, Q. Yuan and J. Zhang, 'Dark Side of Institutional Shareholder Activism in Emerging Markets: Evidence from China's Split Share Structure Reform' (2011) 40(2) *Asia–Pacific Journal of Financial Studies* 240, 259.

[73]   C. Xi, 'Institutional Shareholder Activism in China: Law and Practice (Part 1)' (2006) 17(10) *International Company and Commercial Law Review* 251, 253; see also S. Estrin and M. Prevezer, 'The Role of Informal Institutions in Corporate Governance: Brazil, Russia, India, and China Compared' (2011) 28(3) *Asia Pacific Journal of Management* 41.

[74]   Art. 151 of Chinese Company Law 2018.

[75]   F.X. Hong and S.H. Goo, 'Derivative Action in China: Problems and Prospectus' (2009) 4 *Journal of Business Law* 376, 388.

fidence of public investors in the company and could affect the reputation of the company.[76] Information asymmetry has also proved to be a major practical obstacle for joint derivative action claimants, who need to acquire sufficient information about their fellow shareholders.

6.6   COURT FEES

As illustrated in Figure 6.3 below, litigation fees for derivative actions in China are charged based on a sliding scale system,[77] where the litigation fee is in proportion to the amount of damages the defendants seek to claim. According to Article 13(1) of the Measure on Payment of Litigation,[78] RMB 50 shall be paid for each case seeking damages of no more than RMB 10,000. After the initial RMB 10,000, different percentages (starting at 2.5 per cent) of the damages sought (starting from amounts between RMB 10,000 and RMB 100,000) will be charged for different damage amounts. The lowest percentage of 0.5 per cent will be charged for damages of more than RMB 20 million.

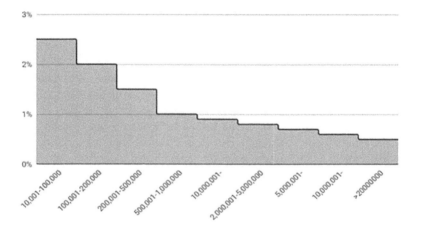

Figure 6.3   Court fees

---

[76]   J. Liu, 'Experience of Internationalization of Chinese Corporate Law and Corporate Governance: How to Make the Hybrid of Civil Law and Common Law Work?' (2015) 26(1) *European Business Law Review* 107, 119.

[77]   This approach is similar to the litigation calculation rules adopted in Japan before the 1993 Commercial Code.

[78]   Section 6, Measure on Payment of Litigation [诉讼费用交纳办法] 2007.

Positively, following the UK rule of the 'indemnity order' which was first made legitimate in *Wallersteiner v Moir (No. 2)*,[79] successful shareholders may be indemnified for investigation fees, assessment fees, notary fees and other reasonable costs incurred from the litigation.[80] Therefore, if the court supports the claim, either fully or partially, in the first instance and no appeal is raised by the defendant, the shareholder may recover fees from the defendant. However, the claimant shareholder may need to pay an additional sum of money for the enforcement of the judgment.

In derivative actions, claimants may have to pay huge amounts in litigation fees if the claimed damages are high. This is particularly likely to be the case for listed companies due to their size, capitalisation and the seriousness of potential damage. In China, through historical evidence related to case numbers it was concluded that the current sliding system served as 'a robust disincentive to prospective shareholders suing derivatively on behalf of the company'.[81]

It is worth looking at the Japanese experience, as a reference for reform, where the sliding scale system has historically adopted but proven to be a barrier to shareholder derivative claims.[82] The *Nikko Securities* case created an impetus for a palpable increase in derivative suits.[83] The court supported the shareholders' argument that the stamp fee for bringing a derivative action should be tailored to a normal fixed rate, because the economic benefit to shareholders from derivative actions is in practice incalculable.[84] As a result, filing a derivative action was given a flat fixed fee of 8,200 Yen, subsequently revised to 13,000 Yen, for litigation where damages sought do not exceed 1.6 million Yen.[85] This amendment is regarded as one of the most influential events in Japanese corporate governance history.[86] This welcome change in

---

[79] *Wallersteiner v Moir (No. 2)* [1975] QB 373; see also *Masri v Consolidated Contractors International Co SAL* [2011] EWHC 1024; *Air Canada v Secretly of State for Trade (No. 2)* [1983] WLR 494.

[80] Art. 35, Provision IV.

[81] F. Meng, 'Funding Derivative Action in China: Lessons from *Wallersteiner v Moir* (No.2) for the Court' (2010) 31(1) *Company Lawyer* 29, 29.

[82] M. Blomstrom and S. La Croix, *Institutional Change in Japan*, (London: Routledge 2006) 241.

[83] S. Kawashima, and S. Sakurai, 'Shareholder Derivative Litigation in Japan: Law, Practice, And Suggested Reforms' (1997) 33 (1) *Stanford Journal of International Law* 1, 9.

[84] *Shiryou–ban Shouji–Houmu* 70 (Tokyo High Court, 30 March 1993); see also art. 267 (4), Japanese Commercial Code.

[85] Art. 4(2) Law on the Fee of Civil Lawsuits of Japan.

[86] T. Fujita, 'Transformation of the Management Liability Regime in Japan in the Wake of the 1993 Revision' in H. Kanda (ed.) *Transforming Corporate Governances in East Asia*, (Abington: Routledge 2008) 13, 15–16.

Japan gives us insight into the possibilities of partly transplanting that rule to promote accessibility and effectiveness of the derivative action mechanism in China.

However, based on our observation in Figure 6.4 below, compared with Japan, the filing fees for derivative cases in China are highly variable with a high standard deviation. Therefore, it might be unreasonable to adopt a one-size-fits-all approach. Also, a fixed fee may lead to an increased litigation fee for smaller claims and discourage litigating shareholders in small cases.

We use a box plot in Figure 6.4 to describe the distribution of filing fees for derivative actions in our cohort. As shown by the box plot, the mean (average) of the data (represented by the dotted line) is 53,274 RMB and the median (represented by the line within the box) is 12,221 RMB. The upper fence of the data is 101,084 RMB, which indicates that in 90 per cent of the cases filing fees are lower than this amount, with a minimum amount of 40 RMB. The data above the upper fence are outliers, indicating extremely high costs in many cases. The highest filing fee in our sample is 1,802,760 RMB.[87]

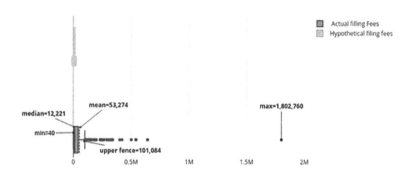

Figure 6.4   Litigation fees

In order to encourage all qualified shareholders to bring legitimate derivative actions, we propose a fixed ceiling on filing fees. Hypothetically, if the maximum amount is fixed at 12,221 RMB (the median of the actual filing

---

[87]   *Zhejiang Dianxin Electronic Development Co. Ltd. et al. v Tonghe Investment Property Co. Ltd. et al.* (2008 MinerZhongZi No. 123) [浙江和信电力开发有限公司、金华市大兴物资有限公司与通和置业投资有限公司、广厦控股创业投资有限公司、上海富沃企业发展有限公司损害公司权益纠纷上诉案 (民二终字第123号)].

fees), extremely high values could be eliminated and the total amount of the filing fees could be reduced to 15 per cent of the actual amount (see the plot for hypothetical filing fees). This means that in total, claimants in our sample could save 85 per cent in filing fees if the filing fees were capped at 12,221 RMB. The ceiling for filing fees could even be set lower than this amount, considering the filing fee for derivative actions in Japan is as low as 13,000 Yen (825 RMB). However, additional empirical research is needed to ascertain the most suitable amount.

6.7   DEMAND REQUIREMENT

With the reference to the procedural rules for bringing a derivative action in China, the mechanism of the demand requirement is adopted to strike a balance between improving shareholder remedies and preventing vexatious suits.[88] This is a screening process for the supervisor, the supervisory board, the board of directors or the executive directors, who have access to more resources in the company as well as information about the behaviour and decisions of directors. This current law and our findings on the application of the rule will be discussed, followed by some reform proposals.

6.7.1   The Current Law

Shareholders may request, in writing, the board of supervisors or the board of directors (the supervisors or the executive director of a LLC without such a board) to bring a derivative action. Only when these requests are refused, or shareholders receive no response within 30 days, or the situation is too urgent, are the shareholders allowed to lodge an action themselves.[89] This demand is 'a nod to the principle of exhaustion of intra-corporate remedies'.[90] The opportunity of correcting the misconducts of corporate controllers should be given to the company before the intervention of the court, because the company is the party that has suffered directly. The supervisor, the supervisory board, the board of directors or the executive director, when assessing the importance and possibilities of continuing a claim, should consider a number of issues, such as the cost of the proceedings and damage to the company's reputation, before making their decision. If a company employs other approaches to solve

---

[88]   H. Huang, 'Shareholder Derivative Litigation in China: Empirical Findings and Comparative Analysis' (2012) 27(4) *Banking and Finance Law Review* 619, 652.

[89]   Art. 151 of Chinese Company Law 2018.

[90]   S. Lin, *Derivative Actions in Chinese Company Law*, (Alphen ann den Rijin: Kluwer Law International 2015) p.114.

Table 6.4   Demand requirement

Satisfied demand?	Number of cases	Percentage
Yes	194	42%
No	188	40%
Unknown	84	18%
Total	466	100%

the problem, there is no need to resort to judicial recourse. The wrong can be corrected by the company itself, which may benefit the company.[91]

6.7.2   Our Findings and Three Observations

As illustrated in Table 6.4 below, we found that 42 per cent (194/466) of the cases in our cohort satisfied the demand requirement, whereas 40 per cent (188/466) failed to meet the requirement with the rest of the cases unknown. Notable circumstances where shareholders failed the demand requirement include making a demand of a single supervisor while there were two supervisors,[92] the supervisory board not receiving the demand letter,[93] and the reflection of the supervisory board after demands were made on the previous board.[94] The rest of the case reports did not clarify whether the plaintiffs had made a demand or not.

In addition to the percentage of satisfying the demand requirement, we have a few interesting observations. First, failure to meet the demand requirement is the main ground for refusing to accept derivative cases. Second, we identified 20 cases where claimants had dual identities, namely shareholders who are also supervisors. Only seven of these 20 cases were accepted by the courts. In some of the cases accepted by the courts, judicial reasoning relied on the rationale that a supervisor could file an action on behalf of the company, and

---

[91] D.A. Demott, 'Shareholder Litigation in Australia and the United States: Common Problems, Uncommon Solutions' (1986) 11 *Sydney Law Review* 259, 262.

[92] *Yang Guiping v Jiangsu Kaiyuan Zhongxin Toys Co. Ltd.* (2013 JuhouShangchuZi No. 0142 [杨桂平诉江苏开元众鑫玩具有限公司利益责任纠纷案 (2013)句后商初字第 0142 号].

[93] *Shandong Hengkang Real Estate Co. Ltd. v Jiangsu Chunhui Ecological Agriculture & Forestry Co. Ltd.* (2015 GaoShangchuZi No. 762) [山东恒康置业有限公司等诉江苏春辉生态农林股份有限公司公司利益责任纠纷案 (2015)高商初字第 762号].

[94] *Zheng Hua et al. v Cui Jinping* (2014 ChaoMinchuZi No. 9320) [郑华等诉崔金萍公司利益责任纠纷案 (2014)朝民初字第 9320 号].

such action would be a company's action,[95] which does not require a demand requirement.[96] In other cases, the courts have allowed the actions to proceed as derivative actions and exempted the shareholder/supervisor from the demand requirement.[97] Thus, courts have been inconsistent in determining whether the demand requirement has been fulfilled, especially when the plaintiff has the dual identity of shareholder and supervisor. When a shareholder is the only supervisory in the company, there is controversy as to whether a shareholder/ supervisor should make a demand to themselves first. Third, follow-up investigations of the cases rejected by the courts revealed an inconsistent application of the law. Some courts adhered to the strict application of the law by insisting that the shareholder(s)/supervisor(s) must make a demand in writing to themselves,[98] and others took a more functional and efficient approach by stating that the plaintiff should have brought the action in their capacity of a supervisor instead of a shareholder.[99]

6.7.3 Function of the Demand Requirement and Business Judgements: A Comparative Analysis of the US and the UK Approaches

The demand requirement is problematic under Chinese law because the law does not specify when cases might be excused from the demand requirement, and judicial practice is inconsistent without clearly defined guidelines. This rigid and inconsistent judicial approach indicates a lack of understanding of the function of the demand requirement, for example, under what circumstances, the requirement is not necessary and it would be more efficient and just to be

---

[95] For the difference between a company action and a derivative action, see art. 23 of Provision IV and previous discussion.

[96] *Zhuhai Pu Enrui Electric Power Technology Co. Ltd. vs Wang Lei et al.* (2017 Yue 04 Minzhong No. 2588) [珠海普恩瑞电力科技有限公司诉王磊、珠海普恩瑞信息技术有限公司损害公司利益案（2017）粤 04 民终 2588号]; *Fu Weiyong v Hu Xiaojian* (2015 YuMinErZhongZi No. 126) [符伟勇与胡小剑损害公司利益案（2015）余民二终字第 126 号].

[97] *Qu Quyin v Qu Zhenming* (2017 Yue 06 Minzhong No. 3876) [区焜栩因与区振明、区浩源损害公司利益案（2017）粤 06 民终 3876 号]; *Huang Wei Yin v Pan Zhonghe* (2017 Yue 03 Minzhong No. 874) [黄伟因与潘中和损害公司利益案（2017）粤 03 民终 874 号]; *Liao Xianghua v Liao Xianggu* (2016 Yue 16 Minzhong No. 6970) [廖香花与廖香姑损害公司利益案 （2016）粤 19 民终 6970 号].

[98] *Liu Wei et al. v Zhang Shenghua et al.* (2016 Yu 0811 Minchu No. 968) [刘巍、范卫国与张胜华、焦作瑞彤科技有限 公司损害公司利益责任纠纷案 (2016)豫 0811 民初 968 号].

[99] *Zhang Yueliang v Wang Weiguo et al.* (2016 Yue 0306 Minchu 24966) [张岳良与王维国、冯军华、深圳新思维电工器材有限公司损害公司利益案 (2016)粤0306 民初 24966 号].

exempted from it. A comparative analysis of UK and US law may shed light on the rationale and function of this requirement when it applies in the derivative action mechanism.

In the US, claimants are also required to make a demand to the board before bringing a derivative action[100] in order to exhaust internal remedies.[101] The demand requirement can be excused if the shareholders can demonstrate that it is futile to make a demand.[102] Unlike the Chinese law, US courts, relying on the business judgement rule,[103] are inclined to defer to internal governance or board decisions when considering whether it is futile to make a demand on the board. The judicial review is usually limited to the scrutiny of the decisions of a special litigation committee, which is formed within the company and made up of disinterested directors. The committee will handle a shareholder's claim and decide whether pursuing a derivative action is in the company's best interest. The committee's recommendation to dismiss a shareholder's demand will be subject to the scrutiny of the court.[104]

In *Aronson v Lewis*,[105] the Delaware Supreme Court developed a two-pronged test for considering whether demand on the board is futile and should be excused: (1) whether the directors are disinterested and independent on the subject; or (2) whether the challenged transaction is otherwise the product of a valid exercise of business judgement. This test, centred on the business judgement rule, has been widely accepted by state law.[106] The demand requirement will be excused for futility if a majority of the board is either interested or can be shown to be controlled by the interested director under this test. Where the plaintiff cannot raise issues as to the independence of directors, the decision-making process can also be challenged for not being a valid exercise of business judgement.[107]

---

[100] MBCA § 7.42.

[101] *Hawes v Oakland*, 104 U.S. 450 (1881), 460.

[102] W. Chen, *A Comparative Study of Funding Shareholder Litigation*, (London: Springer 2017) 46.

[103] For example, see *Auerbach v Bennett*, 393 N.E.2d 994 (NY 1979); *Sinclair Oil Corp. v Levien*, 280 A.2d 717 (Del. 1971); *Shlensky v Wrigley*, 237 N.E.2d 776 (Ill. App. Ct. 19). Australia has a statutory business judgement rule; see Corporations Act 2001 (Australia), s. 180.

[104] *Zapata Corp. v Maldonado*, 430 A.2d 779, 786–87(Del. 1981). Also see C.F. Wilder, 'The Demand Requirement and the Business Judgment Rule: Synergistic Procedural Obstacles to Shareholder Derivative Suits' (1984) 5(3) *Pace Law Review* 633.

[105] *Aronson v Lewis*, 473 A.2d 805 (Del. 1984).

[106] W. Chen, *A Comparative Study of Funding Shareholder Litigation*, (London: Springer 2017) 46.

[107] D.A. Skeel Jr., 'The Accidental Elegance of Aronson v Lewis' (2007) 7(28) *University of Pennsylvania Institute for Law & Econ Research Paper* 182 Available at

Without the demand requirement, the statutory derivative action codified under the UK CA 2006 contains a two-stage permission procedure[108] that requires the court to consider six factors in deciding whether to continue a derivative action after a *prima facie* case is established.[109] Significantly, permission to continue will not be granted where a defendant has performed her duty to promote the success of the company as specified by section 172 of the UK CA 2006.[110] This means that the courts will respect directors' business decisions that increase the company's value in the long term for the interests of shareholders.

It can be observed, when considering whether to permit a derivative action to proceed, that courts will place priority on the company's interests. Courts will always defer to directors' business decisions, as justified by the *de facto* business judgement rule.[111] This is particularly the case in the US, where the business judgement rule functions as a significant safeguard for the authority of the board. It prevents judges from second-guessing directors' business decisions, as judges lack knowledge about business and might be subject to hindsight bias. More importantly, the business judgement rule is justified by encouraging directors to take risks and thereby improving the value of the company.[112]

In stark contrast, Chinese courts seem to lack reasonable and consistent principles or rules for their decisions. Their reluctance to exempt plaintiffs from the demand requirement and accept derivative actions results largely from a dearth of clear-cut legal rules, not from an interest in protecting directors' business decisions. Due to insufficient knowledge, weak authority, worrying directors' competence and the absence of *stare decisis*, it is challenging for Chinese courts to apply discretionary rules transplanted from common law jurisdictions.[113] However, the business judgement rule is seen as something that has strong applicability to corporate China and the application

---

SSRN: https://ssrn.com/abstract=1027010 or http://dx.doi.org/10.2139/ssrn.1027010 (accessed 25 July 2022).

[108] Sections 261–263, UK CA 2006.

[109] Sections 261(2), UK CA 2006.

[110] Sections 263(3)(b), UK CA 2006. Section 172, UK CA 2006.

[111] A. Keay and J. Loughrey, *The Concept of Business Judgment* (2019) 39(1) *Legal Studies* 36; A. Keay, J. Loughrey, T. Mcnulty, F. Okanigbuan and A. Stewart, 'Business Judgment and Director Accountability: a Study of Case-law Over Time' (2020) 20(2) *The Journal of Corporate Law Studies* 359.

[112] A. Gurrea–Martínez, 'Re-examining the Law and Economics of The Business Judgment Rule: Notes for Its Implementation In Non-US Jurisdictions' (2018) 18(2) *The Journal of Corporate Law Studies* 417.

[113] G. Xu, T. Zhou, B. Zeng and J. Shi, 'Directors' Duties in China' (2013) 14(1) *European Business Organization Law Review* 57.

will 'help the Chinese judiciary tackle professionalization and independence issues',[114] including those in derivative action. Furthermore, it may be beneficial to adopt interim measures to ease the tension. The effectiveness of demand requirements in China may benefit from more detailed interpretations to guide judicial practice from the SPC to promote the accessibility and effectiveness of the mechanism. The SPC should consider the commercial substance and adopt realistic approaches in relation to the demand requirement. In addition, the SPC should also issue clarifications as to the general circumstances under which the demand requirement is excused. As demonstrated by experience in the UK and the US, the courts need to achieve a balance between preventing misconduct that harms a company's interests and supporting valid business decisions that foster the company's value.

Besides, the existing 30-day period, which is designed to avoid postponement or neglect by the boards, has been argued to be unreasonable.[115] The 30-day period could be particularly problematic in collective actions with a large number of claimants, which may involve more time for investigation before a decision can be made. Boards may be pushed to reach an uninformed and unreasonable judgement. In order to maintain a balance between the accessibility of the mechanism for shareholders and the effectiveness of boards' judgements, it is suggested that the court should be given the discretion to extend such a time period to accommodate all scenarios.[116]

6.8   COURT DECISIONS

As illustrated in Table 6.5 below, we have categorised court decisions into the headings of Refuse (*caiding bohui qisu* 裁定驳回起诉), Reject and Accept. Refusal refers to a ruling that dismisses a case for non-compliance with procedural requirements.[117] Reject refers to the decision to dismiss the merits of the claimant's claim. Accept refers to cases accepted by the courts including cases where the merits of the claim are considered and those without a substantive ruling by application of the law.[118]

---

[114] C.X. Weng, 'Assessing the Applicability of the Business Judgment Rule and the Defensive Business Judgment Rule in the Chinese Judiciary: A Perspective on Takeover Dispute Adjudication' (2010) 34(1) *Fordham International Law Journal* 124, 147.

[115] F. Ma, 'The Deficiencies of Derivative Actions in China' (2010) 31(5) *Company Lawyer* 150, 153.

[116] See S. Lin, *Derivative Actions in Chinese Company Law* (Alphen ann den Rijin: Kluwer Law International 2015).

[117] P. Tian, *Civil Procedural Law* [民事诉讼法] (Beijing: Law Press: 2005) 186.

[118] For example, see *Guo Mouhai et al. v Danzhou City Government* (2012 HainanErZhonghangZhongZi No. 13) [郭某海等诉儋州市人民政 府土地行政登记

Table 6.5   *Decisions of all cases*

Decision	Count	Percentage
Reject (substantial)	138	30%
Refuse to accept (procedural)	167	36%
Accept	161	34%
Total	466	100%

Comparing the support/acceptance rates of the cases collected by Lin before 2006 (70 per cent support/acceptance) and from 2006 to 2013 (46 per cent), the support/acceptance rate has dropped. We think multiple reasons could explain this curve, which may not necessarily show the conservative judicial attitude of Chinese courts. First, the number of cases has increased, and the decline of the acceptance rate may actually demonstrate that the courts are becoming more relaxed in accepting cases. A relaxed attitude within the capability of the courts' workload would be helpful to promote the accessibility of the mechanism for a more balanced judicial attitude. However, shareholders also need to be prepared to invest time and money, which they may claim in reimbursement from the company, into the litigation to challenge the potential misconduct of the controller.

Second, more support should be offered to eligible shareholders to enable them to bring derivative actions with confidence. We propose a unique enforcement format to regard derivative action to be a private enforcement mechanism supported by the public enforcer. In addition to promoting the accessibility and effectiveness of derivative action mechanism, the support from public enforcers will help vulnerable shareholders who lack knowledge, resources and information, and help to gather willing shareholders to initiate collective actions. For example, with the assistance of the China Securities Investor Services Centre (ISC, 中证中小投资者服务中心),[119] a not-for-profit organisation established in 2014 under the supervision of the CSRC,[120] the accessibility of derivative action could be greatly promoted through the services provided by the ISC, including delivering education, legal, information, technology and other services for small and medium investors to safeguard their rights. This is promising and in line with the nature of administrative

---

案（2012）海南二中行终字第 13号]; *Huang Weiyin v Pan Zhonghe* (2016 Yue 0304 Minchu No. 20545) [黄伟因与潘中和损害公司利益责任（2016）粤 0304 民初 20545 号].

[119] See the official website of the ISC: http://www.isc.com.cn/ (accessed 25 July 2022).

[120] A ministerial-level public institution and public enforcer in China directly under the State Council by imposing administrative and criminal liabilities.

corporate governance in China, which is instituted by the government and is featured with governmental control and intervention.[121] Government policy in China has placed increasing importance on establishing a market economy with the shift towards a rule-based framework. We believe that government policy and its administrative power will have an impact on the effective use of the derivative actions by promoting the educational and communication role played by the ISC and the CSRC.

To date, the ISC has supported three false representation actions brought by investors in listed companies. The ISC has played an essential role in these actions by organising investors, collecting evidence and providing legal services.[122] In the future, the ISC could also contribute to the development of derivative actions in listed companies by monitoring listed companies and facilitating collective action among shareholders. In order to exercise shareholders' rights on behalf of small investors, the ISC has purchased a small package of shares (100 shares) from all the listed companies on both the Shenzhen and the Shanghai Stock Exchanges. As a shareholder, the ISC can monitor listed companies and demand the board of directors/supervisors take action against wrongdoers. If such a demand is unanswered, the ISC may organise minority shareholders to fulfil the 1 per cent shareholding requirement and initiate a derivative action.[123] The role of the ISC in derivative actions and private enforcement of company law and securities laws in China will be further discussed in Section 7.4.

6.9   CAUSE OF ACTION

Theoretically, in a derivative action, Article 151 should be cited together with other provisions in relation to breach of duty or duties by directors or share-

---

[121] A. Keay and J. Zhao, 'Transforming Corporate Governance in Chinese Corporations: A Journey Not A Destination' (2018) 38(2) *Northwestern Journal of International Law and Business* 187, 195.

[122] R.H. Huang, 'Rethinking the Relationship between Public Regulation and Private Litigation: Evidence from Securities Class Action in China' (2018) 19(1) *Theoretical Inquiries in Law* 333; J. Du and H. Fan, 'Development of Securities Supporting Litigation [论证券支持诉讼的专业化发展]' [2017] 2 *On Civil Procedure [民事程序法研究]* 74.

[123] *Framework of the Shareholder Rights of the ISC [投服中心公益股东权的配置及制度建构]*, IOLAW, http://www.iolaw.org.cn/showArticle.aspx?id=5439 (1 January 2018) (accessed 25 July 2022); *People's Republic of China : Financial Sector Assessment Program – Detailed Assessment of Observance of the Iosco Objectives and Principles of Securities Regulation*, IMF, https://www.imf.org/en/Publications/CR/Issues/2017/12/26/Peoples–Republic–of–China–Financial–Sector–Assessment–Program–Detailed–Assessment–of–45517 (26 December 2017) (accessed 25 July 2022).

holders. This is because Article 151 only states that shareholders are allowed to bring a derivative action against directors on behalf of the company, but the cause of action needs to be found in other provisions of the Chinese Company Law.

We found that Article 151 (art. 152 previously)[124] was cited 450 (out of 466 cases) times in our sample (see Figure 6.5 below). This means that judicial practice in China is generally consistent but sometimes inaccurate; sometimes Article 151 was not cited in judgments even where cases were characterised as derivative actions.[125] Further, the main cause of action seems to be a breach of duty by directors; since provisions regarding directors' duties (arts 147–150) were cited most frequently (152 times out of 466 cases). Breach of duty by shareholders was also a major cause of action, as shown by the fact that the articles on shareholders' duty (art. 20) and shareholders/directors' related relationships (art. 21) were cited 35 and 13 times respectively. Articles on the power of the supervisor (art. 53) were featured 13 times, and Articles regarding the revocation of resolutions (art. 22) and the withdrawal of capital (art. 36) were also mentioned (four times each).

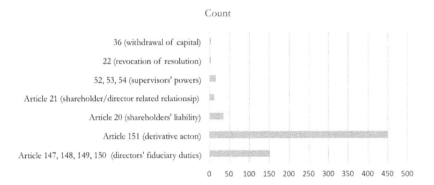

Figure 6.5   *Cause of action and law provision*

These findings have further shed light on the classic scenario of a derivative action in China. Although shareholders are not explicitly mentioned as potential defendants by Article 151, it is clear from our findings that controlling

---

[124] The Chinese Company Law was amended in 2013 and the numbering of the article has been changed.

[125] *Shanghai Hengsheng EE Co. Ltd. v Ye Mou* (2011 HongMinerShangchuZi No. 182) [上海恒生电讯工程有限公司诉叶某纠纷案 (2011虹民二商初字第 182 号)]; *Yu Ru v Wang Dong* (2016 Hu 0112 Minchu No.8831) [于茹诉王东损害股东利益责任纠 (2016)沪 0112 民初 8831 号].

shareholders are commonly sued for causing losses to the company, and in fact they are the main defendants in derivative actions (Figure 6.2 above). Combining the finding demonstrated in Figures 6.2 and 6.5, we conclude that in a typical scenario for a derivative action in China a single individual shareholder will claim against a defendant who is director-shareholder in a LLC for breaching his/her duties. This is consistent with the finding in our sample that more than half of the shareholder defendants held the position of directors. To a large extent, derivative action has addressed the oppression problem in LLCs in China.[126] We agree that the mechanism has been used as an effective way to enforce directors' duties, at least in LLCs. It also has great potential for resolving agency problems in JSLCs.

This classic scenario demonstrates the double agency problem in China, including the vertical one between shareholders and directors and the horizontal problem between majority and minority shareholders.[127] In LLCs, ownership is only marginally separated from control. A dialogue channel is normally established between the board of directors and the shareholders, owing to their close ties. A problem with these ties is confusion about claims against shareholders in derivative actions. Bringing a derivative claim action against a shareholder who is not a director seems to require the claimant to rely on provisions for shareholders' duties (e.g., arts 20 or 21) in addition to Article 151.[128] If the plaintiff only cites Article 151 in making a claim against the shareholder, the court may reject the claim on the grounds that an action under Article 151 is mainly intended to address wrongs done by directors, supervisors or senior managers, and such an action cannot be initiated against shareholders.[129] Therefore, the substantial reason for such claims is perplexing: Did the controllers breach their duties as shareholders or as directors? These actors owe very different duties to the company under company law.

---

[126] N.C. Howson, 'Twenty-Five Years On – The Establishment and Application of Corporate Fiduciary Duties in PRC Law' (*University of Michigan Law & Econ Research Paper No. 17–024*) SSRN, https://papers.ssrn.com/sol3/papers.cfm?abstract _id=3102551 (accessed 25 July 2022).

[127] S. Lin, 'Double Agency Costs in China: A Legal Perspective' (2012) 9 *The Asian Business Lawyer* 116, 119.

[128] *HNA Hotel Holdings Group Co. Ltd. v Zhao Xiaohai* (2016 ShanMinzhong No. 228) [海航酒店控股集团有限公司与被人赵小海损害公司利益责任 纠纷一案（2016）陕民终 228 号].

[129] *Yan Lixin & Feng Ruquan v Shandong Tianan Chemical Co. Ltd.* (2015 LinShangchuZi No. 1332) [隋立新与冯如泉、山东天安化工 股份有限公司股权转让纠纷案 (2015)临商初字第 1332 号]; *Hangzhou Ruili Real Estate Group Co. Ltd. v Hangzhou Xinsheng Real Estate Development Co. Ltd.* (2014 HangBinShangchuZi No. 640) [杭州瑞立房地产集团有限公司诉杭州欣盛房地产开发有限公司等 利益责任纠纷案 (2014)杭滨商初字第 640号].

For example, shareholders do not owe fiduciary duties to the company. The controlling shareholder may owe duties towards minority shareholders, either directly or indirectly, but that duty should be used as the standing for bringing derivative action.

Moreover, the range of reasons that shareholders can use to bring derivative actions seems very broad based on stipulations in Chinese Company Law 2006, which may include any violations of 'laws, administrative regulations or the articles of association during the course of performing his duties'. Therefore, the shareholders will be able to challenge any breach of the duties by directors according to law, regulations or articles of association. These may include breaches of fiduciary duties or duty of diligence with broad scope in the new Chinese Company Law.[130] Article 5 of Chinese Company Law 2006 states that 'a company must, when engaging in business activities, abide by the laws and administrative regulations, observe social morals and business ethics, be in integrity and good faith, accept regulation of the government and the public, and undertake social responsibilities'. Comparatively modern terms such as 'business ethics' and 'social responsibilities' are introduced in the general provisions of Chinese Company Law for the first time. It is implied in Article 5 that apart from the interests of shareholders, employees and other stakeholders, the performance and activities of the company have a deep impact on the market's economic rules and public social interests. Therefore, when company directors and supervisors pursue company interests for their shareholders, they have to be socially responsible and responsible to internal and external stakeholders.[131] As far as legislative tenets are concerned, it is stipulated in Article 1 of Chinese Company Law 2006 that this legislation is enacted in order to 'standardise the organisation and activities of companies, to protect the legitimate rights and interests of companies, shareholders and creditors, to maintain socio-economic order and to promote the development of the social-ist market economy'.[132] However, these socially related responsibilities and legislative tendencies in protecting creditors' interests were first introduced as a guiding principle for future detailed stipulations regarding directors' duties, such as their detailed responsibilities towards various stakeholders, their duties towards stakeholders in realising these responsibilities, and the liability of corporations and directors if they are in breach of these duties. Directors' duties relating to the social aspects required in Chinese Company

---

[130] Arts 147 and 148 of Chinese Company Law 2018.

[131] J. Zhao, 'The Regulation and Steering of Corporate Social Responsibility in China: Stories after the Enforcement of Chinese Company Law' (2011) 22(12) *International Commercial and Company Law Review* 399.

[132] Art. 1 of Chinese Company Law 2018.

Law 2006 are immature, unclear and extremely difficult to enforce.[133] It is overly demanding for directors to enforce these duties in accordance with the legislative principles, and the danger of being held liable for the negligence of these responsibilities could be an onerous burden for directors and deter them from taking risky decisions.

Furthermore, the duty of diligence and duty of loyalty have been introduced into Chinese Company Law. Directors might be held responsible for breaching these duties simply by making bad business decisions and these onerous burdens will have a negative impact on directors when they are trying to make risky management decisions for the long-term interests of corporations. If shareholders are allowed to bring a claim against directors based on infringements of such unclear duties, this may lead to a large number of malicious suits. To counter this defect, efforts should be made to make these provisions regarding directors' duties more accessible and easier to understand for directors, especially those in small- and medium-sized businesses. The improvement can be achieved by various measures, including clearer interpretations, broader enrichment with systematic codification of relevant legislation on directors' duties, and more judicial regulations and explanations from the SPC. Also, in terms of the enforcement of directors' duties for more socially responsible corporations, establishing a sound corporate governance model with a clearer corporate objective is critical for the efficient and sustainable performance of Chinese companies.

It is also recommended that Chinese courts should adopt the concept of the business judgement rule, which was designed in the US to 'stimulate risk taking, innovation and other creative entrepreneurial activities'[134] with the purpose of striking a good 'balance between the need to ensure that directors comply with the duty of diligence and the need to allow directors to take certain

---

[133] L.W. Lin, 'Corporate Social Responsibility in China: Window Dressing or Structural Change' (2010) 28(1) *Berkeley Journal of International Law* 64.

[134] See Section 4.01 of American Law Institute, *Principles of Corporate Governance: An Analysis and Recommendations*, Proposed Final Draft (1992); see also J.E. Kerr, 'Sustainability Meets Profitability: The Convenient Truth of How the Business Judgment Rule Protects a Board's Decision to Engage in Social Entrepreneurship' (2007) 29(2) *Cardozo Law Review* 623; C.X. Weng, 'Assessing the Applicability of the Business Judgment Rule and the 'Defensive' Business Judgment Rule in the Chinese Judiciary: A Perspective on Takeover Dispute Adjudication' (2010) 34(1) *Fordham International Law Journal* 124; R. Sprague and A.J. Lyttle, 'Shareholder Primacy and the Business Judgment Rule: Arguments for Expanded Corporate Democracy' (2010) 16(1) *Stanford Journal of Law, Business & Finance* 1; see also *Percy v Millaudon* (1829) 8 Mart. (n.s.) 68; *Revlon, Inc. v MacAndrews & Forbes Holdings, Inc.* (1986) 506 A.2d 173 and more recently cases like *Gantler v Stephens*, (Del. 2009) 965 A.2d 695.

risks in the exercise of their discretion'.[135] The business judgement rule was introduced more than 180 years ago as a common law standard.[136] It has been regarded as the principle that directors can employ to shield their decisions from judicial scrutiny.[137] The most distinctive contribution of the business judgement rule is that it prevents the judiciary from meddling in managerial decisions.[138] In this sense, the rule may be helpful in protecting directors from personal liability for claims made against them because of errors of judgement or wrong business decisions, protecting them against shareholders' derivative actions based on their negligence.[139] Both academics and practitioners in China have realised the importance of the concept of business judgement, and it is suggested that Chinese judges should reference the principle in managing their discretions when they judge whether directors are in breach of the duties imposed in Chinese Company Law 2006.[140]

---

[135] F. Ma, 'The Deficiency of Derivative Action in China' (2010) 31(5) *Company Lawyer* 150, 153; see also D.M. Branson, 'A Business Judgment Rule for Incorporating Jurisdictions in Asia' (2011) 23 *Singapore Academy of Law Journal* 687; J.H. Farrar, 'Directors' Duties of Care – Issues of Classification, Solvency and Business Judgment and Dangers of Legal Transplant' (2011) 23 *Singapore Academy of Law Journal 745*.

[136] See, S.S. Arusht, 'The Business Judgment Rule Revisited' (1979) 8(1) *Hofstra Law Review* 93, 93.

[137] See, J. Hinsey, 'Business Judgment and the American Law Institute's Corporate Governance Project: The Rule, the Doctrine and the Reality' (1983) 52 *George Washington Law Review* 609, 610.

[138] C.X. Weng, 'Assessing the Applicability of the Business Judgment Rule and the Defensive Business Judgment Rule in the Chinese' (2010) 34(1) *Fordham International Law Journal* 124.

[139] M.B. Hemraj, 'The Business Judgment Rule in Corporate Law' (2004) 15(6) *International Company and Commercial Law Review* 192, 198.

[140] F. Deng, 'A Legal Analysis of Leadership Accountability: An Approach from the Director's Duty of Care in Corporate Law' (2007) 28(1) *Social Science in China* 3.

7. Synchronising norms and institutions – towards a more effective, balanced and accessible settings of derivative action scheme in China

This chapter, examines the force of socio-cultural specialties in shaping the distinct nature of laws in a comparative manner, in particular, the historical and cultural emending and implications. Furthermore, the chapter contextualises these findings and reaffirm proposals against the 'triple criteria' of: (1) accessibility; (2) effectiveness; and (3) a balanced mechanism in the unique Chinese context. We will also consider how private enforcement backed by a public regulator can improve derivative actions along each of the three criteria. presents eight key findings of our empirical analysis, with follow-up reflections and reform proposals.

7.1 UNDERSTANDING THE SOIL IN WHICH THE DERIVATIVE ACTION TAKES ROOT – HISTORICAL AND CULTURAL EMBEDDINGS AND IMPLICATIONS

In China, the historic 'Confucian' philosophy and the dominance of the state as a shareholder have had a profound effect on the development of Chinese corporate governance. Confucian philosophy rests on two primary facets: *Ren* and *Li*. *Ren* is variously described as benevolence, philanthropy, and humaneness, while *Li* reflects the rules and norms of society that dictate acceptable behaviour.[1] Therefore, it is not hard to see that Confucianism embodies rich stakeholder and CSR principles which are voluntary in nature. However, these traditional ideas are challenged by the long history of war taking place in neoteric China, the Cultural Revolution from 1966 to 1976 and the introduction of Western culture, thoughts and values after the adoption of a reform and opening up policy in 1978.[2] As a result, the impact of Confucianism has grad-

---

[1]   K. Zi (552–479 BC), *Lun Yu*.
[2]   Y. Gao, 'Corporate Social Performance in China: Evidence from Large Companies' (2009) 89(1) *Journal of Business Ethics* 23, 26.

ually been weakening, both on Chinese society in general and on the Chinese corporate governance system in particular.[3]

The characteristics of corporate governance are determined by political institutions and the culture practised in a jurisdiction. This is particularly true in China. China's feudal history has had a strong impact on the Chinese legal system due to path dependence. Chinese society has been traditionally and heavily influenced by values related to Confucianism, which are keen to promote a strict system of norms and propriety directing and guiding human behaviour. It is recognised that cultural heritage may have a direct impact on the development and efficiency of corporate governance.[4] Networks form an important aspect of doing business in China, and one often hears of *guanxi, mianzi* and *renqing*.[5] They are forms of social capital which we need to investigate critically as they create and enhance value, but they also might well hinder free market competition and the functioning market forces.

Over the past few decades, a great deal of literature has been produced regarding the importance of *guanxi,* which is variously translated as social relations, personal connections or particular ties.[6] As noted already, it plays an important role in Chinese culture, and it has long been established that national culture is a deeply rooted causal factor shaping corporations' forms,

---

[3]   H. Chaibong, 'The Culture Challenge to Individualism' (2000) 11(1) *Journal of Democracy* 127; G. Rozman, 'Can Confucianism Survive in an Age of Universalism and Globalization?' (2002) 75(1) *Public Affairs* 11.

[4]   See C. Lam and S.H. Goo, 'Confucianism: A Fundamental Cure to the Corporate Governance Problems in China' (2014) 35(2) *Company Lawyer* 52; J. Zhao and S. Wen, 'Gift Giving, Guanxi and Confucianism in a Harmonious Society: What Chinese Law Could Learn from English Law on Aspects of Directors' Duties' (2013) 34(12) *Company Lawyer* 381; W. Qu and P. Leung, 'Culture Impact on Chinese Corporate Disclosure – A Corporate Governance Perspective' (2006) 21(3) *Managerial Auditing Journal* 241; L. Wang and H. Justin, 'The Impact of Chinese Culture on Corporate Social Responsibility: The Harmony Approach' (2009) 88(3) *Journal of Business Ethics* 433; D. Smith, '*Guanxi, Mianzi* and Business: The Impact of Culture on Corporate Governance in China' (2012) 26 *Private Sector Opinion* 1; available at: http://www.ifc .org/wps/wcm/connect/aeae62804b7321708fcdcfbbd578891b/IFC+PSO+26+052112 .pdf?MOD=AJPERES (last accessed on 12 July 2016); J. Nolan, 'Good *Guanxi*, Bad *Guanxi*: Western Bankers and the Role of Network Practices in Institutional Change in China'(2011) 22(16) *The International Journal of Human Resource Management* 3357.

[5]   Y. Yan, *The Flow of Gifts: Reciprocity and Social Networks in a Chinese Village,* (Stanford: Stanford University Press 1996) 74–122.

[6]   A.B. Kipins, 'The Language of Gift: Managing Guanxi in a North China Village' (1996) 22(3) *Modern China* 285, 285; for more discussion on the importance of *guanxi* in contemporary Chinese society see D. Hwang and A. Staley, 'An Analysis of Recent Accounting and Auditing Failures in the United States on US Accounting and Auditing in China' (2005) 20(3) *Managerial Auditing Journal* 227.

customs and performance.[7] *Guanxi*, a system of tight, close-knit networks among people,[8] has played a significant role in the Confucian-dominated Chinese society for almost 2,000 years. With the impact of Chinese history and culture, the concept of *guanxi* and other closely related cultural issues make the Chinese definition of social capital unique. These cultural issues have a direct relationship with what occurs in the business world and their impact on corporate profits,[9] efficiency in reaching agreement about sales contracts,[10] companies' accounting and market performance,[11] and of course the area that we are considering in this book: corporate governance.

Guanxi is, in essence, a coalition-based network of stakeholders sharing resources for survival, and it plays an important role in achieving business success in China. It has been defined in various ways and the literature contains no consensus as to its definition or translation.[12] It has been described as 'tight, close-knit networks',[13] 'interpersonal connections',[14] or a 'gate or pass'.[15] Etymologically, *guan* is a derivative word for 'door' or 'pass' and *xi* is a rather old word with the connotation of hierarchy. *Guanxi* literally means

---

[7]   E.g., A. Licht, 'The Mother of All Path Dependencies: Towards a Cross-cultural Theory of Corporate Governance Systems', (2001) 26(1) *Delaware Journal of Corporate Law* 147; A. Licht, 'The Maximands of Corporate Governance: A Theory of Values of Cognitive Style', (2003) European Corporate Governance Institute, Law Working Paper, 16, ECGI.

[8]   I.Y.M. Yeung and R.L. Tung, 'Achieving Business Success in Confucian Societies: The Importance of *Guanxi* (Connections)' (1996) 25(2) *Organization Dynamics* 54; U. Braendle, T. Casser and J. Noll, 'Corporate Governance in China – Is Economic Growth Potential Hindered by *Guanxi*?' (2005) 110(4) *Business and Society Review* 389.

[9]   J. Ai, 'Guanxi Networks in China: Its Importance and Future Trends' (2006) 14(5) *China and World Economy* 105.

[10]   Y. Luo, 'Guanxi and Performance of Foreign-Invested Enterprises in China: An Empirical Inquiry' (1997) 37(1) *Management International Review* 51.

[11]   Y. Lou and M. Chen, 'Does Guanxi Influence Firm Performance?' (1997) 14(1) *Asia Pacific Journal of Management* 1.

[12]   A.S. Tsui, and J L. Farh, 'Where *Guanxi* Matters: Relational Demography and *Guanxi* in the Chinese Context' (1997) 24(1) *Work & Occupations* 56, 59–61.

[13]   I.Y.M Yeung and R. L. Tung, 'Achieving Business Success in Confucian Societies: The Importance of Guanxi (Connections)' (1996) 25(2) *Organization Dynamics* 54, 54.

[14]   K.R. Xin and L.P. Jone, 'Guanxi: Connections as Substitutes for Formal Institutional Support' (1996) 39(6) *Academy of Management Journal* 1641, 1641.

[15]   I.Y.M Yeung and R. L. Tung, 'Achieving Business Success in Confucian Societies: The Importance of Guanxi (Connections)' (1996) 25(2) *Organization Dynamics* 54, 54.

door into a hierarchy or group.[16] It has always been regarded by Westerners as a 'mysterious, yet vital, ingredient in successful Chinese business activities'.[17] A mechanism can be established through *guanxi* which enables companies to seek and develop working partnerships in an environment characterised by uncertainty and a relatively weak legal framework.[18] *Guanx*i is a double-edged sword.[19] There are arguable benefits of building an extensive *guanxi* network,[20] such as reducing: transaction costs, operational uncertainty, information costs, contextual hazards and competitive threats. Other benefits include enhancing institutional support, better economic returns, business effectiveness, organisational legitimacy and strategic capability, in order to provide more efficient mechanisms for transactions by acting as the catalyst for the development of new market channels and investment opportunities.[21] Nevertheless, it can also be argued that *guanxi* is closely related to corruption, bribery, reciprocal favours and gift-giving targeted at illicit transactions.[22] Notwithstanding this, it has been asserted that *guanxi* differs from bribery and corruption as the former focuses on long-term relationships and the relationship is more important than the material interests that might be exchanged while the latter is focused on what is exchanged, with the relationship simply being a means to an end.[23] Moreover, *guanxi* does accommodate an emotional element but this is not the case in bribery or corruption.[24] Maintaining *guanxi* is normally related to an

---

[16] H. Chee and C. West, *Myths about Doing Business in China*, (Basingstoke: Palgrave 2004) 63.

[17] Y.L. So and A. Walker, *Explaining Guanxi: The Chinese Business Network*, (London: Routledge 2006) 1.

[18] Y. Luo, 'Industrial Dynamics and Managerial Networking in an Emerging Market: the Case of China' (2003) 24(13) *Strategic Management Journal* 1315.

[19] U. Braendle, T. Casser and J. Noll, 'Corporate Governance in China – Is Economic Growth Potential Hindered by *Guanxi*?' (2005) 110(4) *Business and Society Review* 389, 390.

[20] D. Lee, J.H. Pac and Y.H. Wong, 'A Model of Close Business Relationship in China (guanxi)' (2001) 35(2) *European Journal of Marketing* 51; see also S.L. Lovett, C. Simmons and R. Kali, 'Guanxi Versus the Market: Ethics and Efficiency' (1999) 30(2) *Journal of International Business Studies* 231.

[21] Y. Luo, *Guanxi and Business* (New Jersey and London: World Scientific 2000) 48–49.

[22] P. Wright, W.F. Szeto and L.T.W. Cheng, 'Guanxi and Professional Conduct in China: A Management Development Perspective' (2002) 13(1) *International Journal of Human Resource Management* 156, 166; D. Nile and A. Lamsa, 'The Leader-Member Exchange Theory in the Chinese Context and the Ethical Challenge of Guanx1' (2015) 128(4) *Journal of Business Ethics* 851, 857.

[23] M. Yang, 'The Resilience of Guanxi and its New Deployment: A Critique of Some New *Guanxi* Scholarship' (2002) 170 *The China Quarterly* 459, 465.

[24] S. Lovett, L. Simmons and R. Kali, "Guanxi versus the Market, Ethics and Efficiency" (1999) 30(2) *Journal of International Business Studies* 231, 234.

indirect, ultimate purpose of establishing long-term relationships with individuals or organisations and doing this might be regarded, in some contexts, as leading to improper actions. Also *guanxi* has the potential, on the one hand, to engender trust, but on the other hand it can also threaten trust, particularly in organisations like companies.[25]

Chinese businesspersons have spent a significant amount of time, money and energy on cultivating close *guanxi* with people who have political and bargaining power. *La* (establishing) *guanxi* is regarded as the most common strategy applied by the Chinese in order to establish networks. The effects are to build up relationships with others where there was no pre-existing relationship between them, or where an existing relationship is not close enough to be useful. The impact of *guanxi xue* (relationology) percolates through the political, economic, social, cultural and other spheres of life.[26] *Guanxi* has been identified as one of the most uniquely crucial factors in business relationships and networks in China; these relationships are successful and sustainable where entrepreneurs have extensive networks of connections with senior government officials. At its essence it involves building, maintaining and expanding deep, private and complicated interpersonal relationships and bonds between individuals based on mutual trust, respect and sometimes mutual interests.

One study of *guanxi* in the late 1990s found that managers in China were divided as to whether they felt that *guanxi* was decreasing in importance.[27] As for the relationship between corporate performance and *guanxi*, it is argued by Law, Tse and Zhou that the role played by *guanxi* declined in relation to companies' performance in China.[28] With the globalisation of the Chinese economy and accession to the WTO, it is questionable whether *guanxi* still matters in relation to doing business in China. But, looking at the historical development and recent social and economic transformation in China, it appears that *guanxi* is still deeply rooted in China, just as is Confucius philosophy, and it will remain so indefinitely.[29]

---

[25] C. Chen and X. Chen, "Negative Externalities of Close Guanxi Within Organizations" (2009) 26(1) *Asia Pacific Journal of Management* 37, 39.

[26] M. Chen, *Asian Management Systems*, (London: Thomson, 2nd ed. 2004) 45.

[27] D. Guthrie, 'The Declining Significance of Guanxi in China's Economic Transition' (1998) 154 *China Quarterly* 254.

[28] K.S Law, D.K. Tse and N. Zhou, 'Does Human Resource Management Matter in an Emerging Economy? The Example of the PRC' (2003) 34(3) *Journal of International Business Studies* 255.

[29] See J.H. Dunning and C. Kim, 'The Cultural Roots of Guanxi: An Exploratory Study' (2007) 30(2) *The World Economy* 329; C.C. Chen, X.-P. Chen and S. Huang, 'Chinese Guanxi: An Integrative Review and New Directions for Future Research' (2013) 9(1) *Management and Organization Review* 167.

Other cultural derivatives from *guanxi* include factors such as *renqing*, which means gaining advantages from a relationship. If we look at '*ren*' and '*qing*' as two separate words, we find that *ren* means people/humans and *qing* means feelings. Therefore, the direct translation of *renqing* is human feelings. Related to these human feelings, the concept of *renqing* is about reciprocity in established relationships, and it is obviously closely related to the gift-giving and *guanxi* culture in China. This means that *renqing* constitutes the favours that are offered through well-regarded *guanxi*. *Renqing* is regarded as investment for social capital, with the expectation that the beneficiary will remember it and pay it back when the benefactor is in need. There are unspoken assumptions that both parties have based a relationship on mutual trust and common understanding,[30] and this recognition provides credentials which entitle people to various kinds of credit. In terms of *renqing*, as unpaid obligations resulting from invoking a *guanxi* relationship, reciprocity obligations are also formed by the hierarchically structured *guanxi*.[31] Therefore 'the personal investment required to develop and maintain good social relations is accepted as an unavoidable fact of life',[32] achieved through interpersonal accommodation and negotiation. *Renqing* is regarded as a key form of social capital that obliges people and companies to reciprocate through *guanxi* networks.

The concept of *guanxi* is also closely related to the 'gift culture' in China since giving and receiving gifts appropriately is vital in building and sustaining *guanxi*. Knowing how to give and how to receive gifts is critical in building and sustaining relationships, while each gift carries a piece of *renqing* and all 'accounts' are kept carefully and strictly. Favour and obligations are weighed prudently and accordingly.[33] Through interacting and exchanging favours (*renqing*), individuals and business organisations build credibility and establish trust, gradually creating more useful *guanxi* that will normally be mutually beneficial for both parties.

The balance owed via the reciprocity principle by way of *renqing* is normally silently recorded on both sides, and may be discharged in various ways. Parties who do not fulfil their obligations are considered disloyal and dishonest, and

---

[30] W. Jia, 'The Wei (Positioning) – Ming (Naming) – Lianmian (Face) – Guanxi (Relationship) – Renqing (Humanised Feelings) Complex in Contemporary Chinese Culture', in P.D. Hershock and R.T. Ames, *Confucian Cultures of Authority*, (New York: State University of New York Press 2006) 49–64.

[31] K. Hwang and X. Hu, *Face and Favor: The Chinese Power Game* [面子：中国人的权力游戏] 1–3.

[32] J. Zhang and N. Pimpa, 'Embracing Guanxi: The Literature Review' (2010) 1(1) *International Journal of Asian Business and Information Management* 23, 25.

[33] H. von Weltzine Hoivik, 'East Meets West: Tacit Message about Business Ethics in Stories Told by Chinese Managers' (2007) 74(4) *Journal of Business Ethics* 457, 462.

will suffer loss of moral and social face (*mianzi*).[34] *Renqing* can be interpreted as feelings that are found within friendship, family and kin relationships with regard to favours, etiquette and customs.[35] Furthermore, *mainzi*, which means face, also provides the leverage one needs to successfully expand and manipulate a *guanxi* network.[36] Not losing face and saving of others are key components for cultivating a sustainable *guanxi* network. *Xinren* (trust) is regarded as an important element in dynamic *guanxi* because it limits the possibilities of opportunistic behaviour in a business environment that lacks established rules of law or sound enforcement of laws. These elements are not only important in life generally in China, they are major aspects of Chinese commercial life.[37] One of the positive aspects of *guanxi* is that it will engender greater trust in the corporate governance system in that relationships have been developed and individuals and groups might feel that they can trust others more.

It is important for us to discuss the board structure and characteristics of corporate governance in China before we can critically address the relationship between corporate governance, accountability and cultural factors such as *guanxi*. Besides having a management board of directors, a LLC in China is required by the Company Law 2005 to have a supervisory board composed of no less than three members,[38] who are to supervise 'the acts of the directors and senior executives performing their functions'.[39] The composition of the supervisory board should include shareholders' representatives, who are elected by the shareholders' general meeting, and an appropriate percentage of employee

---

[34]   For discussion of *mianzi* and its relationship with *guanxi* and *renqing* see K.K. Hwang, 'Face and Favor: The Chinese Power Game' (1987) 92(2) *American Journal of Sociology* 944; C.F. Yang, 'A Critical Review of the Conceptualization of Guanxi and Renqing' in C.F. Yang (ed.) *The Interpersonal Relationship Affection and Trust of the Chinese: From an Interactional Perspective*, (Taipei: Yuan Liou Publishing 2001) 3; W. Jia, *The Remaking of the Chinese Character and Identity in the 21st Century: The Chinese Face Practices*, (Westport: Ablex Publishing 2001).

[35]   S. Ruehle, 'Guanxi as Competitive Advantages during Economic Crises: Evidence from China during the Recent Financial Crisis' in X. Fu (ed.), *China's Role in Global Economic Recovery*, (London and New York: Routledge 2012) 60.

[36]   Y. Luo, *Guanxi and Business*, (New Jersey and London: World Scientific, 2nd ed. 2007) 29.

[37]   J. Dunning and C. Kim, 'The Cultural Roots of *Guanxi*: An Exploratory Study' (2007) 30(2) *The World Economy* 329, 329.

[38]   Art. 51, Chinese Company Law 2018.

[39]   Art. 53(2), Chinese Company Law 2018. The supervisory board, as an independent board, offers independent opinions on corporate decisions and monitors the directors' executive management, while the board of directors makes the main decisions on the day-to-day operations of the company.

representatives, so that at least one-third of the supervisory board should be democratically elected by the employees of the company.[40]

Thus China has adopted a two-tier board system which is similar to the German insider model.[41] Membership of the supervisory board must include representatives of the staff and workers of the company.[42] For SOEs, the top executives are normally appointed by the Communist Party (the Party).[43] Apart from their directorship position, the top executives normally have an official title within government that is endorsed by government, and this will be at a level that matches their company's position. Many of them return to government positions after a stint as executives. In SOEs members of the supervisory board are civil servants, and despite the fact that there has been improvement since 2010[44] in their education levels and qualifications, they are normally lower than those of the directors on the main board.[45] They also tend to have limited knowledge about the company itself.[46]

While the two-tier system is representative of the corporate governance of many civil law systems,[47] China has also adopted an element that is found in

---

[40]   Art. 51, Chinese Company Law 2018.

[41]   Centre for Financial Market Integrity, *China Corporate Governance Survey* (2007) 8.

[42]   Arts 44, 108, Chinese Company Law 2018.

[43]   A.G. Walder, 'From Control to Ownership: China's Managerial Revolution' (2009) 7(1) *Management and Organization Review* 19, 31.

[44]   W. Li, *China's Corporate Governance and Development Report 2014*, (Beijing: Beijing University Press 2014) pp.178–179.

[45]   Corporate Governance Research Group of Nan–kai University and Chinese Commission of Economy and Trade, *The Internal Corporate Governance Survey of Chinese Listed Corporations* (2005); see also J. Dahya, Y. Karbhari, J.Z. Xiao and M. Yang, 'The Usefulness of the Supervisory Board Report in China' (2003) 11(4) *Corporate Governance: An International Review* 308.

[46]   H. Wang, 'Research on Problems and Countermeasures in Operation of the Board of Supervisors System in China' (2015) 31 *Reformation and Strategy* 15; L. Guo, 'Revisiting the Chinese Styled Board of Supervisors: How It Gets Failed? – An International Comparative Perspective' [2016] 29 *Journal of Comparative Law (*比较 法研究*)* 74.

[47]   Typically it is regarded as typical character of German system. See J. Kay and A. Silberston, 'Corporate Governance' (1995) 153 *National Institute Economic Review* 84; the *Aktiengesetz* mandates a two-tier board with supervisory board (Aufsichtsrat in §100 AktG) and management board (Vorstand in §76 (3) AktG); see also §1, 7, 27, 31 MitbestG; three co-determination regimes are currently enforced under current German Law including co-determination pursuant to the Montan Co-Determination Act, co-determination pursuant to the DrittelbG 2004 and co-determination under the Co-Determination Act 1976, historically, voluntary formation of labour councils at the factory level by an amendment to Business Practice Act in 1890 (*Gewerbeordnung* or GewO); art. 165 of the Weimar Constitution of 1919 which guaranteed employees the right to cooperate with employers on an equal basis in the regulation of

most common law systems which embrace a one-tier board model, namely the appointment of independent directors.[48] These are non-executive directors who are there to hold the executive directors more accountable and to undertake the supervisory aspect of the function of non-executive directors. Independent directors are to be independent from the listed company that employs them and the company's major shareholders. They are not able to hold any other position apart from the independent directors in the company.[49] The Corporate Governance Code provides that all listed companies should have at least three independent directors.[50] An independent director should chair the audit committee, the nomination committee and the remuneration and appraisal committee.[51]

Just like other corporate governance models with a dual board, the management board is accountable to the supervisory board in China.[52] The supervisory board of a listed company is accountable to all shareholders.[53] Meanwhile, the board of directors is also accountable to shareholders.[54] Therefore, management boards are accountable to both shareholders and the supervisory board while the shareholders or shareholders' meeting seems to be the parties that both boards are accountable to as far as the corporate governance code and company law are concerned.[55] Individual directors and managers of the corpo-

---

wages and working conditions; and the Labour Management Relationship Act 1952 (*Betriebsverfassungsegesetz* 1952, or BetrVG 1952) which introduced the principle of one-third representation of the management board for all other industries. See also G. Cromme, 'Corporate Governance in German and the German Corporate Governance Code' (2005) 13(3) *Corporate Governance: An International Review* 362; M. Goergen, M.C. Manjoin and L. Renneboog, 'Corporate Governance in Germany' in K. Keasey, S. Thompson and M. Wright (eds) *Corporate Governance: Accountability, Enterprise and International Comparisons,* (Chichester: John Wiley & Sons 2005) 285.

[48]   J.N. Gordon, 'The Rise of Independent Directors in the United States, 1950–2005: Of Shareholder Value and Stock Market Price' (2007) 59(6) *Stanford Law Review* 1465; for the discussion on Chinese independent directors regime see D.C. Clarke, 'The Independent Directors in Chinese Corporate Governance' (2006) 31(1) *Delaware Journal of Corporate Law* 125.

[49]   See art. 49, Code of Corporate Governance for Listed Companies in China, 2001.

[50]   Ibid.

[51]   Ibid, art. 52 of Code of Corporate Governance for Listed Companies in China, 2001.

[52]   A. Belcher and T. Naruisch, 'The Evolution of Business Knowledge in the Context of Unitary and Two-Tier Board Systems' [2005] 7 *Journal of Business Law* 443, 451.

[53]   China Securities Regulatory Commission, *Code of Corporate Governance for Listed Companies in China,* 2001, art. 59.

[54]   Ibid, art. 42.

[55]   See also art. 46, Chinese Company Law 2006.

ration are accountable to the management board. These relationships will be taken into account in the next part of the chapter.

Guanxi and other cultural derivatives are obviously closely related to the notions of reciprocity, obligation and indebtedness, as well as trust, and they are essential for personal relationships in China. The concentric *guanxi* circle is established through *renqing,* gift-giving and *xinren* by inventing and re-inventing relationships in an ongoing process of social engineering.[56] It has been argued that *guanxi* is a mixture of *ganqing* (sentiments) and *renqing,* while *renqing* is the precondition for establishing *guanxi* and provides a moral foundation for the reciprocity and equity that are implicit in all *guanxi* relationships.[57] The traditional Chinese social culture surrounding business practices, including the key roles of *guanxi* and *renqing,* still plays a significant role in the remarkable and recent growth of the Chinese economy and increasing cross-border business opportunities. Logically, *guanxi* and other cultural derivatives will also have an impact on the relationship between the two boards, independent directors, and shareholders to whom they are accountable.

The interaction between *guanxi* and its derivatives, as in other collectivist cultures, has been viewed by many scholars as an idiosyncratic cultural phenomenon within which Confucianism is the major life philosophy.[58] Personal relationships have always played a key role in the process of business transactions in China in initiating, negotiating and closing a deal. It is a matter of trust and reliance on networking opportunities, and the maintenance of well-established relationships.[59] One interesting feature of *guanxi* is that the exchange of favours tends to benefit the weaker side, who usually expects to receive more help than he or she can reciprocate.[60] This unequal exchange 'reflects the Confucian principle of family cohesion, in which family ties demand mutual assistance'.[61] Therefore, it may be worth considering the

---

[56] A.Y. King, 'Kuan-his and Network Building' (1991) 120(2) *Daedalus* 69; see also J. Luo and Y. Yeh, 'Neither Collectism nor Individualism: Trust in the Chinese *Guanxi* Circle' (2012) 2(1) *Journal of Trust Research* 53.

[57] Y. Luo, *Guanxi and Business* (New Jersey and London: World Scientific 2000) 15.

[58] D.J. Lee, J.H. Pae and Y.H. Wong, 'A Model of Close Business Relationship in China (Guanxi)' (2001) 35(2) *European Journal of Marketing* 51, 53; see also M.M. Yang, *Gift Favors and Banquets: The Art of Social Relationships in China,* (New York: Cornell University Press 1994).

[59] A. Young, 'Conceptualising a Chinese Corporate Governance Framework: Tension between Tradition, Ideologies and Modernity' (2009) 20(7) *International Company and Commercial Law Review* 235, 237.

[60] M. Chen, *Asian Management Systems,* (London: Thomson, 2nd ed. 2004) 44.

[61] J.P. Alston, 'Wa, Guanxi, and Inhwa: Managerial Principle in Japan, China, and Korea' (1989) 32(2) *Business Horizon* 26, 28.

parties that are comparatively weaker in the scenario of accountability within the corporate governance framework. These parties could be at a disadvantage or in positions of vulnerability, especially when we are discussing *guanxi* in the context of accountability.

It is our task in this section to find out whether China's culture and traditions, including *guanxi* will continue to influence the development of Chinese corporate governance, and in particular where they fit in relation to the *wenze* system of accountability. The Chinese corporate governance system currently in place owes a lot to the longstanding and deeply-held Chinese value of upholding the importance of flexibility, resulting in tolerance of certain degrees of freedom in decision-making.[62] Within corporate governance this is described as 'low structure, high ambiguity', in which the ambiguity allows for culture, traditions and values to decide what is fair and what is right for corporations.[63] The higher degree of autonomy and ambiguity allow culture to play a greater role. Preferences and interpretations of culture are permitted to interfere with corporate governance.

It is also argued that culture is as an amorphous concept which is hard to define but is fundamental.[64] In many places in China the government and the Party still play an important role in governing and interfering in corporate decisions, so that the existing culture may need to play a greater role in corporate governance. For example, the *guanxi* between the civil servants who represent the state or a state agency and shareholders and stakeholders are particularly important in a society that exhibits high levels of collectivism and the avoidance of uncertainty.[65] It is crucial to point out that the essence of *guanxi* must be cultivated over time, and the process of establishing *guanxi* is the processing of exchanging *renqing,* gift-giving and establishing *xinren.* While contracts are regarded as the core legal documents in the Western business world, cultural elements play a rudimentary role in China in the process of reaching business agreements. Discussions of these cultural issues are particularly important in corporate governance since these issues serve as a form of

---

[62]   S.H. Goo and A. Carve, 'Law Structure, High Ambiguity: Selective Adaption of International Norms of Corporate Governance Mechanisms in China', in M. Nakamura (ed.) *Changing Corporate Governance in China and Japan: Adaptions of Anglo–American Practices*, (Basingstoke: Palgrave Macmillan 2008) 206, 207.

[63]   Ibid.

[64]   M. Lebas and J. Weigenstein, 'Management Control: The Roles of Rules, Markets and Culture' (1986) 23(3) *Journal of Management Studies* 259, 264.

[65]   D. Hay, S.M. Adnan and C. Staden, 'Culture, Governance Structure and Corporate Social Responsibility (CSR) reporting: Evidence from China, India, Malaysia and the United Kingdom.' Paper presented at the 2010 AFAANZ (Accounting and Finance Association of Australia and New Zealand) Conference, Christchurch, New Zealand.

insurance in a relatively risky business environment.[66] While the enforcement of law is relatively weak and the involvement of government is comparatively strong in China, having *guanxi* with suppliers, banks, government supervisory agencies, retailers and customers could help tremendously by offering them a number of benefits.

7.2   ASCERTAINING THE THEMES

This chapter chooses to assess the derivative action law in China according to three criteria: accessibility, balance, and effectiveness.

7.2.1   Accessibility

Accessibility to shareholders is essential for improving the effectiveness of derivative actions. This requires a basic awareness of available remedies and access to courts without excessive litigation fees or unreasonable procedural barriers.[67] Measured against this criterion, derivative actions mechanism in China still encounter many deficiencies as revealed by our study: such as high litigation fees, standing requirements, and barriers brought by difficulties in initiating overcome collective action in JSLCs. As the result, most existing derivative action cases have single, natural person claimants, and cases for JSLCs with dispersed ownership are extremely rare.

In addition, the unbalanced relationship between minority shareholders and the board/majority shareholders is also a major barrier. The board or majority shareholders manage the company and control the companies' resources and usually have an informational and financial advantage over minority share-holders. They are usually more sophisticated or are supported by professionals. Through their advantageous position, the board or majority shareholders can have the court strike out derivative cases and obstruct the rights of minority shareholders. We found that less than half of all cases satisfied the demand requirement and the overall success rate of derivative cases is low.

Accessibility of the derivative action could be further undermined by legal transplant effects in China and other developing countries. As an imported

---

[66]   R.Y.J. Chua and M.W. Morris, 'Dynamics of Trust in Guanxi Networks' in Y. Chen, (ed.) *National Culture and Groups*, (Bingley: Emerald Group Publishing Limited 2006) 95, 98.

[67]   This definition of availability is borrowed from the definition of 'access to justice' in the World Justice Project Rule of Law index. See https://worldjusticeproject .org/our–work/wjp–rule–law–index/wjp–rule–law–index–2017%E2%80%932018 (accessed 25 July 2022).

law, it might be less effective than internally developed law[68] as people might be unaware of their legal rights or less willing to make such a non-traditional claim.[69] We found that these are all somehow unbalanced phenomena that hinder the accessibility of the mechanism.

In order to address these obstacles to accessibility, we make a number of reform proposals, including a maximum cap for filing fees, a more enabling litigating environment to facilitate a more active role for institutional investors, and a supporting role for a public enforcer. Compared with individuals who are usually 'one shot litigants', institutional investors are usually 'repeat players' and thus have the legal experience and bargaining power to challenge the board and majority shareholders.[70] The role of institutional investors is particularly important in JSLCs as they are more likely to overcome the collective action problem and meet the 1 per cent shareholding threshold. A public enforcer in China such as the CSRC could assist shareholders by providing education, legal representation, and other resources. The establishment of the ISC under the auspices of the CSRC might be the start of a promising new model of derivative action – private enforcement supported by a public enforcer.

7.2.2   Balance

The effectiveness of derivative actions should also be assessed against a balanced mechanism, namely to strike a balance between strengthening shareholder protection and respecting corporate internal governance. Derivative actions should give shareholders remedies against abuse by the controllers, but if courts are overly liberal in accepting these actions, the company might lose the opportunity to resolve conflicts through internal procedures, and the decision-making power of the board will be compromised.[71] Compared to internal remedies, derivative actions can be lengthy and costly and damage the company's reputation. An abundance of lawsuits might also become a drain on judicial resources.[72]

---

[68]   J. Torpman and F. Jörgensen, 'Legal Effectiveness: Theoretical Developments Concerning Legal Transplants' (2005) 91(4) *Archives for Philosophy of Law and Social Philosophy* 515.

[69]   B.G. Garth and M. Cappelletti, 'Access to Justice: The Newest Wave in the Worldwide Movement to Make Rights Effective' (1978) 27 *Buffalo Law Review* 181.

[70]   Ibid.

[71]   In both the UK and the US, the board has not only the power, but also a defensible right to manage affairs of the company. See M. Moore, *Corporate Governance in the Shadow of the State* (London: Bloomsbury Publishing 2013) 29.

[72]   J. Kirkbride, S. Letza and C. Smallman, 'Minority Shareholders and Corporate Governance: Reflections on the Derivative Action in the UK, the USA and in China' (2009) 51(4) *Intentional Journal of Law & Management* 206.

The unique corporate governance model and mix of shareholders in China also necessitate a flexible and balanced approach for derivative actions. In contrast to the UK and US, the corporate governance problems in China are fundamentally different in that the main agency problem is one caused by the abuse by controlling shareholders, rather than the conflict between the board and shareholders. Nevertheless, experience from the UK and US highlights the importance of respecting the internal governance of companies, particularly through the business judgement rule.

In the case of LLCs, a balance should be slightly tilted towards the accessibility of derivative actions. Due to the lack of an open market, regulatory oversight, and a fully-fledged oppression remedy, derivative actions in LLCs should offer more protection to less sophisticated shareholders. For example, the demand requirement should be excused in a case brought by the only supervisor of a small company who is also a shareholder. At the other end of the spectrum are listed JSLCs, where derivative actions should tilt towards protecting board discretion and the companies' collective interests. Even so, we have observed that the eligibility requirements could be loosened to create a more balanced derivative action mechanism.[73]

Another necessary aspect of balance in derivative actions is the balance between litigation and alternative dispute resolution mechanisms. It is important to preserve established, long-term relationships within companies, especially given the central role of *guanxi* and *mianzi* in Chinese society. We observe that the prevalence of derivative action cases in JSLCs and LLCs is quite unbalanced. In LLCs, shareholders usually have their personal relationships and business relationships intertwined. A formal action in court might lead to a breakdown of the relationships, and therefore, a derivative action might not be the best method for resolving conflicts in some cases. To complement derivative actions, alternative dispute resolution mechanisms such as arbitration and the out-of-court settlement may be encouraged. These methods may be more cost-effective and may preserve long-term relationships among shareholders.[74]

---

[73] For example, reform proposals have been put forward to lower the 1 per cent to 0.1 per cent to enhance the accessibility in J. Zhao and S. Wen, 'The Eligibility of Claimants to Commence Derivative Litigation on Behalf of China's Joint Stock Limited Companies' (2018) 48(2) *Hong Kong Law Journal* 687.

[74] I.K.L. Mak, *Alternative Dispute Resolution of Shareholder Disputes in Hong Kong: Institutionalizing Its Effective Use*, (Cambridge: Cambridge University Press 2017) 130.

7.2.3   Effectiveness

If the law is viewed as a tool for social engineering, i.e., regulating or shaping the behaviours of members of society, the effectiveness of law must be measured by the extent to which it fulfils its objectives. The aims of law can be divided into preventive or curative objectives. For a preventive law, it is effective if it can deter undesirable behaviours and prevent wrongs from happening. For a curative law, it is effective if it can remedy wrongs *ex post facto* and compensate the wronged parties.[75] The effectiveness of the derivative action law should be measured according to both preventive and curative objectives, for it has a dual nature. First, the law seeks to deter directors and controlling shareholders from causing damage to the company and shareholders. Second, the law also seeks to compensate shareholders who have suffered losses. By deterring and compensating, the law can ameliorate agency problems in companies and strengthen corporate governance.[76]

7.3   INTEGRATING PROBLEMS, PROPOSALS WITH THEMES

We believe that the criteria stated above are key for addressing problems and promoting sound corporate governance and operative corporate law. These criteria can be addressed through the reform proposals in this chapter. For example, accessibility can be improved through the reform of substantive and procedural rules, including more relaxed claimant eligibility for JSLCs, capped litigation fees in order to improve the predictability and consistency of the legislation in reducing cultural and reputational hindrances. We have studied various aspects of derivative actions and proposed various reforms, all of which bear on one or more of the stated criteria. These correspondences are detailed in Tables 7.1 and 7.2 below.

In order to institute a comprehensive picture all these criteria, the following matrix has been developed, demonstrated in Figure 7.1 through a hypothetical model, to establish the link between these three criteria: accessibility, balance, and effectiveness. We assume that accessibility and balance are normally distributed variables, and effectiveness is the bivariate normal distribution made

---

[75]   A. Allott, 'The Effectiveness of Law' (1980) 15(2) *Vanderbilt University Law Review* 229.

[76]   S.P. Ferris, T. Jandik and R.M. Lawless, 'Derivative Lawsuits as a Corporate Governance Mechanism: Empirical Evidence on Board Changes Surrounding Filings' (2007) 42(1) *Journal of Financial and Quantitative Analysis* 143.

Table 7.1   *Aspects of derivative actions studied and their bearings on accessibility, effectiveness, and balance*

Aspect	Accessibility	Balance	Effectiveness
Number of cases	x		x
Regional distribution	x		x
Type of company (mostly LLCs)	x	x	x
Type of company (few JSLCs)	x	x	x
Claimant	x		x
Defendant	x		x
Cause of action	x	x	x
Court fees	x		x
Demand requirement	x	x	
Court decision	x		x

Table 7.2   *Reform proposals and their bearings on accessibility, effectiveness, and balance*

Reform	Accessibility	Balance	Effectiveness
Consistent judicial approach	x	x	x
Increasing use of derivative action for JSLCs	x		x
Maximum cap for filing fees	x		x
Balanced approach to the demand requirement	x	x	x
Statutory business judgement rule		x	x
Private enforcement supported by public enforcer	x		x

up of these two variables.[77] We assume that these criteria are normally distributed because extreme cases are rare as it is difficult for a derivative action in one jurisdiction being extremely accessible, balanced, and effective while one jurisdiction is quite the opposite.

Here the X axis represents accessibility, with balance on the Y axis. The vertical axis represents effectiveness. Accessibility and balance are both positively correlated with effectiveness as both can improve the outcome

---

[77]   A bivariate normal distribution may be used to analyse the relationship between two normally distributed variables – e.g., the relationship between fathers' heights and the heights of their eldest sons. For the maths, see https://brilliant.org/wiki/mul tivariate–normal–distribution/#applications (accessed 25 July 2022).

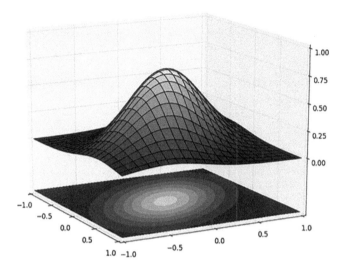

Figure 7.1   Model for availability, balance, and effectiveness

and effects of derivative actions. The diagram shows that as accessibility and balance increase, effectiveness is also increasing. However, accessibility and balance are and, in our opinion, should be negatively correlated in the model. This is because when derivative action mechanism becomes increasingly or overly accessible to shareholders, it will be difficult to maintain a balance because of boards' discretion and accessibility of remedies against boards.

There is a peak in the curve representing the maximum value for effectiveness, and after reaching this peak effectiveness will decrease as accessibility or balance increase. This means that there is an optimal combination of effectiveness and balance that will lead to the result with maximum effectiveness. It should be noted that here we only present a crude model with hypothetical values without precise analysis on dialectical relations values. Future studies might try to clarify the precise relationships between accessibility, balance and effectiveness, including their distributions and correlations.

7.4   PRIVATE ENFORCEMENT BACKED BY PUBLIC REGULATOR IN CHINA: THE CASE OF INVESTOR SERVICES CENTRE FOR SUPPORTING DERIVATIVE ACTIONS

In a unique hybrid corporate governance model with inevitable and necessary government interference, we think it is important to have a section with more detailed analysis on public enforcement supported by a public enforcer. Before considering how private enforcement can be facilitated by a public enforcer, we first need to stress that both private and public enforcements are important and complementary to each other. On the one hand, La Porta et al. argued that private enforcement can facilitate the development of stock markets, whereas public enforcement has little impact.[78] Their argument provides the theoretical underpinning for policy makers, such as the World Bank, that promote private enforcement and deregulation over public regulation.[79] On the other hand, Jackson found that public enforcement is at least as significant as private enforcement and is correlated with the development of financial markets.[80] Contrary to La Porta et al.'s finding that 'legal origin matters', it is argued that regulatory institutions are more important for robust securities markets than the traditional rules of the common law, such as fiduciary duties.[81] Common law jurisdictions have more intensive financial regulation than civil law countries. The financial regulation in the US is more intensive than that in Britain, but the financial regulation in Britain is significantly more intensive than in civil law countries.[82] Regardless of legal origin, countries should adopt effective public enforcement in addition to disclosure rules in order to protect investors.

From the above discussion, it can be seen that both private enforcement and public enforcement are important and that the effectiveness of the law relies on their combined effort. Private enforcement and public enforcement can be viewed as two basic forms of social control. Social controls imposed on businesses can be classified into four categories: market discipline; private litigation; public enforcement; and state ownership. The purpose of social control is to reduce two kinds of costs: those of dictatorship and those of disorder. The disorder is the ability of private parties to impose external costs on each

---

[78]   R. La Porta, F. Lopez-de-Silane and A. Shleifer, 'What Works in Securities Law?' (2006) 61(1) *The Journal of Finance* 1.

[79]   G. McCormack, 'Why 'Doing Business' with the World Bank May Be Bad for You' (2018) 19(3) *European Business Organisation Law Review* 649.

[80]   H.E. Jackson, 'Variation in the Intensity of Financial Regulation: Preliminary Evidence and Potential Implications' (2007) 24(2) *Yale Journal on Regulation* 254.

[81]   Ibid.

[82]   Ibid.

other, while dictatorship results in costs imposed by public officials on private parties. From market discipline to state ownership, the costs of disorder decline as those of dictatorship increase. An efficient choice of institution differs from country to country and depends on the precise trade-offs between disorder and dictatorship.[83] It is important to consider the traditions, political constraints, and reform processes in different countries and their effects on the choices and enforcement of rules.[84]

In developing countries such as China where the law is incomplete, public enforcement usually plays a more important role than private enforcement. Compared with judges who are reactive, regulators are proactive enforcers.[85] Regulators also have more expertise and political incentive to sanction socially undesirable behaviours. Evidence of the important role of the public regulator can be observed in China, where the judiciary is weak and the CSRC has played a dominant role in enforcing securities laws and fiduciary duties of directors in listed companies.

However, relying solely on public enforcement can be problematic. Regulators might not pursue public interest only and can be captured by industries. Rather than correcting market failures, regulation can be used to create barriers to competition.[86] Under such circumstances, the costs of dictatorship might outweigh those of disorder. Public regulation imposes too many *ex ante* controls in China, whereas the *ex post* enforcement remains poor. For example, scholars question the 'regulatory intensity' of the CSRC and argue that its enforcement is weak, particularly when imposing sanctions against directors and supervisors in listed companies.[87] With serious regulatory capture problems, the power of a financial regulator is proportional to the degree of corruption.[88]

---

[83] S. Djankov et al., 'The New Comparative Economics' (2003) 31(4) *Journal of Comparative Economics* 595.

[84] H.E. Jackson, 'Variation in the Intensity of Financial Regulation: Preliminary Evidence and Potential Implications' (2007) 24(2) *Yale Journal on Regulation* 254; K. Pistor, 'Patterns of Legal Change: Shareholder and Creditor Rights in Transition Economies' (2000) 1(1) *European Business Organization Law Review* 59.

[85] C. Xu and K. Pistor, 'Law Enforcement under Incomplete Law: Theory and Evidence from Financial Market Regulation' (LSE STICERD Research Paper No. TE442), https://papers.ssrn.com/sol3/papers.cfm?abstract_id=1160987 (2003) (accessed 25 July 2022).

[86] G.J. Stigler, 'The Theory of Economic Regulation' (1971) 2(1) *The Bell Journal of Economics and Management Science* 3.

[87] F. Zhang and X. Li, 'Empirical Analysis of the Regulatory Intensity of the CSRC [对证监会执法强度的实证分析]' (2016) 1 *Modern Law Science [现代法学]* 38.

[88] P. Xie and L. Lu, *Economic Analysis on Financial Corruption in China [中国金融腐败的经济学分析]*, (Beijing: CITIC Press Group 2005).

Given the limitations of public regulation, it is necessary to promote stronger private enforcement in China. Private enforcement can complement public enforcement and improve the effectiveness of law in two aspects: first, private enforcement constitutes an additional deterrence to misbehaviour; second, private enforcement can provide compensation for claimants who cannot be compensated through public sanctions.[89] In addition, a more effective private enforcement mechanism will reduce the need for public regulation, unnecessary *ex ante* control and, consequently, the risk of regulatory capture. After years of reform, company law and securities regulation in China is evolving towards 'completeness'. A myriad of legal rules for private enforcement, including derivative actions, has been introduced for investor protection. The problem is that these legal rules remain law on the books and are not well-used, as confirmed by our findings. One of the main reasons for the marginalisation of private enforcement in China is the dominant role played by public regulation and public regulators such as the CSRC, who are quasi-legislators with wide regulatory powers.[90] To achieve a balanced combination of private and public enforcement, it is necessary to promote private enforcement and curtail the power of public regulators.

We have found that derivative actions are rarely used by listed companies and it is difficult for shareholders to surmount the shareholding/procedural/financial obstacles in bringing derivative actions. Therefore, private enforcement supported by a public regulator is the most suitable model for derivative actions in China, and this is compatible with the institutional and political environment of the country. The ISC is an example in the right direction. Although the mission and functions of the ISC, a newly established organisation, are still unclear, it could become a quasi-public regulator that constitutes an extension of the CSRC and enforces its orders. As such, the ISC may become too politicised to escape 'regulatory capture', like the CSRC itself. We think it would be better if the ISC becomes like a public institutional investor that is actively involved in corporate governance in order to achieve the following missions.

First, as a public institutional investor, the ISC can improve the accessibility of derivative actions for listed companies. It provides education and information to shareholders so as to increase awareness of the derivative action mechanism part of shareholders' rights. The ISC could also assist shareholders in bringing derivative actions by coordinating collective actions, providing information and legal representation, and preserving a fund that could provide financial assistance to claimants. In addition, by becoming a shareholder in

---

[89]   Ibid.

[90]   L. Lin, *Annual Report on China's Rule of Law No.15*, (Beijing: Social Sciences Academic Press 2017).

listed companies, the ISC would be a legitimate party to monitor corporate governance and initiate derivative actions against misbehaviour as the claimant. It has been found that public institutional investors such as public pension funds are instrumental in improving the effectiveness of class actions and are more active than private institutional investors in the corporate governance process.[91] The public nature of these funds seems to have made them different from private institutional investors, who are discouraged by free-rider problems and the prospect of bearing the litigation costs. The managers in public pension funds are 'political entrepreneurs' who are motivated by political gains in addition to economic gains. In pursuing actions for the benefit of all shareholders, public institutional investors actually provide a public good that private investors are unwilling to fund.[92]

Second, the ISC can be instrumental in achieving a balance between accessibility and other considerations such as respecting internal governance, maintaining long-term relationships, and saving judicial resources. As a public institutional shareholder, the ISC has an informational advantage and is more likely to exhaust internal remedies before starting lawsuits. Consequently, derivative actions initiated by the ISC may be more likely to be meaningful and achieve the corrective justice as the goal and value of private law.[93] Additionally, the ISC could even facilitate other dispute settlement measures.

Third, the ISC can initiate more cases, which will facilitate the development of more consistent legal rules. For example, our empirical findings demonstrate that the demand requirement has been applied rigidly and inconsistently by Chinese courts. This reflects overly formalised judicial procedure and curtailed judicial discretion in civil law countries.[94] It is impracticable to expand the discretion of the Chinese courts so that they could develop legal rules for excusing the demand requirement based on the business judgement rule as the courts in the US. If not corrected, it could lead to more uncertainty, inconsistency, delay, corruption or miscarriage of justice.[95] Instead, corrective guidance from the SPC is only possible with an accumulation of judicial practice.

---

[91]   J.D. Cox and R. S. Thomas, 'Does the Plaintiff Matter – An Empirical Analysis of Lead Plaintiffs in Securities Class Actions' (2006) 106(7) *Columbia Law Review* 1587.

[92]   R. Romano, 'Public Pension Fund Activism in Corporate Governance Reconsidered' (1993) 93(4) *Columbia Law Review* 795.

[93]   E.J. Weinrib, *The Idea of Private Law* (Oxford: Oxford University Press 1995) 56–58; P. Cane, 'Review: Corrective Justice and Correlativity in Private Law' (1995) 16(3) *Oxford Journal of Legal Studies* 471.

[94]   A. Shleifer, 'Understanding Regulation' (2005) 11(4) *European Financial Management* 439.

[95]   Ibid.

Fourth, the ISC can act as a bridge between the CSRC and courts, facilitating communication between the governmental agency and judges. This would help to coordinate administrative sanctions and civil litigations against wrongdoers. In particular, the ISC could channel experience from the CSRC to courts regarding fiduciary duties in listed companies, as the CSRC has been the main enforcer of fiduciary duties in listed companies in China.[96] However, public enforcement is insufficient for deterring or compensating and bringing reputational damage to the company. Therefore, in order to provide a better remedy for shareholders, the ISC should actively enforce fiduciary duties through derivative actions, with support from the CSRC. Moreover, although the ISC only represents shareholders in listed companies, its enforcement of fiduciary duties will also be beneficial for shareholders in LLCs. The derivative action is the main method for challenging controlling shareholder in LLCs in China. Derivative actions brought by the ISC will help courts, generally, to develop more specific rules of fiduciary duties and clarify procedural rules for derivative actions.

Fifth, the ISC can also promote shareholder activism by monitoring disclosures of listed companies and preventing abuse *ex ante*. As a shareholder, the ISC can exercise its shareholder rights by participating in shareholders' meetings and inspecting financial documents. In China, it is common for listed companies to require shareholders to provide documents in addition to those provided by law and regulations and thereby impose illegal obstacles against minority shareholders to attend shareholder meetings and vote. The involvement of the ISC can reduce such practices and safeguard the rights of minority shareholders.

In Taiwan, the experience of a counterpart of the ISC can be instructive. The second-tier stock market in Taiwan is similar to that in Mainland China in that the majority of shareholders are individual shareholders. There are many 'financial consumers' that need heightened protection, compared with institutional investors.[97] In order to strengthen protection for minority and individual shareholders, the SFIPC (Securities and Futures Investors Protection Center) was established in 2003 with a similar role to that of the ISC. Funded by the government with key personnel appointed by the government, the SFIPC has a role similar as the ISC, including mediating, bringing actions for breach of

---

[96] G. Xu, T. Zhou, B. Zeng and J. Shi, 'Directors' Duties in China' (2013) 14(1) *European Business Organization Law Review* 57.

[97] D. Lamb, 'A Specter is Haunting the Financial Industry – The Specter of the Global Financial Crisis: A Comment on the Imminent Expansion of Consumer Financial Protection in the United States, the United Kingdom, and the European Union' (2011) 31(1) *Journal of the National Association of Administrative Law Judiciary* 213.

company law or securities regulations, and suing in its own name. The SFIPC also owns shares of listed companies.[98]

The SFIPC has played an active and relatively successful role in protecting minority shareholders of listed companies. It has also obtained large settlements for shareholders. In addition to leading 'shareholding activism', the SFPIC has also provided education for ordinary shareholders and collaborated with the public regulator.[99] However, the SFPIC has focused its efforts on enforcing securities regulations rather than fiduciary duties. The SFIPC can bring both class actions and derivative actions. As of the end of 2018, the SFIPC had filed 54 derivative actions and the Center was able to force wrongdoers to compensate companies for the total amount of NT$1.57 billion, thereby protecting the interests of companies and their shareholders.[100]

However, the main problem of the SFIPC is that it is more of a quasi-public regulator than a public institutional shareholder. The SFIPC has been criticised for assuming conflicting roles, representing shareholders and public interest at the same time. Furthermore, while it is funded by public resources, it lacks transparency and efficiency. However, in the 2018 report, the positive observation is that the degree of transparency has been improved with a detailed report from independent auditors.[101]

The lessons provided by the SFIPC remind us of the importance of a clear definition of roles. In an economy that is transitioning from a planned economy to a market economy, the main role of the ISC should be facilitating private enforcement, rather than strengthening public enforcement. To ensure that the ISC can provide 'public good' for ordinary shareholders, the public nature of the ISC needs to be recognised by law. First, the ISC should be exempt from the shareholding percentage and time requirements in JSLCs. As a public institutional shareholder, the ISC presumably represents the interests of shareholders as a whole and should not be forced to solicit support from other shareholders in order to meet the shareholding requirement.[102] This has been confirmed by the revised Securities Law which passed on 28 December 2019

---

[98]   C.C. Chen, *Enforcement of The Duties of Directors by The Securities and Futures Investors Protection Center in Taiwan*, Research Collection School of Law, https://papers.ssrn.com/sol3/papers.cfm?abstract_id=2588254 (accessed 25 July 2022).

[99]   Ibid.; Y. Miao, *Enforcement Mechanisms of Securities Law in P. R. China [*中国证券法律实施机制研究*]* Chapter 5 (Beijing: Beijing University Press 2017).

[100]   SFIPC, *2018 Annual Report* 21.

[101]   SFIPC, 2018 *Annual Report* 26–35.

[102]   In Taiwan, the SFIPC is entitled to the exemption of the shareholding requirement for bringing the derivative action for listed companies so that it could save time and costs; see J., Chen, 'Framework of the Shareholder Rights of the ISC [投服中心公益股东权的配置及制度建构]', IOLAW, http://www.iolaw.org.cn/showArticle.aspx?id=5439 (2017) (accessed 25 July 2022).

by the National People's Congress Standing Committee and will be effective on 1 March 2020. According to the Chinese Securities Law 2020, where the issuer's director, supervisor or senior executive violates the provisions of any law or administrative regulation or the company's bylaws in the performance of corporate duties, causing any loss to the company, investor protection institution formed in accordance with the provisions of laws, administrative regulations or the provisions issued by the securities regulatory authority of the State Council, this obviously includes ISC, may file a lawsuit with a people's court in its own name for the interests of the company, the shareholding ratio and shareholding period shall not be subject to the restriction prescribed in the Chinese Company Law of the People's Republic of China.[103]

Second, in addition to raising claims as a shareholder, the ISC should be allowed to bring litigation in the form of 'public interest litigation' (公益集团 诉讼*Gongyi Jituan Susong*), which can enjoy reduced litigation fees. Public interest litigation was introduced by the amendment to the Chinese Civil Procedure Law in 2012.[104] It refers to litigation brought by a third party for the interests of a large group of people, such as consumers of defective products and environmental victims. As individual investors in the Chinese stock market can be viewed as 'financial consumers', it is possible for public interest organisations to bring litigation on their behalf. This has been confirmed by the Chinese Securities Law 2020 as an investor protection institution may, as entrusted by 50 or more investors, participate in legal proceedings as a representative.[105] With the approval of the CSRC, investor protection organisations can bring public interest litigation against breach of securities laws. The ISC should be explicitly authorised to bring public interest litigations.

Third, the public nature of the ISC indicates that it might act with political incentives rather than protecting the public interest. The ISC might become a mere extension of the CSRC and bring lawsuits selectively, as instructed by the CSRC.[106] Consequently, it might entrench the power of the public regulator and fail to improve the effectiveness of private enforcement. Furthermore, like a public regulator, the ISC could incur administrative costs and might be subject to regulatory capture. Therefore, governance mechanisms within the ISC are necessary to improve its transparency and accountability. Most importantly, the ISC should explain or give account of its actions, how it uses public resources, the costs and benefits of litigation compared with other rem-

---

[103] Arts 90 and 94, Chinese Securities Law 2020.
[104] Art. 55, Civil Procedure Law 2012
[105] Art. 95, Chinese Securities Law 2020.
[106] Art. 55, Civil Procedure Law 2012.

edies, and how its actions could contribute to the goal of investor protection.[107] Strengthening organisations such as the ISC can promote private enforcement backed by a public regulator and is crucial for creating trust and confidence in the Chinese financial market.

7.5   THE ESTABLISHMENT OF A MORE EFFICIENT DERIVATIVE ACTION SCHEME IN CHINA

Effective from 2006, the derivative claim action system embedded in Chinese Company Law was designed to improve the Chinese corporate governance system and provide a weapon against insider and controlling shareholder abuse in newly corporatised listed companies in China.[108] Since the enforcement of the Chinese Company Law enacted in 2006, the demand for minority shareholder protection has increased as the result of demand from several directions. With the increasing number of dividable shareholders, largely due to the expansion of the securities market, the rights and liabilities of investors are promoted by the public media in the aftermath of corporate scandals and market turbulence.[109] The focus on the development of the stock market in order to ease the pressures on loan capital from banking finance is making shareholders' rights and remedies increasingly important.

The conversion of SOEs enables the government to be less concerned about providing guidance and privileges to SOEs, and by extension the state as the biggest shareholder in SOEs.[110] China has experienced an unprecedented wave of corporatisation and privatisation since implementing the Chinese Company Law 1993.[111]The corporatisation of business organisations with decreased government interference under Chinese Company Law 2006, in comparison with Chinese Company Law 1993, means that corporate governance theory is closely related to the protection of the shareholder in China.

Systematic corporate governance reform is becoming increasingly important in the emerging Chinese market, which is moving towards a more free

---

[107] J. Bird, 'Regulating the Regulators: Accountability of Australian Regulators' (2011) 35(3) *Melbourne University Law Review* 739.
[108] D.C. Clarke and N.C. Howson, 'Pathway to Minority Shareholder Protection: Derivative Action in the People's Republic of China' in D. Puchniak, H. Baum and M. Ewing-Chow (eds) *The Derivative Action in Asia: A Comparative and Functional Approach* (Cambridge: Cambridge University Press 2012) 243.
[109] X. Tang, 'Protecting Minority Shareholders in China: A Task for Both Legislations and Enforcement' Chapter 9 in C. Milhaupt, K. Kim and H. Kanda (eds) *Transforming Corporate Governance in East Asia* (London: Routledge 2009) 151–177.
[110] Ibid.
[111] Y. Wei, 'The Development of Securities Market and Regulations in China' (2005) 27(3) *Loyola of Los Angeles International and Comparative Law Review* 479.

market system.[112] Shareholder derivative claims are always used as a 'case study' for the relationship between institutions and the norms of corporate governance.[113] Chinese government officials and commentators believe that shareholder derivative claim actions will promote better corporate governance in China,[114] and it is an 'almost unanimous understanding' that China has to institute a system for shareholder derivative suits.[115] Conversely, however, corporate governance theories could be adopted as an effective way of illuminating an improved institutionalised derivative claim system. The lack of a shareholder remedy contributed the inefficient corporate governance system in China, especially for minority shareholders.[116] Proponents of derivative action describe it as 'the chief regulator of corporate management'.[117] It plays a significant role in deterring managerial misconduct, and thereby reduces the agency cost inherent in corporate management.[118] It is predicted that the adoption of the actions will be 'a major development of Chinese company legislations" with "far reaching implication for corporate governance'.[119] However, the effectiveness of transplanting the derivative action rule into China may not always lead to the intended consequences and results.

---

[112] S.C. Jain, *Emerging Economies and the Transformation of International Business*, (Cheltenham: Edward Elgar 2006) 383–386.

[113] See examples such as: D.C. Clarke, 'The Ecology of Corporate Governance in China', The George Washington University Law and Legal Theory Working Paper No. 433; A. Keay, 'The Ultimate Objective of the Public Company and the Enforcement of the Entity Maximisation and Sustainability Model' (2010) 10(1) *Journal of Corporate Law Studies* 369; S.P. Ferris, T. Jandik, R.M. Lawless and A. Makhija, 'Derivative Lawsuits as a Corporate Governance Mechanism: Empirical Evidence on Board Changes Surrounding Filings' (2009) 42(1) *Journal of Financial and Quantitative Analysis* 143; R. Romano, 'The Shareholder Suit: Litigation Without Foundation?' (1991) 7(1) *Journal of Law Economics and Organization* 55; A.S. Ginevri, 'The Rise of Long-Term Minority Shareholders' Rights in Publicly Held Corporations and Its Effect on Corporate Governance' (2011) 12(4) *European Business Organization Law Review* 587.

[114] J. Deng, 'Building an Investor-Friendly Shareholder Derivative Lawsuit System in China' (2005) 46(2) *Harvard International Law Journal* 347, 349.

[115] G. Yu, 'Using Western Law to Improve China's State Owned Enterprise: Of Takeover and Securities Fraud' (2004) 39(2) *Valparaiso University Law Review* 339, 340.

[116] G. Yu, 'Towards an Institutional Competition Model of Comparative Corporate Governance Studies' (2003) 6 *Journal of Chinese and Comparative Law* 31, 56.

[117] *Cohen v Beneficial industrial Corp.*, 337 U.S. 541 (1949), p. 548.

[118] J. Coffee and D. Schwartz, 'The Survival of the Derivative Suit: An Evaluation and a Proposal for Legislative Reform' (1981) 81 *Columbia Law Review* 261.

[119] H. Huang, 'The Statutory Derivative Action in China: Critical Analysis and Recommendations for Reform' (2007) 4(2) *Berkeley Business Law Journal* 227, 242.

Corporate governance theories including agency theory and path dependence theory can help to explain the Chinese derivation action with unique 'Chinese characteristics'. China's economy is in a critical transitional phase with changes in the enterprise system and the securities market. This places the Chinese corporate governance system in a unique position to adopt the derivative action rule. The company law system in China, including civil procedural law, economic transformation, current legal enforcement problems, qualification of practitioners and judges, Chinese traditions and history, will have to be considered collectively with the corporate governance system to determine the effectiveness of adopting a derivative action system.

'The judiciary is weak, unsophisticated and riddled with corruption' in China.[120] Furthermore, Chinese judges are often criticised for their inadequate qualifications, poor training and lack of knowledge and skills. The reputation and authority of the judiciary has been negatively compromised as a result of corruption and political interference in judicial processes. *Guanxi* and *Renqing* make the supervisory board, which does not have power over the managerial board and has no remit to elect or dismiss managerial directors, even less efficient. Institutional shareholders and other non-controlling shareholders in China, who may be able to bring such actions, will normally be reluctant to do so because of *Guanxi* and *Renqing* due to the controlling shareholders and management. These factors make the introduction of path dependence theory necessary as a theoretical base for the unique problems of establishing and enforcing an efficient derivative action system in China.

The Chinese corporate governance system is a control-based model, in which the controlling shareholders 'tightly control the list companies through concentrated ownership [and] management friendly boards'.[121] If derivative action is to play any role, the question is what, if any, are the net benefits of these actions for companies, shareholders and stakeholders from a social or economic perspective. It is important to introduce agency theory to the discussions of Chinese shareholding structure and the problems of derivative action, in order to make this legal scheme more enforceable and popular, especially for public companies, and reduce the agency cost. With the unique characteristics of Chinese SOEs and the close *Guanxi* between government and corporations, derivative claims are a reasonable remedy and provide an alternative way of protecting the interests of shareholders, particularly minority shareholders.

---

[120] Z. Zhang, 'The Shareholder Derivative Action and Good Corporate Governance in China: Why the Excitement is Actually for Nothing' (2011) 28(2) *UCLA Pacific Basin Law Journal* 175, 175.

[121] Q. Liu, 'Corporate Governance in China: Current Practices, Economic Effects and Institutional Determinants' (2006) 52(2) *CESifo Economic Studies* 415, 429.

There is a strong need for China to adopt a workable derivative action system due to the current context of rapid economic transformation, as well as a high incidence of directors and majority members harming the interests of the company or the minority shareholders. In the following section, corporate governance theories will be used to discuss the possible ways of enabling legislators and regulators to make derivative action rules accessible, enforceable and efficient for Chinese investors within the unique Chinese system.

7.5.1 Agency Theory

Derivative claims by shareholders are closely related to the question of control of the corporate form, and of the steps being taken on behalf of shareholders to redress the imbalance in modern corporations between the control exercised by directors and that exercised by shareholders.[122] It is argued that derivative actions generate agency costs, and the risk and fear of being sued might hinder corporate directors from accepting the position in the first place.[123] On the other hand, derivative actions can reduce agency costs as the claims work to 'deter mismanagement by imposing the threat of liability and therefore align the interests of managers and shareholders'.[124] The adoption of the derivative claim principle will increase the costs that companies have to incur in order to attract good directors. A manager's net return from his job must equal some 'reservation' level for him to be willing to work for the company based on market forces.[125]

However, it is necessary to expand the scope of shareholder remedies towards a derivative action system because of the difficulty of winning a proxy fight by getting sufficient numbers of shareholders at the requisite meeting, regardless of the fact that shareholders have their own contractual remedies which manifest themselves in positive control.[126] Under these circumstances, shareholders must revert to negative legal control measures to redress the imbalance in control between the owner and directors of the company, in

---

[122] D. McDonough, 'Proposed New Statutory Derivative Action – Does it Go Far Enough' (1996) 8(1) *Bond Law Review* 47.

[123] Section 2.2.1 of R.R. Kraakman, P. Davies, H. Hansmann, G. Hertig, K.J. Hopt, H. Kanda and E.B. Rock (eds) *The Anatomy of Corporate Law: A Comparative and Functional Approach*, (New York: Oxford University Press 2004).

[124] I. Ramsay 'Corporate Governance, Shareholder Litigation and the Prospects for a Statutory Derivative Action' (1992) 15(1) *University of New South Wales Law Journal* 149, 152.

[125] A. Reisberg, *Derivative Actions and Corporate Governance Theory and Operation*, (Oxford: Oxford University Press 2007) p.48.

[126] Section 168, UK CA 2006.

order to obtain a balance of control and accountability.[127] Due to the fact that shareholders are liable to suffer the consequences of any wrongdoing carried out by the directors in their name, they should be authorised to issue any type of instructions to the directors concerning the performance of their duties.[128]

Different mechanisms and principles established with the purpose of reducing agency cost problems are adopted in different legal systems.[129] In China, the very high concentration of ownership is directly linked to control from the board of directors, which is regarded as a critical connection between ownership and control in the current Chinese corporate governance scheme.[130] Efforts have been made by the government to reduce the over-concentration of state shareholding. Notwithstanding a general objective to create a more dispersed and competitive shareholding structure, corporatisation and ownership diversification have also led to the emergence of new owners such as individual minority shareholders, institutional investors, and employee-shareholders.[131] However, state ownership still prevails in most listed enterprises where the state still holds a high percentage of ownership.[132] These unique characteristics of Chinese corporate governance make derivative action a particularly important remedy for minority shareholders because of the difficulties of removing the directors or bringing about other changes.

Chinese corporate governance is at a primitive stage, and serious misbehaviour on the part of the board of directors is the major problem.[133] Deterrence by way of legal sanction is the solution, since voluntary market discipline would not function as efficiently in China as in countries with a mature market

---

[127] I Ramsay 'Corporate Governance, Shareholder Litigation and the Prospects for a Statutory Derivative Action' (1992) 15(1) *University of New South Wales Law Journal* 149, 151; see also P. Willcocks, *Shareholders' Rights and Remedies,* (New York: Federation Press 1991) 16.

[128] A. Carver, 'Corporate Governance – Capitalism's Fellow Traveler' in F.M. Patfield (ed.) *Perspectives on Company Law* Volume 2, (London: Kluwer Law International 1997) 69, 74–75.

[129] See E. Glaeser and A. Shlefier, 'The Rise of the Regulatory State' (2003) 41(2) *Journal of Economic Literature* 401.

[130] L.H. Tan and J.Y. Wang, 'Modeling an Efficient Corporate Governance System for China's Listed State–Owned Enterprises: Issues and Challenges in a Transitional Economy' (2007) 7(1) *Journal of Corporate Law Studies* 143, 147.

[131] S. Tenev, C. Zhang and L. Brefort, *Corporate Governance and Enterprise Reform in China: Building the Institutions of Modern Market,* (Washington D.C.: World Bank and the International Finance Corporation 2002) 2–3.

[132] C.J. Milhaupt, 'The State as Owner—China's Experience' (2020) 36(2) *Oxford Review of Economic Policy* 362.

[133] J. Zhao, 'The Regulation and Steering of Corporate Social Responsibility in China: Stories after the Enforcement of Chinese Company Law' (2011) 22(12) *International Commercial and Company Law Review* 400.

economy.[134] Therefore, minority shareholders in China are forced to rely on negative control through legal litigation as opposed to positive control by voluntary measures. If this negative control can be used efficiently by shareholders, it will have a positive effect on enhancing managerial efficiency and accountability.

No shareholder wants to be liable for uncertain or very high costs but receive only a *pro rata* share of the gains from success, while other shareholders free ride on their efforts. In order to enable shareholders to use negative control to its fullest extent, reasonable ligation costs are one of the key requirements. It is claimed that the effectiveness of shareholder litigation as a governance mechanism is hampered by collective action problems, because the cost of bringing a lawsuit, although less than the shareholders' aggregate gain, is typically greater than a shareholder's *pro rata* benefit as a claimant.[135] The problem of financial incentives to police management raises a principal-agent problem; the attorney's incentives need not coincide with the shareholders' interests. As far as litigation cost is concerned, fixed litigation fees will encourage shareholders to sue on behalf of the company in order to reduce the agency cost. The fixed fee will also help to reduce monitoring costs incurred by shareholders, since in the case of derivative action, shareholder coordination is not necessary and fixed litigation fees will make the shareholders' decision easier even without any coordination. It seems reasonable that 'the availability of this action economises on costs that otherwise would be necessarily incurred if shareholders were required to take collective action'.[136]

Corporate governance is a process, a monitoring device and a mechanism to minimise problems that may be brought about in the agent-principal-third-party relationship. However, in a derivative claim, a new agent-principal-third-party relationship can be observed. The shareholder who brings the claim replaces the directors as the agent of the company as the principal, acting in the collective interests of all the shareholders. If the shareholder who brings the action, the agent in the new agency relationship, brings a derivative action on behalf of the company who is the direct beneficiary, the company is logically required to indemnify the cost of the claim simply because the litigation is brought for the company in the name of the shareholder, as is the case in a disclosed agency

---

[134] Z. Zhang, 'Legal Deterrence: The Foundation of Corporate Governance—Evidence from China' (2007) 15(5) *Corporate Governance — An International Review* 741.

[135] R. Romano, 'The Shareholder Suit: Litigation Without Foundation?' (1991) 7(1) *Journal of Law Economics and Organization* 55, 55.

[136] A. Reisberg, *Derivative Actions and Corporate Governance Theory and Operation*, (Oxford: Oxford University Press 2007) 24.

relationship. It is the general rule that where a person contracts as an agent for a principal, the contract is the contract of the principal, not of the agent.

In China, the minority shareholder's right and incentive to bring an action on behalf of the company becomes more important because of the shareholding ownership structure and *Guanxi* between directors and minority shareholders. A reasonable and encouraging cost system is important for a more accessible derivative action system. Agency theory can be used as theoretical support for a more sensible fee arrangement, including fixed litigation costs and the adoption of indemnity orders.

7.5.2   Path Dependence Theory

Path dependence, a comparatively new theory originating in the 1980s, suggests that an outcome or decision is shaped in specific and systematic ways by the historical path leading to it, as well as by other factors within the socio-economic context.[137] While convergence theorists predict that countries, especially countries with weak legal systems, will adopt certain legal rules that have been demonstrably efficient in other jurisdictions, theorists who adhere to path dependence normally argue that divergence will still exist because legal rules are shaped by pre-existing political and social forces. [138] As part of the domestic legal and financial framework, a corporate law system has significant sources of path dependence, which include historical accidents as well as economic and political particulars of the domestic system.[139] The persistence of these sources significantly contributes to the stability of the domestic corporate governance system in any local socio-economic environment.

Path dependence theory can be regarded as a theoretical base for the adoption of a derivative action system with many unique characteristics shaping a particular nation's unique corporate governance model, corporate law background, enforcement process, shareholder structure, civil procedure law, and stage of economic development. It has been argued by Bebchuk and Roe that the initial ownership structure in a country will directly influence the subsequent development of ownership structure and laws.[140] Furthermore, these authors developed the theory to suggest that the interested parties possessing the power to influence ownership structure and corporate law will have both

---

[137]   O.A. Hathaway, 'The Course and Pattern of Legal Change in a Common Law System' (2001) 88 *Iowa Law Review* 1, 103–104.

[138]   K. Pistor, 'Patterns of Legal Changes: Shareholder and Creditor Rights in Transition Economies' (2000) EBRD working paper 49/2000.

[139]   L. Bebchuk and M.J. Roe, 'A Theory of Path Dependence in Corporate Governance and Ownership' (1999) 52(1) *Stanford Law Review* 127.

[140]   Ibid.

the incentive and the power to impede changes that might improve efficiency but are contrary to their private control interests.[141]

In China, the term 'listed company' normally refers to listed SOEs, and the largest shareholder normally refers to the state, which dominates the shareholding in Chinese listed companies. The very high concentration of state ownership is directly linked to control from the board of directors, who are regarded as a critical link between ownership and control in the current Chinese corporate governance scheme.[142] However, when the SOEs are listed, the local office of the Bureau of State Asset Management or its local subsidiaries always act as the largest shareholders, and the chairman of the board of directors is usually a representative from the Bureau who will consult with the board and nominate the directors of the SOEs.[143] Therefore, the decisions made by the board will be closely focused on the largest shareholder's interests. This unique shareholding structure makes derivative lawsuits from minority shareholders particularly valuable while the prevalence of SOEs and the concentrated ownership structure renders minority shareholders extremely vulnerable.

Furthermore, the legal environment for the protection of minority shareholders is important in determining the strength of a country's capital markets.[144] The stock market in China is under-developed and market forces are very weak.[145] The reason for most shareholder investment in China is to gain immediate profits from dividends. Minority shareholders are always ignorant of company performance and information disclosed, and they own stock for a relatively short shareholding period.

The arguments concerning modifications of the standing requirement in JSLCs seem to be reasonable and consistent with the Chinese corporate governance framework. The unique shareholding structure and the dominant position of directors and controlling shareholders make it necessary to adapt current company law to offer efficient remedies to minority shareholders and ensure

---

[141] Ibid, 132.

[142] L.H. Tan and J.Y. Wang, 'Modeling an Efficient Corporate Governance System for China's Listed State-Owned Enterprises: Issues and Challenges in a Transitional Economy' (2007) 7(1) *Journal of Corporate Law Studies* 143, 147.

[143] J.F. Huchet and X. Richer, 'China in Search of an Efficient Corporate Governance System: International Comparison and Lessons' Centre for Economic Reform and Transformation, Herriot-Watt University, Edinburgh, Discussion Paper No 99/01 (11 Feb 1999).

[144] R. Tomasic and N. Andrews, 'Minority Shareholder Protection in China's Top 100 Listed Companies' (2007) 9(1) *Australian Journal of Asian Law* 88; see also H. Cai, 'Bonding, Law Enforcement and Corporate Governance in China' (2007) 13(1) *Stanford Journal of Law, Business and Finance* 82.

[145] M. Xu aand S. Neftci, *China's Financial Markets*, (London: Elsevier 2007) 218.

effective supervision of directors. The speculative business virtue of minority shareholders' investment and their remote distance from business operations in China make these reforms even more necessary. The rule-oriented protection of minority shareholders in the domain of corporate law shows its merits in comparison with market forces in China.

There is another argument based on path dependence theory that could explain the relationship between the unique corporate governance system in China and its derivative claim system. In terms of problems funding the litigation cost, a solution that has been advanced and practiced elsewhere is the establishment of a foundation that processes a certain amount of the shares from each listed company in that jurisdiction.[146] Corporate governance-related litigations funded by similar non-profit organisations have proved reasonably successful in Taiwan, Japan and South Korea.[147] However, it is doubtful whether this system could be enforced in China because of the Chinese corporate governance and business organisation structures. The transplant of the system into China would be hindered by the government's tight control over civil society instructions.[148]

More generally speaking, China's listed companies face a set of very different ownership, business and financial conditions in comparison with companies operating under the Anglo-American model, and institutional conditions for the successful operation of the Chinese corporate governance framework are either absent or undeveloped.[149] Fiduciary duties of directors are not clearly addressed in Chinese Company Law and issues of standards of liability for independent directors and directors in general remain unclear.[150] The legal system of the People's Republic of China, with little more than half a century's history, is still in its infancy compared with many continental European or Anglo-American law systems. The division between the supervisory power of the Chinese Securities Regulatory Commission and the authority of stock exchanges is unclear, leading to confusion in the regulation of the securities

---

[146] P. Jiang, The Development of Corporate Law from the 19th to the 20th Century (*Gongsifa Cong 19 Shiji Dao 20 Shiji de Fazhan*) in F. Guo and J. Wang, *An Comprehensive Study of Company Law Reform (Gongsifa Xiugai Zongheng Tan) [《公司法》修改纵横谈]* (Beijing: Law Press China 2000) 204.

[147] C.J. Milhaupt, 'Nonprofit Organisation as Investor Protection: Economic Theory, and Evidence from East Asia' (2004) 29(1) *Yale Journal of International Law* 169.

[148] D.C. Clarke, 'The Ecology of Corporate Governance in China' The George Washington University Law and Legal Theory Working Paper No. 433, p.55.

[149] O.K. Tam, 'Ethical Issues in the Evolution of corporate governance in China' (2002) 37(3) *Journal of Business Ethics* 303, 311.

[150] D.C. Clarke, 'The Independent Directors in Chinese Corporate Governance' (2006) 31(1) *Delaware Journal of Corporate Law* 125, 224.

market and corporations.[151] The enforcement of Chinese law is regarded as one of the most challenging problems for the government, despite the high priority which has been placed on judicial development.

The enforcement of law and regulations for corporate governance will also be different in China than they are elsewhere. Little judicial independence can be observed even in modern China because the judiciary is 'parallel to rather than superior to, other units of the Chinese bureaucracy'.[152] The courts in China are 'people's courts', they are financed by the government and are administratively and institutionally accountable to the government.[153] There is a lack of thorough understanding and sufficient experience on the part of directors, judges,[154] solicitors and other practitioners regarding actual legal meanings, the nature and scope of their duties and how to enforce them through management policies. However, transplanting the derivative action system to China and making it enforceable will involve a long process based on a more solid and thorough understanding of the nature and scope of the directors' duties codified in Chinese Company Law 2006, together with more expertise from judges and more in-depth academic research. Thus, whether shareholders' derivative action in Chinese Company Law 2006 will truly enable shareholders to recover from mismanagement remains uncertain, and the accessibility of the system is particularly important in China due to the doubtful ability of the courts, as well as a lack of confidence in the courts on the part of minority shareholders and the public. China is the first Communist nation in the world to have a stock exchange, and the only socialist country to initiate the creation of a market-style modern enterprise system since 1990, through a corporatisation and shareholding framework but without privatising its state-owned enterprises. China needs a unique system of its own, shaped by the 'socialist market economy with Chinese characteristic'. This is also the case for a putative Chinese derivative action system.

---

[151]   Y. Wei, 'The Development of the Securities Market and Regulations in China' (2005) 27(3) *Loyola of Los Angeles International and Comparative Law Review* 479, 485.

[152]   M.A. Layton, 'Is Private Securities Litigation Essential for the Development of China's Stock Market?' (2008) 83(6) *New York University Law Review* 1948, 1957–1958.

[153]   Ibid., 1958.

[154]   With more than 170,000 law graduates every year gaining their LL.B degree from universities, the qualifications of Chinese judges are worrying. Only 19.1 per cent of them have a Bachelor's degree or higher, while many have not graduated from law school and a substantial number graduating so through continuing education; see M. Zhang, 'International Civil Litigation in China: A Practical Analysis of the Chinese Judicial System' (2002) 25 *Boston College International & Comparative Law Review* 59, 94–95.

8. Conclusion to derivative actions and corporate governance in China

Clark labeled the shareholder derivative suit as 'one of the most interesting and ingenious accountability mechanisms' for large companies.[1] The introduction of the shareholder derivative action system in Chinese Company Law 2006 has been regarded as a milestone for Chinese Company Law and corporate governance reform.[2] The new Chinese Company Law 2006 offered many changes to various aspects of corporate governance, and made it easier to start and conduct business by using corporations as a form of business organisation in China. The statutory derivative action framework enacted in China is, just like most of its predecessors, designed to correct the difficulties faced by minority shareholders who are faced with controllers who have misused their power within the company. With the dramatic increase in investments from foreign institutional investors in the emerging market, from $25 billion in 1990 to $300 billion in 2005,[3] the acceptance of shareholder derivative litigation demonstrates the way in which emerging economies like that in China are seeking to attract domestic and foreign investors and compete with developed economies for capital.[4] The new law also enhances the protection of disadvantaged groups such as minority shareholders and various stakeholders, addressing some of the issues arising from ineffective corporate governance systems and the abuse of power from boards and controlling shareholders. The derivative action system offers a legitimate platform to redress corporate misbehaviour in the interests of minority shareholders and the company at large.

---

[1] R.C. Clark, *Corporate Law*, (New York: Aspen Publisher 1986) para. 15.1.

[2] N. Krause and C. Qin, 'An Overview of China's New Company Law' (2007) 28(10) *The Company Lawyer* 316, 319; see also M. Gu, *Understanding Chinese Company Law*, (Hong Kong: Hong Kong University Press, 2nd ed. 2010) Chapter 6.

[3] T. Moss, V. Ramachandran and S. Standley, 'Why Doesn't Africa Get More Equity Investment? Frontier Stock Market, Firm Size and Asset Allocation of Global Emerging Market Fund' 1, Centre for Global Development, Working Paper No. 112 (2007); available at http://ideas.repec.org/p/cgd/wpaper/112.html (accessed 25 July 2022).

[4] A.M. Scarlett, 'Investors Beware: Assessing Shareholder Derivative Litigation in India and China' (2011) 33(1) *University of Pennsylvania Journal of International Law* 173, 177.

Compared with pre-existing legislations, uncertainties about derivative suits in China[5] have been reduced by the amendments brought in by Chinese Company Law 2006. However, in terms of the newly established derivative action, ineffective aspects within the new statutory system stipulated in Chinese Company Law 2006 still hinder the enforcement of an investor-friendly derivative lawsuit system in China. Doctrinal and political obstacles severely limit the function and efficacy of the derivative suit as a device for policing management malfeasance.[6] These deficiencies rest on the standing, scope and the cost of litigation. Reform suggestions have been made regarding each deficiency of the system, with the purpose of building a new and efficient framework by maintaining a balance between granting rights to minority shareholders while at the same time avoiding frivolous suits. The suggestions were made clearer by discussions of theoretical support from corporate governance theories including agency theory and path dependence theory. It is concluded that derivative action in China must include a few specific local variations to fit with the many unique characteristics of China's history, economy and society. The relationship between the interests of shareholders, stakeholders, the company, directors, agency theory and stakeholder theory can be seen in the Figure 8.1 below.

Priority should be placed on encouraging shareholders to take derivative action and address the misconduct of company management teams, rather than on restricting the scope of derivative action. However, there is still a long way to go before China can fully adopt a derivative action litigation system with efficient Chinese civil procedures, thereby offering shareholders better and more practical remedies.

Throughout our studies on the cases and follow up investigation on the institutional environment for reform, we have considered many path dependencies deeply embedded in China, such as judicial resources, juridical attitudes, Chinese cultural attributes such as *Guanxi*, the shareholding structure, shareholder activism or passivity, and the availability of alternative remedies. Our findings have led us to believe that the derivative action in China is unique. Our goal is to promote derivative action as a widely recognised and appropriately used mechanism, which should achieve a reputation for being

---

[5]   The uncertainties can be observed in statutory instruments and also in cases: e.g., arts 111 and 63 of Chinese Company Law 1993, art. 42 of Chinese Securities Law 1999, art. 4 of Principles of Corporate Governance for Listed Companies, *Zhangjiagang Fiber Company* Case (1994), *Shanghai Yanzhong Water Company* Case (1997), *Xiamen Xinda Network Company* Case (1997), *Zhejiang Wu Fang Zhai Company* Case (2001) and more recent *Sanjiu Pharmaceutical Company* Case (2003).

[6]   D.C. Clarke, 'The Ecology of Corporate Governance in China' The George Washington University Law and Legal Theory Working Paper No. 433, 47.

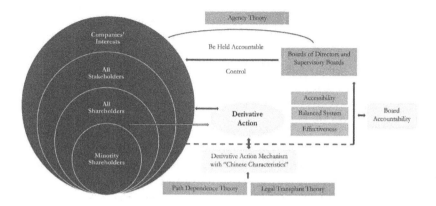

Figure 8.1   *Corporate actors, corporate decisions, and corporate governance theories*

user-friendly, with legal practitioners willing to suggest it and shareholders willing to seek remedies relying on it.

From our empirical research on derivative actions, based on 466 cases in China, we have found that:

(1)   there is a rising number of derivative action cases in China from 2006 to 2020, but the mechanism may still be underused;

(2)   there is a disparity in the regional distribution of derivative action cases, most of which are concentrated in economically developed areas;

(3)   disparity also exists in the type of companies involved, with the overwhelming majority of cases brought for LLCs;

(4)   the most typical scenario of a derivative action in China involves a shareholder in a LLC suing the controlling shareholder who also acts as the director;[7]

(5)   the demand requirement and court fees are the major obstacles in bringing derivative actions, as less than half of all cases have satisfied the demand requirement and court fees can be extremely high;

(6)   the success rate for raising a derivative action is relatively low, at 35 per cent;

(7)   court fees are highly variable with a high standard deviation;

---

[7]   We concluded this scenario from the findings that 50 per cent of cases have single, natural person claimants, the largest group of defendants are shareholders and the principal cause of action is breach of directors' duties.

(8) derivative actions are difficult in China because of collective action problems, but these problems can be overcome by shareholders with established *guanxi*.

In response to these findings, and to build a more effective framework by maintaining a balance between minority shareholder rights and avoiding frivolous suits, we have made a few proposals for a more accessible derivative action mechanism:

(1) The judiciary should develop a more consistent approach towards derivative actions, particularly in terms of interpreting the demand requirement, directors' duties, and shareholders' duties. The legitimacy of the judiciary and ultimately the rule of law depends on a consistent and predictable application of law.
(2) Derivative actions should be made more accessible to shareholders in JSLCs by lowering the shareholding requirement, reducing litigation fees, giving a more active role to institutional shareholders, and better coordinating collective actions, which can be supported by quasi-public organizations such as the ISC.
(3) A maximum cap for filing fees should be implemented.
(4) When considering whether to accept a derivative action case, instead of using a rigid application of the demand requirement, courts should make a comprehensive and balanced consideration regarding the costs of proceedings, company's reputation, judicial resources, and alternative remedies (e.g., internal remedies and settlements) and guidance from SPC is desirable.
(5) A statutory business judgement rule should be introduced as a complementary system.
(6) The derivative action system in China should be consolidated as a private enforcement measure supported by a public enforcer. The investor protection institution should play an educational and supporting role for shareholders, especially minority shareholders to facilitate derivative action in JSLC, especially listed ones.

As one of the legal regimes with high expectations, working side by side with statutory oppression remedies,[8] we believe that the derivative action has the

---

[8] Art. 20, Chinese Company Law 2018. When the first Company Law was introduced in China in 1993 as a result of the economic reconstruction that placed the reform of SOEs at the top of the agenda, some Western concepts were introduced including private ownership, the ownership of shares and the diversification of enterprise ownership; see O.K. Tam, *The Development of Corporate Governance in China*, (Cheltenham: Edward Elgar 1999) 1.

potential to become an effective and ingenious accountability mechanism for both LLCs and JSLCs. As a milestone for Chinese Company Law and corporate governance reform,[9] the derivative action system in China must be established with some specific local variations to fit with the many unique characteristics of China's history, economy, and society.

Under the three criteria of accessibility, balance, and effectiveness, derivative actions in China should be developed to serve these competing goals. On one hand, it should encourage a variety of shareholders, individually as well as collectively, to participate in litigation to deter misconduct among management personnel. On the other hand, it should constrain shareholders from abusing derivative actions that may easily encroach upon the powers of corporate management and impose unnecessary burdens on them.

Finally, we believe that case law in China offers a precious opportunity to fill in the gap between 'law in books' and 'law in action'. Judicial precedent is becoming increasingly important in China since the traditional view about the role of courts is changing.[10] However, it is dangerous to exaggerate the function of case law in China, considering the inconsistent and inaccurate application of the law in courts at various levels.

---

[9]   N. Krause and C. Qin, 'An Overview of China's New Company Law' (2007) 28(10) *The Company Lawyer* 316, 319; see also M. Gu, *Understanding Chinese Company Law*, (Hong Kong: Hong Kong University Press, 2nd ed. 2010) Chapter 6.

[10]   S. Lin, 'Private Enforcement of Chinese Company Law: Shareholder Litigation and Judicial Discretion' (2016) 4 *China Legal Science* 73.

Index